Lecture Notes in Computer Science   6721

Commenced Publication in 1973
Founding and Former Series Editors:
Gerhard Goos, Juris Hartmanis, and Jan van Leeuwen

W0246073

Wolfgang De Meuter
Gruia-Catalin Roman (Eds.)

Coordination Models and Languages

13th International Conference, COORDINATION 2011
Reykjavik, Iceland, June 6-9, 2011
Proceedings

 Springer

Volume Editors

Wolfgang De Meuter
Vrije Universiteit Brussel, Faculty of Sciences
Pleinlaan 2, 1050 Brussels, Belgium
E-mail: wdmeuter@vub.ac.be

Gruia-Catalin Roman
Washington University, Department of Computer Science and Engineering
Campus Box 1045, 1 Brookings Drive, St. Louis, MO 63130-4899, USA
E-mail: roman@wustl.edu

ISSN 0302-9743   e-ISSN 1611-3349
ISBN 978-3-642-21463-9   e-ISBN 978-3-642-21464-6
DOI 10.1007/978-3-642-21464-6
Springer Heidelberg Dordrecht London New York

Library of Congress Control Number: 2011928244

CR Subject Classification (1998): D.2, C.2, C.2.4, F.1.2, I.2.8, I.2.11, C.3

LNCS Sublibrary: SL 2 – Programming and Software Engineering

Typesetting: Camera-ready by author, data conversion by Scientific Publishing Services, Chennai, India

Printed on acid-free paper

Springer is part of Springer Science+Business Media (www.springer.com)

Foreword

In 2011 the 6th International Federated Conferences on Distributed Computing Techniques (DisCoTec) took place in Reykjavik, Iceland, during June 6–9. It was hosted and organized by Reykjavik University. The DisCoTec series of federated conferences, one of the major events sponsored by the International Federation for Information processing (IFIP), included three conferences: Coordination, DAIS, and FMOODS/FORTE.

DisCoTec conferences jointly cover the complete spectrum of distributed computing subjects ranging from theoretical foundations to formal specification techniques to practical considerations. The 13th International Conference on Coordination Models and Languages (Coordination) focused on the design and implementation of models that allow compositional construction of large-scale concurrent and distributed systems, including both practical and foundational models, run-time systems, and related verification and analysis techniques. The 11th IFIP International Conference on Distributed Applications and Interoperable Systems (DAIS) elicited contributions on architectures, models, technologies and platforms for large-scale and complex distributed applications and services that are related to the latest trends in bridging the physical/virtual worlds based on flexible and versatile service architectures and platforms. The 13th Formal Methods for Open Object-Based Distributed Systems and 31st Formal Techniques for Networked and Distributed Systems (FMOODS/FORTE) together emphasized distributed computing models and formal specification, testing and verification methods.

Each of the three days of the federated event began with a plenary speaker nominated by one of the conferences. On the first day, Giuseppe Castagna (CNRS, Paris 7 University, France) gave a keynote titled "On Global Types and Multi-Party Sessions." On the second day, Paulo Verissimo (University of Lisbon FCUL, Portugal) gave a keynote talk on "Resisting Intrusions Means More than Byzantine Fault Tolerance." On the final and third day, Pascal Costanza (ExaScience Lab, Intel, Belgium) presented a talk that discussed "Extreme Coordination—Challenges and Opportunities from Exascale Computing."

In addition, there was a poster session, and a session of invited talks from representatives of Icelandic industries including Ossur, CCP Games, Marorka, and GreenQloud.

There were five satellite events:

1. The 4th DisCoTec workshop on Context-Aware Adaptation Mechanisms for Pervasive and Ubiquitous Services (CAMPUS)
2. The Second International Workshop on Interactions Between Computer Science and Biology (CS2BIO) with keynote lectures by Jasmin Fisher (Microsoft Research - Cambridge, UK) and Gordon Plotkin (Laboratory for Foundations of Computer Science - University of Edinburgh, UK)

3. The 4th Workshop on Interaction and Concurrency Experience (ICE) with keynote lectures by Prakash Panangaden (McGill University, Canada), Rocco de Nicola (University of Florence, Italy), and Simon Gay (University of Glasgow, UK)

4. The First Workshop on Process Algebra and Coordination (PACO) with keynote lectures by Jos Baeten (Eindhoven University of Technology, The Netherlands), Dave Clarke (Katholieke Universiteit Leuven, Belgium), Rocco De Nicola (University of Florence, Italy), and Gianluigi Zavattaro (University of Bologna, Italy)

5. The 7th International Workshop on Automated Specification and Verification of Web Systems (WWV) with a keynote lecture by Elie Najm (Telecom Paris, France)

I believe that this rich program offered each participant an interesting and stimulating event. I would like to thank the Program Committee Chairs of each conference and workshop for their effort. Moreover, organizing DisCoTec 2011 was only possible thanks to the dedicated work of the Publicity Chair Gwen Salaun (Grenoble INP - INRIA, France), the Workshop Chairs Marcello Bonsangue (University of Leiden, The Netherlands) and Immo Grabe (CWI, The Netherlands), the Poster Chair Martin Steffen (University of Oslo, Norway), the Industry Track Chairs Björn Jónsson (Reykjavik University, Iceland), and Oddur Kjartansson (Reykjavik University, Iceland), and the members of the Organizing Committee from Reykjavik University: Árni Hermann Reynisson, Steinar Hugi Sigurðarson, Georgiana Caltais Goriac, Eugen-Ioan Goriac and Ute Schiffel. To conclude I want to thank the International Federation for Information Processing (IFIP), Reykjavik University, and CCP Games Iceland for their sponsorship.

June 2011   Marjan Sirjani

Preface

The 13th International Conference on Coordination Models and Languages, part of the IFIP federated event on Distributed Computing Techniques, took place in Reykjavik, June 6-9, 2011. The conference focused on the design and implementation of models that allow compositional construction of large-scale concurrent and distributed systems, including both practical and foundational models, runtime systems, and related verification and analysis techniques.

The Program Committee received more than 45 abstracts eventually followed by 35 full paper submissions, covering a varied range of topics including parallel and multicore programming, coordination of mobile systems, (session) types, context management, and programming and reasoning about distributed and concurrent software. Each paper was reviewed anonymously by at least three Program Committee members. After a careful and thorough review process, the Program Committee selected 14 papers for publication, based on their significance, originality, and technical soundness. The review process included a shepherding phase whereby some of the papers received active guidance by one of the Program Committee members in order to produce a high-quality final version.

The program was further enhanced by an inspiring invited talk by Pascal Costanza of the Intel ExaScience Lab. The presentation was entitled "Extreme Coordination—Challenges and Opportunities from Exascale Computing."

The success of Coordination 2011 was due to the dedication of many people. We thank the authors for submitting high-quality papers, and the Program Committee (and their co-reviewers) for their careful reviews, lengthy discussions, and balanced deliberations during the final selection process. We thank the providers of the EasyChair conference management system, which was used to run the review process and to facilitate the preparation of these proceedings. Finally, we thank the Distributed Computing Techniques Organization Committee (led by Marjan Sirjani) for their enormous contribution in making the logistic aspects of Coordination 2011 a success.

June 2011

Wolfgang De Meuter
Gruia-Catalin Roman

Organization

Program Committee

Farhad Arbab	CWI and Leiden University, The Netherlands
Carlos Canal	University of Málaga, Spain
Dave Clarke	Katholieke Universiteit Leuven, Belgium
Wolfgang De Meuter	Vrije Universiteit Brussel, Belgium
Rocco De Nicola	University of Florence, Italy
Susan Eisenbach	Imperial College, UK
Patrick Eugster	Purdue University, USA
John Field	IBM Research, USA
Robert Hirschfeld	Hasso-Plattner-Institut, Germany
Jean-Marie Jacquet	University of Namur, Belgium
Doug Lea	SUNY Oswego, USA
Jay A. Mccarthy	Brigham Young University, USA
Sun Meng	Peking University, China
Mark Miller	Google, USA
Gruia-Catalin Roman	Washington University in St. Louis, USA
Manuel Serano	INRIA, France
Marjan Sirjani	School of Computer Science, Reykjavik University, Iceland
Carolyn Talcott	SRI International, USA
Vasco Vasconcelos	University of Lisbon, Portugal
Mirko Viroli	Università di Bologna, Italy

Additional Reviewers

Malte Appeltauer	Francisco Martins
Lorenzo Bettini	Ronaldo Menezes
Laura Bocchi	Dimitris Mostrous
Behnaz Changizi	Andrea Omicini
Francisco Couto	Michael Perscheid
Ali Hong	Rosario Pugliese
Mohammad Izadi	Tamara Rezk
Sung-Shik Jongmans	Alessandro Ricci
Narges Khakpour	Manuel Serrano
Ramtin Khosravi	Bastian Steinert
Jens Lincke	Francesco Tiezzi
Michele Loreti	

Table of Contents

Fault in the Future*

Einar Broch Johnsen[1], Ivan Lanese[2], and Gianluigi Zavattaro[2]

[1] Department of Informatics, University of Oslo, Norway
einarj@ifi.uio.no
[2] Focus Team, Università di Bologna/INRIA, Italy
{lanese, zavattar}@cs.unibo.it

Abstract. In this paper we consider the problem of fault handling inside an object-oriented language with asynchronous method calls whose results are returned inside futures. We present an extension for those languages where futures are used to return fault notifications and to coordinate error recovery between the caller and callee. This can be exploited to ensure that invariants involving many objects are restored after faults.

1 Introduction

Concurrent and distributed systems demand flexible communication forms between distributed processes. While object-orientation is a natural paradigm for distributed systems [14], the tight coupling between objects traditionally enforced by method calls may be criticized. Concurrent (or active) objects have been proposed as an approach to concurrency that blends naturally with object-oriented programming [1,18,27]. Several slightly differently flavored concurrent object systems exist for, e.g., Java [5,25], Eiffel [8,22], and C++ [21]. Concurrent objects are reminiscent of Actors [1] and Erlang processes [4]: objects are inherently concurrent, conceptually each object has a dedicated processor, and there is at most one activity in an object at any time. Thus, concurrent objects encapsulate not only their state and methods, but also a single (active) thread of control. In the concurrent object model, *asynchronous method calls* may be used to better combine object-orientation with distributed programming by reducing the temporal coupling between the caller and callee of a method, compared to the tightly synchronized (remote) method invocation model. Intuitively, asynchronous method calls spawn activities in objects without blocking execution in the caller. Return values from asynchronous calls are managed by so-called *futures* [12,19,27]. Asynchronous method calls and futures have been integrated with, e.g., Java [17] and Scala [11] and offer a large degree of potential concurrency for deployment on multi-core or distributed architectures.

In the event-driven communication model of Actors and Erlang processes, fault recovery is typically managed by linking processes together [4] or by monitors [2,26]. These approaches do not address asynchronous method calls and

---

* Partly funded by the EU project FP7-231620 HATS and the ANR-2010-SEGI-013 project AEOLUS.

W. De Meuter and G.-C. Roman (Eds.): COORDINATION 2011, LNCS 6721, pp. 1–15, 2011.

futures. In this paper, we extend the Java approach [17] with mechanisms for error recovery developed in the context of web services. Futures are used to identify calls, so they provide a natural means to distribute fault notifications and kill requests. We introduce also primitives for defining and invoking compensations allowing one to undo already completed method executions. In this way, we obtain a symmetric framework where caller and callee can notify their failure to the partner and manage the incoming notifications. This supports distributed error recovery policies programming.

The work reported in this paper is based on ABS, a formal modeling language for distributed concurrent objects which communicate by asynchronous method calls and futures, to take advantage of its formal semantics and simplicity. ABS is a variant of Creol [9, 16], and it is the reference language of the European Project HATS [13]. Creol has been shown to support compositional verification of concurrent software [3, 9], in contrast to multi-threading. A particular feature of ABS is its cooperative scheduling of method activations inside concurrent objects, which allows different activities to be pursued within the object in a controlled way; in particular, active and reactive object behaviors are easily and dynamically combined. In ABS, any method may be called both synchronously and asynchronously. Recently, this notion of cooperative scheduling has been integrated in Java by means of concurrent object groups [25].

We work with an ABS kernel language for distributed concurrent objects in which asynchronous method calls and futures form the basic communication constructs. The proposed kernel language combines the concurrency model of ABS with explicit language constructs for error recovery. In particular, both the caller and callee may signal a failure: the caller by performing a $x := f$.**kill** operation (reminiscent of the **cancel** method of Java futures) on the future f identifying the call, while the callee by executing the **abort** n command (n describes the kind of failure). If the callee aborts, then it will definitely terminate its activities. On the contrary, if the caller performs $x := f$.**kill**, it expects that the callee will react by executing some compensating activity (in contrast to Java, where the call is just interrupted). Such activities are attached to the **return** statement, that we replace with the new command **return** e **on compensate** s (where s is the compensation code). This is the main novelty of our proposal: when a callee successfully completes, it has not definitely completed its activity as it will possibly have to perform its compensation activity in case of failure of the caller. This mechanism is inspired by the compensation mechanisms adopted in service orchestration languages like WS-BPEL [23] or Jolie [10]. A compensation can return to the caller some results: to this aim we use a new future which is freshly created and assigned to x by $x := f$.**kill**.

Paper structure. Section 2 introduces our ABS kernel language (without error handling) and presents its syntax and semantics. Section 3 proposes fault-handling primitives for ABS and discusses by simple examples the typical patterns of interaction between the caller and callee under our model of failures. Section 4 discusses the operational semantics of the new primitives and their impact on the ABS type system. Section 5 concludes the paper.

2 A Language for Distributed Concurrent Objects

We consider *ABS*, an abstract behavioral specification language for distributed concurrent objects (modifying Creol [9, 16] by, e.g., excluding class inheritance and dynamic class upgrades). Characteristic features of ABS are that: (1) it allows abstracting from implementation details while remaining executable; i.e., a *functional sub-language* over abstract data types is used to specify internal, sequential computations; and (2) it provides *flexible concurrency and synchronization mechanisms* by means of asynchronous method calls, release points in method definitions, and cooperative scheduling of method activations.

Intuitively, concurrent ABS objects have dedicated processors and run in a distributed environment with asynchronous and unordered communication. Communication between objects is based on asynchronous method calls. (There is no remote field access.) Calls are asynchronous as the caller may decide at runtime when to synchronize with the reply from a call. Method calls may be seen as triggers, spawning new concurrent activities (so-called *processes*) in the called object. Thus, an object has a set of processes to be executed, which stem from method activations. Among these, at most one process is *active*. The others are *suspended* in a process pool. Process scheduling is non-deterministic, but controlled by *processor release points* in a cooperative way.

An ABS *model* defines interfaces, classes, datatypes, and functions, and a main method to configure the initial state. We elide the definition of data types and functions to focus on the concurrency and communication aspects of ABS models. Objects are dynamically created instances of classes; their declared attributes are initialized to arbitrary type-correct values. This paper assumes that models are well-typed, so method binding is guaranteed to succeed.

The concurrent object language of ABS is given in Fig. 1. Here, an interface *IF* has a name I and method signatures Sg. A class implements interfaces specifying types for its instances. A class CL has a name C, interfaces $\overline{I}$, class parameters and state variables x of type T, and methods M. (The *attributes* of the class are its parameters and state variables.) A method signature Sg declares the return type T of a method with name m and formal parameters $\overline{x}$ of types $\overline{T}$. M defines a method with signature Sg, local variable declarations $\overline{x}$ of types $\overline{T}$, and a body with statement s. Statements may access attributes of the current class, locally defined variables, and the method's formal parameters.

Right-hand side expressions *rhs* include object creation **new** $C(\overline{e})$, communication constructs (discussed below), and expressions e. Expressions include Boolean expressions, the read-only self-reference **this**, references x to attributes and local variables, and functional terms (omitted here). Statements are standard for assignment $x := rhs$, sequential composition $s_1; s_2$, **skip**, **if**, **while**, and **return** constructs. The **release** statement unconditionally releases the processor, suspending the active process. In **await** g **do** $\{s\}$, the guards g control processor release and consist of Boolean conditions b and return tests $x?$ (see below). If all guards g evaluate to false, the processor is released and the process *suspended*. When the processor is idle, any enabled process from the object's pool of suspended processes may be scheduled.

Syntactic categories.	Definitions.

C, I, m in Names

g in Guard

s in Statement

e in Expression

b in Bool Expression

$IF ::= \textbf{interface } I \{ \overline{Sg} \}$

$CL ::= \textbf{class } C\, [(\overline{T\ x})]\, [\textbf{implements } \overline{I}]\, \{ \overline{T\ x};\ \overline{M} \}$

$Sg ::= T\ m\ (\overline{T\ x})$

$M ::= Sg\{\overline{T\ x};\ s\}$

$g ::= b \mid x? \mid g \wedge g \mid g \vee g$

$e ::= b \mid x \mid \textbf{this} \mid \ldots$

$s ::= s; s \mid x := rhs \mid \textbf{release} \mid \textbf{await } g \textbf{ do } \{s\} \mid \textbf{skip}$
$\quad \mid \textbf{if } b \textbf{ then} \{s\} [\textbf{else} \{s\}] \mid \textbf{while } b \{s\} \mid \textbf{return } e$

$rhs ::= e \mid \textbf{new } C[(\overline{e})] \mid e!m(\overline{e}) \mid x.\textbf{get}$

Fig. 1. ABS syntax for the concurrent object language

Communication in ABS is based on asynchronous method calls, denoted $o!m(\overline{e})$. After an asynchronous call $x := o!m(\overline{e})$, the caller may proceed with its execution without blocking on the call. Here x is a future variable, o is an object (an expression typed by an interface), and $\overline{e}$ are expressions. A future variable x refers to a return value which has yet to be computed. There are two operations on future variables, which control external synchronization in ABS. First, a return test $x?$ evaluates to false unless the reply to the call can be retrieved. (Return tests are used in guards.) Second, the return value is retrieved by the expression $x.\textbf{get}$, which blocks execution in the object until the return value is available. The statement sequence $x := o!m(\overline{e});\ v := x.\textbf{get}$ encodes a blocking, *synchronous call*, abbreviated $v := o.m(\overline{e})$ whereas the statement sequence $x := o!m(\overline{e});\ \textbf{await } x?\ \textbf{do } v := x.\textbf{get}$ encodes a non-blocking, *preemptable call*, abbreviated $\textbf{await } v := o.m(\overline{e})$.

2.1   Operational Semantics

The operational semantics of ABS is presented as a transition system in an SOS style [24]. The rules, given in Fig. 2, apply to subsets of configurations (the standard context rules are not listed). For simplicity we assume that configurations can be reordered to match the left hand side of the rules (i.e., matching is modulo associativity and commutativity as in rewriting logic [20]). We denote by $\llbracket e \rrbracket_{\sigma}^{cn}$ a confluent and terminating reduction system which reduces expressions e to data values (from a set Val) in a substitution σ and a configuration cn. (In particular, $\llbracket x? \rrbracket_{\sigma}^{cn} = \text{true}$ if $\llbracket x \rrbracket_{\sigma}^{cn} = f$ and $fut(f, v) \in cn$ for some value $v \neq \bot$, otherwise $\llbracket x? \rrbracket_{\sigma}^{cn} = \text{false}$. The remaining cases are fairly straightforward.)

Configurations cn are sets of objects, invocation messages, and futures. The associative and commutative union operator on configurations is denoted by whitespace. Configurations live inside curly brackets; in the term $\{cn\}$, cn captures the *entire* configuration. An *object* is a term $ob(o, a, p, q)$ with identifier o, an attribute mapping a representing the object's fields, an *active process* p, and a *pool of suspended processes* q. A process p consists of a mapping l of local variable bindings and a list s of statements, denoted by $\{l|s\}$ when convenient. In an *invocation message* $invoc(o, f, m, \overline{v})$, o is the callee, f the future to which the call's result is returned, m the method name, and $\overline{v}$ the call's actual parameter

$$(\text{Assign1})$$
$$\frac{x \in \text{dom}(l) \quad v = [\![e]\!]^\varepsilon_{(a \circ l)}}{\begin{array}{l} ob(o, a, \{l|x := e; s\}, q) \\ \rightarrow ob(o, a, \{l[x \mapsto v]|s\}, q) \end{array}}$$

$$(\text{Assign2})$$
$$\frac{x \in \text{dom}(a) \quad v = [\![e]\!]^\varepsilon_{(a \circ l)}}{\begin{array}{l} ob(o, a, \{l|x := e; s\}, q) \\ \rightarrow ob(o, a[x \mapsto v], \{l|s\}, q) \end{array}}$$

$$(\text{Bind-Mtd})$$
$$\frac{p' = \text{bind}(o, f, m, \overline{v})}{\begin{array}{l} ob(o, a, p, q) \; invoc(o, f, m, \overline{v}) \\ \rightarrow ob(o, a, p, \text{enqueue}(p', q)) \end{array}}$$

$$(\text{Async-Call})$$
$$\frac{o' = [\![e]\!]^\varepsilon_{(a \circ l)} \quad \overline{v} = [\![\overline{e}]\!]^\varepsilon_{(a \circ l)} \quad \text{fresh}(f)}{\begin{array}{l} ob(o, a, \{l|x := e!m(\overline{e}); s\}, q) \\ \rightarrow ob(o, a, \{l|x := f; s\}, q) \\ invoc(o', f, m, \overline{v}) \; fut(f, \bot) \end{array}}$$

$$(\text{Return})$$
$$\frac{v = [\![e]\!]^\varepsilon_{(a \circ l)} \quad l(\text{destiny}) = f}{\begin{array}{l} ob(o, a, \{l|\text{return } e; s\}, q) \; fut(f, \bot) \\ \rightarrow ob(o, a, \{l|s\}, q) \; fut(f, v) \end{array}}$$

$$(\text{Await1})$$
$$\frac{[\![g_i]\!]^{cn}_{(a \circ l)}}{\begin{array}{l} \{ob(o, a, \{l|\text{await } \overline{g_i \; \textbf{do} \; s_i}; s\}, q) \; cn\} \\ \rightarrow \{ob(o, a, \{l|s_i; s\}, q) \; cn\} \end{array}}$$

$$(\text{Await2})$$
$$\frac{\forall i. \neg [\![g_i]\!]^{cn}_{(a \circ l)}}{\begin{array}{l} \{ob(o, a, \{l|\text{await } \overline{g_i \; \textbf{do} \; s_i}; s\}, q) \; cn\} \\ \rightarrow \{ob(o, a, \{l|\text{release}; \text{await } \overline{g_i \; \textbf{do} \; s_i}; s\}, q) \; cn\} \end{array}}$$

$$(\text{Read-Fut})$$
$$\frac{v \neq \bot \quad f = [\![e]\!]^\varepsilon_{(a \circ l)}}{\begin{array}{l} ob(o, a, \{l|x := e.\text{get}; s\}, q) \; fut(f, v) \\ \rightarrow ob(o, a, \{l|x := v; s\}, q) \; fut(f, v) \end{array}}$$

$$(\text{Release})$$
$$\begin{array}{l} ob(o, a, \{l|\text{release}; s\}, q) \\ \rightarrow ob(o, a, \text{idle}, \\ \text{enqueue}(\{l|s\}, q)) \end{array}$$

$$(\text{Activate})$$
$$\frac{p = \text{select}(q, a, cn)}{\begin{array}{l} \{ob(o, a, \text{idle}, q) \; cn\} \\ \rightarrow \{ob(o, a, p, q \backslash p) \; cn\} \end{array}}$$

Fig. 2. ABS semantics

values. A *future* $fut(f, v)$ has an identifier f and a reply value v (which is $\bot$ when the reply value has not been received). Values are object and future identifiers, Boolean expressions, and null (as well as expressions in the functional language). For simplicity, classes are not represented explicitly in the semantics, but may be seen as static tables. We assume given a function $bind(o, f, m, \overline{v})$ which returns a process resulting from the activation of m in the class of o with actual parameters $\overline{v}$, callee o and associated future f; and a predicate $fresh(i)$ asserts that a name i is globally unique (where i may be an identifier for an object or a future). Let *idle* denote any process $\{l|s\}$ where s is an empty statement list.

Transition Rules. There are different assignment rules for expressions (*Assign1* and *Assign2*), method calls (*Async-Call*), and future dereferencing (*Read-Fut*). Rules *Assign1* and *Assign2* assign the value of expression e to a variable x in the local variables l or in the fields a, respectively. Here and in the sequel, the variable s will match any (possibly empty) statement list. (We omit the standard rules for skip, if-then-else, and while and the rule for object creation.)

Process Suspension and Activation. Three operations manipulate a process pool q: enqueue(p, q) adds a process p to q, $q \backslash p$ removes the process p from q, and select(q, a, cn) selects a process from q (if q is empty or no process is *ready*, this is the idle process [16]). The different possible definitions correspond to different process scheduling policies. Let $\emptyset$ denote the empty pool. Rule *Release* suspends the active process to the pool, leaving the active process idle. Rule *Await1* consumes the await statement if one of the guards evaluates to true in the current state and selects the related continuation, rule *Await2* adds a release to suspend the process if all the guards evaluate to false. Rule *Activate* selects

$$
\begin{array}{llll}
s ::= & \ldots & & \textit{Standard statements} \\
& | & \textbf{abort } n & \text{(Abort)} \\
& | & \textbf{return } e \textbf{ on compensate } s & \text{(Return)} \\
& | & \textbf{on } x := f.\textbf{get do } s\ \overline{\textbf{on fail } n\ s} & \text{(Get)} \\
\\
rhs ::= & \ldots & & \textit{Standard rhs} \\
& | & f.\textbf{kill} & \text{(Kill)}
\end{array}
$$

Fig. 3. Primitives for error handling

a process from the pool for execution if this process is *ready* to execute, i.e., if it would not directly be resuspended or block the processor [16].

Communication. Rule *Async-Call* sends an invocation message to o' with the unique identity f (by the condition fresh(f)) of a new future, the method name m, and actual parameters $\overline{v}$. The return value of the new future f is undefined (i.e., $\perp$). Rule *Bind-Mtd* consumes an invocation method, placing the process corresponding to the method activation in the callee's process pool. A reserved local variable 'destiny' stores the identity of the future associated with the call. Rule *Return* places the return value in the call's associated future. Rule *Read-Fut* dereferences the future f if $v \neq \perp$, otherwise the object is *blocked*.

3 Primitives for Error Handling

In this section we describe the syntax and the informal semantics of the primitives we propose for distributed error handling. As already said, ABS communication is asynchronous and based on futures. Thus we extend this idea to allow also for error notification and management. We assume to have a set *Err* of fault names, ranged over by n. The sets *Err* of fault names and *Val* of values are disjoint. Consider a method invocation $x := o!m(\overline{e})$. The caller will use future x inside all primitives related to handling errors for this method invocation. In the callee instead the used future is implicit, since each method execution has an attached future, i.e. the one where the return value is put.

In order to deal with errors, we mainly have to extend statements s and right-hand sides *rhs* w.r.t. Fig. 1. Small extensions will be needed also for method signatures and types. The extended syntax for statements and right-hand sides is described in Fig. 3. One may have a look to Fig. 4 and Fig. 5, described in detail later, to see how those primitives can be used.

We have a new primitive, **abort** n, to be used by the callee to signal its failure to its caller. Name n is used to notify the kind of error, and is reminiscent of exception types in e.g. Java[1]. The **abort** statement concludes the execution of the method. Also, the primitive **return** is extended with the clause **on compensate** s. This clause declares that, after the **return** has been executed and the method's normal execution completed, if compensation of this

---

[1] Our approach can be generalized to exception types, we choose to have just names for simplicity.

method call is needed, code s has to be executed. No continuation different from a compensation is allowed after **return**. Compensation s will be executed in the same environment of the method body.

The two primitives above are executed by the callee. The caller has primitives for detecting the result of an invocation and for killing/compensating a past invocation. For detecting the result of the invocation we extend the $x := f.$**get** primitive of ABS (we use f for an expression that evaluates to a future). It becomes part of the construct **on** $x := f.$**get do** s $\overline{\textbf{on fail}\ n_i\ s_i}$, which executes $x := f.$**get** as before, but then it executes s if the future f contains a value v, or the clause s_i if f contains a fault name n_i. In the first case the value v is assigned to variable x, otherwise x is unchanged.

The primitives described so far allow errors generated in the callee to be managed. On the other side, the caller may enter an error situation that requires to annul the effect of the call. This is done using the statement $x := f.$**kill**. Here f is the future corresponding to the method call to be annulled while x is a variable that will contain the fresh future f' to be used to interact with the compensation. The annul request is asynchronous, and the result can be tested by using the normal **await** and **get** primitives. Upon the execution of $x := f.$**kill** the value of f becomes the special value $kill(f')$, denoting that a kill request has been sent, and a reply is expected in f'. The identity of future f' is stored in x and f' is initialized to $\bot$. The annul request will be managed by the target method call either before it starts, or at its end. In the first case the method is not executed at all. In the second case, if execution was successful then the compensation code is executed, otherwise no code is executed (only successful executions can be compensated). The value of future f' is changed to a normal value v or to an error notification n depending on the result of the compensation code. Since f' is a future, one may even ask to kill an ongoing compensation. Two special fault notifications may be returned in such a future: Ann, specifying that either the method call has been annulled before starting or that it aborted on its own, and NoC, specifying that the killed method defined no compensation.

Note that both values and fault notifications unlock the **await** statement.

We clarify the error handling style induced by these primitives with a simple bank transfer example and a speculative parallelism example[2].

Example 1 (Bank transfer). Assume that a bank A wants to transfer some amount of money *money* from one of its accounts *accNoA* to an account *accNoB* of a bank B. Clearly, the interaction has to guarantee that money is neither created nor destroyed, and this should hold even in case of failures.

The codes of the caller and callee are in Fig. 4 and Fig. 5, respectively. The caller asks for the transfer by invoking method MAKETRANSFER (Fig. 4, line 3). If later on it finds a problem (e.g., there is not enough money in the

---

[2] For simplicity, we avoid in the examples the typing of faults: this is considered in the following. We also shorten $x := x + e$ (resp. $x := x - e$) into $x\ += e$ (resp. $x\ -= e$).

```
1   bool TRANSFER (int accNoA, int accNoB, int money)
2   { bool x, y;
3     f := bankB!MAKETRANSFER (int accNoB, int money);
4     if accountsA[accNoA].balance < money then
5         { f' := f.kill;
6           on x := f'.get
7               do return false
8               on fail no-money abort lost-money
9               on fail Ann return false
10        }
11    else
12        { await f? do
13            on y := f.get
14                do accountsA[accNoA].balance -= money;
15                    return x
16                on fail no-acc
17                    return false
18  }   }
```

Fig. 4. Bank transfer example: caller

source account[3]) it kills the MAKETRANSFER computation (Fig. 4, line 5). If the computation has already failed then nothing has to be done, and the clause **on fail** Ann (Fig. 4, line 9) is executed. If the MAKETRANSFER computation has not started yet, it is annulled and the same clause line **on fail** Ann is executed on the caller. If the MAKETRANSFER computation has successfully terminated then a compensation has been installed and its execution is started (when the scheduler decides to schedule it). When executing the compensation one does not know whether the received money is still available. In fact, the lock has been released after completion of method MAKETRANSFER, and another method of bank B may have used the money. If the money is still available then compensation is successful (we will see that the invariant has been preserved), clause **do** is executed on the caller (Fig. 4, line 7), and value *false* is given as a result. If the money is no longer available then the **abort** *no-money* (Fig. 5, line 12) statement triggers the **on fail** *no-money* clause on the caller (Fig. 4, line 8). In the caller this will cause an **abort** *lost-money* signaling at the upper level that error recovery has not been successful. This is the only case where money is not preserved, but this is notified by a failure to the upper level. Note that in case of successful termination of the caller (which may happen even if the call failed), the TRANSFER method returns true if the transfer has been performed, false otherwise.

Example 2 (Speculative parallelism). As an additional example of the usage of the error handling primitives, we consider a typical pattern of service composition —the so-called *speculative parallelism*. This pattern generalizes client-server

---

[3] This particular problem could have been checked before the invocation, but this is useful to show in a small example most of the error recovery mechanisms.

```
1   bool MAKETRANSFER (int accNo, int money)
2   { if not valid(accNo) then
3        { abort no-acc }
4     else
5        { accountsB[accNo].amount += money;
6          return true
7            on compensate
8              if accountsB[accNo].amount >= money then
9                { accountsB[accNo].amount -= money;
10                 return false }
11             else
12               { abort no-money }
13   }     }
```

Fig. 5. Bank transfer example: callee

interaction to cases in which several servers can provide to the client the required reply. In these cases, the client asynchronously calls all the possible (alternative) servers, and then waits for the replies. The first reply will be accepted, while the other calls will be killed.

Consider, for instance, a concert ticket reservation method (the client of the pattern is specified in Fig. 6) that invokes two possible reservation services (Fig. 6, lines 2-3). The servers are specified in Fig. 7. When one of the two requests succeeds, the other is canceled. If the first one fails, the second one is waited for. Only if both of them abort (Fig. 6, lines 10 and 17), the failure *no_ticket* is propagated to the upper level. In case both of them will succeed, only one request will be considered (according to which of the two branches of the **await** clause will be selected): the other one will be compensate via the **kill** mechanism (Fig. 6, lines 6 and 13).

4   Semantics for Error Handling

In this section we extend the ABS semantics in Fig. 2 to include the error handling primitives discussed above. The rules defining the semantics for error handling in Fig. 8 are to be added to the ones of Fig. 2, but for rules *Return* and *Read-Fut*, which are supposed to replace the homonymous rules in Fig. 2.

In order to understand the rules, one has to keep in mind the different states a future can have. Futures are created with a value $\perp$, saying that no result from the invoked method is available yet. The callee can store in the future either a value $v \in Val$ specifying the return value of a successful method, or a failure notification $n \in Err$ in case of abort of the method call. On the other side the caller can store in the future the kill request $kill(f')$ where f' is the fresh future used for receiving the result of the kill request.

Rules *Return-Comp1* and *Return-Comp2* model successful return and installation of a compensation. The two rules differ since in the first case the return value is stored in the future, in the second case it is discarded because of a

```
1   int CONCERT_TICKET (int concert_code)
2   { f1 := service1!RESERVE_TICKET (int concert_code);
3     f2 := service2!RESERVE_TICKET (int concert_code);
4     await f1? do
5        on x := f1.get
6           do { f3 := f2.kill;
7                return x }
8           on fail no_ticket
9              on y := f2.get do return y
10                          on fail no_ticket abort no_ticket,
11    f2? do
12       on x := f2.get
13          do { f3 := f1.kill;
14               return x }
15          on fail no_ticket
16             on y := f1.get do return y
17                          on fail no_ticket abort no_ticket
18  }
```

Fig. 6. Client in the "speculative parallelism" example

```
1   int RESERVE_TICKET (int concert_code)
2   { await x := this.AVAILABLE(concert_code)
3            //returns the ticket code or -1
4     if (x = -1)
5        then abort no_ticket
6        else return x on compensate f := this!CANCEL(concert_code,x)
7   }
```

Fig. 7. Server in the "speculative parallelism" example

kill request. The compensation is installed by letting it precede by a **release**, forcing the terminated method to release the lock, and by an **onkill** f statement. This last is runtime syntax. Its semantics is defined by rules *Onkill1* and *Onkill2*. In case there is a $kill(f')$ inside future f the effect of **onkill** f is to change the special local variable *destiny* to f' so specifying that the result of the compensation will be advertised on future f'. Otherwise it releases the lock and checks again later. Notice that the standard **return** statement corresponds just to a **return** installing the default compensation **abort** NoC (rule *Return*).

Rules *Abort1* and *Abort2* define the **abort** n primitive. Essentially, it stores the fault name n in the future and releases the lock. In case the future contains $kill(f')$ instead the fault name is not stored, and f' is set to fault name Ann.

Rules *Kill1* and *Kill2* perform **kill**. In *Kill1* future f (containing a value, possibly $\bot$) is set to $kill(f')$ and future f' is created and set to $\bot$. In *Kill2* instead f contained a failure notification, thus f' is set to Ann. Rule *Kill3* deals with killing of an already killed method call: simply the existing reference to the result of the **kill** is assigned to the variable. Thus **kill** is essentially idempotent.

$$(\textsc{Return})$$
$$ob(o,a,\{l|\text{return }e\},q)$$
$$\to ob(o,a,\{l|\text{return }e \text{ on compensate abort } \textsc{NoC}\},q)$$

$$(\textsc{Return-Comp1})$$
$$\frac{v = \llbracket e \rrbracket^{\varepsilon}_{(a \circ l)} \quad l(\text{destiny}) = f}{ob(o,a,\{l|\text{return }e \text{ on compensate }s\},q)\ \mathit{fut}(f,\bot)}$$
$$\to ob(o,a,\{l|\text{release};\text{onkill }f;s\},q)\ \mathit{fut}(f,v)$$

$$(\textsc{Return-Comp2})$$
$$\frac{l(\text{destiny}) = f}{ob(o,a,\{l|\text{return }e \text{ on compensate }s\},q)\ \mathit{fut}(f,\text{kill}(f'))}$$
$$\to ob(o,a,\{l|\text{release};\text{onkill }f;s\},q)\ \mathit{fut}(f,\text{kill}(f'))$$

$$(\textsc{Onkill1})$$
$$ob(o,a,\{l|\text{onkill }f;s\},q)\ \mathit{fut}(f,\text{kill}(f'))$$
$$\to ob(o,a,\{l[\text{destiny}\mapsto f']|s\},q)\ \mathit{fut}(f,\text{kill}(f'))$$

$$(\textsc{Onkill2})$$
$$\frac{y \neq \text{kill}(f')}{ob(o,a,\{l|\text{onkill }f;s\},q)\ \mathit{fut}(f,y)}$$
$$\to ob(o,a,\{l|\text{release};\text{onkill }f;s\},q)\ \mathit{fut}(f,y)$$

$$(\textsc{Abort1})$$
$$\frac{l(\text{destiny}) = f}{ob(o,a,\{l|\text{abort }n\},q)\ \mathit{fut}(f,\bot)}$$
$$\to ob(o,a,\{l|\text{release}\},q)\ \mathit{fut}(f,n)$$

$$(\textsc{Abort2})$$
$$\frac{l(\text{destiny}) = f}{ob(o,a,\{l|\text{abort }n\},q)\ \mathit{fut}(f,\text{kill}(f'))\ \mathit{fut}(f',x)}$$
$$\to ob(o,a,\{l|\text{release}\},q)\ \mathit{fut}(f,\text{kill}(f'))\ \mathit{fut}(f',\text{Ann})$$

$$(\textsc{Kill1})$$
$$\frac{f = \llbracket e \rrbracket^{\varepsilon}_{(a \circ l)} \quad \text{fresh}(f') \quad v \in \mathit{Val}}{ob(o,a,\{l|x := e.\text{kill};s\},q)\ \mathit{fut}(f,v)}$$
$$\to ob(o,a,\{l|x := f';s\},q)\ \mathit{fut}(f,\text{kill}(f'))\ \mathit{fut}(f',\bot)$$

$$(\textsc{Kill2})$$
$$\frac{f = \llbracket e \rrbracket^{\varepsilon}_{(a \circ l)} \quad \text{fresh}(f') \quad n \in \mathit{Err}}{ob(o,a,\{l|x := e.\text{kill};s\},q)\ \mathit{fut}(f,n)}$$
$$\to ob(o,a,\{l|x := f';s\},q)\ \mathit{fut}(f,\text{kill}(f'))\ \mathit{fut}(f',\text{Ann})$$

$$(\textsc{Kill3})$$
$$\frac{f = \llbracket e \rrbracket^{\varepsilon}_{(a \circ l)}}{ob(o,a,\{l|x := e.\text{kill};s\},q)\ \mathit{fut}(f,\text{kill}(f'))}$$
$$\to ob(o,a,\{l|x := f';s\},q)\ \mathit{fut}(f,\text{kill}(f'))$$

$$(\textsc{Pre-Kill})$$
$$invoc(o,f,m,\overline{v})\ \mathit{fut}(f,\text{kill}(f'))\ \mathit{fut}(f',\bot)$$
$$\to \mathit{fut}(f,\text{kill}(f'))\ \mathit{fut}(f',\text{Ann})$$

$$(\textsc{Read-Fut})$$
$$\frac{v \in \mathit{Val} \quad v \neq \bot \quad f = \llbracket e \rrbracket^{\varepsilon}_{(a \circ l)}}{ob(o,a,\{l|\text{on }x := e.\text{get do }s' \overline{\text{ on fail }n_i\ s_i};s\},q)\ \mathit{fut}(f,v)}$$
$$\to ob(o,a,\{l|x := v;s';s\},q)\ \mathit{fut}(f,v)$$

$$(\textsc{Read-Err})$$
$$\frac{n_j \in \mathit{Err} \quad f = \llbracket e \rrbracket^{\varepsilon}_{(a \circ l)} \quad (\text{on fail }n_j\ s_j) \in \overline{\text{on fail }n_i\ s_i}}{ob(o,a,\{l|\text{on }x := e.\text{get do }s' \overline{\text{ on fail }n_i\ s_i};s\},q)\ \mathit{fut}(f,n_j)}$$
$$\to ob(o,a,\{l|s_j;s\},q)\ \mathit{fut}(f,n_j)$$

Fig. 8. ABS semantics for error handling

Rule *Pre-Kill* discards a method invocation which has not started yet and which has to be killed. The future waiting for the result is set to Ann.

The last two rules are used for getting the result of a method invocation (or of a kill). If the value in the future is a non $\bot$ data value (rule *Read-Fut*) then it is assigned to the variable x and clause **do** is executed. If it is an error notification (rule *Read-Err*) instead the corresponding clause **on fail** is executed.

$$
\begin{array}{ccc}
\text{(GET)} & \text{(RETURN)} & \text{(ASSIGN)} \\[2pt]
\dfrac{\Gamma \vdash x : \mathbf{fut}\langle T\rangle}{\Gamma \vdash x.\mathbf{get} : T} &
\dfrac{\Gamma \vdash e : \Gamma(\text{return})}{\Gamma \vdash \mathbf{return}\ e} &
\dfrac{\Gamma \vdash e : T' \quad T' \preceq \Gamma(v)}{\Gamma \vdash v := e}
\end{array}
$$

Fig. 9. Sample typing rules for ABS

4.1   Typing

ABS relies on a type system guarenteeing that method binding always succeeds. One can extend the type system to additionally ensure that faults are managed in a correct way, in particular that all the faults that may be raised by a method invocation are managed by the caller.

While referring to [15] for a full description of the type system, we report in Fig. 9 the more interesting rules, and extend them to deal with error handling.

We use typing contexts which are mappings from names (of variables, interfaces and classes) to types. The reserved name *return* is bound to the return type of the current method. Relation $\preceq$ is the subtyping relation.

To check the correctness of error management, one has essentially to tag a method with the list of failures it can raise. Also, one has to specify the behavior of the compensation, including (recursively) its ability to throw faults. According to this idea, the signature Sg of a method m becomes:

$$
\begin{aligned}
Sg &::=\ T\ m\ (\overline{T\ x})\ ED \\
ED &::=\ \mathbf{throws}\ \overline{n}\ [\mathbf{on\ comp}\ T\ ED]
\end{aligned}
$$

Here $\overline{n}$ is the list of names of faults method m may throw. The optional clause **on comp** $T\ ED$ specifies the typing of the compensation. It is omitted if the compensation is not present. In this case it stands for the (infinite) unfolding of the type **on comp null throws** NoC **rec** $X.$**on comp null throws** $\varepsilon\ X$ where **null** is a subtype of any data type and ε the empty list.

As an example, the signatures of methods TRANSFER in Fig. 4 and MAKE-TRANSFER in Fig. 5 are respectively:

```
bool TRANSFER(int accNoA, int accNoB, int money)
     throws lost-money
bool MAKETRANSFER(int accNo, int money)
     throws no-acc on comp bool throws no-money
```

Similarly, futures have to declare the kinds of faults they are supposed to manage. The type declaration of a future becomes:

$$
T ::= \ \ldots\ \mid\ \mathbf{fut}\langle T\rangle\ ED \qquad \text{where } ED \text{ is as before.}
$$

We show in Fig. 10 the main typing rules for error recovery. We need two reserved names: $faults$, bound to the list of faults that the current method can throw, and $comp$, bound to the typing of the current compensation. Rule *T-Abort* simply checks that the thrown fault is allowed. Rule *T-Get* verifies that the returned value has the correct type, and that all faults that may be raised

$$\frac{\text{(T-Abort)}}{n \in \Gamma(\text{faults})} \qquad \frac{\text{(T-Get)}}{\Gamma \vdash x : T \quad \Gamma \vdash f : \textbf{fut}\langle T' \rangle \textbf{ throws } \overline{n_i} \; CM \quad T' \preceq T \quad \Gamma \vdash s \quad \Gamma \vdash s_i}{\Gamma \vdash \textbf{on } x := f.\textbf{get do } s \textbf{ on fail } n_i \; s_i}$$

$$\frac{\text{(T-Return)}}{\Gamma \vdash e : \Gamma(\text{return}) \qquad \Gamma(comp) = T \textbf{ throws } \overline{n} \; CM}{\Gamma[return \mapsto T, faults \mapsto \overline{n}, comp \mapsto CM] \vdash s}$$
$$\Gamma \vdash \textbf{return } e \textbf{ on compensate } s$$

$$\frac{\text{(T-Kill)}}{\Gamma \vdash x : T' \qquad \textbf{fut}\langle T \rangle \textbf{ throws } \overline{m_i}, \text{Ann } CM \preceq T'}{\Gamma \vdash f : \textbf{fut}\langle T'' \rangle \textbf{ throws } \overline{n_i} \textbf{ on comp } T \textbf{ throws } \overline{m_i} \; CM}$$
$$\Gamma \vdash x := f.\textbf{kill}$$

Fig. 10. Sample typing rules for error management in ABS

by the callee are managed. Rule *T-Return* checks the type of the returned value, and ensures that the compensation has the expected behavior. Finally rule *T-Kill* controls that variable x can store the result of the **kill**, including the possibility for it to be Ann.

The subtyping relation $\preceq$ has to be defined also on the new types for futures. It can be defined by:

$$\frac{\text{(Fut-Sub)}}{T \preceq T' \quad \overline{n} \supseteq \overline{n'} \quad T_1 \preceq T_1' \quad ED \preceq ED'}{\textbf{fut}\langle T \rangle \textbf{ throws } \overline{n} \text{ [on comp } T_1 \; ED] \preceq \textbf{fut}\langle T' \rangle \textbf{ throws } n' \text{ [on comp } T_1' \; ED']}$$

The type system is easily extended from statements to configurations. Then, a standard subject reduction theorem holds for configurations, ensuring that well-typed configurations evolve to well-typed configurations. Finally, it is possible to prove that in well-typed configurations whenever a **get** statement receives a fault n, it provides a corresponding **on fail** n s clause for managing it.

5 Conclusion and Future Work

Taking inspiration from models and languages for fault and compensation handling like the Sagas calculi [6] and the orchestration languages WS-BPEL [23] and Jolie [10], we have presented an extension of the concurrent object-oriented language ABS (the reference language in the European Projects HATS [13]) with primitives for error handling. Callee side faults are similar to exceptions as in e.g. Java, while the use of compensations for managing caller side kill requests is novel for the object-oriented world as far as we know. Our main contribution has been to combine these two mechanisms in a coherent way, suitable for a language with asynchronous communication based on futures. This approach has been developed by ensuring that the main principles underlying ABS were preserved, in particular concerning collaborative scheduling and asynchronous method execution. These features of ABS are needed so to allow compositional correctness proofs based on invariants, similarly e.g. to what done in [3, 9]. In fact, under collaborative scheduling processes may ensure that an invariant holds only at release points. If all pieces of code ensure that the invariant holds before any release point by assuming that it holds at the beginning of their execution, then the invariant holds under any possible scheduling, without any need to check for interferences.

Invariants shed some light on a typical problem of the compensation approach, namely compensation correctness. In fact, compensations are supposed to take the process back to a consistent state which is however different from the state where the process started. In other words, the rollback is not perfect. For instance, in [7] this is kept into account by relying on an user-defined equivalence on states: the compensations should lead the program to a state which is equivalent to the one where the program itself started. In a world where programs are equipped with invariants, compensation correctness becomes clearer: compensation should restore the invariant which has been broken by the failure.

Let us consider Example 1. There we have a distributed invariant specifying that the sum of the money in the source and target accounts should not change. Since this invariant involves two distinct objects, it may not hold when there are pending method invocations, kills or when at least one of the objects has not released the lock. It is easy to check that the invariant is preserved by the normal execution, where no fault happens. Interestingly, it is also preserved in case of faults which are handled. In fact, in case of fault in the callee the money is never removed from the starting account, and in case of failure in the caller the compensation withdraws the excess of money from the callee. The only case where the invariant is violated is if the caller wants to compensate the call, but this is no more possible because the money has already been used by the callee. This is also the only case where method TRANSFER aborts. Thus one can say that the code satisfies the invariant above in the sense that either it aborts, or the invariant holds when the call is terminated, independently on the number of (successfully managed) failures. In this sense we can say that the compensation code in the example is correct w.r.t. this specific invariant.

As future work, we plan to develop general techniques for proving correctness of compensations using invariants. Moreover, to better evaluate the practical impact of our proposal, we will implement the proposed primitives in ABS and we will investigate the possibility to apply our fault handling model in other object-oriented languages with futures.

References

1. Agha, G., Hewitt, C.: Actors: A conceptual foundation for concurrent object-oriented programming. In: Research Directions in Object-Oriented Programming, pp. 49–74. MIT Press, Cambridge (1987)
2. Agha, G., Ziaei, R.: Security and fault-tolerance in distributed systems: an actor-based approach. In: Proc. of CSDA 1998, pp. 72–88. IEEE Computer Society Press, Los Alamitos (1998)
3. Ahrendt, W., Dylla, M.: A system for compositional verification of asynchronous objects. Science of Computer Programming (2010) (in press)
4. Armstrong, J.: Programming Erlang: Software for a Concurrent World. Pragmatic Bookshelf (2007)
5. Baduel, L., et al.: Programming, Composing, Deploying, for the Grid. In: Grid Computing: Software Environments and Tools. Springer, Heidelberg (2006)

6. Bruni, R., Melgratti, H., Montanari, U.: Theoretical foundations for compensations in flow composition languages. In: Proc. of POPL 2005, pp. 209–220. ACM Press, New York (2005)
7. Caires, L., Ferreira, C., Vieira, H.T.: A process calculus analysis of compensations. In: Kaklamanis, C., Nielson, F. (eds.) TGC 2008. LNCS, vol. 5474, pp. 87–103. Springer, Heidelberg (2009)
8. Caromel, D.: Service, Asynchrony, and Wait-By-Necessity. Journal of Object Oriented Programming, 12–22 (November 1989)
9. de Boer, F.S., Clarke, D., Johnsen, E.B.: A complete guide to the future. In: De Nicola, R. (ed.) ESOP 2007. LNCS, vol. 4421, pp. 316–330. Springer, Heidelberg (2007)
10. Guidi, C., Lanese, I., Montesi, F., Zavattaro, G.: Dynamic error handling in service oriented applications. Fundam. Inform. 95(1), 73–102 (2009)
11. Haller, P., Odersky, M.: Scala actors: Unifying thread-based and event-based programming. Theoretical Computer Science 410(2-3), 202–220 (2009)
12. Halstead Jr., R.H.: Multilisp: A language for concurrent symbolic computation. ACM Trans. Prog. Lang. Syst. 7(4), 501–538 (1985)
13. European Project HATS, http://www.cse.chalmers.se/research/hats/
14. International Telecommunication Union. Open Distributed Processing — Reference Model parts 1–4. Technical report, ISO/IEC, Geneva (July 1995)
15. Johnsen, E.B., Kyas, M., Yu, I.C.: Dynamic classes: Modular asynchronous evolution of distributed concurrent objects. In: Cavalcanti, A., Dams, D.R. (eds.) FM 2009. LNCS, vol. 5850, pp. 596–611. Springer, Heidelberg (2009)
16. Johnsen, E.B., Owe, O.: An asynchronous communication model for distributed concurrent objects. Software and Systems Modeling 6(1), 35–58 (2007)
17. JSR166: Concurrency utilities, http://java.sun.com/j2se/1.5.0/docs/guide/concurrency
18. Lavender, R.G., Schmidt, D.C.: Active object: an object behavioral pattern for concurrent programming. In: Pattern Languages of Program Design 2, pp. 483–499. Addison-Wesley Longman Publishing Co., Inc., Amsterdam (1996)
19. Liskov, B.H., Shrira, L.: Promises: Linguistic support for efficient asynchronous procedure calls in distributed systems. In: Proc. of PLDI 1988, pp. 260–267. ACM Press, New York (1988)
20. Meseguer, J.: Conditional rewriting logic as a unified model of concurrency. Theoretical Computer Science 96, 73–155 (1992)
21. Morris, B.: CActive and Friends. Symbian Developer Network (November 2007), http://developer.symbian.com/main/downloads/papers/CActiveAndFriends/CActiveAndFriends.pdf
22. Nienaltowski, P.: Practical framework for contract-based concurrent object-oriented programming. PhD thesis, Department of Computer Science, ETH Zurich (2007)
23. Oasis. Web Services Business Process Execution Language Version 2.0, http://docs.oasis-open.org/wsbpel/2.0/wsbpel-v2.0.html
24. Plotkin, G.D.: A structural approach to operational semantics. Journal of Logic and Algebraic Programming 60-61, 17–139 (2004)
25. Schäfer, J., Poetzsch-Heffter, A.: JCoBox: Generalizing active objects to concurrent components. In: D'Hondt, T. (ed.) ECOOP 2010. LNCS, vol. 6183, pp. 275–299. Springer, Heidelberg (2010)
26. Venkatasubramanian, N., Talcott, C.L.: Reasoning about meta level activities in open distributed systems. In: Proc. PODC 1995, pp. 144–152. ACM Press, New York (1995)
27. Yonezawa, A.: ABCL: An Object-Oriented Concurrent System. MIT Press, Cambridge (1990)

Revisiting Glue Expressiveness in Component-Based Systems*

Cinzia Di Giusto and Jean-Bernard Stefani

INRIA Rhône Alpes, Grenoble, France

Abstract. We take a fresh look at the expressivity of BIP, a recent influential formal component model developed by J. Sifakis et al. We introduce a process calculus, called CAB, that models composite components as the combination of a *glue* (using BIP terminology) and subcomponents, and that constitutes a conservative extension of BIP with more dynamic forms of glues. We study the Turing completeness of CAB variants that differ only in their language for glues. We show that limiting the glue language to BIP glues suffices to obtain Turing-completeness, whereas removing priorities from the control language loses Turing-completeness. We also show that adding a simple form of dynamic component creation in the control language without priorities is enough to regain Turing completeness. These results complement those obtained on BIP, highlighting in particular the key role of priorities for expressivity.

1 Introduction

Component-based software engineering is by now well entrenched in various areas, from embedded systems to Web applications, and is supported by numerous standards, including UML. Its central tenet is that complex systems can be built by composing, or *gluing* together possibly independently developed components.

In their paper on glue expressiveness [3] Bliudze and Sifakis have proposed to look at the expressive power of *glues* or composition operators in an effort to assess the relative merits of different component frameworks with respect to their composition capabilities. In essence, the criterion they use to compare two sets $\mathcal{G}_1$ and $\mathcal{G}_2$ of composition operators is whether it is possible, given a family of primitive components $\mathcal{B}$ and an equivalence relation $\sim$ between these components, to find, for a given operator $g_1 \in \mathcal{G}_1$, a corresponding operator $g_2 \in \mathcal{G}_2$ such that all their compositions are equivalent, i.e. $\forall B_1, \ldots, B_n \in \mathcal{B} :$ $g_1(B_1, \ldots, B_n) \sim g_2(B_1, \ldots, B_n)$. As a notable result, they showed that their BIP component framework, whose glues feature multiparty synchronization and priorities, is universal with respect to a family of operators defined by inference rules in a subset of the GSOS format.

This work, however, leaves open a number of questions, in particular regarding the form glues can take, and their intrinsic expressivity. Indeed, the notion of

---

* Research partially funded by ANR Project PiCoq, Fondation de Coopération Scientifique Digiteo Triangle de la Physique, and Minalogic Project Mind.

W. De Meuter and G.-C. Roman (Eds.): COORDINATION 2011, LNCS 6721, pp. 16–30, 2011.

glue in [3] is essentially a static one. One may legitimately argue in favor of more dynamic forms of composition, e.g. to allow the creation of new components or the replacement of existing ones to accommodate different forms of software update. Even without considering full dynamic reconfiguration, one may take into account changes in configuration or interconnection between components, e.g. to accommodate different *modes* of operation, where the notion of mode is loosely understood as a collection of execution states [9]. It thus appears beneficial to consider not just static glues but glue processes in their own right.

In the paper, we adopt this view: we model component assemblages as terms in a process calculus, called CAB (for Components And Behaviors). A component assemblage (or composite component) in CAB takes the form $l[C_1; \ldots; C_n \triangleright B]$, where l is the name of the composite, $C_1, \ldots, C_n$ are the subcomponents of the composite, i.e. the components that are glued together (using BIP terminology) in the assemblage, and B is the *glue* – a term in a simple process calculus which we call the *glue language*. By construction, we recover BIP glues as essentially single state processes of our glue language.

With this view of glues as terms of a glue language, new expressivity questions arise, such as:

1. What is the expressivity of the resulting process calculus (in particular, if we restrict the glue language to terms corresponding to BIP glues only)?
2. What is the expressivity of the calculus if we remove the possibility of specifying priority constraints in the glue language ?
3. What is the expressivity of the calculus if we add more dynamic forms of control, such as component creation, in the glue language ?

In this paper we (begin to) answer these questions using classical Turing-completeness as our benchmark for expressivity. Following BIP, the CAB calculus is parametric over a family $\mathcal{P}$ of primitive components. So if we considered a large enough family, these questions would be trivial. Instead, we restrict our primitive components to be given by terms from the glue language itself – which form a strict non-Turing-complete subset of CCS – so as to characterize the intrinsic expressivity of the glue language. The questions then become non-trivial, and we obtain answers that may even appear surprising. Indeed, we first show that even with the restricted glue language consisting of static BIP glues only, the resulting variant of CAB is Turing-complete. Second, we show that this expressivity is lost if one restricts oneself to a subset of the glue language without priority constraints. These results confirms the expressive power of priorities, which was pointed out but not necessarily as clearly apparent in earlier works on BIP and process calculi with priorities. Finally, as a first answer to the last question, we show that we recover Turing-completeness if we add a very simple form of component creation in our glue language without priorities.

To summarize, our contributions are the following:

- We introduce a new process calculus, CAB, that extends the BIP framework with dynamic composition (or glue) capabilities.
- We demonstrate the expressiveness of priorities in the BIP framework by showing that BIP glues, composing simple CCS processes, is enough to

obtain a Turing-complete language, and that Turing completeness is lost
if we remove priorities.
– We show that Turing-completeness can be retained if we introduce more dynamic aspects in the language, namely a simple form of component creation.

The paper is organized as follows. Section 2 introduces the CAB process calculus and defines its operational semantics in SOS style. Section 3 proves our first result: CAB, restricted to a control language consisting of BIP glues, is Turing-complete. Section 4 proves our two other results: dropping priorities from CAB results in a non Turing-complete language; adding component creation to the control language without priorities is enough to regain Turing-completeness. Section 5 concludes the paper and discusses some related works.

2   CAB: Syntax and Semantics

We introduce in this section the CAB process calculus. In order to explain its constructs, as well as to make its relationship with the BIP framework clear, we begin by recalling the definition of the latter.

The BIP framework. We rely on the description of the BIP framework provided by [2,3]. A BIP component is simply a labeled transition system (LTS), whose labels are ports[1].

Definition 1. *A component is an LTS $B = (Q, P, \rightarrow)$ where*

1. *Q is a set of states*
2. *P is a set of ports*
3. *$\rightarrow \subseteq Q \times P \times Q$ is a set of transitions. We use $q \xrightarrow{a} q'$ to denote $(q, a, q') \in \rightarrow$.*

Components can be composed (glued) to form systems. A composition is given by a set of rules (the glue) that enforce synchronization and priority constraints among them.

Definition 2. *A BIP system S that glues together n components $B_i = (Q_i, P_i, \rightarrow_i)$ where ports and states are pairwise disjoint, is an LTS $S = (\mathbb{Q}, \mathbb{P}, \rightarrow_S)$ where $\mathbb{Q} = \prod_{i=1}^{n} Q_i$, $\mathbb{P} = \bigcup_{i=1}^{n} P_i$ and where $\rightarrow_S$ is a relation derivable as the least relation satisfying a finite set of rules[2] obeying the following format:*

$$r : \frac{\{B_i \xrightarrow{a_i} B_i'\}_{i \in I} \quad \{B_j \xrightarrow{b_j^k} \mid k \in [1..m_j]\}_{j \in J}}{(B_1, \ldots, B_n) \xrightarrow{a}_S (B_1', \ldots, B_n')} \tag{1}$$

where I and J are sets of indexes in $[1, n]$, $B_i' = B_i$ if $I \notin I$, and $I \neq \emptyset$ (i.e. there is at least one positive premise).

---

[1] This is a difference with the definition in [3], where labels are defined to be *sets* of ports. We have adopted labels as simple ports in this paper to simplify the presentation. Our results are not impacted by this decision, however, for our processes only have a fixed finite number of distinct ports, so that we can always bijectively map a set of ports onto a single port.

[2] The finiteness of the set of rules defining a glue seems implicit in [3].

Note that by definition there is at most one positive premise for each B_i in a rule in BIP format. The key features of the BIP framework are: (i) the ability to build hierarchical components; (ii) the concept of an explicit entity (the glue) responsible for the composition of components; (iii) the support of multipoint synchronizations, manifested by the positive premises in glue rules; (iv) The presence of priority constraints, given by the negative premises in glue rules.

The CAB calculus. As indicated in the introduction, we retain for CAB the general structure of composite components suggested by the BIP framework: a component in CAB takes the form $l[C_1; \ldots; C_n \rhd B]$, where l is the name of the component, $C_1, \ldots, C_n$ are its subcomponents and B is the glue. In contrast to glues in BIP, a glue in CAB can evolve over time, corresponding to changes in the synchronization and priority constraints among components, and is given by a term of a process calculus we call the *glue language*. We adopt in this paper a very simple glue language featuring:

- *Action prefix* $\alpha.B$, where α is an action, and B a continuation glue. The presence of action prefix in our glue language allows the definition of dynamic glues.
- *Parallel composition* $B_1 \parallel B_2$, where B_1 and B_2 are two glues. The parallel composition of glues can be interpreted as an *and* operator combining the synchronization and priority constraints embodied by B_1 and B_2. It is important to note that the two branches B_1 and B_2 in a parallel composition $B_1 \parallel B_2$ do *not* interact.
- *Recursion* $recX.B$, where X is a process variable, and B a glue. This allows the definition of glues with cyclic behaviors.

Formally, let $\mathcal{N}_P = \{a, b, c \ldots\}$ and $\mathcal{N}_C = \{h, k, l \ldots\}$ be denumerable sets of ports names and components names respectively. The CAB calculus is parametric over a set $\mathcal{P}$ of *primitive components* defined as labeled transition systems with labels in $\mathcal{N}_P$. We define CAB($\mathcal{P}$) processes as follows:

Definition 3 (CAB). *The set of CAB($\mathcal{P}$) processes is described by the following grammar, where P denotes an element of $\mathcal{P}$:*

$$
\begin{aligned}
S &::= l[C \rhd B] \mid l[P] & Act &::= \emptyset \mid \{evt\} \\
C &::= \mathbf{0} \mid S \mid C; C & evt &::= l : a \mid evt, evt \\
B &::= \mathbf{0} \mid \langle Act, Tag, Act \rangle.B \mid B \parallel B \mid recX.B \mid X & Tag &::= \tau \mid a
\end{aligned}
$$

In order to simplify notation we write $l : a$ instead of $l : \{a\}$, and a instead of $l : a$ when it is clear from the context which component is providing event a. We abbreviate $\alpha.\mathbf{0}$ to α. We define $S.\mathbf{nm} = l$ if $S = l[P]$ or $S = l[C \rhd B]$ for some P, C, B (i.e. the function $\mathbf{nm}$ returns the name of an individual component S).

Actions in our glue language differ from those in classical process calculi, such as CCS, for they play different roles: they embody synchronization and priority constraints that apply to subcomponents in a composition, and they provide a form of label renaming. An action is a triplet of the form $\langle pr, tag, syn \rangle$, where

$$\text{REC } \frac{B\{X/rec\,X.B\} \xrightarrow{\alpha} B'}{rec\,X.B \xrightarrow{\alpha} B'} \qquad \text{PAR1 } \frac{B \xrightarrow{\alpha} B'}{B \parallel B_2 \xrightarrow{\alpha} B' \parallel B_2} \qquad \text{PAR2 } \frac{B \xrightarrow{\alpha} B'}{B_2 \parallel B \xrightarrow{\alpha} B_2 \parallel B'}$$

$$\text{ACT } \langle pr, tag, syn \rangle.B \xrightarrow{\langle pr, tag, syn \rangle} B$$

$$\text{TAU } \frac{C_i \xrightarrow{\tau} C_i'}{l[C_1; \ldots; C_i; \ldots; C_m \rhd B] \xrightarrow{\tau} l[C_1; \ldots; C_i'; \ldots; C_m \rhd B]}$$

$$\text{BEH } \frac{C_{i_1} \xrightarrow{a_1} C_{i_1}' \ldots C_{i_n} \xrightarrow{a_n} C_{i_n}' \quad B \xrightarrow{\langle pr, tag, \{l_{i_1}:a_1, \ldots, l_{i_n}:a_n\}\rangle} B' \quad C_1 \ldots C_m \vdash pr}{l[C_1; \ldots; C_m \rhd B] \xrightarrow{tag} l[C_1'; \ldots; C_m' \rhd B']}$$

where $I = \{i_1, \ldots, i_n\} \subseteq [1, m], \forall i \in I, C_i.\mathbf{nm} = l_i$ and $\forall j \in [1, m] \setminus I, C_j' = C_j$

Fig. 1. A labeled transition system semantics for $\text{CAB}(\mathcal{P})$

pr is a priority constraint (i.e. events in subcomponents which would preempt the synchronization syn), syn is a synchronization constraint (i.e. events to be synchronized between subcomponents), and tag is an event made visible by the composite as a result of a successful syn synchronization.

Hence a glue B of the form $\langle\{l : a\}, t, \{l_1 : c_1, l_2 : c_2\}\rangle.B'$ specifies a synchronization constraint between two subcomponents l_1 and l_2: if the first one is ready to perform event c_1, and the other is ready to perform event c_2, then the composition is ready to perform event t, provided that subcomponent l is not ready to perform event a. When the event t of the composite is performed (implying the two subcomponents l_1 and l_2 have performed events c_1 and c_2, respectively), a new glue B' is then put in place to control the behavior of the composite. Note that tag t can be either τ (which denotes an internal event) or a port (an event). Hence a tag $t = \tau$ results in a synchronization between subcomponents that takes place silently, with no implication from the environment of the composite. A tag $t \neq \tau$ subjects the evolution of the composite to the availability of an appropriate synchronization on t in the environment of the composite.

The operational semantics of $\text{CAB}(\mathcal{P})$ is defined as the least labeled transition relation derivable by the inference rules in Figure 1. Rules for parallel composition and recursion are defined as usual. Rules BEH and TAU define the evolution of an aggregation of components inside a composite named l. Rule BEH stipulates that if a glue B is ready to perform an action $\langle pr, tag, \{l_1 : a_1, \ldots, l_n : a_n\}\rangle$ and components named $l_1, \ldots, l_n$ are ready to perform $a_1, \ldots, a_n$ respectively, then their composition is ready to perform action tag, provided priority constraint pr is satisfied. Having a priority constraint satisfied is defined as follows. Let $pr = \{l_{j_1} : c_{j_1}, \ldots, l_{j_k} : c_{j_k}\}$ with $J = \{j_1 \ldots j_m\} \subseteq [1, m]$, we say that $C_1 \ldots C_m \vdash pr$ iff for every $i \in J$, $S_i \xrightarrow{c_i} $ with $S_i.\mathbf{nm} = l_i$ and $S_i \in \{C_1, \ldots, C_m\}$. If $pr = \emptyset$ we are not imposing any priority policy on the synchronization.

Similarly, with an action of the form $\langle pr, tag, \emptyset \rangle$ there is no synchronization requirement, but the environment of the composite must be ready to perform tag in order for the system to evolve.

Notation 1. *We denote with* $!\alpha.P$ *the process* $rec\,X.\,\alpha.(P \parallel X)$. *We use* $\longrightarrow$ *to denote the relation* $\xrightarrow{\tau}$. *We use* $\prod_{i=1}^{n} B_i$ *to denote* $B_1 \parallel \ldots \parallel B_n$[3].

Encoding BIP. The operational semantics, and in particular rule BEH, above was defined so as to mimic very closely the capabilities of glues in BIP. We now clarify the relationship between $\mathrm{CAB}(\mathcal{P})$ and BIP systems defined over a set $\mathcal{P}$ of components. We can encode a BIP glue G in $\mathrm{CAB}(\mathcal{P})$ as follows. By definition, G is given by a finite set of rules r that obey the format given in Definition 2. Let r be such a rule:

$$r : \frac{\{C_i \xrightarrow{a_i} C_i'\}_{i \in I} \quad \{C_j \xrightarrow{c_j^k} \mid k \in [1..m_j]\}_{j \in J}}{(C_1, \ldots, C_n) \xrightarrow{tag} (C_1', \ldots, C_n')}$$

where I and J are set of indexes in $[1, n]$. The encoding $[\![r]\!]$ of rule r in $\mathrm{CAB}(\mathcal{P})$ is defined as:

$$[\![r]\!] = !\langle \{h_j : c_j^k \mid k \in [1, m_j]\}_{j \in J}, tag, \{h_i : a_i\}_{i \in I}\rangle$$

A BIP composition S with glue rules $r_1, \ldots, r_p$ and components $C_1, \ldots, C_n \in \mathcal{P}$ can thus be encoded as follows:

$$[\![S]\!] = l[h_1[C_1]; \ldots; h_n[C_n] \triangleright \prod_{i=1}^{p} [\![r_i]\!]]$$

By construction, we obtain:

Theorem 2. *BIP systems defined over a set* $\mathcal{P}$ *of components can be encoded in CAB(P): any BIP system* S *is strongly bisimilar to its encoding* $[\![S]\!]$.

3   Turing-Completeness of CAB

In this section as in the rest of the paper, we work within $\mathrm{CAB}(\emptyset)$, which, for simplicity, we denote CAB. We show the Turing-completeness of CAB by proving we can encode Minsky machines into it. This gives us a result on the *intrinsic* expressive power of the CAB glue language, in the sense that it does not depend on the presence of primitive components: we only construct component systems using glue language terms. Note that this is equivalent to considering only primitive components which are labeled transition systems defined by CAB terms of the form $l[\mathbf{0} \triangleright B]$, where B is a term with actions of the form $\langle \emptyset, a, \emptyset \rangle$. For reference, these primitive processes are given by terms of the following grammar, whose operational semantics is given by rules REC, PAR1, PAR2, and ACT in Figure 1:

$$B ::= \mathbf{0} \mid \langle \emptyset, a, \emptyset \rangle.B \mid B \parallel B \mid rec\,X.B \mid X.$$

---

[3] The parallel operator $\parallel$ is commutative and associative modulo strong bisimilarity.

$$
\text{M-Inc} \; \frac{i : \texttt{INC}(r_j) \quad m'_j = m_j + 1 \quad m'_{1-j} = m_{1-j}}{(i, m_0, m_1) \longrightarrow_{\text{M}} (i+1, m'_0, m'_1)}
$$

$$
\text{M-Dec} \; \frac{i : \texttt{DECJ}(r_j, s) \quad m_j \neq 0 \quad m'_j = m_j - 1 \quad m'_{1-j} = m_{1-j}}{(i, m_0, m_1) \longrightarrow_{\text{M}} (i+1, m'_0, m'_1)}
$$

$$
\text{M-Jmp} \; \frac{i : \texttt{DECJ}(r_j, s) \quad m_j = 0}{(i, m_0, m_1) \longrightarrow_{\text{M}} (s, m_0, m_1)} \qquad \text{M-Halt} \; \frac{i : \texttt{HALT}}{(i, m_0, m_1) \nrightarrow_{\text{M}}}
$$

Fig. 2. Semantics of Minsky machines

Minsky Machines. Minsky machines [10] provide a Turing-complete model of computation. A Minsky machine is composed of a set of sequential, labeled instructions, and at least two registers. Registers r_j ($j \in \{0, 1\}$) can hold arbitrarily large natural numbers. Instructions $(1 : I_1), \ldots, (n : I_n)$ can be of two kinds: $\texttt{INC}(r_j)$ adds 1 to register r_j and proceeds to the next instruction; $\texttt{DECJ}(r_j, s)$ jumps to instruction s if r_j is zero, otherwise it decreases register r_j by 1 and proceeds to the next instruction. A Minsky machine includes a program counter p indicating the label of the instruction being executed. In its initial state, the machine has both registers initialized to m_0 and m_1 respectively, and the program counter p is set to the first instruction. The Minsky machine stops whenever the program counter is set to the $\texttt{HALT}$ instruction. A *configuration* of a Minsky machine is a tuple (i, m_0, m_1); it consists of the current program counter and the values of the registers. Formally, the reduction relation over configurations of a Minsky machine , denoted $\longrightarrow_{\text{M}}$, is defined in Figure 2.

The encoding. The encoding of Minsky machines in CAB, denoted $[\![\cdot]\!]_1$, is given in Figure 3. We now give some intuitions on it. Given a Minsky machine M, we encode it as a system m. m contains three components: the two registers r_0 and r_1, and the program counter. The instructions of the machine are encoded in the glue of m. Numbers inside registers are encoded in the glue as the parallel composition of as many occurrences of the unit process $\langle \emptyset, u_j, \emptyset \rangle$ as the number to be encoded. An increment simply adds an occurrence of the unit process $\langle \emptyset, u_j, \emptyset \rangle$ to the register. The decrement and jump is encoded as the parallel composition of the two branches. The decrement branch simply removes one occurrence of the unit process $\langle \emptyset, u_j, \emptyset \rangle$, if such occurrence is available. The jump branch is guarded by the priority $r_j : u_j$. In other words, to be able to execute the jump, it is necessary to check that the register is indeed empty. If this is the case the program counter is updated accordingly. More formally, the encoding of a configuration in the Minsky machine is defined as follows:

$$\llbracket R_j = m \rrbracket_1 = r_j [\mathbf{0} \triangleright \prod_1^m \langle \emptyset, u_j, \emptyset \rangle \; \Vert ! \langle \emptyset, z_j, \emptyset \rangle \; \Vert ! \langle \emptyset, inc_j, \emptyset \rangle . \langle \emptyset, u_j, \emptyset \rangle]$$

INSTRUCTIONS $(i : I_i)$

$\llbracket (i : \text{INC}(r_j)) \rrbracket_1 \quad = ! \langle \emptyset, \tau, \{p_i, inc_j, next_{i+1}\} \rangle$

$\llbracket (i : \text{DECJ}(r_j, s)) \rrbracket_1 = ! \langle \emptyset, \tau, \{p_i, u_j, next_{i+1}\} \rangle \; \Vert ! \langle r_j : u_j, \tau, \{p_i, z_j, next_s\} \rangle)$

$\llbracket (i : \text{HALT}) \rrbracket_1 \quad\quad = \langle \emptyset, halt, p_i \rangle$

Fig. 3. Encoding of Minsky machines into CAB

Definition 4. *Let M be a Minsky machine and (k, m_0, m_1) one of its configurations. The encoding of $\llbracket k, m_0, m_1 \rrbracket_1$ is defined as*

$$m[\llbracket R_0 = m_0 \rrbracket_1; \llbracket R_1 = m_1 \rrbracket_1; pr[\mathbf{0} \triangleright \prod_{i=1}^n ! \langle \emptyset, next_i, \emptyset \rangle . \langle \emptyset, p_i, \emptyset \rangle];$$

$$pr[\mathbf{0} \triangleright \langle \emptyset, p_k, \emptyset \rangle \; \Vert \prod_{i=1}^n ! \langle \emptyset, next_i, \emptyset \rangle . \langle \emptyset, p_i, \emptyset \rangle] \triangleright \prod_{i=1}^n \llbracket i : I_i \rrbracket_1]$$

where the encoding of registers and instructions is defined in Figure 3.

Notice that in order to synchronize at the same time p_i and $next_i$ we have to duplicate the component representing the program counter. This does not introduce non determinism as only one instance of the action $\langle \emptyset, p_i, \emptyset \rangle$ is available at every step.

The correctness of the encoding follows by a case analysis on the type of instruction performed when the program counter reaches k. This is formalized by the following Lemma.

Lemma 1. *Let M be a Minsky machine and (k, m_0, m_1) one of its configuration then $(k, m_0, m_1) \longrightarrow_M (k', m_0', m_1')$ iff $\llbracket k, m_0, m_1 \rrbracket_1 \longrightarrow \llbracket k', m_0', m_1' \rrbracket_1$.*

Proof (Sketch). Here we show only that if $(k, m_0, m_1) \longrightarrow_M (k', m_0', m_1')$ then $\llbracket k, m_0, m_1 \rrbracket_1 \longrightarrow \llbracket k', m_0', m_1' \rrbracket_1$ when the k-th instruction is a decrement on register $m_0 > 0$. The other cases and the other direction are similar or simpler.

Then, from Definition 4, we have that

$$m[\llbracket R_0 = m_0 \rrbracket_1; \llbracket R_1 = m_1 \rrbracket_1; pr[\mathbf{0} \triangleright \prod_{i=1}^n ! \langle \emptyset, next_i, \emptyset \rangle . \langle \emptyset, p_i, \emptyset \rangle];$$

$$pr[\mathbf{0} \triangleright \langle \emptyset, p_k, \emptyset \rangle \; \Vert \prod_{i=1}^n ! \langle \emptyset, next_i, \emptyset \rangle . \langle \emptyset, p_i, \emptyset \rangle] \triangleright \prod_{i=1}^n \llbracket i : I_i \rrbracket_1]$$

where the k-th instruction is encoded as

$$! \langle \emptyset, \tau, \{p_k, u_0, next_{k+1}\} \rangle \; \Vert ! \langle r_0 : u_0, \tau, \{p_k, z_0, next_s\} \rangle)$$

and $m_0' = m_0 - 1$, $k' = k + 1$. In this case, the only possible evolution is the one that synchronizes the program counter p_k, the unit u_0 inside register r_0 and $next_{k+1}$, evolving into the system:

$$m[\llbracket R_0 = m_0 - 1 \rrbracket_1; \llbracket R_1 = m_1 \rrbracket_1; pr[\mathbf{0} \rhd \langle \emptyset, p_{k+1}, \emptyset \rangle \parallel \prod_{i=1}^{n} !\langle \emptyset, next_i, \emptyset \rangle . \langle \emptyset, p_i, \emptyset \rangle];$$

$$pr[\mathbf{0} \rhd \prod_{i=1}^{n} !\langle \emptyset, next_i, \emptyset \rangle . \langle \emptyset, p_i, \emptyset \rangle] \rhd \prod_{i=1}^{n} \llbracket i : I_i \rrbracket_1]$$

Now, it is easy to see that the system above corresponds to $\llbracket k', m_0', m_1' \rrbracket_1$.   □

By means of the previous lemma, we can state the operational correspondence between M and its encoding $\llbracket M \rrbracket_1$.

Theorem 3. *Let M be a Minsky machine and $\llbracket M \rrbracket_1$ as defined in Definition 4. Then M halts with registers $R_i = m_i'$ for $i \in [0,1]$ iff $\llbracket M \rrbracket_1 \xrightarrow{halt}$ and locations r_i for $i \in [0,1]$ is $\llbracket R_i = m_i' \rrbracket_1$.*

It is important to notice that our encoding relies on elementary components of the form $l[\mathbf{0} \rhd B]$, which are glued together by glue terms which are essentially in BIP format, as discussed in Section 2. The above theorem gives us actually a stronger result which says that the subset of CAB where glues are restricted to be in BIP format, and where primitive components correspond to labeled transition systems given by elementary components of the form $l[\mathbf{0} \rhd B]$, is Turing-complete.

4   Expressivity of CAB Variants

We have shown that CAB is Turing powerful. We now investigate the sources of expressiveness in the language. The first thing we show is that in the encoding given in Section 3 the presence of priorities is essential. Indeed we can prove that if we consider a fragment of CAB without priorities the resulting language is not Turing powerful anymore. This can be proven by providing an encoding into Petri nets, a well known non Turing-powerful model.

4.1   CAB without Priorities

A *Petri net* (see e.g. [6]) is a tuple $N = (P, T, m_0)$, where P and T are finite sets of *places* and *transitions*, respectively. A finite multiset over the set S of places is called a *marking*, and m_0 is the initial marking. Given a marking m and a place p, we say that the place p contains $m(p)$ *tokens* in the marking m if there are $m(p)$ occurrences of p in the multiset m. A transition is a pair of markings written in the form $m' \Rightarrow m''$. The marking m of a Petri net can be modified by means of transitions firing: a transition $m' \Rightarrow m''$ can fire if $m(p) \geq m'(p)$ for every place $p \in S$; upon transition firing the new marking of the net becomes

$n = (m \setminus m') \uplus m''$ where $\setminus$ and $\uplus$ are the difference and union operators for multisets, respectively. This is written as $m \to n$.

We denote the fragment of CAB without priorities as CAB^{-p}. This fragment is obtained by replacing production $\langle Act, Tag, Act \rangle$ with $\langle \emptyset, Tag, Act \rangle$ in Definition 3. Before presenting the encoding into Petri Nets, we introduce some more terminology: we define a notion of top level actions in the glue of a component.

Definition 5 (*top*). *Let* $l[C \triangleright B]$ *be a system in CAB. top(B) is defined inductively on the structure of the glue* B *as follows:*

$$top(\mathbf{0}) = top(X) ::= \emptyset \qquad top(\langle pr, tag, syn \rangle.B) ::= \{\langle pr, tag, syn \rangle\}$$
$$top(recX.B) ::= top(B) \qquad top(B_1 \parallel B_2) ::= top(B_1) \cup top(B_2)$$

We also define how to build the graph of precedence of a glue B:

Definition 6. *Let* $l[C \triangleright B]$ *be a system in CAB. The graph of* B, *denoted with* $\mathcal{G}(B) = (Nodes(B), Edges(B))$, *is a directed graph, inductively defined as:*

$$\mathcal{G}(\mathbf{0}) \qquad ::= Nodes(B) = \{\mathbf{0}\},$$
$$Edges(B) = \emptyset$$
$$\mathcal{G}(\langle act \rangle.B_1) ::= Nodes(B) = \{\langle act \rangle\} \cup Nodes(B_1),$$
$$Edges(B) = \{\langle act \rangle \to x \mid x \in top(B_1)\} \cup Edges(B_1)$$
$$\mathcal{G}(B_1 \parallel B_2) ::= Nodes(B) = Nodes(B_1) \cup Nodes(B_2),$$
$$Edges(B) = Edges(B_1) \cup Edges(B_2)$$
$$\mathcal{G}(recX.B_1) ::= Nodes(B) = Nodes(B_1)$$
$$Edges(B) = Edges(B_1) \text{ where every time we encounter}$$
$$X \text{ we add an edge to the nodes in } top(B_1)$$

Let $n \in Nodes(B)$, *we denote with* $Adj(n)$ *the list of nodes adjacent to* n.

The idea is that every system is a Petri Net and the marking represents the components that are ready to interact at a given instant. Transitions mimic the semantics of CAB^{-p} systems. The construction of the Petri Net is inductive on the hierarchy of components: let $S = l_S[S_1; \ldots; S_m \triangleright B_S]$ be a system in CAB^{-p}. We assume that k is the maximum number of levels of nesting in S. We decorate every location in S with the corresponding level of nesting in S, from 1 the innermost, to k the outermost level.

Let $\mathcal{PN}(S_i) = (P(S_i), T(S_i), m_0(S_i))$ be the Petri Net for the subsystem S_i for all $i \in [1, m]$. $\mathcal{PN}(S)$ is built by taking:

- as set of places, the set of all places of the subnets for $S_1 \ldots S_n$ plus all the nodes in the graph of the behavior B_S:

$$P(S) = \bigcup_{i=1}^{n} P(S_i) \cup \{[l_S^k : \langle \emptyset, tag, syn \rangle] \mid \langle \emptyset, tag, syn \rangle \in Nodes(B_S)\};$$

Notice that there is a bijection between nodes in the graphs of glues and the places in the Petri Net. Hence for every node n in the graph of glue located at l in level j there exists a distinctive place $[l^j : n]$ and vice-versa.

– as set of transitions all the transitions of subnets $\mathcal{PN}(S_1) \ldots \mathcal{PN}(S_n)$ plus
  for all nodes $\langle \emptyset, tag, syn \rangle$ in $Nodes(B_S)$ where $tag = \tau$ we add a set of
  transitions that:
  • Take as precondition, recursively on the part syn of the nodes considered,
    all the places $[l^j : \langle \emptyset, t, s \rangle]$ for $j \in [1, k-1]$ and such that $l : t$ appears
    in the synchronization part syn in one of the nodes. Notice that, this
    accounts in considering in a single transition all the components involved
    in a τ step: i.e. the places involved in the precondition correspond to all
    the leafs in the derivation tree of the τ step.
  • Take as postcondition all the places built from nodes in the adjacent list
    of all the nodes obtained by places in the preconditions.
  For instance, consider the system

$$l^3[l^2[l^1[\mathbf{0} \rhd \langle \emptyset, a, \emptyset \rangle.\mathbf{0}] \rhd \langle \emptyset, b, \{l^1 : a\} \rangle.\mathbf{0}] \rhd \langle \emptyset, \tau, \{l^2 : b\} \rangle.\mathbf{0}]$$

  here there is a single transition that takes as precondition the places: $\{[l^3 :$
  $\langle \emptyset, \tau, \{l^2 : b\} \rangle], [l^2 : \langle \emptyset, b, \{l^1 : a\} \rangle], [l^3 : \langle \emptyset, a, \emptyset \rangle]\}$ and as post condition the
  places $\{[l^1 : \mathbf{0}], [l^2 : \mathbf{0}], [l^3 : \mathbf{0}]\}$
– as initial marking, the initial marking of all subnets plus the nodes corresponding to the top level actions in B_S:

$$m_0(S) = \uplus_{i=1}^n m_0(S_i) \uplus \{[l_S^k : n] \mid n \in top(B_S)\}$$

The correctness of the above construction follows by induction on the nesting
of components.

Theorem 4. *Let $S = l_S[S_1; \ldots; S_m \rhd B_S]$ be a system in CAB^{-p}, and $\mathcal{PN}(S) = (P(S), T(S), m_0(S))$ the corresponding Petri Net. Then $S \longrightarrow S'$ iff there exists a marking m' such that $m_0(S) \Rightarrow m'$ and m' is a marking that takes all the top level actions in S'.*

Proof. Here we show only the correctness direction, soundness is similar. Let
$S = l_S[S_1; \ldots; S_m \rhd B_S]$ be a system in CAB^{-p}, and $m_0(S)$ the initial marking in
the Petri Net constructed as described above. The proof proceeds by induction on
the nesting of components in S. If $S \longrightarrow S'$ then we have that either rule BEH or
TAU has been used. The case of TAU follows by inductive hypothesis. Instead if
the τ step comes from BEH , we have that there exists an action $\langle \emptyset, \tau, \{a_1 \ldots a_n\} \rangle$
at top level in B_S. Moreover we have $C_{i_1} \ldots C_{i_n}$ components that are offering
actions $a_1 \ldots a_n$ respectively. Hence at top level in these components we have an
action $\langle \emptyset, a_{i_j}, syn \rangle$ for $j \in [1, n]$. Therefore, by construction we have a token in
all these places and the transition can fire, moving all tokens in the successors
of the action: i.e. in all the nodes of the adjacency list, that by construction
corresponds to the new action at top level in S'.   □

4.2   Recovering Expressiveness

We, now, introduce a new construct to CAB^{-p} to recover the loss of expressiveness due to the absence of priorities. We consider an operator that adds new

$$\begin{aligned}
\llbracket R_j = 0 \rrbracket_2 &::= r_j[a[\mathbf{0} \rhd \langle \emptyset, act_j, \emptyset \rangle \; |||\, !\langle \emptyset, zero_j, \emptyset \rangle.\langle \emptyset, act_j, \emptyset \rangle] \rhd Fwd \parallel Z \parallel INC] \\
Fwd &::= !\langle \emptyset, inc_j, inc_j \rangle \; |||\, !\langle \emptyset, dec_j, dec_j \rangle \\
Z &::= !\langle \emptyset, z_j, act_j \rangle.\langle \emptyset, \tau, zero_j \rangle \\
INC &::= !\langle \emptyset, inc_j, act_j \rangle.new \; Level \\
Level &::= a[a[\mathbf{0} \rhd \langle \emptyset, act_j, \emptyset \rangle] \rhd Fwd \parallel DEC \parallel INC] \\
DEC &::= \langle \emptyset, dec_j, act_j \rangle.\langle \emptyset, act_j, \emptyset \rangle
\end{aligned}$$

INSTRUCTIONS $(i : I_i)$

$$\begin{aligned}
\llbracket (i : \mathtt{INC}(r_j)) \rrbracket_2 &= !\langle \emptyset, \tau, \{p_i, inc_j, next_{i+1}\} \rangle \\
\llbracket (i : \mathtt{DECJ}(r_j, s)) \rrbracket_2 &= !\langle \emptyset, \tau, \{p_i, dec_j, next_{i+1}\} \rangle \; |||\, !\langle \emptyset, \tau, \{p_i, z_j, next_s\} \rangle) \\
\llbracket (i : \mathtt{HALT}) \rrbracket_2 &= \langle \emptyset, halt, p_i \rangle
\end{aligned}$$

Fig. 4. Encoding of Minsky machines into CAB without priorities

components inside a system. To this aim, we add to Definition 3 the following production:

$$B ::= new \; S$$

with this operational semantics:

$$\text{NEW} \; new \; S \xrightarrow{new \; S} \mathbf{0} \qquad \text{CRE} \; \frac{B \xrightarrow{new \; S} B'}{l[C \rhd B] \xrightarrow{\tau} l[C; S \rhd B']}$$

Thanks to the interplay between the creation of new components and recursion we can re-obtain Turing equivalence. The result, similarly to the one in Section 3, is obtained by resorting to an encoding of Minsky machines. We proceed by giving some intuitions on the encoding given in Figure 4. Registers are encoded as a hierarchy of components that handle both the representation of the number and a mechanism to increment or decrement. The nesting of these components represents the number contained. At every instant, the mechanism controlling the register is placed in the innermost position. Thus, whenever an increment takes place, a new component is created inside the deepest level and all the control is transfered to the newly created object: this is the role of $a[\mathbf{0} \rhd \langle \emptyset, act_j, \emptyset \rangle]$ which activates the current instance. On the contrary, in case of a decrement, the current instance is deactivated: i.e. it remains as garbage but it cannot be used anymore and a signal is passed to the upper component so to activate decrements and increments at the proper level of nesting. Notice, that in order to communicate with the active instance, it is necessary to equip every level of the nesting with a process Fwd. This process is responsible for forwarding increment and decrement events to reach the component that controls the simulation of the computation. Without loss of generality, we assume that registers are initialized to zero. The following definition formalizes the encoding of a Minsky machine M:

Definition 7. *Let M be a Minsky machine with registers initialized to 0 and program counter set to 1: its encoding $\llbracket M \rrbracket_2$ is*

$$m[\![R_0 = 0]\!]_2; [\![R_1 = 0]\!]_2; pr[\mathbf{0} \triangleright \prod_{i=1}^{n} !\langle \emptyset, next_i, \emptyset \rangle.\langle \emptyset, p_i, \emptyset \rangle];$$

$$pr[\mathbf{0} \triangleright \langle \emptyset, p_1, \emptyset \rangle \parallel \prod_{i=1}^{n} !\langle \emptyset, next_i, \emptyset \rangle.\langle \emptyset, p_i, \emptyset \rangle] \triangleright \prod_{i=1}^{n} [\![i : I_i]\!]_2]$$

where the encoding of registers and instructions is defined in Figure 4.[4]

Similarly as before, the correctness of the encoding follows by a case analysis on the type of instruction performed when the program counter reaches k. Notice that, depending on the specific computation there can be components as $a[a[\mathbf{0} \triangleright \mathbf{0}] \triangleright Fwd \parallel INC]$ "floating" in the system. Nevertheless this garbage can be ignored as it is never re-used: i.e. it cannot interact with the rest of the system.

Lemma 2. *Let M be a Minsky machine and (k, m_0, m_1) one of its configuration then $(k, m_0, m_1) \longrightarrow_M (k', m_0', m_1')$ iff $[\![k, m_0, m_1]\!]_2 \longrightarrow [\![k', m_0', m_1']\!]_2$.*

Proof (Sketch). Here we show only that if $(k, m_0, m_1) \longrightarrow_M (k', m_0', m_1')$ then $[\![k, m_0, m_1]\!]_2 \longrightarrow [\![k', m_0', m_1']\!]_2$ when the k-th instruction is a decrement on register $m_0 > 0$. The other cases and the other direction are similar or simpler.

We first define $[\![k, m_0, m_1]\!]_2$, for the sake of simplicity we will not consider the occurrences of garbage objects, taking for grant that those will not interfere with the computation.

$$[\![k, m_0, m_1]\!]_2 ::= m[\![R_0 = m_0]\!]_2; [\![R_1 = m_1]\!]_2; pr[\mathbf{0} \triangleright \prod_{i=1}^{n} !\langle \emptyset, next_i, \emptyset \rangle.\langle \emptyset, p_i, \emptyset \rangle];$$

$$pr[\mathbf{0} \triangleright \langle \emptyset, p_k, \emptyset \rangle \parallel \prod_{i=1}^{n} !\langle \emptyset, next_i, \emptyset \rangle.\langle \emptyset, p_i, \emptyset \rangle] \triangleright \prod_{i=1}^{n} [\![i : I_i]\!]_2]$$

where

$$[\![R_j = m_j]\!]_2 ::= r_j[a[\mathbf{0} \triangleright \langle \emptyset, act_j, \emptyset \rangle \parallel !\langle \emptyset, zero_j, \emptyset \rangle.\langle \emptyset, act_j, \emptyset \rangle],$$
$$C[\ldots C[a[a[\mathbf{0} \triangleright \langle \emptyset, act_j, \emptyset \rangle] \triangleright Fwd \parallel DEC \parallel INC]]\ldots] \triangleright Fwd \parallel Z \parallel INC]$$

and $C[\bullet] = a[a[\mathbf{0} \triangleright \mathbf{0}], \bullet \triangleright Fwd \parallel DEC \parallel INC]$ is repeated m_j times. The k-th instruction is encoded as

$$!\langle \emptyset, \tau, \{p_k, dec_0, next_{k+1}\} \rangle \parallel !\langle r_0 : u_0, \tau, \{p_k, z_0, next_s\} \rangle)$$

and $m_0' = m_0 - 1$, $k' = k + 1$. In this case, the only possible evolution is the one that synchronizes the program counter p_k, the message dec_0 inside register r_0 and $next_{k+1}$, evolving into the system:

---

[4] Notice that the interplay of recursion and creation of new components is implicit in the definition of INC and $Level$. The same thing could have been written as: $!recX\langle \emptyset, inc_j, act_j \rangle.new\ a[a[\mathbf{0} \triangleright \langle \emptyset, act_j, \emptyset \rangle] \triangleright Fwd \parallel DEC \parallel X]$.

$$m[\![R_0 = m_0 - 1]\!]_2; [\![R_1 = m_1]\!]_2; pr[\mathbf{0} \rhd \langle \emptyset, p_{k+1}, \emptyset \rangle \parallel \prod_{i=1}^{n} !\langle \emptyset, next_i, \emptyset \rangle.\langle \emptyset, p_i, \emptyset \rangle];$$

$$pr[\mathbf{0} \rhd \prod_{i=1}^{n} !\langle \emptyset, next_i, \emptyset \rangle.\langle \emptyset, p_i, \emptyset \rangle] \rhd \prod_{i=1}^{n} [\![i : I_i]\!]_2$$

Notice that the message on dec_0 will start a chain of synchronizations between components $a[\ldots]$ through the Fwd event to reach the deepest component and then activate the real decrement. It is easy to conclude that the system above corresponds to $[\![k', m_0', m_1']\!]_2$.   □

The previous lemma allows us to conclude:

Theorem 5. *Let M be a Minsky machine and $[\![M]\!]_2$ as defined in Definition 7. Then M halts with registers $R_i = m_i'$ for $i \in [0,1]$ iff $[\![M]\!]_2 \xrightarrow{halt}$ and locations r_i for $i \in [0,1]$ is $[\![R_i = m_i']\!]_2$.*

5   Final Remarks

We have taken in this paper a decidedly process algebraic view of glues in component-based systems, introducing an alternate view, and an extension, of the BIP framework in the form of the CAB process calculus. We have studied the expressiveness of CAB, which gave us a way to characterize the intrinsic (i.e. not relatively to a predefined family of components) expressive power of its glue language. We have shown that, while being very simple, the calculus is Turing-complete thanks mainly to the presence of priorities. As a matter of fact, we have shown that the fragment of CAB where priorities have been removed is only as expressive as Petri nets, which is a testament to the gain in expressive power obtained through the use of priorities. However expressiveness can be recovered in a calculus without priorities if dynamic operators are added to the language.

We have already discussed in the introduction the relations with the BIP framework and seen how the present paper brings new light on BIP expressiveness. Here we relate our paper to other works studying the expressiveness of multiparty synchronization or priority. Multiparty synchronization has been proposed in several process calculi. One of the first proposals is CSP [7] where synchronization can take place among all processes that share a channel with the same name. A recent work by Laneve and Vitale [8] has shown that a calculus able to synchronize on n channels is strictly more expressive than one that can only synchronize up to $n-1$ channels. [5] shows a similar result in the context of a concurrent logic calculus. In the current paper we have mostly shown the benefit of priorities for expressiveness. However we suspect that multiparty synchronization is also important for expressiveness. In our two encodings of Minsky machines in Section 3 and in Section 4, we rely decisively on 3-way synchronization; whether it is absolutely required is a question for further study.

Several works tackle the problem of adding priority mechanisms in a process calculus [4]. In [11] it has been shown that CCS enriched with a form of priority guards is strictly more expressive than CCS: essentially, it is possible to model the leader election problem in CCS with priorities, which is not the case with plain CCS. Analogously, [12] shows that a core calculus similar to CCS, if extended with several kinds of priorities, can model the leader election problem while the core calculus can not. Both these studies state the impossibility to encode the calculus with priorities in the plain calculus. In contrast, we show in this paper an absolute increase in expressiveness from Petri Nets to Minsky machines. Closer to the present work is the paper in [1], where the authors show that CCS without restriction, and with replication instead of recursion, can be encoded into Petri Nets while the same calculus enriched with priorities and a weak form of restriction is Turing-powerful. Compared to [1] we are considering recursive processes instead of replicated ones thus the drop of expressiveness when not using priorities is stronger in our case.

As for future work, we plan to investigate other, more involved, forms of dynamic configuration of components. Moreover we are interested in understanding if our result of Turing completeness can be related to the ability of simulating all recursively enumerable LTSs thus making unnecessary the presence of the parameter $\mathcal{P}$ in the full calculus $CAB(\mathcal{P})$.

References

1. Aranda, J., Valencia, F., Versari, C.: On the expressive power of restriction and priorities in CCS with replication. In: de Alfaro, L. (ed.) FOSSACS 2009. LNCS, vol. 5504, pp. 242–256. Springer, Heidelberg (2009)
2. Bliudze, S., Sifakis, J.: The algebra of connectors - structuring interaction in bip. IEEE Trans. Computers 57(10), 1315–1330 (2008)
3. Bliudze, S., Sifakis, J.: A notion of glue expressiveness for component-based systems. In: van Breugel, F., Chechik, M. (eds.) CONCUR 2008. LNCS, vol. 5201, pp. 508–522. Springer, Heidelberg (2008)
4. Cleaveland, R., Lüttgen, G., Natarajan, V.: Priority in process algebra. Technical report, Nasa (1999)
5. Di Giusto, C., Gabbrielli, M., Meo, M.C.: On the expressive power of multiple heads in chr. To appear in ACM Transactions on Computational Logic (2010)
6. Esparza, J., Nielsen, M.: Decidability issues for petri nets - a survey. Bulletin of the EATCS 52, 244–262 (1994)
7. Hoare, C.A.R.: Communicating Sequential Processes. Prentice Hall International Series in Computer Science (1985)
8. Laneve, C., Vitale, A.: The expressive power of synchronizations. In: LICS 2010, pp. 382–391. IEEE Computer Society, Washington, DC (2010)
9. Maraninchi, F., Rémond, Y.: Mode-automata: a new domain-specific construct for the development of safe critical systems. Sci. Comput. Program 46(3) (2003)
10. Minsky, M.: Computation: Finite and Infinite Machines. Prentice-Hall, Englewood Cliffs (1967)
11. Phillips, I.: CCS with priority guards. J. Log. Algebr. Progr. 75(1), 139–165 (2008)
12. Versari, C., Busi, N., Gorrieri, R.: An expressiveness study of priority in process calculi. Mathematical. Structures in Comp. Sci. 19, 1161–1189 (2009)

Encoding Context-Sensitivity in Reo into Non-Context-Sensitive Semantic Models

Sung-Shik T.Q. Jongmans[1,*], Christian Krause[2,**], and Farhad Arbab[1]

[1] Centrum Wiskunde & Informatica (CWI), Amsterdam, The Netherlands
jongmans@cwi.nl
[2] Hasso Plattner Institute (HPI), University of Potsdam, Germany

Abstract. Reo is a coordination language which can be used to model the interactions among a set of components or services in a compositional manner using *connectors*. The language concepts of Reo include synchronization, mutual exclusion, data manipulation, memory and context-dependency. Context-dependency facilitates the precise specification of a connector's possible actions in situations where it would otherwise exhibit nondeterministic behavior. All existing formalizations of context-dependency in Reo are based on extended semantic models that provide constructs for modeling the presence and absence of I/O requests at the ports of a connector.

In this paper, we show that context-dependency in Reo can be encoded in basic semantic models, namely connector coloring with two colors and constraint automata, by introducing additional fictitious ports for Reo's primitives. Both of these models were considered as not expressive enough to handle context-dependency up to now. We demonstrate the usefulness of our approach by incorporating context-dependency into the constraint automata based Vereofy model checker.

1 Introduction

Over the past decades, *coordination languages* have emerged for modeling and implementing interaction protocols between two or more software components. One example is Reo [1], a language for compositional construction of *connectors*. Connectors are software entities that coordinate the communication between components; they constitute the *glue* that holds components together, and become, once considered at a higher level of abstraction, components themselves.

Connectors have several behavioral properties; for instance, they may manipulate data items that pass through them. Another property is *context-dependency* or *context-sensitivity*: whereas the behavior of a context-*in*sensitive connector depends only on its own state, the behavior of a context-sensitive connector depends also on the presence or absence of I/O-requests at its ports—its *context*. To illustrate context-sensitivity, we consider the LossySync connector, which coordinates the interaction between two components: a *writer* and a *taker*. If the

---

* Corresponding author.
** Supported by the research school in 'Service-Oriented Systems Engineering' at HPI.

taker is prepared to receive data, LossySync properly relays a data item from the writer to the taker. If the taker, however, refuses to receive, LossySync loses the data item sent by the writer. Since LossySync's behavior depends on the taker's willingness to receive data, that is, the presence or absence of a request for input, LossySync exhibits context-dependent behavior.

Several formal models for describing the behavior of Reo connectors exist, but not all of them have constructs for context-dependency. For example, the early models (e.g., an operational model based on *constraint automata* [2]), although attractive because of their simplicity, lack such constructs. These models implement context-sensitivity as non-determinism. In an attempt to mend this deficiency, more recent models incorporate constructs for context-dependency, but at the cost of more complex formalisms (e.g., the *3-coloring model* [3]). As a result, the algorithms for their simulation and verification suffer from a high computational complexity, which makes these models less attractive in practice.

In this contribution, we show that context-dependency in fact *can* be captured in simple semantic models, namely the *2-coloring model* [3] and constraint automata: we define an operator that transforms a connector with 3-coloring semantics to one with 2-coloring semantics, while preserving its context-sensitive behavior. Furthermore, we prove the transformation's correctness, and, to illustrate its merits, we show how our approach enables the verification of context-dependent connectors with the Vereofy model checker (impossible up to now). Other applications of our approach include context-sensitive *connector decomposition* [4], and, as we speculate, an improved implementation of Reo's interpreter.

The paper is organized as follows. In Section 2, we briefly discuss Reo and connector coloring. In Section 3, we present the transformation from 3-coloring models to 2-coloring models. In Section 4, we present an application of our approach to Vereofy. We discuss related work in Section 5. Section 6 concludes the paper.

2   Reo Overview

In this section, we discuss connectors in Reo and the coloring models for describing their behavior. A comprehensive overview appears in [1,5].

The simplest connectors, called *primitives*, consist of a number of input and output *nodes* to which components can connect and at which they can issue *write* and *take* requests for data items. Data items *flow* through a primitive from its input node(s) to its output node(s); if data flow through a node, this node *fires*. The semantics of a primitive specifies its behavior by describing how and when data items flow through the primitive's nodes. To illustrate this, we now present some common primitives and sketch their semantics informally.

The Sync primitive consists of an input node and an output node. Data items flow through this primitive only if these nodes have pending write and take requests. The LossySync primitive behaves similarly, but, as described in Section 1, loses a data item if its input node has a pending write request, while its output node has no pending take request. In contrast to the previous two memoryless primitives, primitives can have *buffers* to store data items in. Such primitives

Table 1. Common primitives

	Sync	LossySync	FIFO$_1$ (Empty)	FIFO$_1$ (Full)
	$A \longrightarrow B$	$A \dashrightarrow B$	$A \;\square\; B$	$A \;\blacksquare\; B$
2-Col	(diagram)	(diagram)	(diagram)	(diagram)
3-Col	(diagram)	(diagram)	(diagram)	(diagram)

exhibit different states, while the internal configuration of Sync and LossySync always stays the same. For instance, the FIFO$_1$ primitive consists of an input node, an output node, and a buffer of size 1. In the EMPTY state, a write request on the input node of FIFO$_1$ causes a data item to flow into the buffer (i.e., the buffer becomes full), while a take request on its output node remains pending. Conversely, in the FULL state, a write request on its input node remains pending, while a take request on its output node causes a data item to flow from the buffer to the output node (i.e., the buffer becomes empty). The first row of Table 1 depicts the three primitives discussed. In general, we define primitives as follows. Let $\mathcal{N}$ode be a denumerable set of nodes.

Definition 1 (Primitive). *A primitive P of arity k is a list $(n_1^{j_1}, \ldots, n_k^{j_k})$ such that $n_i \in \mathcal{N}$ode, $j_i \in \{\text{``i''}, \text{``o''}\}$, and $[if\ i \neq i',\ then\ n_i \neq n_{i'}]$ for all $1 \leq i, i' \leq k$.*

One can construct complex connectors from simpler constituents using *composition*. In this view, a connector consists of a set of nodes, a set of primitives connecting these nodes, and a subset of *boundary nodes* on which components can perform I/O-operations. Although primitives have only boundary nodes, this generally does not hold for composed connectors. For instance, composing LossySync and FIFO$_1$, by *joining* the former's output node with the latter's input, causes their shared node to become *internal* to the composed connector. This connector, called LossyFIFO$_1$, appears in the top–left cell of Table 2. We proceed with the formal definitions.

Definition 2 (Connector). *A connector C is a tuple $\langle N, B, E \rangle$ such that N is the set of nodes occurring in C, $\emptyset \neq B \subseteq N$ is a set of boundary nodes, and E is a set of primitives.*

Definition 3 (Composition of connectors). *Let $C_1 = \langle N_1, B_1, E_1 \rangle$ and $C_2 = \langle N_2, B_2, E_2 \rangle$ be connectors such that $E_1 \cap E_2 = \emptyset$. Their composition, denoted $C_1 \times C_2$, is defined as: $C_1 \times C_2 = \langle N_1 \cup N_2, (B_1 \cup B_2) \setminus (B_1 \cap B_2), E_1 \cup E_2 \rangle$.*

Thus, to compose two connectors, we merge their sets of nodes, compute a new set of boundary nodes, and merge the primitives that constitute them.

Thus far, we presented only the structure of connectors; next, we focus on their behavior. More specifically, we discuss *connector coloring* [3], the most relevant

Table 2. Empty LossyFIFO$_1$ and its $\mathcal{M}$-transformation

	LossyFIFO$_1$		$\mathcal{M}$(LossyFIFO$_1$)	
	A $\qquad\qquad$ B $\qquad\qquad$ C		A $\qquad\qquad$ B $\qquad\qquad$ C	

(2-Col. / 3-Col. colorings shown at left; 2-Coloring shown at right — figure)

model to this paper, in some detail; we mention other models in Section 5. Connector coloring works by assigning *colors* to the nodes of a connector. These colors specify whether data items may flow at a node. For instance, when using two colors, one color expresses that data can flow at a node (i.e., the flow-color: ——), while the other expresses the opposite (i.e., the no-flow color: - - - -). We call a total map from the nodes of a connector to colors a *coloring*.

Definition 4 (Coloring [3]). *Let $N \subseteq \mathcal{N}$ode and $\mathcal{C}$olors a set of colors. A coloring over N, denoted c, is a total map $N \to \mathcal{C}$olors. We denote c's domain by $\mathsf{dom}(c)$.*

To model a connector's different behavior in different states, we use *coloring tables*. A coloring table consists of a number of colorings and corresponds to a configuration of a connector; each coloring describes one way in which nodes can fire synchronously in this configuration.

Definition 5 (Coloring table [3]). *A coloring table, denoted T, is a set of colorings with mutually equal domains, denoted $\mathsf{dom}(T)$, and co-domains.*

When certain nodes fire synchronously, a connector's configuration may change (e.g., a full FIFO$_1$ can become empty). We use *next functions*, which describe transitions from one coloring table to the next, to model this change.

Definition 6 (Next function [5]). *Let S be a set of coloring tables such that $\mathsf{dom}(T_1) = \mathsf{dom}(T_2)$ for all $T_1, T_2 \in S$. A next function over S, denoted η, is a map $S \times \{\mathsf{dom}(S) \to \mathcal{C}$olors$\} \to S$ in which $\mathsf{dom}(S) = [\mathsf{dom}(T)$ for any $T \in S]$ is the domain of any coloring in $\bigcup_{T \in S} T$.*

Coloring tables that consist of 2-colorings for the previously discussed primitives appear in the third row of Table 1. For instance, the top coloring of Sync denotes the presence of flow between A and B; its bottom coloring denotes the absence of flow. The middle coloring of LossySync denotes that data items flow only at A, causing them to get lost before reaching B.

To compute the behavior of a composed connector whose constituents have coloring tables and next functions as semantic model, we use the composition operators for coloring tables and next functions. The formal definitions appear below; shortly, we discuss an example (LossySync).

Definition 7 (Composition of colorings [3]). *Let c_1 and c_2 be colorings such that $c_1(n) = c_2(n)$ for all $n \in \mathsf{dom}(c_1) \cap \mathsf{dom}(c_2)$. Their composition, denoted $c_1 \cup c_2$, is defined as:*

$$c_1 \cup c_2 = \left\{ n \mapsto \kappa \,\middle|\, n \in \mathsf{dom}(c_1) \cup \mathsf{dom}(c_2) \ \text{ and } \ \kappa = \left(\begin{array}{l} c_1(n) \text{ if } n \in \mathsf{dom}(c_1) \\ c_2(n) \text{ otherwise} \end{array} \right) \right\}$$

Definition 8 (Composition of coloring tables [3]). *Let T_1 and T_2 be coloring tables. Their composition, denoted $T_1 \cdot T_2$, is defined as:*

$$T_1 \cdot T_2 = \left\{ c_1 \cup c_2 \,\middle|\, \begin{array}{l} c_1 \in T_1 \ \text{ and } \ c_2 \in T_2 \ \text{ and} \\ c_1(n) = c_2(n) \ \text{ for all } \ n \in \mathsf{dom}(c_1) \cap \mathsf{dom}(c_2) \end{array} \right\}$$

Definition 9 (Composition of next functions [5]). *Let η_1 and η_2 be next functions over sets of coloring tables S_1 and S_2, respectively, and let $S_1 * S_2 = \{ T_1 \cdot T_2 \mid T_1 \in S_1 \ \text{ and } \ T_2 \in S_2 \}$. Their composition, denoted $\eta_1 \otimes \eta_2$, is defined as:*

$$\eta_1 \otimes \eta_2 = \left\{ (T_1 \cdot T_2, c_1 \cup c_2) \mapsto \eta_1(T_1) \cdot \eta_2(T_2) \,\middle|\, \begin{array}{l} T_1 \cdot T_2 \in S_1 * S_2 \\ \text{and } c_1 \cup c_2 \in T_1 \cdot T_2 \end{array} \right\}$$

The expressiveness of connector coloring depends on the instantiation of $\mathcal{C}olors$ in Definitions 4, 5, and 6. With two colors, we obtain *2-coloring models* in which $\mathcal{C}olors = \{ \text{———} , \text{- - - -} \}$. Whereas 2-coloring models can express synchronization, they cannot express context-dependency: to model context-sensitive connectors, three colors seem necessary. With three colors, we obtain *3-coloring models* in which $\mathcal{C}olors = \{ \text{———} , \text{- -▷- -} , \text{- -◁- -} \}$. Instead of one no-flow color as in 2-coloring models, two colors to express the absence of flow exist in 3-coloring models. As a result, in 3-coloring models, one can express *why* data does not flow, whereas in 2-coloring models, one can express only *that* data does not flow. More precisely, in 3-coloring models, the direction of the arrow of the no-flow colors indicates where the reason for the absence of flow comes from. Loosely speaking, an arrow pointing in the same direction as the flow indicates that a node has no pending write requests, while an arrow pointing in the opposite direction indicates that a node has no pending take requests. In text, we associate - -▷- - with the former case and - -◁- - with the latter. We prefix "coloring" by "2-" (respectively, "3-") if $\mathcal{C}olors$ in Definitions 4, 5, and 6 accords with 2-coloring (respectively, 3-coloring) models.

To illustrate the previous, 3-colorings for Sync, LossySync and FIFO_1 appear in the fourth row of Table 1, and composed 2-coloring and 3-coloring tables for $\mathsf{LossyFIFO}_1$ appear in the two bottom–left cells of Table 2. The middle coloring in the 2-coloring table of the empty $\mathsf{LossyFIFO}_1$ describes an inadmissible behavior: if A fires, but B does not, LossySync loses a data item between A and B despite the empty buffer. Such a coloring does not exist in the 3-coloring table of the empty $\mathsf{LossyFIFO}_1$. Thus, 3-coloring models can capture

Table 3. $\mathcal{M}$-transformation of common primitives

	$\mathcal{M}$(Sync)	$\mathcal{M}$(LossySync)	$\mathcal{M}$(FIFO$_1$) (Empty)	$\mathcal{M}$(FIFO$_1$) (Full)

context-dependency—through the propagation of the reason for the absence of flow—whereas 2-coloring models cannot.

Finally, we define *colored connectors* (respectively, 2-colored, 3-colored connectors), which are connectors whose semantics are defined in terms of a coloring model (respectively, 2-coloring model, 3-coloring model), and their composition operator, which preserves well-formedness by Proposition 3.3.5 in [5].

Definition 10 (Colored connectors). *A colored connector over a set of coloring tables S, denoted $\mathcal{C}^{\mathsf{Col}}$, is a tuple $\langle C, \eta \rangle$ in which $C = \langle N, B, E \rangle$ is a connector, and η is a next function over S such that $\mathsf{dom}(S) = N$.*

Definition 11 (Composition of colored connectors). *Let $\mathcal{C}_1^{\mathsf{Col}} = \langle C_1, \eta_1 \rangle$ and $\mathcal{C}_2^{\mathsf{Col}} = \langle C_2, \eta_2 \rangle$ be colored connectors. Their composition, denoted $\mathcal{C}_1^{\mathsf{Col}} \times \mathcal{C}_2^{\mathsf{Col}}$, is defined as: $\mathcal{C}_1^{\mathsf{Col}} \times \mathcal{C}_2^{\mathsf{Col}} = \langle C_1 \times C_2, \eta_1 \otimes \eta_2 \rangle$.*

3   From Three to Two Colors

In the literature, 2-coloring models are considered not expressive enough to capture context-dependency of connectors. In this section, however, we show the converse: at the expense of making the models of the primitives more complex, we encode context-dependent behavior using only two colors (and without altering the existing composition operators for coloring models). Our encoding comprises a generic transformation from 3-colored connectors to 2-colored connectors. Essentially, we trade a more complex semantic model—i.e., 3-coloring—with simple primitives for a simpler semantic model—i.e., 2-coloring—with more complex primitives. We start by introducing our transformation operator, denoted $\mathcal{M}$, which we liberally overload for different types of arguments for notational convenience. In Section 3.1, we prove the correctness of the transformation by showing that flow through nodes of a 3-colored connector $\mathcal{C}^{\mathsf{Col}}$ implies corresponding flow through its transformation $\mathcal{M}(\mathcal{C}^{\mathsf{Col}})$ (a 2-colored connector); in Section 3.2, we discuss the distributivity properties—important for compositionality—of $\mathcal{M}$.

We begin with the $\mathcal{M}$-transformation for connectors. Informally, this transformation clones all nodes in a connector and inverts the direction of the flow through these clones. The latter facilitates the backwards propagation of the reason for the absence of flow in case the connector lacks appropriate take requests (in a similar spirit as the $- \!\!-\!\!\prec\!\!- \!\!-$ color). Henceforth, we call a node n of the original connector a *base node* and its unique clone, denoted $\overline{n}$, a *context node*. Base and context nodes correspond *one-to-one*, and we consider them each other's *duals*. Next, let N be a set of base nodes. We define its $\mathcal{M}$-transformation, denoted $\mathcal{M}(N)$, as $\mathcal{M}(N) = \bigcup_{n \in N} \{n, \overline{n}\}$, that is, the set of base nodes and their duals. Finally, let inv be the inverse map of "i" and "o", that is, $inv = \{\,\text{"i"} \mapsto \text{"o"}, \text{"o"} \mapsto \text{"i"}\,\}$. We can now define $\mathcal{M}$ for connectors, starting with a definition of $\mathcal{M}$ for primitives.

Definition 12 ($\mathcal{M}$-transformation of primitives). *Let* $P = (n_1^{j_1}, \ldots, n_k^{j_k})$ *be a primitive. Its $\mathcal{M}$-transformation, denoted $\mathcal{M}(P)$, is defined as:* $\mathcal{M}(P) = \left(n_1^{j_1}, \ldots, n_k^{j_k}, \overline{n}_1^{\,inv(j_1)}, \ldots, \overline{n}_k^{\,inv(j_k)}\right)$.

Definition 13 ($\mathcal{M}$-transformation of connectors). *Let* $C = \langle N, B, E \rangle$ *be a connector. Its $\mathcal{M}$-transformation, denoted $\mathcal{M}(C)$, is defined as:* $\mathcal{M}(C) = \langle \mathcal{M}(N), \mathcal{M}(B), \mathcal{M}(E) \rangle$ *in which* $\mathcal{M}(E) = \{\, \mathcal{M}(P) \mid P \in E \,\}$.

One can straightforwardly show that $\mathcal{M}$ for primitives yields primitives, that is, preserves well-formedness with respect to Definition 1 [6]. The same holds for $\mathcal{M}$ for connectors (the proof uses preservation of well-formedness by $\mathcal{M}$ for primitives).

Proposition 1 ($\mathcal{M}$-transformation of primitives and connectors preserves well-formedness). *$\mathcal{M}$-transforming a primitive yields a primitive. $\mathcal{M}$-transforming a connector yields a connector.*

The $\mathcal{M}$-transformations of Sync, LossySync, and FIFO_1 appear in the first row of Table 3, while the top–right cell of Table 2 depicts the $\mathcal{M}$-transformation of $\mathsf{LossyFIFO}_1$. The figures exemplify that data flow in the opposite direction through context nodes when compared with the direction of the flow through base nodes. As mentioned before, this resembles how the 3-coloring model communicates the reason for no-flow backwards through the connector. Furthermore, context nodes nowhere communicate with base nodes: they form a *context circuit* that influences the behavior of the *base circuit* and vice versa, but data items cannot flow from one of these circuits to the other. The $\mathcal{M}$-transformation of LossySync exemplifies this influence: the new dotted arrow tangent to the original dashed arrow indicates that data may disappear between A and B iff data flow through $\overline{B}$.

To describe the behavior of $\mathcal{M}$-transformed connectors, we proceed with the definition of $\mathcal{M}$ for colorings, coloring tables, and next functions. We first present their formal definitions, and clarify these afterwards.

Definition 14 ($\mathcal{M}$-transformation of colorings). *Let c be a 3-coloring. Its $\mathcal{M}$-transformation, denoted $\mathcal{M}(c)$, is defined as:*

$$\mathcal{M}(c) = \bigcup_{n \in \mathrm{dom}(c)} \begin{cases} \{\, n \mapsto \text{-\,-\,-\,-}, \overline{n} \mapsto \text{-\,-\,-\,-} \,\} & \text{if } c(n) = \text{-\,-▷-\,-} \\ \{\, n \mapsto \text{-\,-\,-\,-}, \overline{n} \mapsto \text{———} \,\} & \text{if } c(n) = \text{-\,-◁-\,-} \\ \{\, n \mapsto \text{———}, \overline{n} \mapsto \text{-\,-\,-\,-} \,\} & \text{if } c(n) = \text{———} \end{cases}$$

Definition 15 ($\mathcal{M}$-transformation of coloring tables). *Let T be a 3-coloring table. Its $\mathcal{M}$-transformation, denoted $\mathcal{M}(T)$, is defined as: $\mathcal{M}(T) = \{\, \mathcal{M}(c) \mid c \in T \,\}$.*

Definition 16 ($\mathcal{M}$-transformation of next functions). *Let η be a next function over a set of 3-coloring tables S. Its $\mathcal{M}$-transformation, denoted $\mathcal{M}(\eta)$, is defined as: $\mathcal{M}(\eta) = \{\, (\mathcal{M}(T), \mathcal{M}(c)) \mapsto \mathcal{M}(\eta(T,c)) \mid T \in S \text{ and } c \in T \,\}$.*

Informally, $\mathcal{M}$ applied to a 3-coloring c clones its domain (similar to the way $\mathcal{M}$ for connectors clones nodes) and maps each node in the new domain to either ——— or -\,-\,-\,-. The idea behind these mappings follows below.

- If c maps n to ———, $\mathcal{M}(c)$ also maps n to ———, while it maps $\overline{n}$ to -\,-\,-\,-. This ensures that data never flow through the same parts of the base and the context circuits synchronously. If we would allow such synchronous flow, for instance, data items could flow between the base nodes and through the context circuit of a LossySync (i.e., this LossySync has pending write and take requests) at the same time. This would mean, however, that this LossySync may lose the data item flowing through its base circuit *without reason* (because of the pending take request). This is inadmissible behavior.
- If c maps n to -\,-◁-\,- (i.e., the no-flow color indicating that n lacks take requests), $\mathcal{M}(c)$ maps n to -\,-\,-\,- (because flow cannot appear out of nowhere), while it maps $\overline{n}$ to ——— (because the absence of pending take requests may cause lossy channels to lose data items).
- If c maps n to -\,-▷-\,- (i.e., the no-flow color indicating that n lacks write requests), $\mathcal{M}(c)$ maps n to -\,-\,-\,- (because flow cannot appear out of nowhere), and the same holds for $\overline{n}$ (because the absence of pending write requests may never cause loss of data).

Next, we discuss preservation of well-formedness [6]. Let c be a 3-coloring. We make two observations: (i) because context nodes correspond one-to-one to base nodes, $\mathcal{M}(c)$ maps all nodes in $\mathcal{M}(\mathrm{dom}(c))$ exactly once, and (ii) $\mathcal{M}(c)$ maps all nodes in its domain to either ——— or -\,-\,-\,-. Hence, $\mathcal{M}(c)$ defines a 2-coloring over the set $\mathcal{M}(\mathrm{dom}(c))$. Well-formedness of $\mathcal{M}$ for 3-coloring tables then follows immediately. Finally, we argue that $\mathcal{M}$ for next functions preserves well-formedness; let η be a next function over a set of 3-coloring tables S. Since $\mathcal{M}$ for 3-colorings (respectively, 3-coloring tables) yields well-formed 2-colorings (respectively, 2-coloring tables), and since S is a set of 3-coloring tables, $\mathcal{M}(\eta)$ defines a map from [2-coloring tables and 2-colorings] to 2-coloring tables. Hence, $\mathcal{M}(\eta)$ defines a next function over a set of 2-coloring tables.

Proposition 2 ($\mathcal{M}$-transformation of colorings, coloring tables, and next functions preserves well-formedness). *$\mathcal{M}$-transforming a 3-coloring c yields a 2-coloring over $\mathcal{M}(\mathsf{dom}(c))$. $\mathcal{M}$-transforming a 3-coloring table yields a 2-coloring table. $\mathcal{M}$-transforming a next function over a set of 3-coloring tables S yields a next function over a set of 2-coloring tables $\mathcal{M}(S) = \{\ \mathcal{M}(T) \mid T \in S\ \}$, and $\mathsf{dom}(\mathcal{M}(S)) = \mathsf{dom}(\mathcal{M}(T))$ for any $T \in S$.*

Finally, we present the $\mathcal{M}$-transformation of colored connectors. Both the definition and its preservation of well-formedness turn out straightforwardly. To $\mathcal{M}$-transform a colored connector, we take the $\mathcal{M}$-transformations of its constituents; preservation of well-formedness then follows from Propositions 1 and 2.

Definition 17 ($\mathcal{M}$-transformation of colored connectors). *Let $\mathcal{C}^{\mathsf{Col}} = \langle C, \eta \rangle$ be a colored connector over a set of 3-coloring tables. Its $\mathcal{M}$-transformation, denoted $\mathcal{M}(\mathcal{C}^{\mathsf{Col}})$, is defined as: $\mathcal{M}(\mathcal{C}^{\mathsf{Col}}) = \langle \mathcal{M}(C), \mathcal{M}(\eta) \rangle$.*

Proposition 3 ($\mathcal{M}$-transformation of colored connectors preserves well-formedness). *$\mathcal{M}$-transforming a colored connector over a set of 3-colorings yields a colored connector over a set of 2-colorings.*

3.1 Correctness of $\mathcal{M}$

In this subsection, we show the *correctness* of $\mathcal{M}$ for colored connectors. To define "correctness" in this context, we first introduce the concept of *paintings*, which are, essentially, (infinite) executions of a colored connector.

Definition 18 (Painting). *Let $\mathcal{C}^{\mathsf{Col}} = \langle C, \eta \rangle$ be a colored connector over S and $T_0 \in S$ the coloring table corresponding to its initial configuration. A painting of $\mathcal{C}^{\mathsf{Col}}$ is a sequence $[T_0, c_0, T_1, c_1, \ldots]$ such that $c_i \in T_i$, and $T_{i+1} = \eta(T_i, c_i)$ for all $i \geq 0$. The set of all $\mathcal{C}^{\mathsf{Col}}$'s paintings is denoted $\mathsf{Painting}(\mathcal{C}^{\mathsf{Col}})$.*

We call $\mathcal{M}$ for colored connectors correct if, for each painting of $\mathcal{C}^{\mathsf{Col}}$, there exists a *corresponding* painting of $\mathcal{M}(\mathcal{C}^{\mathsf{Col}})$ and vice versa; paintings correspond if, for all indexes, (i) the respective colorings assign flow to the same shared nodes—i.e., nodes that occur in both of the colored connectors—and (ii) the respective coloring tables correspond to the same configuration. We formulate our correctness theorem more formally below; a proof follows shortly.

Theorem 1 (Correctness of $\mathcal{M}$). *Let $\mathcal{C}^{\mathsf{Col}} = \langle C, \eta \rangle$ be a colored connector over a set of 3-coloring tables S and $\mathcal{M}(\mathcal{C}^{\mathsf{Col}}) = \langle \mathcal{M}(C), \mathcal{M}(\eta) \rangle$ a colored connector over a set of 2-coloring tables $\mathcal{M}(S)$ (by Proposition 3). Then:*

I. *if:* $[T_0, c_0, \ldots] \in \mathsf{Painting}(\mathcal{C}^{\mathsf{Col}})$
   then: $[\mathcal{M}(T_0), \mathcal{M}(c_0), \ldots] \in \mathsf{Painting}(\mathcal{M}(\mathcal{C}^{\mathsf{Col}}))$ *such that for all $0 \geq i$:*
   $$\{\ n \mid c_i(n) = \text{------}\ \} = \{\ n \in \mathsf{dom}(c_i) \mid (\mathcal{M}(c_i))(n) = \text{------}\ \}$$

II. *if:* $[\mathcal{M}(T_0), \mathcal{M}(c_0), \ldots] \in \mathsf{Painting}(\mathcal{M}(\mathcal{C}^{\mathsf{Col}}))$
    then: $[T_0, c_0, \ldots] \in \mathsf{Painting}(\mathcal{C}^{\mathsf{Col}})$ *such that for all $0 \geq i$:*
    $$\{\ n \mid c_i(n) = \text{------}\ \} = \{\ n \in \mathsf{dom}(c_i) \mid (\mathcal{M}(c_i))(n) = \text{------}\ \}$$

Later, we sketch a proof by induction that establishes the theorem. For the sake of conciseness, however, we first move large parts of the inductive step to the following two lemmas. Lemma 1 states that $\mathcal{M}$ for next functions over 3-coloring tables preserves the flow behavior of the connector. That is, if an untransformed coloring assigns flow to some base node, the $\mathcal{M}$-transformed coloring (i) exists, and (ii) also assigns flow to this base node. The same must hold in the opposite direction. Lemma 2 states that $\mathcal{M}$ for next functions preserves transitions from one configuration to the next. Note that these two lemmas correspond to the two conditions for "correspondence" given above.

Lemma 1 ($\mathcal{M}$ for colored next functions preserves flow). *Let η be a next function over a set of 3-coloring tables S, let $\mathcal{M}(\eta)$ be its $\mathcal{M}$-transformation, that is, a next function over a set of 2-coloring tables $\mathcal{M}(S)$ (by Proposition 2), and let $n \in \mathsf{dom}(S)$ be a node. Then:*

$$\begin{pmatrix} T \in S \ \text{and} \ c \in T \\ \text{and} \ c(n) = \text{---} \end{pmatrix} \text{ iff } \begin{pmatrix} \mathcal{M}(T) \in \mathcal{M}(S) \ \text{and} \ \mathcal{M}(c) \in \mathcal{M}(T) \\ \text{and} \ (\mathcal{M}(c))(n) = \text{---} \end{pmatrix}$$

Proof. We first prove the left-to-right direction (ONLY IF), and proceed with the right-to-left direction (IF).

ONLY IF — *We start by deriving the first two conjuncts of the right-hand side (RHS) from the first two conjuncts of the left-hand side (LHS). This turns out straightforwardly: $T \in S$ implies $\mathcal{M}(T) \in \mathcal{M}(S)$ by the definition of $\mathcal{M}(S)$ in Proposition 2, and $c \in T$ implies $\mathcal{M}(c) \in \mathcal{M}(T)$ by Definition 15 of $\mathcal{M}$ for 3-coloring tables. Finally, we derive the RHS's third conjunct from the third conjunct of the LHS. By the premise, $c(n) = \text{---}$. Then, by Definition 14 of $\mathcal{M}$ for 3-colorings, $\{ n \mapsto \text{---} , \overline{n} \mapsto \text{- - - -} \} \subseteq \mathcal{M}(c)$. Hence, $(\mathcal{M}(c))(n) = \text{---}$.*

IF — *The first two conjuncts of the LHS follow from the first two conjuncts of the RHS similar to the ONLY IF case. Next, by the premise, $(\mathcal{M}(c))(n) = \text{---}$, that is, $n \mapsto \text{---} \in \mathcal{M}(c)$. By Definition 14 of $\mathcal{M}$ for 3-colorings, this happens only if $c(n) = \text{---}$.* □

Lemma 2 ($\mathcal{M}$ for colored next functions preserves transitions). *Let η be a next function over a set of 3-coloring tables S, let $\mathcal{M}(\eta)$ be its $\mathcal{M}$-transformation, that is, a next function over a set of 2-coloring tables $\mathcal{M}(S)$ (by Proposition 2), and let $n \in \mathsf{dom}(S)$ be a node. Then:*

$$\begin{pmatrix} T, T' \in S \ \text{and} \ c \in T \\ \text{and} \ \eta(T, c) = T' \end{pmatrix} \text{ iff } \begin{pmatrix} \mathcal{M}(T), \mathcal{M}(T') \in \mathcal{M}(S) \ \text{and} \ \mathcal{M}(c) \in \mathcal{M}(T) \\ \text{and} \ (\mathcal{M}(\eta))(\mathcal{M}(T), \mathcal{M}(c)) = \mathcal{M}(T') \end{pmatrix}$$

Proof. The implication, in both directions, follows from the definition of $\mathcal{M}(S)$ in Proposition 2 (first conjunct), Definition 15 of $\mathcal{M}$ for 3-coloring tables (second conjunct), and Definition 16 of $\mathcal{M}$ for next functions (third conjunct). □

Finally, given the previous two lemmas, we sketch a proof of Theorem 1.

Proof (Of Theorem 1; Sketch). Both I. and II. follow from induction on the length of a painting's prefix. The base case (prefix of length 1) follows from preservation of well-formedness of $\mathcal{M}$ for next functions (recall $\mathcal{M}(S) = \{\ \mathcal{M}(T) \mid T \in S\ \}$), and because $T_0 \in S$ by Definition 18. To prove the inductive step, first, suppose there exists a painting with prefix of length $2j - 1$ on which the theorem holds, for some $j \geq 1$ (note that the $(2j - 1)$-th element is a coloring table). Next, apply Lemma 1 to establish that there exists a painting with a prefix of length $2j$ on which the theorem holds (note that the $(2j)$-th element is a coloring). Finally, apply Lemma 2 to establish that there exists a painting with a prefix of length $2j + 1 = 2(j + 1) - 1$ on which the theorem holds. $\qquad\square$

3.2   Distributivity of $\mathcal{M}$

Previously, we showed that by applying $\mathcal{M}$ to a 3-colored connector, we obtain a corresponding 2-colored connector. Though an essential result, it not yet suffices: to properly construct a complex 2-colored connector from context-dependent constituents, we still must compose a corresponding 3-colored connector from 3-colored primitives first. Only thereafter, we can apply $\mathcal{M}$ to obtain the desired 2-colored connector. Instead, we would prefer (i) to apply $\mathcal{M}$ only once to the 3-colored primitives (yielding, among others, the primitives in Table 3), and (ii) to construct context-dependent 2-colored connectors by composing these $\mathcal{M}$-transformed primitives. We prefer this approach, because we speculate that an implementation of Reo that operates on 2-coloring models can compute connector composition more efficiently than an implementation that operates on 3-coloring models. In this section, we develop the theory that accommodates this: we show the *compositionality* of $\mathcal{M}$. This means that it does not matter whether we (a) first apply $\mathcal{M}$ to 3-colored connectors and then the composition operator on the resulting 2-colored connectors, or (b) first apply the composition operator on 3-colored connectors and then $\mathcal{M}$ to the resulting composition. Specifically, we show that $\mathcal{M}$ distributes over composition of connectors (Definition 2) and composition of next functions (Definition 9). Distributivity over composition of colored connectors (Definition 10) then follows straightforwardly.

   We start, however, with a proposition stating that $\mathcal{M}$ for sets of nodes (defined in the second paragraph of Section 3) distributes over the set operators $\cup$, $\cap$, and $\setminus$. Our complete proof [6] consists of a series of straightforward applications of the definitions and the distributivity laws of these operators, while making use of the one-to-one correspondence between base and context nodes.

Proposition 4 ($\mathcal{M}$ for sets of nodes distributes over $\cup, \cap, \setminus$ for sets). *Let $N_1, N_2 \subseteq \mathcal{N}\text{ode}$ be sets of nodes. Then: $\mathcal{M}(N_1) \cup \mathcal{M}(N_2) = \mathcal{M}(N_1 \cup N_2)$, $\mathcal{M}(N_1) \cap \mathcal{M}(N_2) = \mathcal{M}(N_1 \cap N_2)$, and $\mathcal{M}(N_1) \setminus \mathcal{M}(N_2) = \mathcal{M}(N_1 \setminus N_2)$.*

We proceed with a compositionality lemma that concerns $\mathcal{M}$ for connectors.

Lemma 3 ($\mathcal{M}$ for connectors distributes over $\times$ for connectors). *Let C_1 and C_2 be connectors. Then: $\mathcal{M}(C_1) \times \mathcal{M}(C_2) = \mathcal{M}(C_1 \times C_2)$.*

Proof. Suppose $C_1 = \langle N_1, B_1, E_1 \rangle$ and $C_2 = \langle N_2, B_2, E_2 \rangle$ (without loss of generality). Applying Definition 13 of $\mathcal{M}$ for connectors and Definition 2 of $\times$ to rewrite the above equation, we obtain the following:

$$
\left\langle
\begin{array}{l}
\mathcal{M}(N_1) \cup \mathcal{M}(N_2), \\
\mathcal{M}(B_1) \cup \mathcal{M}(B_2) \setminus \mathcal{M}(B_1) \cap \mathcal{M}(B_2), \\
\mathcal{M}(E_1) \cup \mathcal{M}(E_2)
\end{array}
\right\rangle
=
\left\langle
\begin{array}{l}
\mathcal{M}(N_1 \cup N_2), \\
\mathcal{M}(B_1 \cup B_2 \setminus B_1 \cap B_2), \\
\mathcal{M}(E_1 \cup E_2)
\end{array}
\right\rangle
\quad
\begin{array}{l}
\text{(I)} \\
\text{(II)} \\
\text{(III)}
\end{array}
$$

Sub-equations (I) and (II) follow from Proposition 4. Sub-equation (III) holds because, by Definition 13 of $\mathcal{M}$ for sets of primitives: $\mathcal{M}(E_1) \cup \mathcal{M}(E_2) = \{ \mathcal{M}(P) \mid P \in E_1 \} \cup \{ \mathcal{M}(P) \mid P \in E_2 \} = \{ \mathcal{M}(P) \mid P \in E_1 \cup E_2 \} = \mathcal{M}(E_1 \cup E_2) = \mathcal{M}(E_1 \cup E_2)$. □

To show that $\mathcal{M}$ distributes over composition of next functions, we, as before, start with a proposition. More specifically, Proposition 5 states that $\mathcal{M}$ distributes over composition of colorings and coloring tables. We consider our complete proofs [6], though rather technical and detailed, straightforward. They rely on the following observations: (i) context nodes correspond one-to-one to base nodes, (ii) the colors assigned to a base node and its dual context node by an $\mathcal{M}$-transformed 2-coloring uniquely define the color assigned to the base node by the 3-coloring (by Definition 14 of $\mathcal{M}$ for 3-colorings), and (iii) each context node that corresponds to a base node in the domain-intersection of two untransformed 3-colorings occurs in the domain-intersection of their $\mathcal{M}$-transformations.

Proposition 5 ($\mathcal{M}$ for colorings and coloring tables distributes over $\cup$ for colorings and $\cdot$ for coloring tables). *Let c_1 and c_2 be 3-colorings. Then, $\mathcal{M}(c_1) \cup \mathcal{M}(c_2) = \mathcal{M}(c_1 \cup c_2)$. Let T_1 and T_2 be 3-coloring tables. Then, $\mathcal{M}(T_1) \cdot \mathcal{M}(T_2) = \mathcal{M}(T_1 \cdot T_2)$.*

We proceed with a compositionality lemma that concerns $\mathcal{M}$ for next functions.

Lemma 4 ($\mathcal{M}$ for next functions distributes over $\otimes$ for next functions). *Let η_1 and η_2 be next functions over sets of 3-coloring tables S_1 and S_2. Then: $\mathcal{M}(\eta_1) \otimes \mathcal{M}(\eta_2) = \mathcal{M}(\eta_1 \otimes \eta_2)$.*

Proof. Follows from Table 4. □

Finally, we present the compositionality theorem of $\mathcal{M}$, which states that $\mathcal{M}$ distributes over composition of colored connectors. As mentioned before, this result follows straightforwardly from the previous lemmas.

Theorem 2 (Compositionality of $\mathcal{M}$). *Let $\mathcal{C}_1^{\mathsf{Col}}$ and $\mathcal{C}_2^{\mathsf{Col}}$ be colored connectors over sets of 3-coloring tables. Then: $\mathcal{M}(\mathcal{C}_1^{\mathsf{Col}}) \times \mathcal{M}(\mathcal{C}_2^{\mathsf{Col}}) = \mathcal{M}(\mathcal{C}_1^{\mathsf{Col}} \times \mathcal{C}_2^{\mathsf{Col}})$.*

Proof. Suppose $\mathcal{C}_1^{\mathsf{Col}} = \langle C_1, \eta_1 \rangle$ and $\mathcal{C}_2^{\mathsf{Col}} = \langle C_2, \eta_2 \rangle$ (without loss of generality). Applying Definition 17 of $\mathcal{M}$ for 3-colored connectors and Definition 11 of $\times$ to rewrite the above equation, we obtain the following:

$$
\left\langle
\begin{array}{l}
\mathcal{M}(C_1) \times \mathcal{M}(C_2), \\
\mathcal{M}(\eta_1) \otimes \mathcal{M}(\eta_2)
\end{array}
\right\rangle
=
\left\langle
\begin{array}{l}
\mathcal{M}(C_1 \times C_2), \\
\mathcal{M}(\eta_1 \otimes \eta_2)
\end{array}
\right\rangle
\quad
\begin{array}{l}
\text{(I)} \\
\text{(II)}
\end{array}
$$

Sub-equation (I) follows immediately from Lemma 3, while sub-equation (II) follows from Lemma 4. □

Table 4. Proof: $\mathcal{M}(\eta_1) \otimes \mathcal{M}(\eta_2) = \mathcal{M}(\eta_1 \otimes \eta_2)$

$\mathcal{M}(\eta_1) \otimes \mathcal{M}(\eta_2)$

$= \ /^*$ By Definition 9 of $\otimes \ _*/$

$$\left\{ \begin{array}{c} \langle \mathcal{M}(T_1) \cdot \mathcal{M}(T_2), \mathcal{M}(c_1) \cup \mathcal{M}(c_2) \rangle \\ \updownarrow \\ (\mathcal{M}(\eta_1))(T_1, c_1) \cdot (\mathcal{M}(\eta_2))(T_2, c_2) \end{array} \middle| \begin{array}{c} \mathcal{M}(T_1) \cdot \mathcal{M}(T_2) \in \mathcal{M}(S_1) \cdot \mathcal{M}(S_2) \\ \text{and} \\ \mathcal{M}(c_1) \cup \mathcal{M}(c_2) \in \mathcal{M}(T_1) \cdot \mathcal{M}(T_2) \end{array} \right\}$$

$= \ /^*$ By the distributivity of $\mathcal{M}$ over $\cup$ and $\cdot$ in Proposition 5 $_*/$

$$\left\{ \begin{array}{c} \langle \mathcal{M}(T_1 \cdot T_2), \mathcal{M}(c_1 \cup c_2) \rangle \\ \updownarrow \\ (\mathcal{M}(\eta_1))(T_1, c_1) \cdot (\mathcal{M}(\eta_2))(T_2, c_2) \end{array} \middle| \begin{array}{c} \mathcal{M}(T_1 \cdot T_2) \in \mathcal{M}(S_1 \cdot S_2) \\ \text{and} \\ \mathcal{M}(c_1 \cup c_2) \in \mathcal{M}(T_1 \cdot T_2) \end{array} \right\}$$

$= \ /^*$ Because, by the definition of $\mathcal{M}(S)$ in Proposition 2, $\mathcal{M}(T') \in \mathcal{M}(S)$ iff $T' \in S$, and because, by Definition 15 of $\mathcal{M}$ for 3-coloring tables, $\mathcal{M}(c) \in \mathcal{M}(T)$ iff $c \in T$ $_*/$

$$\left\{ \begin{array}{c} \langle \mathcal{M}(T_1 \cdot T_2), \mathcal{M}(c_1 \cup c_2) \rangle \\ \updownarrow \\ (\mathcal{M}(\eta_1))(T_1, c_1) \cdot (\mathcal{M}(\eta_2))(T_2, c_2) \end{array} \middle| \begin{array}{c} T_1 \cdot T_2 \in S_1 \cdot S_2 \\ \text{and} \\ c_1 \cup c_2 \in T_1 \cdot T_2 \end{array} \right\}$$

$= \ /^*$ Because, by Definition 16 of $\mathcal{M}$ for next functions, $(\mathcal{M}(\eta_1))(T_1, c_1) = \mathcal{M}(\eta_1(T_1, c_1))$ and $(\mathcal{M}(\eta_2))(T_2, c_2) = \mathcal{M}(\eta_1(T_2, c_2))$ $_*/$

$$\left\{ \begin{array}{c} \langle \mathcal{M}(T_1 \cdot T_2), \mathcal{M}(c_1 \cup c_2) \rangle \\ \updownarrow \\ \mathcal{M}(\eta_1(T_1, c_1)) \cdot \mathcal{M}(\eta_2(T_2, c_2)) \end{array} \middle| \ T_1 \cdot T_2 \in S_1 \cdot S_2 \ \text{and} \ c_1 \cup c_2 \in T_1 \cdot T_2 \right\}$$

$= \ /^*$ By the distributivity of $\mathcal{M}$ over $\cdot$ in Proposition 5 $_*/$

$$\left\{ \begin{array}{c} \langle \mathcal{M}(T_1 \cdot T_2), \mathcal{M}(c_1 \cup c_2) \rangle \mapsto \\ \mathcal{M}(\eta_1(T_1, c_1) \cdot \eta_2(T_2, c_2)) \end{array} \middle| \ T_1 \cdot T_2 \in S_1 \cdot S_2 \ \text{and} \ c_1 \cup c_2 \in T_1 \cdot T_2 \right\}$$

$= \ /^*$ By Definition 16 of $\mathcal{M}$ for next functions, $_*/$

$$\mathcal{M}\left(\left\{ \begin{array}{c} \langle T_1 \cdot T_2, c_1 \cup c_2 \rangle \mapsto \\ \eta_1(T_1, c_1) \cdot \eta_2(T_2, c_2) \end{array} \middle| \ T_1 \cdot T_2 \in S_1 \cdot S_2 \ \text{and} \ c_1 \cup c_2 \in T_1 \cdot T_2 \right\} \right)$$

$= \ /^*$ By Definition 9 of $\otimes \ _*/$

$\mathcal{M}(\eta_1 \otimes \eta_2)$

---

4 Application: Context-Dependency in Vereofy

As an application, we present an implementation of our encoding in a constraint automata based model checker, which is considered as not expressive enough for the verification of context-dependent connectors. Specifically, we extend the Vereofy [7] model checking tool for the analysis of Reo connectors, developed at the TU of Dresden.[1] Vereofy uses two input languages: the *Reo Scripting Language* (a textual version of Reo) and the guarded command language *CARML* (a textual version of constraint automata). Vereofy allows the verification of temporal properties expressed in LTL and CTL-like logics and supports bisimulation equivalence checks. Moreover, it can generate counterexamples and provides a GUI integration with the Eclipse Coordination Tools (ECT).[2]

---

[1] Vereofy homepage: `http://www.vereofy.de`

[2] ECT homepage: `http://reo.project.cwi.nl`

```
1  #include "builtin"                    8  #include "builtin_CD.carml"
2  // Non-deterministic LossyFIFO:       9  // Context-dependent LossyFIFO:
3  CIRCUIT LOSSY_FIFO_ND {              10  CIRCUIT LOSSY_FIFO_CD {
4     new LOSSY_SYNC_ND(A;M);           11     new LOSSY_SYNC_CD(A,nM;M,nA);
5     new FIFO1(M;B);                   12     new FIFO1_CD(M,nB;B,nM);
6     M = NULL;                         13     M = NULL; nM = NULL;
7  }                                    14  }
```

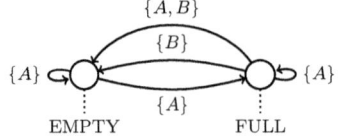

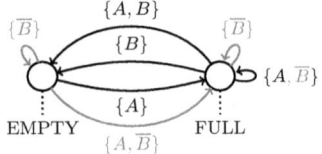

Fig. 1. Non-deterministic (left) vs. context-dependent (right) LossyFIFO$_1$ in Vereofy

Vereofy operates on constraint automata and, thus, does not natively support context-dependent behavior. However, in the previous section, we showed that we can transform 3-colored connectors to 2-colored connectors, while preserving their context-sensitive semantics. Moreover, 2-coloring models and constraint automata correspond to each other (informal arguments appear in [3,5], while [6] contains a formal account). Hence, by using the $\mathcal{M}$-transformation, we can construct context-dependent constraint automata as follows. First, we transform the 3-colored primitives to context-dependent 2-colored primitives. Next, we compute the constraint automata corresponding to the resulting 2-colored primitives. Note that the resulting automata can have context-sensitive behavior (because the 2-colored primitives to which they correspond can have such behavior). Finally, we compose the resulting constraint automata to form more complex context-sensitive connectors (possible due to Theorem 2). Although simple and straightforward, this recipe enables the analysis of context-sensitive connectors in Vereofy. For this purpose, we have adapted Vereofy's library of built-in primitives: using the $\mathcal{M}$-transformation, we wrote a new library containing context-dependent versions of the basic Reo primitives.[3]

As an example, Figure 1 depicts a listing of the non-deterministic and the context-dependent versions of the LossyFIFO$_1$ example, and two constraint automata generated from them using Vereofy. For simplicity, we have hidden the internal node M, used a singleton set as data domain, and removed all data constraints in the generated automata. The constraint automata on the left and right correspond to the non-deterministic and the context-dependent versions, respectively. The latter uses our new context-dependent primitives. The crucial difference between the two is that the non-deterministic version contains an illegal transition via port A in the EMPTY state. This corresponds to the connector losing a data item in a situation where the FIFO$_1$ buffer is empty and should, in any case, accept the data item. In the context-sensitive version, however, this illegal transition does not exists. (Note that if we hide all context nodes—i.e., disregard all gray transitions in Figure 1—we obtain the non-deterministic automaton without the illegal transition.)

---

[3] CD-Library and examples: http://reo.project.cwi.nl/vereofy_CD.tar.gz

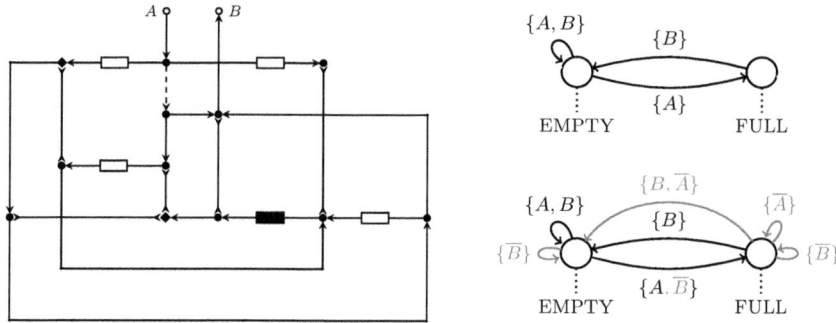

Fig. 2. SyncFIFO$_1$: its composition (left), its ordinary constraint automaton (top–right), and its context-dependent constraint automaton (bottom–right)

A more complex example concerns SyncFIFO$_1$, a connector with an input node, an output node, and a buffer of size 1. SyncFIFO$_1$ behaves identically to FIFO$_1$, except for the case in which it has an empty buffer and pending I/O-requests on both of its nodes: then, SyncFIFO$_1$ routes a data item from its input node *past its buffer* to its output node in one atomic step (thus behaving as a Sync). Instead of modeling SyncFIFO$_1$ as a primitive without inner structure, we can construct it by composing other primitives as depicted in Figure 2 (left); for reasons of space, we do not discuss the interaction and characteristics of the primitives involved in this composition (more details appear in [6]).

A first attempt to model SyncFIFO$_1$ using our library of context-sensitive primitives failed due to the presence of *causality loops* in the resulting composition.[4] Since one cannot detect and remove causality loops from constraint automata, we removed the colorings that contain causality loops from the composed 3-coloring model of SyncFIFO$_1$ and, afterwards, applied $\mathcal{M}$ to this filtered model. This process yielded a 2-coloring model, whose equivalent constraint automaton we encoded in CARML. In Figure 2, we depict the constraint automaton resulting from the procedure just sketched (bottom–right). Additionally, we depict the constraint automaton that one obtains when composing the ordinary primitives (top–right) instead of the context-sensitive ones. (As before, we hide internal nodes.) At first sight, these automata seem very similar. In fact, if we hide all context nodes in the context-dependent constraint automaton—i.e., disregard its gray transitions—we obtain two identical automata.

The crux of the difference between the two automata, therefore, lies exactly in these context nodes: in contrast to LossyFIFO$_1$, SyncFIFO$_1$ itself exhibits context-dependent behavior (instead of only the primitives that constitute it, namely LossySync). Recall that in the EMPTY state, if output node B lacks a take

---

[4] Causality loops may occur if a composed connector has one or more circular sub-circuits (as in the case of SyncFIFO$_1$) and can cause, among other anomalous phenomena, a reason for the absence of flow to appear out of nowhere. Colorings that contain causality loops, therefore, describe inadmissible behavior. In [5], Costa proposes an algorithm for the detection of colorings that contain causality loops.

request, a write request on A causes a data item to flow into the buffer. However, if B has a pending take request, a write request on A causes a data item to flow immediately to node B. The ordinary constraint automaton of $\mathsf{SyncFIFO}_1$ does not capture this difference, which means that an implementation of this constraint automaton would non-deterministically choose one of these two options in case of a pending write request on A and a pending take request on B. In contrast, an implementation of the context-dependent constraint automaton of $\mathsf{SyncFIFO}_1$ always chooses the appropriate option, because in the absence of a take requests on B, data items with irrelevant content—i.e., *signals*—flow through $\overline{B}$. To illustrate this, we encourage the interested reader to compose $\mathsf{SyncFIFO}_1$ and FIFO_1 in the same way we composed $\mathsf{LossySync}$ and FIFO_1.[5]

5   Related Work

In [8], Arbab et al. introduce a coalgebra-based semantic model—the first—for Reo. Some years later, in [2], Baier et al. present an automaton-based approach, namely constraint automata (CA), and prove correspondences with the coalgebra-based model. In [3], however, Clarke et al. observe that neither of these models can handle context-sensitivity, and they introduce the 2-coloring and 3-coloring models to mend this deficiency. Since then, other semantic models with the same aim have come to existence. In [5], Costa introduces *intentional automata* (IA) as an operational model with constructs for context-dependency. Unlike CA, whose states correspond one-to-one to the internal configurations of connectors, IA have more states than the connectors they model; each state of an IA contains information about not only the configuration of the connector, but also about the nodes that *intend* to fire (i.e., with a pending I/O-request). Similarly, transition-labels consist of two sets of nodes: those that intend to fire, and those that actually fire. By maintaining information about I/O-request on nodes, IA capture context-dependency. The number of states, however, quickly grows large, whereas our approach yields succinct CA. In [9], Bonsangue et al. introduce *guarded automata* (GA) as another automaton-based model for capturing context-dependency. Like CA, the states of GA correspond one-to-one to the configurations of connectors, which makes them significantly more compact than IA. To encode context-sensitivity, every transition-label of a GA consists of a *guard* and a *string*. Together, they express which nodes can fire (the string), given the presence and absence of requests at certain nodes (the guard). Guarded automata seem very similar to the CA we obtain with our approach: instead of

---

[5] The constraint automaton that results from composing the ordinary constraint automata of $\mathsf{SyncFIFO}_1$ and FIFO_1 includes a transition that describes an inadmissible behavior in which, in case both $\mathsf{SyncFIFO}_1$ and FIFO_1 have empty buffers, the input node of $\mathsf{SyncFIFO}_1$ fires and causes its own buffer to become full (while the buffer of FIFO_1 remains empty). The constraint automaton that results from composing the context-dependent constraint automata of $\mathsf{SyncFIFO}_1$ and FIFO_1, in contrast, does not include such a transition: if the input node of $\mathsf{SyncFIFO}_1$ fires when both $\mathsf{SyncFIFO}_1$ and FIFO_1 have empty buffers, the buffer of FIFO_1 becomes full (while the buffer of $\mathsf{SyncFIFO}_1$ remains empty).

guards that contain negative occurrences of (base) nodes to specify that these nodes have no pending I/O-requests, we make these negative occurrences explicit with the introduction of (flow through) context nodes.

Besides Vereofy, other approaches to model checking Reo connectors exist. In [10], Kokash et al. employ the mCRL2 toolset, developed at the TU of Eindhoven, for model checking connectors, combined with a translation tool that automatically generates mCRL2 specifications from graphical models of Reo connectors. The tool's original algorithm operated on constraint automata, making it impossible to verify context-dependent connectors using this approach. Later, however, Kokash et al. incorporated (3-)coloring information in the tool, thus facilitating verification of context-dependent connectors. This advantage of mCRL2 over Vereofy, which could not handle context-dependent connectors up to now, seems no longer valid as we have shown how to encode context-sensitivity in Vereofy. An advantage of Vereofy over mCRL2, on the other hand, is its ability to generate *counterexamples*, which mCRL2 cannot do. In [11], Kemper introduces a SAT-based approach to model checking *timed constraint automata* (TCA). In her work, Kemper represents TCA as formulas in propositional logic and uses existing SAT solvers for verification. This approach allows for model checking timed properties of Reo connectors, but it cannot handle context-dependency. In [12], Mousavi et al. develop a structural operational semantics in Plotkin's style for Reo, encode this semantics in the Maude term-rewriting language, and use Maude's LTL model checking module to verify Reo connectors. In [13], Khosravi et al. introduce a mapping from Reo to Alloy, a modeling language based on first-order relational logic, and apply the Alloy Analyzer for verification. Although the approach can handle some context-dependent connectors—using a *maximal progress rule* that removes undesired behavior—Khosravi et al. admit to have considerable performance issues.

6   Conclusions and Future Work

We showed how to encode context-sensitivity in the 2-coloring model and constraint automata by adding fictitious nodes to primitives, while both these models are considered incapable of capturing context-dependent behavior. Our approach, constituted by the $\mathcal{M}$-transformation, enables the application of tools and algorithms devised for such simpler semantic models to context-dependent connectors. As an example, we demonstrated how Vereofy can model check context-sensitive connectors, which seemed impossible up to now.

With respect to future work, we would like to investigate whether Reo's implementation can benefit from the results presented in this paper. We speculate that algorithms for the computation of connector composition run faster on $\mathcal{M}$-transformed 2-colored connectors (or their corresponding constraint automata) than on the original 3-colored connectors, because of the simpler semantic model. Furthermore, we would like to study the relation between other formalisms for Reo that facilitate the proper modeling of context-dependent behavior (e.g., intentional automata and guarded automata).

Acknowledgments. We are grateful to the Vereofy team for their support.

References

1. Arbab, F.: Reo: A channel-based coordination model for component composition. Mathematical Structures in Computer Science 14, 329–366 (2004)
2. Baier, C., Sirjani, M., Arbab, F., Rutten, J.: Modeling component connectors in Reo by constraint automata. Science of Computer Programming 61(2), 75–113 (2006)
3. Clarke, D., Costa, D., Arbab, F.: Connector colouring I: Synchronisation and context dependency. Science of Computer Programming 66(3), 205–225 (2007)
4. Pourvatan, B., Sirjani, M., Arbab, F., Bonsangue, M.: Decomposition of constraint automata. In: Proceedings of the 7th International Workshop on Formal Aspects of Component Software (FACS 2010). LNCS. Springer, Heidelberg (to appear, 2011)
5. Costa, D.: Formal Models for Component Connectors. PhD thesis, Vrije Universiteit Amsterdam (2010)
6. Jongmans, S.S., Krause, C., Arbab, F.: Encoding context-sensitivity in Reo into non-context-sensitive semantic models. Technical Report SEN-1105, Centrum Wiskunde & Informatica (2011)
7. Baier, C., Blechmann, T., Klein, J., Klüppelholz, S.: Formal verification for components and connectors. In: de Boer, F.S., Bonsangue, M.M., Madelaine, E. (eds.) FMCO 2008. LNCS, vol. 5751, pp. 82–101. Springer, Heidelberg (2009)
8. Arbab, F., Rutten, J.: A coinductive calculus of component connectors. In: Wirsing, M., Pattinson, D., Hennicker, R. (eds.) WADT 2003. LNCS, vol. 2755, pp. 34–55. Springer, Heidelberg (2003)
9. Bonsangue, M.M., Clarke, D., Silva, A.: Automata for context-dependent connectors. In: Field, J., Vasconcelos, V.T. (eds.) COORDINATION 2009. LNCS, vol. 5521, pp. 184–203. Springer, Heidelberg (2009)
10. Kokash, N., Krause, C., de Vink, E.P.: Verification of context-dependent channel-based service models. In: de Boer, F.S., Bonsangue, M.M., Hallerstede, S., Leuschel, M. (eds.) FMCO 2009. LNCS, vol. 6286, pp. 21–40. Springer, Heidelberg (2010)
11. Kemper, S.: SAT-based verification for timed component connectors. ENTCS 255, 103–118 (2009)
12. Mousavi, M.R., Sirjani, M., Arbab, F.: Formal semantics and analysis of component connectors in Reo. ENTCS 154(1), 83–99 (2006)
13. Khosravi, R., Sirjani, M., Asoudeh, N., Sahebi, S., Iravanchi, H.: Modeling and analysis of Reo connectors using Alloy. In: Lea, D., Zavattaro, G. (eds.) COORDINATION 2008. LNCS, vol. 5052, pp. 169–183. Springer, Heidelberg (2008)

The Context of Coordinating Groups in Dynamic Mobile Networks

Christine Julien

The University of Texas at Austin
Austin, Texas, USA
c.julien@mail.utexas.edu

Abstract. Context-awareness in dynamic and unpredictable environments is a well-studied problem, and many approaches handle sensing, understanding, and acting upon context information. Entities in these environments are not in isolation, and oftentimes the manner in which entities coordinate depends on some (implicit) notion of their *shared* context. In this paper, we are motivated by the need to explicitly construct notions of the *context of a group* that can support better coordination within the group. First we identify an efficient representation of context (both of an individual and of a group) that can be shared across wireless connections without incurring a significant communication overhead. Second we provide precise semantics for different types of groups, each with compelling use cases in these dynamic computing environments. Finally, we define and demonstrate protocols for efficiently computing groups and their context in a distributed manner.

1 Introduction

In this paper, we motivate the need to share context information in a local neighborhood that is a subset of a larger dynamic mobile or pervasive computing environment. Existing context-aware approaches tend to be exclusively ego-centric, focusing on how to sense the context of a single entity and how to use that sensed context to create better behavior of that single entity. We posit that the context of a *group* of entities within a dynamic network can be just as important if not more important to the overall behavior of the system.

There are many situations in which knowledge about the context of a group is invaluable, not the least of which are emerging social scenarios. Consider a dynamic and opportunistic network of mobile devices in a public space like a park; a group context that identifies a group of people interested in a pick-up game of football and having a similar skill level could support ad hoc formation of groups in physical space. A device on an automobile on a highway may want to generate an individualized group containing nearby automobiles that have a potential to collide with it. Knowledge about network protocols used in a neighborhood of a dynamic mobile computing network can support regional protocol selection [15]. While these groups are all fundamentally very different in structure and purpose, in all of these situations, the group is defined by the context

W. De Meuter and G.-C. Roman (Eds.): COORDINATION 2011, LNCS 6721, pp. 49–64, 2011.

of the situation, and the group itself exhibits an aggregated context that can in turn affect the behavior of its component entities (and perhaps the definition of the group itself). These notions of groups, context, and their intersection are all fundamental pieces of coordinated mobile and pervasive computing applications. Consider again the selection of a network protocol based on network context. Any single node observing just its own context may choose a protocol that ends up incurring more overhead or delay given the network context beyond the node itself; the ability to efficiently acquire information about a wider context of a group of network nodes allows a more informed, *coordinated*, decision.

A well recognized challenge in realizing such a notion of group context is in how to efficiently share context without overburdening an already constrained communication environment (where wireless links create serious bandwidth and energy limitations). While recent approaches have recognized the need for efficient context-awareness, they have largely focused on the acquisition of an ego-centric view of context and not on the view of the context of a group or on sharing information among entities to generate a distributed shared view of the context of that group. We tackle both of these challenges in this paper.

Consider university students' pervasive computing devices. An individual student's context (collected and maintained by his device(s)) can include his courses, his participation in activities, and his individual context (e.g., he is in the library studying, he is part of a particular group project, he is distracted, he is hungry). Existing work has created mechanisms to clearly understand, represent, and use individual context [11,23]. What is equally interesting is the context of a *group* of students. Such group context may be symmetric (shared and coordinated among the group members) or asymmetric (egocentric and individualized to a particular entity); applications demand both forms to enable entities within groups to understand, support, and adapt coordination behaviors. As an example of a symmetric group context, given a group of students enrolled in the same course, a context measure that represents the students' aggregate understanding of the course material can provide feedback to the instructor; there is only a single view of the group's context, regardless of the perspective of the entity looking at the context. As an example of an asymmetric context, a particular student studying in the library may be interested in which the students at nearby tables have a copy of a the textbook. The latter is defined with respect to the student looking for the textbook; students in different locations in the library will have different views for the same group context definition. In the asymmetric case, the group membership is determined by the relationship between the defining entity's context and other entities' contexts; in the symmetric group, membership is defined by the aggregate relationship among all of the entities' contexts.

Abstracting the pervasive computing entities, their physical environment, and the networks that connect them into measures of *context* and *group context* eases the development of application logic, allowing one to focus on how such context measures can be used to aid entities' activities. We provide an expressive definition of a group and its context, delegate the construction of the group and the computation of its context to a middleware, and provide easy interface from the application logic to the group context infrastructure. In this paper, we demonstrate the feasibility of providing a variety of definitions of groups and their contexts. Given the resource constrained devices and networks that comprise emerging environments, it is essential that computation and sharing of groups and their contexts is highly space and communication efficient. Our architecture enables future work in expressive coordination among these groups that can easily rely on the group's context for enhancing the coordination activities.

This paper makes three fundamental contributions. In Section 2, we design a space-efficient context summary that can be communicated and shared in multi-hop wireless networks, evaluate its space efficiency, and give a simple framework for communicating these summaries efficiently. In Sections 3 and 4 we define *groups* in these coordinating environments and create precise formulations of the *context* of groups. We create space- and communication-efficient protocols for distributed determination of *group context*; we demonstrate and evaluate these approaches in Section 5. We argue that supporting expressive coordination among networked entities with complex social, spatial, and temporal relationships requires a formal understanding of groups and their shared context.

2   A Space Efficient Context Summary

Sharing context can add significant overhead; communicating detailed context, which is necessary for determining arbitrary groups and their contexts, has remained too expensive for practical implementations. In this section, we describe an efficient representation of context that can be shared with limited overhead.

Summary Data Structures. Our context summary is based on a derivative of a Bloom filter [2], which succinctly represents set membership using a bit array m and k hash functions. To add an element to a Bloom filter, we use k hash functions to get k positions in m and set each position to 1. To test whether an element e is in the set, we check whether the positions associated with e's k hash values are 1. If any position is *not* 1, e is not in the set. Otherwise, e is in the set *with high probability*. False positives occur if inserting other elements happens to set all k positions associated with e's hash values. Bloom filters trade size for false positive rate; a false positive rate of 1% requires 9.6 bits per element.

A *Bloomier filter* [6] associates a value with each element. The intuitive construction consists of a cascade of Bloom filters on each bit of the values. Consider the case where each value is either 0 or 1. Within a Bloomier filter, a Bloom filter A_0 contains all of the keys that map to 0; B_0 contains all of the keys that map to 1. If the value associated with element e is 0, it is inserted in A_0; if the value is 1, it is inserted in B_0. When one queries the Bloomier filter for the value of e', the query checks whether e' is in A_0 and in B_0. There are four possible results. (1) If e' is in neither A_0 or B_0, e' has not been associated with a value in the Bloomier filter. (2) If e' is in A_0 but not B_0, e' was inserted in the Bloomier filter with high likelihood, and when it was inserted, it was associated the value 0. It is possible that e' was not inserted at all (the unlikely false positive), but it was not inserted with value 1. (3) Similarly, if e' is in B_0 but not in A_0, the query returns 1. (4) If e' is in both A_0 and B_0, one of these is a false positive. To handle this fourth case, another pair of Bloom filters attempts to resolve false positives in the first pair. A_1 contains keys that map to 0 and generated false positives in B_0. B_1 contains keys that map to 1 and generated false positives in A_0. The problem is the same as before but with a smaller key set whose size depends on the false positive rates of A_0 and B_0. The Bloomier filter continues to add levels of filters until the key set becomes small enough to store in a map.

To handle longer values, a Bloomier filter uses a cascaded filter for each bit, i.e., when the range of values is $\{0,1\}^r$, it creates r Bloom filter cascades. This has space complexity of $O(rn)$, where n is the number of elements stored and r is the number of bits needed to represent an element's value. This is in comparison to the $O(rn \log N)$ space complexity of enumerating the value of every element in the set (where N is the number of possible context elements). The Bloomier filter has a false positive rate $\epsilon \propto 2^{-r}$. We use this construction, which achieves fast computation with slightly higher than optimal space use; different constructions make varying tradeoffs in space and time complexity [5,21].

Defining Context Summaries. Our context summary must be space efficient while retaining semantic fidelity. We assume every entity has a unique identifier, $node_i$. We also assume that the universe of context types $\mathcal{C}$ is well-known and shared *a priori* among all entities in the network. Let $|\mathcal{C}| = N$. A given entity senses a (small) subset of the possible context types. Let $\mathcal{C}_{node_i} \subseteq \mathcal{C}$ be the types that $node_i$ senses. $|\mathcal{C}_{node_i}| = n$; $n \ll N$. A general statement of context sensing is as a function $context_{node_i} : \mathcal{C}_{node_i} \rightarrow \{0,1\}^r$ where r is the maximum number of bits needed to represent any type in $\mathcal{C}$. Each context item $c \in \mathcal{C}_{node_i}$ has a value $context_{node_i}(c)$ in the range $[0 . . 2^r]$. For any $\bar{c} \notin \mathcal{C}_{node_i}$, $context_{node_i}(\bar{c}) = \perp$. That is, if $node_i$ does not sense $\bar{c}$, the sensed value is null.

We aim to create a summary that, when queried with a context type, returns the relevant state of the entity. If $c' \in \mathcal{C}_{node_i}$, then the summary should return $context_{node_i}(c')$. If $\bar{c'} \notin \mathcal{C}_{node_i}$, the summary should return $\perp$ with high probability. False positives are allowed (but undesirable) for context types that were not sensed by $node_i$. Every summary contains the key cs_id mapped to the value $node\_id$; when a summary is queried with cs_id it will, without fail, return the unique id of the entity whose context is summarized. Our context summary is a straightforward Bloomier filter. This summary achieves a space complexity of $O(rn)$ bits. The time required to traverse the cascaded data structures and retrieve a value is $O(\log \log n)$. With probability $O(2^{-r})$, when the summary is queried with $\bar{c'} \notin \mathcal{C}_{node_i}$, it returns a false positive, i.e., a value that is garbage.

To determine whether a summary contains an attribute's value, we have to poll all N possible attributes. If N is large (and it usually is), this is excessive. The summary can also return false positives (albeit with low probability) that can negatively impact applications that use context. We refine our summary by adding a bit vector bv of length N, each element of which is a flag for a $c \in \mathcal{C}$. If the value for c is included in the summary, $bv[c]$ is 1; otherwise it is 0. This adds overhead, particularly if N is huge, but it removes all false positives. This summary requires $O(N + rn)$ bits; it retains the $O(\log \log n)$ lookup time.

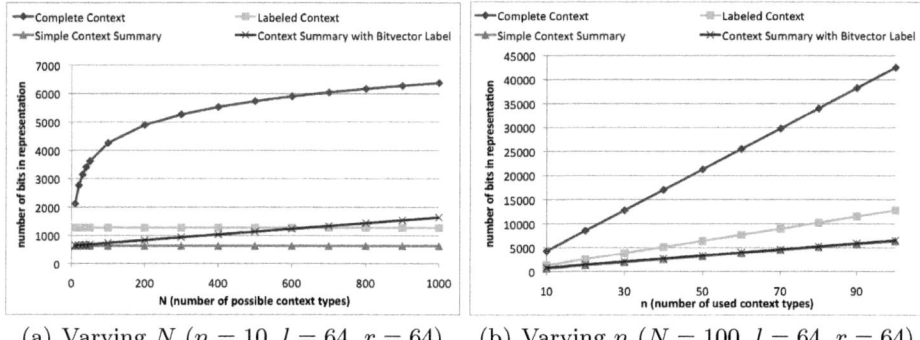

(a) Varying N ($n = 10$, $l = 64$, $r = 64$)   (b) Varying n ($N = 100$, $l = 64$, $r = 64$)

Fig. 1. Number of bits required to represent context using the four different approaches. (l is the length of a context label; r is the the max context size (both in bits).

We adopt some simple notational conveniences to refer to context summaries and their components. Given a context summary CS and a context attribute l and its value v that has been inserted, CS.$l = v$; if an attribute referred to by l has not had a value inserted, CS.$l = \perp$ with high probability. We use the notation CS.$l \leftarrow v$ to insert the value v associated with the key l into CS, e.g. CS.$cs\_id \leftarrow node\_id$. CS.bv refers to the bit vector of the extended context summary; CS.$bv[l]$ is 1 if attribute l is stored in CS and 0 otherwise.

Fig. 1 compares four approaches to context representation analytically. *Simple Context Summary* is our simple Bloomier filter representation. *Context Summary with Bitvector Label* is our approach that extends the simple context summary with a bit vector of length N. *Complete Context* enumerates the value of every element in the set (which requires $O(nr \log N)$ space [6]). *Labeled Context* enumerates only the values of context attributes in $\mathcal{C}_{node_i}$, each labeled with its key (which requires a $O(n(r + l))$ space, where l is the length of a label).

The summary approaches significantly reduce the size of the context representation, especially as N grows (Fig. 1(a)). However, when we hold N constant, but increase n (Fig. 1(b)), sending labels becomes expensive. Fig. 1 assumes context labels that are 64 bits in length (8 characters); longer labels with more semantic information increase this gap. From this analysis, we can conclude that our context summary achieves the highest reduction in size of context representation. In addition, when the number of possible context types remains relatively small, it is reasonable to add a bit vector summary of the context summary.

Communicating Context Summaries. We have reduced the size of the context representation to reduce communication overhead of sharing context in pervasive computing environments. We construct a framework that transparently piggybacks context summaries on outgoing wireless transmissions. Fig. 2 shows our framework's architecture. An application sends context to the *Context Handler* and retrieves context about other entities and groups. The *Context Shim* attaches context summaries to outgoing packets and examines incoming packets for received contexts. The right of Fig. 2 shows the internals of *Context Shim*, which stores MYCONTEXT, this entity's context information. This architecture

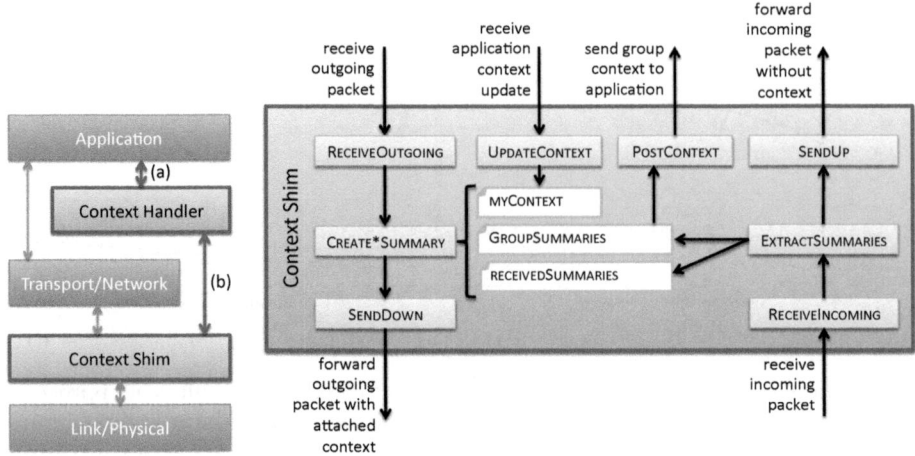

Fig. 2. Architecture for Context Sharing

allows neighboring nodes to exchange context; we also spread summaries beyond one-hop neighbors by inserting an attribute into each summary, *hops*, initialized to 0. Every time the shim receives an incoming summary, it increments this hop count before storing it in RECEIVEDSUMMARIES. As long as the summary's hop count has not surpassed a provided threshold, τ, the receiving node appends the summary to its outgoing packets (in addition to its own summary).

Fig. 3 gives the behavior of the CREATECONTEXTSUMMARY and EXTRACT-SUMMARIES from Fig. 2. The $\oplus$ appends the summary to the packet without altering the packet in any other way. This shows creation of the extended context summary; the simple context summary is the same without line 4.

CREATECONTEXTSUMMARY(*pkt*)
1 **for** $(l, v) \in$ MYCONTEXT
2   **do** CS.$cs\_id \leftarrow node\_id$
3   CS.$l \leftarrow v$
4   CS.$bv[l] = 1$
5   CS.$hops = 0$
6 $pkt' = pkt \oplus$ CS
7 **for** CS $\in$ RECEIVEDSUMMARIES
8   **do if** CS.$hops < \tau$
9   **then** $pkt' = pkt' \oplus$ CS
10 **return** pkt'

EXTRACTSUMMARIES(*pkt*)
1 $pkt' = pkt$
2 **for** CS appended to pkt'
3   **do** CS.$hops \leftarrow$ (CS.$hops + 1$)
4   insert (CS.cs_id, CS)
              in RECEIVEDSUMMARIES
5          $pkt' = pkt' \ominus$ CS
6 **return** pkt'

Fig. 3. Pseudocode for CREATECONTEXTSUMMARY and EXTRACTSUMMARIES

3 Supporting Groups and Their Context

A *group* is a set of nodes (identified by *node_ids* or context summaries). In this section, we define the *context* of such groups using individual context summaries.

The Context of a Group. Given a group of entities and their context summaries, we must devise a space-efficient representation of the aggregate context of the group. Given a set of context summaries, we define an aggregate of those summaries that captures the *context of the group* by summarizing the values included in the individual summaries. Assuming complete knowledge of all of the context summaries of a group g, we define the group context of g as:

$$\text{GROUPCONTEXT}_{g\_id} = \{(l, v_{agg}) : v_{agg} = f_{agg,l}(\{\text{CS}_{n_i}.l : n_i \in g\}), \forall l \in \bigcup_{n_i \in g} \text{CS}_{n_i}\}$$

where $f_{agg,l}$ is an aggregation function associated with the context type l. Different types of context have different forms of aggregation. For example, to aggregate multiple location values, $f_{agg,loc}$ may construct a bounding box. Aggregation functions can be standard functions like average, maximum, or minimum, or they may be defined by the context ontology. We assume the aggregation function for each context label is defined and shared *a priori*. A group context is a set of pairs of labels and values and can be represented by a context summary. In this case, the context attribute cs_id is a unique g_id instead of the $node\_id$. We can construct a group context summary iteratively as shown in Fig. 4.

A group summary tracks the nodes it summarizes to ensure that it does not aggregate information for a node twice. This information is added in line 4 of AGGSUMMARIES (which uses f_{ids} to make a list of included $node\_ids$). Line 3 in CREATEGROUPAGG checks before incorporating CS into GS that GS does not already include the node. Context summaries and group summaries are interchangeable; it

CREATEGROUPAGG(g_id)

1   Create empty group summary GS
2   **for** CS $\in$ RECEIVEDSUMMARIES
3   **do if** $g\_id \in$ CS.$G \wedge \neg$CS.$cs\_id \in$ GS.agg_nodes
            $\wedge$CS.$agg\_nodes \cap$ GS.$agg\_nodes = \emptyset$
4   **then** GS = AGGSUMMARIES(GS, CS)
5   **return** GS

AGGSUMMARIES(CS_1, CS_2)

1   create empty aggregate summary CS_{agg}
2   **for** $l \in (\text{CS}_1.labels \cup \text{CS}_2.labels)$
3   **do if** $l = cs\_id$
4   **then** $\text{CS}_{agg}.agg\_nodes \leftarrow f_{ids}(\text{CS}_1.l, \text{CS}_2.l)$
5   **else if** $l \in \text{CS}_1.labels$ and $l \in \text{CS}_2.labels$
6   **then** $\text{CS}_{agg}.l \leftarrow f_{agg,l}(\text{CS}_1.l, \text{CS}_2.l)$
7   **else if** $l \notin \text{CS}_1.labels$ and $l \in \text{CS}_2.labels$
8   **then** $\text{CS}_{agg}.l \leftarrow \text{CS}_2.l$
9   **else** $\text{CS}_{agg}.l \leftarrow \text{CS}_1.l$
10 **return** CS_{agg}

Fig. 4. Pseudocode to create group context summaries

is possible that a CS $\in$ RECEIVEDSUMMARIES is a group summary; the check on the second half of line 3 in CREATEGROUPAGG ensures that we never include information about the same node more than once in an aggregate summary.

Capturing Connectivity. Our group definitions can be expressed from a global perspective that assumes knowledge of all entities and their contexts. This is unreasonable in a distributed, dynamic environment since it does not account for connectivity, which is necessary for entities to share context and determine groups in a distributed manner. We define connectivity as a binary relation, $\mathcal{K}$, that captures the ability of two entities to communicate via a single network hop. We assume $\mathcal{K}$ is symmetric. We define $\mathcal{K}^*$ to contain pairs of mutually reachable entities (i.e., $(n, n') \in \mathcal{K}^*$ if there exists a (potentially multihop) path between n and n'). Of course, actually carrying out communication across a multihop path may or may not succeed due to dynamics, noise, dropped packets, and subtleties of communication protocols; $\mathcal{K}^*$ represents the *ideal* connectivity. We forward summaries only in a limited region defined by a constraint on the number of hops, τ. While $\mathcal{K}^*$ captures all paths, $\mathcal{K}^\tau$ defines pairs of entities within τ of each other; these entities should mutually know each other's context. Obviously, $\mathcal{K}^\tau \subseteq \mathcal{K}^*$. The summaries stored in RECEIVEDSUMMARIES of entity n should be a subset of the summaries of the entities to which n is related under $\mathcal{K}^\tau$.

4   Defining Groups: A Distributed Emergent Approach

We construct formal definitions of four types of groups that capture coordination needs of entities in dynamic environments. This set is not meant to be complete, but it is expressive. We refine our context handling protocols to create, maintain, and share groups. CS_n is the summary for entity with $node\_id = n$. Every group has a unique id g_id that is also unique from all node ids.

Labeled Groups. The simplest type of group is one in which members are determined *a priori*. Such groups are effectively *labeled*; the group's g_id is a shared unique id (whether public or secreted in some way). As a convenient way for designating that entity n is in group g_id, we use the entity's context summary; for every group of which it is a member, an entity inserts a pair $(\text{Group}i, g\_id)$ in its summary. Labels of the form $\text{Group}i$ are reserved identifying groups; the value of i ranges from 1 to the number of groups of which the entity is a member, and g_id is the (unique) group id for one of these groups. If an entity is a member of three groups with ids g_id_1, g_id_2, and g_id_3, its summary may contain the following three mappings: $(\text{Group}1, g\_id_1)$, $(\text{Group}2, g\_id_2)$, and $(\text{Group}3, g\_id_3)$, though there is no association between the i in $\text{Group}i$ and the group ids. We refer to entity n's groups as $CS_n.G$, where G is a set of group ids. As an application example, consider devices carried by students enrolled in a course. These students may each belong to a group identified by the course name; a student's context summary includes a group id for each enrolled course.

Given the context summaries of all entities, the membership of a labeled group is a set g_{g_id} such that $\forall n' \in g_{g_{id}} : g\_id \in CS_{n'}.G$. For our students, g_{id} contains all of the students enrolled in a course. To refine a labeled group to account for connectivity, we consider only context summaries from entities that are related to n under $\mathcal{K}^*$. The membership of the *partition* of $g_{g_{id}}$ of which n is a member (i.e., $g_{g_{id}}[n]$) is a set of entities such that $\forall n' \in g_{g_{id}}[n] : (n, n') \in \mathcal{K}^* \wedge g\_id \in CS_{n'}.G$. Consider students studying in the library; $g_{g\_id}[n]$ for a student n includes all students reachable via an ad hoc network of their devices.

Since we do not distribute summaries beyond τ, we may not have information about the entire partition $g[n]$. The group membership that a given entity n may know about is defined relative to $\mathcal{K}^\tau$; to capture this, we simply replace $\mathcal{K}^*$ in the above with $\mathcal{K}^\tau$. This use of the connectivity relation is pretty strong; it

CREATELGCONTEXTSUMMARY(*pkt*)

  1 **for** $(l, v) \in$ MYCONTEXT
  2   **do** CS.$l \leftarrow v$
  3   CS.$bv[l] = 1$
  4 $i = 1$
  5 **for** $g\_id \in$ LABELEDGROUPS
  6   **do** CS.("Group"$+i$) $\leftarrow g\_id$
  7   CS.$bv[("Group" + i)] = 1$
  8          $i = i + 1$
  9 $pkt' = pkt \oplus$ CS
10 **for** CS $\in$ RECEIVEDSUMMARIES
11   **do if** CS.$hops < \tau$
12   **then** $pkt' = pkt' \oplus$ CS
13 **return** pkt'

LGEXTRACTSUMMARIES(*pkt*)

  1 $pkt' = pkt$
  2 **for** CS appended to pkt'
  3   **do** CS.$hops \leftarrow$ (CS.$hops + 1$)
  4   insert (CS.cs_id, CS)
             in RECEIVEDSUMMARIES
  5          $pkt' = pkt' \ominus$ CS
  6 $i = 1$
  7 $g\_id =$ MYCONTEXT.("Group"$+i$)
  8 **while** $g\_id \neq \perp$
  9   **do** CS$_{agg}$ =
             CREATEGROUPAGG(g_id)
10   CS$_{agg}$.*Group1* $\leftarrow g\_id$
11   insert (g_id, CS$_{agg}$)
             in RECEIVEDSUMMARIES
12   post group context update
             to application if changed
13          $i = i + 1$
14          $g\_id =$ CS.("Group"$+i$)
15 **return** pkt'

Fig. 5. Pseudocode for CREATELGCONTEXTSUMMARY and LGEXTRACTSUMMARIES

requires that all members of the (partition of the) group must be related to n under $\mathcal{K}^\tau$. In a weaker form, each member must be related under the transitive closure of $\mathcal{K}^\tau$, i.e., $(\mathcal{K}^\tau)^+$: $\forall n' \in g_{g_{id}}[n] : (n, n') \in (\mathcal{K}^\tau)^+ \wedge g\_id \in CS_{n'}.G$.

We replace CREATECONTEXTSUMMARY in Fig. 3 with CREATEDLGCON-TEXTSUMMARY in Fig. 5, which inserts the group id (g_id) for this entity's groups. LGEXTRACTSUMMARIES processes received summaries and computes group membership by determining the group membership(s) of the entities from which received summaries came, updating the aggregate information for those groups, and informing the application of the changed group context. A node only creates group summaries for groups of which it is a member; the group's aggregate context is based on any context summary received from any other entity with the same group id. This implements the weak form of labeled groups; the groups will include entities related by $(\mathcal{K}^\tau)^+$. To create the strong form, we simply remove line 11 of LGEXTRACTSUMMARIES. When line 11 is included, the computed group summary is inserted in RECEIVEDSUMMARIES and will be appended to sent packets. This enables the computation of groups that extend across $(\mathcal{K}^\tau)^+$. When LGEXTRACTSUMMARIES operates over the summaries in RECEIVEDSUMMARIES to compute the aggregate context (lines 9-14), it does not matter if the summary used is an individual context summary or a group summary since AGGSUMMARIES is iterative. The check on line 3 of CREATE-GROUPAGG in Fig. 4 prevents us from aggregating two summaries that include information about the same entity. The result is a heuristic; it may be possible to create a group summary that incorporates information about a larger number of entities, but this is not possible from the summary data we distribute. To maximize the number of entities represented in an aggregate, we can optimize the order in which we incorporate them; we omit these algorithms for brevity.

58   C. Julien

The context of the group of students labeled by course number could represent a variety of factors. As one example, the students' context summaries may also carry a field labeled "understanding of concept A"; this value may be filled in automatically by some assessment applications on the device; the context of a group can then be the group's average understanding of the material.

Asymmetric Groups. Entities can also define ego-centric notions of context, or *asymmetric groups*, known only to the entity at its center. As an example, an application on a car may keep the driver aware of other nearby cars that have the potential for collision. Members of an asymmetric group need not know they are part of the group; if two entities use the same asymmetric group definition, they likely end up with completely different groups. This is the case in our example; two different cars clearly have different perspectives of other cars with a potential for collision. Information about asymmetric groups is not shared (i.e., asymmetric group summaries are not placed in RECEIVEDSUMMARIES). Asymmetric groups can be defined given a function f_n provided by entity n that constrains the relationship between the entity's context and the context of any group member. Specifically, the membership of an asymmetric group is a set g_{f_n} such that $\forall n' \in g_{f_n} : (n, n') \in \mathcal{K}^\tau \wedge f_n(\text{CS}_n, \text{CS}_{n'})$. In our collision-awareness application, f_n may compute the "time to collision" given my velocity and another nearby car's velocity; if this time to collision is over a threshold, f_n returns true.

We use f_n to "tag" the summaries stored in RECEIVEDSUMMARIES that should be part of the asymmetric group and compute the group context for those tagged summaries. When sending summaries from RECEIVEDSUMMARIES, the tags need to be stripped from the summaries. We omit this pseudocode for brevity. The context computed by our car's f_{agg} could be the number of cars within the dangerous zone or their average speed. A more complex f_{agg} could compute the bounding box of dangerous cars to show on a heads-up display.

Symmetric Groups. Entities can share a symmetric definition of a group that constrains the pairwise relationship between any entities in the group. Consider a set of devices forming a mobile ad hoc network that wants to determine the best network protocols given current network conditions. Such a network may wish to form a group of mutually reachable devices whose context determines a set of protocols. A function f_{g_id} shared among entities *a priori* can define membership in the group based on pairwise comparisons of members' contexts. The set $g_{f_{g\_id}}[n]$ of members of n's partition of this group is one such that $\forall n, n' \in g_{f_{g\_id}}[n] : (n, n') \in \mathcal{K}^\tau \wedge f_{g\_id}(\text{CS}_n, \text{CS}_{n'})$. Symmetry refers to the fact that $n' \in g_{f_{g\_id}}[n] \Leftrightarrow n \in g_{f_{g\_id}}[n']$; this is ensured by the symmetry of $\mathcal{K}$ and the shared f_{g_id}. The above provides a strong requirement on connectivity; in the weaker form, each group member must be related to n under $(\mathcal{K}^\tau)^+$. With respect to our mobile ad hoc network example, f_{g_id} may require all of the nodes in the group to be mutually reachable within a specified number of hops or time.

If a receiving entity determines that a received summary is part of one of its symmetric groups, it tags the summary with the group id before inserting it in RECEIVEDSUMMARIES. Like labeled groups (and unlike asymmetric groups), these summaries are inserted in RECEIVEDSUMMARIES and are appended to outgoing packets to enable computation of groups across $(\mathcal{K}^\tau)^+$. Our protocol checks $f_{g\_id}(\text{MYCONTEXT}, \text{CS})$ for any received summary CS, calculates the aggregate context, and updates both RECEIVEDSUMMARIES and the application.

In our application scenario, metrics such as relative mobilities of the nodes, neighbor densities, and communication error rates influence the selection of the best protocol [15]. Given information in the group members' context summaries (e.g., connectivity, velocity, position, error rates), these aggregate measures can be easily calculated and handed to a process that selects the best protocol.

Context-Defined Groups. Context-defined groups require that a group together satisfy some requirement. Consider a network with changing capabilities and an application that wants to leverage network resources to perform a task. A group may be a set of devices, which, in the aggregate, is capable of completing that task. Similarly, imagine using a local network of smart phones to form teams for a pick-up game of football, where each team should have a capable player at each position. As with symmetric groups, such a group is defined by a function over context summaries; in this case, the requirement specifies a property that the group as a whole must uphold. Given f_{g_id} that defines the group constraint(s), $g_{g\_id}[n]$ is valid if and only if $f_{g\_id}(g_{g\_id}[n])$. The strong version of a context-defined group requires all members of $g_{g\_id}[n]$ to be related to n via $\mathcal{K}^\tau$; the weaker version requires each member to be related to n via $(\mathcal{K}^\tau)^+$. Multiple groups defined with the same f_{g_id} may overlap (i.e., a single node could define multiple groups using the same context function).

Summaries for these groups are placed in RECEIVEDSUMMARIES and appended to packets. The more complex piece of determining context-defined groups is the application of f to the RECEIVEDSUMMARIES (both individual and group summaries), shown in Fig. 6. There are several ways one can apply f_{g_id} for a context-defined group. We generate all permutations of RECEIVEDSUMMARIES and look at them from largest to smallest, where the size is the number of nodes for which it contains summary information. We take the largest permutation that satisfies f_{g_id} (if one exists), compute its aggregate context, and return it to the application as the context

CDGROUPEXTRACTSUMMARIES(*pkt*)

```
1   pkt' = pkt
2   for CS appended to pkt'
3       do CS.hops ← (CS.hops + 1)
4           insert (CS.cs_id, CS) in RECEIVEDSUMMARIES
5           pkt' = pkt' ⊖ CS
6   for g_id ∈ CONTEXTDEFINEDGROUPS
7       do for each permutation P of
               RECEIVEDSUMMARIES sorted by size
8           do if f_g_id(P)
9               then CS_agg = AGGSUMMARIES(P)
10                  insert (g_id, CS_agg) in
                        RECEIVEDSUMMARIES
11                  post group context update
                        to application if changed
12                  skip remaining permutations
13  return pkt'
```

Fig. 6. Pseudocode for CDGROUPEXTRACTSUMMARIES

of the group. Different heuristics exist for choosing which of the groups that satisfy f_{g_id} is best, including application-defined metrics for the quality of a group. Evaluating the relative merits of these alternatives is out of the scope of this paper but is an area of future research.

In our examples, the context could capture the quality of the aggregate. For devices providing resource capabilities, the context may be the quality of service the aggregate of entities can provide for the task. For the ad hoc sport team formation, the context may be a measure of the overall quality of a team.

5   Implementation, Demonstration, and Evaluation

We implemented our approaches in C++ using the architecture in Fig. 2. We incorporated this prototype into the OMNeT++ discrete event simulator with the INET framework and used this prototype to define contexts of individual entities, share them, create groups, and define and share the context of those groups[1]. We provide a few demonstrative results, first for the performance of the context summary mechanisms and then for some groups and their context.

Evaluation Settings. We used an available UDP implementation to generate data packets (on top of which context summaries could be piggybacked) and the provided AODV routing implementation to route data packets. While we experimented with a variety of settings, we report results we achieved when using 50 nodes moving according to the random waypoint mobility model with varying speeds (from 0 to 20 m/s). Each node generated UDP traffic at a rate of 10 packets/s and was assigned a different set of destinations (to allow for the AODV protocol to form and reuse existing routes); when a node generated a UDP packet, it selected a destination randomly from this list. Unless specified otherwise, the charts below use a τ of three hops, a context label and value lengths of 64 bits, n of 10, and N of 1000. We show 95% confidence intervals.

Sharing Context Summaries. We implemented the four approaches for context summaries described in Section 2. We executed each on our sample networks; the results given a varying n (the number of contexts used in a context summary) and N (the number of context labels known to the application) are shown in Fig. 7. It is immediately obvious that the shapes of these curves match those in Fig. 1, which indicates that our experience with the context summary structures matches our analytical expectations. These results boost our confidence that our simple Bloomier filter based context summary and the Bloomier filter based context summary with the associated bit vector provide good communication efficiency for sharing context information in a distributed network.

Calculating and Sharing Groups. Fig. 8 shows a labeled group created using context summaries with bit vectors. We varied the fraction of the 50 nodes that were labeled with the group and their speeds. Fig. 8(a) compares the correctness of calculating the groups for a scenario when 15 nodes were labeled as group members. The bottom line in the figure compares the nodes our approach determined to be within the group to 15. The second line compares this to the

---

[1] The code is available at http://www.ece.utexas.edu/~julien/GroupContext.html

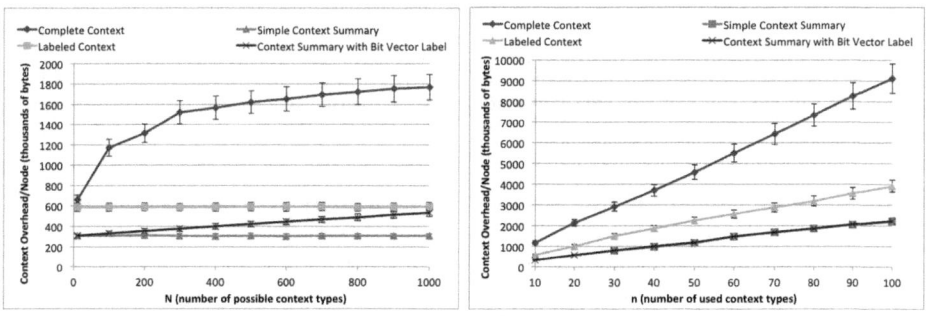

Fig. 7. Context Summary Size in Simulation

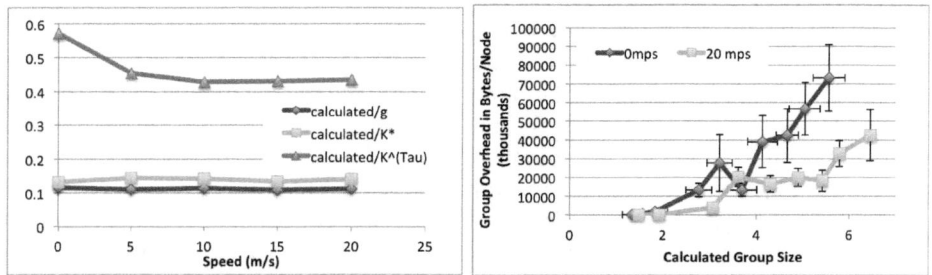

(a) Correctness of group vs. g, K^*, and K^τ (b) Additional overhead of group context

Fig. 8. Calculating and Sharing Groups (Actual Group Size = 15)

number of nodes that were connected (i.e., K^*). The highest line compares the number of group members discovered to the number that were expected to be within range (i.e, K^τ, based on an estimated radio range). The latter is the fair comparison; given the opportunistic distribution of context information, we were able to identify $\sim 50\%$ of the actual group members. Errors in group calculation can be due to communication failures, noise, and stale knowledge (which is impacted by the data rate since summaries are piggybacked on data packets). Further study of the impact of data rates and update intervals for context information may help to better understand the incompleteness of group calculation.

Fig. 8(b) shows the overhead for sharing group contexts. This overhead is higher when nodes are stationary since they are more likely to succeed in calculating the group, thereby generating a summary to share. Future work will investigate heuristics to help reduce this overhead. As one example, in our prototype, we forward both group context summaries *and* the individual context summaries that the group summary is based on. Removing some of this redundant information can lower the cost of context communication, albeit at the expense of having detailed individual information spread further in the network.

6   Related Work

Because of their space efficiency, Bloom filters are widely used in networking [3], for example to succinctly represent coding symbols for efficient erasure coded communication [4] or support uniform distribution of stored data [16]. Bloom filters have been used to gossip cache entries and reduce overlaps in collections in a P2P network [1] and to summarize the shared contents of a group [18]. Similarly, Bloom filters have been used in wireless sensor networks to dynamically create clusters and aggregate data [13] or to efficiently route queries [14]. Dynamic Bloom filters [10] improve upon space efficiency by shrinking their size when possible, specifically for the purpose of representing data shared in a network. These approaches all focus on set membership representations, which cannot represent context values.

The spectral Bloom filter [7] extends the Bloom filter to multisets, allowing one to estimate frequencies, which is applicable to managing per-flow traffic in network routers [17]. Using attenuated Bloom filters, each node stores discounted Bloom filters representing the contents of its neighbors, which it uses to route queries to locations that are likely to store results [22]. This is similar to using context summaries to form asymmetric groups, however we devise a generalized framework instead of tailoring the summary to a given application.

Other approaches have recognized that groups and their context are important. In [9] groups are formed statically or based on co-location, while our groups can be defined in many ways. The approach in [9] also does not focus on efficient representation and sharing of context and is therefore not transferable to resource constrained infrastructureless environments.

The Team Analysis and Adaptation Framework (TAAF) [8] observes the behavior of a distributed collaborative team and introduces constructs to adapt supporting services and team coordination. TAAF assumes the team is already assembled, and the generation of the context of the team is centralized. Context-Aware Ephemeral Groups (CAEG) [24] explore a more abstract definition of groups based solely on social connections that are used to guide users to likely relevant resources and to maintain persistent state among the users in a ubiquitous computing space, though the focus in on function and interface instead of on efficiency of context representation. We argue that the latter is essential in ad hoc environments, which are severely resource constrained. Our work is a complement to CAEG in supporting the necessary efficient exchange of individual and group context information and new ways to support expressive group creation and management (outside of CAEG's social group).

7   Conclusions and Future Work

In this paper, we have tackled the multipart problem of expressively summarizing the context of individual entities in a dynamic environment so that they can be shared efficiently across wireless links. We use these individual context summaries to define and compute groups on-the-fly, dependent on the context and to the compute the aggregate context of the group. The work in this paper is a first step in being able to compute and share such expressive aggregate context information without supporting infrastructure and opens many interesting new research questions. Directly related to the work in this paper are ideas for incorporating additional mechanisms to shrink the summaries further [12,19,20]. In computing the groups, we assumed we used a slightly larger structure (the context summary with a bit vector) that removed all false positives; if the size of this structure is undesirable, it becomes interesting to ask what the impact is of false positives on group formation. These questions and others lay the groundwork for future use of shared distributed context state to support expressive coordination in dynamic environments.

References

1. Bender, M., Michel, S., Triantafillou, P., Weikum, G., Zimmer, C.: Improving collection selection with overlap awareness in p2p search engines. In: SIGIR (2005)
2. Bloom, B.: Space/time tradeoffs in hash coding with allowable errors. Comm. of the ACM 13(7) (1970)
3. Broder, A., Mitzenmacher, M.: Network applications of bloom filters: A survey. Internet Mathematics 1(4) (2004)
4. Byers, J., Considine, J., Mitzenmacher, M., Rost, S.: Informed content delivery across adaptive overlay networks. IEEE/ACM Trans. on Netw. 12(5) (2004)
5. Charles, D., Chellapilla, K.: Bloomier filters: A second look. In: Halperin, D., Mehlhorn, K. (eds.) ESA 2008. LNCS, vol. 5193, pp. 259–270. Springer, Heidelberg (2008)
6. Chazelle, B., Kilian, J., Rubinfeld, R., Tal, A.: The bloomier filter: An efficient data structure for static support lookup tables. In: SIAM (2004)
7. Cohen, S., Matias, Y.: Spectral bloom filters. In: SIGMOD (2003)
8. Dorn, C., Truong, H.L., Dustdar, S.: Measuring and analyzing emerging properties for autonomic collaboration service adaptation. In: Rong, C., Jaatun, M.G., Sandnes, F.E., Yang, L.T., Ma, J. (eds.) ATC 2008. LNCS, vol. 5060, pp. 162–176. Springer, Heidelberg (2008)
9. Ferscha, A., Holzmann, C., Oppl, S.: Context awareness for group interaction support. In: MobiWac (2004)
10. Guo, D., Wu, J., Chen, H., Luo, X.: Theory and network applications of dynamic bloom filters. In: INFOCOM (2006)
11. Hackmann, G., Julien, C., Payton, J., Roman, G.C.: Supporting generalized context interactions. In: SEM (2005)
12. Hagerup, T., Tholey, T.: Efficient minimal perfect hashing in nearly minimal space. In: Ferreira, A., Reichel, H. (eds.) STACS 2001. LNCS, vol. 2010, p. 317. Springer, Heidelberg (2001)
13. Hebden, P., Pearce, A.: Bloom filters for data aggregation and discovery: A hierarchical clustering approach. In: ISSNIP (2005)
14. Jardak, C., Riihijarvi, J., Mahonen, P.: Analyzing the optimal use of bloom filters in wireless sensor networks storing replicas. In: WCNC (2009)
15. Jun, T., Julien, C.: Automated routing protocol selection in mobile ad hoc networks. In: SAC (2007)
16. Kostic, D., Rodriguez, A., Albrecht, J., Vahdat, A.: Bullet: High bandwidth data dissemination using an overlay mesh. In: SOSP (2003)

17. Kumar, A., Xu, J., Wang, J.: Space-code bloom filter for efficient per-flow traffic measurement. IEEE J. on Selected Areas in Comm. 24(12) (2006)
18. Ledlie, J., Taylor, J., Serben, L., Seltzer, M.: Self-organization in peer-to-peer systems. In: SIGOPS European Wkshp. (2002)
19. Mitzenmacher, M.: Compressed bloom filters. IEEE Trans. on Netw. 10(5) (2002)
20. Pagh, A., Pagh, R., Rao, S.: An optimal bloom filter replacement. In: SODA (2005)
21. Porat, E.: An optimal bloom filter replacement based on matrix solving. In: Frid, A., Morozov, A., Rybalchenko, A., Wagner, K.W. (eds.) CSR 2009. LNCS, vol. 5675, pp. 263–273. Springer, Heidelberg (2009)
22. Rhea, S., Kubiatowicz, J.: Probabilistic location and routing. In: INFOCOM (2002)
23. Salber, D., Dey, A.K., Abowd, G.D.: The context toolkit: Aiding the development of context-enabled applications. In: CHI (1999)
24. Wang, B., Bodily, J., Gupta, S.: Supporting persistent social groups in ubiquitous computing environments using context-aware ephemeral group service. In: PerCom (2004)

CSP as a Coordination Language

Moritz Kleine

Technische Universität Berlin,
Institute for Software Engineering and Theoretical Computer Science,
Berlin, Germany
mkleine@cs.tu-berlin.de

Abstract. Coordination languages allow us to separate interaction behavior from the sequential functional aspects of the components of concurrent systems. This helps us to reduce the complexities of such systems
making them easier to design and to understand. However, there is still
a gap between formal approaches to coordination and their implementation in programming languages. For example, CSP is often used as a
coordination model but only subsets of CSP are supported by programming languages (e. g., occam) or frameworks (e. g., JCSP). In this paper,
we present our approach to using a more complete CSP as a coordination
language. Our approach allows us to use standard CSP tools for verifying the coordination processes of a system and to use these processes at
runtime to coordinate the systems' components.

1   Introduction

A major problem in developing concurrent software is that the additional complexity that comes with concurrency often causes unexpected asynchronous
behavior that quite often manifests in subtle bugs. Formal methods such as
Communicating Sequential Processes (CSP) and formal designs help to avoid
such bugs during the design phase of a system. However, finding methods for
deriving implementations from CSP-based models is an active field of research.
It is, for example, not obvious how to integrate CSP with internal actions of a
system, because CSP abstracts from internal actions to a great extent. Coordination languages such as Linda [2] offer an approach to taming the complexities
of concurrent programs. This family of languages targets the description of the
interaction behavior of a system's components separating the interactions from
the sequential functional properties of the components. While coordination languages target the implementation level description of concurrent or distributed
systems, process algebras target their design and are more tailored to (mechan-
ically) verify systems.

In this paper, we present our approach to using CSP as a coordination language. The approach is to coordinate non-atomic actions of a concurrent system
by a CSP-based coordination environment in a noninvasive way. We present a
model of a coordination environment that interprets a process simulating its
truly concurrent semantics (where concurrent events may be performed at the

W. De Meuter and G.-C. Roman (Eds.): COORDINATION 2011, LNCS 6721, pp. 65–79, 2011.

same time and not only interleaved) within the standard interleaving operational semantics of CSP. The abstractions inherent to the process algebra are undone by regarding an event as a terminating (not necessarily atomic) action and a hidden transition as an internal action of the final system. Whenever the coordination environment performs a (possibly hidden) event, it performs the action mapped to that particular event. Actions can implement arbitrary computations, even communication, including shared-memory communication and message-passing. Our approach allows us to use CSP for the design and implementation of concurrent systems by adding a coordination environment to a (sequential) host language. The use of CSP enables us to perform deadlock-checking and more advanced properties (by means of refinement and LTL model checking) at design time.

In the next section, CSP is introduced and approaches using CSP for the engineering of coordinated concurrent systems are presented. Abstractions built into the language and their relevance for coordination are discussed in Section 3. The model of a coordination environment is presented in Section 4. Section 5 presents a proof obligation to ensure data independence of concurrent actions. Important properties of coordination processes are characterized and discussed in Section 6. The Java implementation supporting our approach is presented in Section 7. In that section, we also give pointers to further work. We then present related work in Section 8. The conclusions of this paper are given in Section 9.

2   CSP and Coordination

The process algebra Communicating Sequential Processes (CSP) [6,14], provides an algebraic notation based on *events*, process names and process operators tailored for the concise modeling of current systems. Concurrent systems are modeled as *processes* that perform events. If a process offers an event with which its environment agrees to synchronize, the event is performed. Events are both atomic and instantaneous.

Events are commonly regarded as rendezvous communication between processes. From this viewpoint, processes are anonymous entities communicating synchronously over named channels. Accordingly, an event models the occurrence of a communication identified by the channel name and the message being sent over it. Messages can only be sent if the receiver is willing to accept them. Events can also be regarded as abstractions of atomic actions of a system in the understanding that duration of actions can be modeled by splitting events into start and end events.

CSP is equipped with operational, denotational and algebraic semantics. The concept of refinement facilitates the step-wise development of processes by gradually restricting their behaviors. In this context, CSP enjoys the property of *compositionality*: given a process that satisfies some specification and another process refining a part of the first process, we may replace that part with the second process and obtain a new process that also satisfies the specification. Modeling, exploration and verification of processes is supported by a number of industrial-strength tools. The automatic refinement checker FDR [14], for example, proves or refutes refinement assertions in the denotational models *traces*, *stable failures* and *failures-divergences*.

In [15], Schneider and Treharne present a combination of CSP and B [1] that is now known as CSP‖B. The idea of CSP‖B is to separate the specification of a component into state related and interaction properties. The B method is used to express requirements on state of the components and their coordination is expressed in CSP. CSP events are associated with operations, hence assuming atomicity of operations.

CSP++ [5], is a framework realizing CSP concurrency on top of POSIX threads for C++. The framework defines a whole development life-cycle starting with a CSP_M specification being refined down to a CSP implementation model. The implementation model is finally translated into C++ using the CSP++ framework. This framework implements channels as an inter-process communication primitive and allows us to bind user-coded functions to events that are executed when the event is performed. The CSP++ framework implements the occam-style CSP supporting sequential composition, external choice, interleaving and parallel composition.

JCSP [18] is a well-known Java library offering CSP concepts as a foundation for developing concurrent systems in an event-based style. In this framework, processes communicate over channels which are basically buffers. JCSP realizes CSP's synchronous communication between Java threads by blocking the send operation until the value is read by its receiver. This is realized using the Java primitives *synchronize*, *wait* and *notify*. Processes (implemented as Java threads) are not allowed to invoke each other's methods but they may be combined to wait passively on a number of alternative events. The external generation of such an event triggers the processes into action according to the CSP semantics of the process operator combining the events.

3   Unravelling Abstractions

This section explains, how the abstractions built into CSP can be unravelled to coordinate concurrent systems. The arguments presented here are based on the following assumptions.

1. CSP offers a rich set of operators to facilitate the concise modeling of concurrent systems. This set is intendedly non-minimal and offers different operators to describe semantically equivalent processes. The idea is that the operators model abstractions of different implementations. The coordination environment must be able to unravel these abstractions accordingly.
2. Once a process is proved to satisfy the interaction behavior of the components of a system, the process should be directly usable as a coordination process without being refined further (even if the process is a nondeterministic one).
3. Coordination processes still abstract from data being used in the implementation.

4. Although the standard CSP semantics are interleaving ones, a coordination environment must be able to profit from true concurrency if that is offered by the underlying computing hardware.
5. Coordination processes define the external and internal interactions of a system.

3.1   Timeout, Hiding and Nondeterminism

The operators timeout, hiding and internal choice, offer abstractions that allow us to develop concise models of concurrent systems but which have to be undone for the implementation of a conforming system For example, although

$$P \rhd Q = (P \;\square\; Q) \sqcap Q$$

holds, the timeout operator offers a convenient abstraction of a process that switches automatically to Q if P fails to perform a visible event within a certain time interval. From an implementation point of view this is fundamentally different from $(P \;\square\; Q) \sqcap Q$ which can be understood as a process deciding to offer either the initials of P and Q for synchronization or just the initials of Q. Thus, our approach unravels the abstractions built into the timeout operator differently than that built into its semantically equivalent version. On the implementation level, $P \rhd Q$ is implemented as a timeout (e.g., using a timer), while $(P \;\square\; Q) \sqcap Q$ models a combination of internal and external influences (independent of time).

In the semantic framework of CSP, timeout is introduced by hiding. As explained above, our understanding of a timeout is somewhat different. Analogously, we deal with hiding different from its treatment on the semantic level of CSP. There, hiding abstracts events such that the following equality holds:

$$(a \to STOP) \setminus \{a\} = STOP \,.$$

Nevertheless, in the operational semantics $(a \to STOP) \setminus \{a\}$ performs a hidden action before evolving to STOP. Our approach adopts this understanding and takes hidden actions into account. A coordination process like $P \setminus A$ removes A from the externally visible events and specifies that the system cannot synchronize with its environment on any event from A. However, within P, the events in A are available for synchronization, of course.

A similar argument applies to

$$a \to P \;\square\; a \to Q = a \to (P \sqcap Q) \,.$$

The left-hand side models a system that offers two similar actions for synchronization but its future depends on the external decision which one of the two exclusive actions is chosen. The right-hand side models a system offering a single action to its environment and then decides internally if it continues as P or as Q. Accordingly, $P \sqcap Q$ is understood as a system performing an internal action to make the decision between P and Q. Thus, when used in a coordination process, the internal (nondeterministic) choice gives rise to a single internal action whose outcome determines which one of the processes is chosen. There are more reasons for allowing the internal choice to be used in a coordination process. For example, it is quite often the case that nondeterministic models of a system are sufficient to express certain properties (e. g., deadlock-freedom). Once a process is proved to express the interaction requirements of a system it is clearly desirable to take it as the coordination process and to implement the missing details on the level of some programming language instead of further refining the CSP model.

3.2   Duration, Conflict and Concurrency

Events are assumed to be instantaneous and atomic. In [6], Hoare proposes to unravel this abstraction by splitting an event into start and end event to model duration of the original event. Our approach adopts this idea. Events are split into start and end events and the action that realizes the original event is performed between these two. It is important to note that actions can be of arbitrary granularity (i.e. just a few basic operations of a processing unit or a long running service) and may even be internally concurrent. The single requirement is that it is guaranteed to terminate eventually.

Furthermore, we believe that concurrency must be distinguished from choice for the purposes of a coordination language. Designers of concurrent systems should be able to specify which parts of a system may be executed simultaneously (truly concurrent) and which are mutual exclusive. For example, the processes

$$P = a \rightarrow b \rightarrow STOP \; \Box \; b \rightarrow a \rightarrow STOP$$
$$Q = a \rightarrow STOP \; |_\emptyset| \; b \rightarrow STOP$$

are equivalent in the standard CSP models (e. g., traces, stable failures and failures-divergences) but we think of them as describing different systems. P describes a system that must perform a and b exclusively while Q may perform a and b at the same time. This observation is of theoretical and practical importance for a CSP-based approach to coordination. The theoretical issue is that the standard semantics for CSP are interleaving ones and thus do not distinguish choice from concurrency. The practical issue is that a concurrent program should be able to profit from the gains promised by concurrency instead of being limited to purely sequential runs (due to interleaving).

There are two ways of understanding a CSP event. Either as a hand-shaken communication of parallel processes (or components) or as an abstraction of some sequential action (not necessarily related to communication). The former understanding gives rise to implementations of channels that can be used by software developers to build their programs using CSP-style communication. Operators like hiding or internal choice are not supported by these approaches. As explained above, our approach interprets events as arbitrary actions that are performed between the start and end events of a split event in the coordination process.

Interestingly, as shown in [8], the splitting of events allows us to distinguish choice from concurrency. In that paper, a syntactical transformation T of processes is presented that splits the events in its argument (even the hidden ones)

of its input process into start and end events and relabels them in such a way
that hidden transitions become observable again. T allows us to determine pairs
of possibly concurrent events taking hidden events into account. T distinguishes
concurrency from *conflict* in that start and end events of concurrent events
may interleave while conflict relates to exclusive start evens. The transitions
$x, y \in \Sigma \cup \{\checkmark, \tau\}$, leading from P to the states P_x, P_y, $P_x \neq P_y$ respectively, are
conflicting in P if x cannot fire in P_y or y cannot fire in P_x. This deliberately
includes the case $x = y$, because events can be auto-conflicting (if they lead to
different states). This also extends to τ transitions, because conflicts between
those are also possible (as, e. g., in $(a \rightarrow P \;\square\; b \rightarrow Q) \setminus \{a, b\}$). Furthermore, T
allows us to simulate truly concurrent CSP within the framework of standard
interleaving CSP. This is beneficial because these semantics are well-developed,
well-documented and supported by a number of industrial-strength tools such
as FDR and ProB.

Any of the choices presented in this section is justified by the standard semantics of (untimed) CSP. An important feature is that nondeterminism is supported
on the design level but resolved on the implementation level. The advantage is
simplicity of reasoning about the design (e. g., deadlock-freedom is often provable
on a quite abstract design level).

4   Designing a Coordination Environment

The ideas presented in the previous section are supported by the transformation
T presented in [8]. The transformation splits events into start and end events,
introduces fresh hidden actions for internal choices and timeouts, and takes
internal transitions into account. T gives rise to a coordination environment
that simulates the truly concurrent version of a CSP coordination process at
runtime and starts a user-defined function (UDF) after performing the start
event of a split event and performs the respective end event after termination
of the UDF. A UDF is the implementation of a terminating action provided by
the user.

The intent of the coordination environment is to enable coordination of a
concurrent system in a *noninvasive* way separating *interaction* and *data* independently from a specific target language.

The notion of noninvasiveness means that existing implementations of components do not need to be modified to be coordinated. The coordination is done
on top of the component implementations provided by the user encapsulating
the coordinated components, taking their operations as UDFs implementing the
actions of the final system.

The separation of interaction and data is important with respect to the modeling of the coordination process (which may involve data but which does not
necessarily relate to data being communicated or computed by the actions of the
system) and with respect to the final combination of the coordination process
with the UDFs of the system. The first aspect means that the variables used in
a coordination process are independent of the actual values being communicated

and processed by the system (unlike in CSP∥B [15], for example). The second aspect means that the UDFs being mapped to possibly concurrent events may not modify data being shared amongst themselves.

The design-flow associated with our approach allows the concurrency structure and the UDFs to be developed and verified independently up to the point when the system is assembled to a concrete executable concurrent system (by combining the coordination process with the UDFs implementing the actions). Only then sets of possibly concurrent events must be identified and it must be proved that the UDFs do not introduce data races. This issue is discussed in Section 5. The following subsections present our understanding of how a coordination environment should perform actions and enable actions to be chosen internally or by the environment.

4.1   Performing Actions

The purpose of the coordination environment is not only to coordinate concurrent parts of a system but also to execute UDFs when performing actions and to assign the execution of UDFs to threads. This is done while performing an event or a τ-transition made visible by T.

Since the simulation of the original process P is defined by the operational firing rules of CSP unrolling $T(P)$ while hiding the externalized hidden actions and the end events of visible actions, we do not go into details of unrolling the coordination process here. The important point is that the events are regarded as actions which are associated with UDFs and that these UDFs are executed between the atomic steps of the actions start and its end.

The following cases are to be considered when performing an action. The action either corresponds to a (a) synchronized event, (b) to a hidden event, (c) to a renamed event, or (d) to any other event.

The first case (a) is commonly considered to be a problem when matching actions with events. The argument against performing actions for synchronized events is the following question:

"which of the synchronized components should perform the action?"

This question remained unanswered for some systems. For example the process analysis toolkit PAT [16] allows events – except synchronization events – to be associated with UDFs. Our answer to this question (and our argument in favor of performing actions for synchronized events) is that synchronization primarily affects the order of events and not their ownership. Thus, a single action is performed after the start event in an arbitrarily chosen context (either one of the threads performing the preceding actions, possibly another).

In the second case (b) the original event (being subject to hiding) defines the action to be performed. In the third case (c) the renamed event (not the original one) defines the action to be performed. Although this decision seems to be at odds with case (b), because both renaming and hiding can be regarded as a substitution of the original event's name (in a user-defined way or by τ respectively), the different treatments are necessary for uniquely identifying the

UDFs to be executed. The reason is that hidden events cannot be synchronized on but renamed events are available for synchronization.

In the last case, the event directly identifies the UDF to be performed. It is noteworthy, however, that $\checkmark$ is not associated with a UDF. It solely models termination of a process, is commonly considered to be outside the alphabet of a process, and it is the only event not being split by T.

As an example, the single UDF to be performed by the following coordination process P (being algebraically equivalent to $SKIP$) is the one identified by event a.

$$P = ((b \rightarrow SKIP)[b \leftarrow a] \mid_{\{a\}} \mid a \rightarrow SKIP) \setminus \{a\}$$

This design decisions described above allow us to relinquish the idea that a sequential process models a single thread of control. A sequential process defines the order of its actions but these can be performed by different threads. This gives us great freedom in distributing the actions amongst processing units of the final system. Load balancing could, for example, be realized by statically creating a task queue and distributing the actions dynamically at runtime. Any of these informal descriptions above conforms to the formal definition of T.

4.2   Choosing Events

There must be some additional component added to the coordination environment dealing with the execution of hidden events. Visible events are available for external synchronization and chosen externally. But how to resolve conflicts of hidden actions?

Our solution is to use event listeners that reside above the component performing $T(P)$ and below the one realizing the hiding of externalized hidden actions and the end events of actions. This way, it can be ensured that the e and eh events are immediately performed so that $T(P)$ can proceed and offer any causally dependent s and sh events. The strategy how to choose amongst sh events, however, must be provided by the user of our coordination approach. Like the UDFs realizing the resolution of internal choices, listeners are to be injected into the coordination environment to deal with sh events introduced by hiding (those not being introduced by internal choice or timeout).

This leaves it open to the programmer to decide if hidden actions have priority over visible ones as, e. g., in the tau-priority model presented in [14], and how conflicts of hidden actions are resolved.

It is important to notice that this does not contradict non- invasiveness of our approach. By making hidden events on the outermost process available for internal event listeners, we provide a general way for resolving nondeterminism.

5   Detecting Data Races

CSP can be used as a coordination language independent of the target language. Thus, we do not consider a particular specification language for the UDFs here and present a purely mathematical proof obligation to ensure freedom of data races in a coordinated system. It is defined as a so-called *frame property*, based on our notion of possible concurrency (as presented in [8]), describing the modification behavior of a UDF with respect to another UDF. Refer to [11] for a more in-depth presentation of framing.

Let F be the type of all UDFs and *Var* the type of all modifiable entities (references to objects and primitive types). The mapping of events to UDFs is formally defined as a partial injective function such that its inverse is a total injection. It is

$$udf : \Sigma \rightarrowtail\mkern-14mu\rightarrow F\,, \qquad \text{and its inverse is} \qquad udf^{-1} : F \rightarrowtail \Sigma\,.$$

Hence, a UDF uniquely identifies an event but events do not necessarily identify a UDF. A *data race* is formally expressed using the following functions:

$$shared : F \times F \rightarrow \mathbb{P}\ Var$$

$$shared(f, g) \mathrel{\widehat{=}} (writes(f) \cap rw(g)) \cup (writes(g) \cap rw(f))$$

$$writes, reads, rw : F \rightarrow \mathbb{P}\ Var$$

$$rw(f) \mathrel{\widehat{=}} writes(f) \cup reads(f)$$

Two UDFs f and g suffer from a *data race* if their frames overlap and one modifies data also read or written by the other.

$$race(f, g) \mathrel{\widehat{=}} shared(f, g) \neq \emptyset$$

Let $conc : \Sigma \times \Sigma \rightarrow Bool$ be the predicate telling us whether or not two events are possibly concurrent in a given process P (i.e., $conc(x, y) \leftrightarrow (x, y) \in conc(P)$). This predicate is combined with udf^{-1} to the following predicate telling us whether or not two UDFs are possibly concurrent:

$$conc^{F} : F \times F \rightarrow Bool\,, \quad \text{where} \quad conc^{F}(f, g) \mathrel{\widehat{=}} conc(udf^{-1}(f), udf^{-1}(g))\,.$$

The proof obligation ensuring freedom of data races is

$$\forall f, g \in F : conc^{F}(f, g) \Rightarrow \neg\ race(f, g)\,.$$

A system violating this condition can be corrected by either adjusting the coordination process (by removing possible simultaneity) or modifying the UDFs (by making the frames distinct).

In general, determining the sets *reads* and *writes* of arbitrary UDFs is a hard problem (due to aliasing). Dealing with this issue is beyond the scope of the work presented here. However, it is noteworthy that specialized logics such as separation logic [13] offer a prospective alternative for specifying (and verifying) properties such as the data independence of UDFs.

Besides this data related proof obligation, it must be proved that the UDFs are never called outside their preconditions and that they are guaranteed to terminate to obtain total correctness of a system. Furthermore, it must be proved that the UDFs resolving nondeterministic choices always return a valid process name.

As motivated in the Introduction, the sequential terminating UDFs implementing the sequential parts of the program are oblivious to concurrency modulo the proof obligation presented above. This means that our approach is noninvasive and allows us to turn a verified sequential system into a concurrent one by identifying parts of the program that make up the UDFs, adding a suitable CSP script and mapping events to UDFs. Provided that the additional proof-obligation can be discharged successfully, modular verification remains valid on that program. This implies that the sequential parts do not have to be modified at all. The coordination environment is the entry point to the final program and solely requires implementation of the mapping from events to UDFs.

6   Supported Processes

The approach presented here supports all finite alphabet CSP processes except the ill-formed recursive process $P = P$ (which is sometimes understood as div). This includes infinite state processes as well as diverging ones. The limitation to processes whose alphabet is finite matches the assumption that there are only finitely many UDFs assigned to the events of a process. Our approach to simulation is capable of dealing with any CSP process whose alphabet is finite. Consider the following divergent processes:

$$P = \mu P' \bullet (e \to P') \setminus \{e\} \qquad \text{and} \qquad Q = \mu Q' \bullet (e \to Q' \sqcap SKIP) \setminus \{e\} \,.$$

P models a process that runs forever without any interaction with its environment. This is not a problem in its own right, because, as shown in our case-study on modeling and implementing a workflow server in CSP [7], divergence may naturally arise when modeling server processes. Q may also diverge, but may as well eventually decide to terminate gracefully.

The reason for accepting such processes is that the internal actions resolving the choices can be used to implement local *fairness* conditions. The notion of fairness conditions refers to conditions that 'cure' processes that behave badly under the assumption that repeated (local) choices can always be resolved in the same way. The fact that this is unlikely to happen in reality is expressed by fairness. FDR does not support fairness but PAT explicitly deals with fairness, as described in [17]. Fairness can be specified on different levels of granularities (e. g., local or global) and can be regarded as an abstraction of probabilities.

Consequently, the process Q shown above is not necessarily diverging and might be guaranteed to terminate eventually under certain fairness assumptions. The same applies to other processes containing process control constructs such as internal or external choice, timeout or interrupt allowing the process to eventually exit from cycles of hidden actions.

Both tools FDR and ProB can be used to verify that P unavoidably diverges while Q may eventually terminate. FDR proves this in the traces model because

$$\mathcal{T}[\![P]\!] = \{\langle\rangle\} \qquad \text{and} \qquad \mathcal{T}[\![Q]\!] = \{\langle\rangle, \langle\checkmark\rangle\} \,.$$

In the failures-divergences model $P = Q$ because both processes may diverge initially.

The same result can be obtained using the LTL model checking capabilities of ProB. In ProB's LTL syntax, the formula $\phi = F\ G\ [tau]$ states that a process unavoidably diverges (all of its executions eventually end up in an endless cycle of τ events). Now

$$P \models \phi \qquad \text{but} \qquad Q \not\models \phi.$$

The counterexample found by ProB expectedly shows that Q may eventually perform $\checkmark$. Another interesting example is the infinite state process

$$R = \mu\, R' \bullet (a \to R' \,|||\, b \to STOP).$$

It can be simulated although it is obviously questionable if any reasonable program conforming to this design exists. Infinite state processes such as R are likely to eventually run out of memory, crashing the whole system.

Now, the same mechanism that can be used to implement fairness can be facilitated to turn theoretically infinite state processes into finite state processes. However, this requires knowledge of the structure of the processes when implementing the UDF resolving the internal choices. In the example of process R, the relevant UDF could count the a's and always choose the b if a certain bound is reached.

In this context it is important to observe that CSP_M scripts modeling infinite state systems cannot in general be checked by FDR because compilation of the script to the internal LTS will not terminate. The ProB LTL model checker, however, performs on-the-fly model checking and quite often succeeds in model checking infinite-state systems [12].

7   Implementation and Further Work

The coordination model presented here is given in a target language independent way. In this section, we present its implementation for the target language Java. It simulates a coordination process at runtime and executes user-defined Java code when performing an event. For now, it implements the operational semantics of the process operators *prefixing*, *sequential composition*, *internal choice*, *external choice*, *generalized parallel*, *timeout*, *interrupt*, *hiding*, and *renaming*.

The coordination environment provides the final class *CspEnvironment* encapsulating the coordination process. This class manages the events offered by the coordination process, listeners that deal with changes of offered events, and the mapping of events to UDFs. The mapping of events to UDFs is defined by an implementation of the *CspEventExecutor* interface. The environment immutably references a single instance of a *CspProcessStore* holding the process configurations that describes the coordination process to be simulated. The environment instance is the only object that the implementation synchronizes on when performing the atomic start and end transitions modeling an event of the coordination process. The start transitions of visible events are available for

```
CspEventExecutor cee = ... ;
Filter filter = ... ;
// setup cee and filter
CspProcessStore store = new CspProcessStore ();
// register process configurations
CspEnvironment env = new CspEnvironment(store , cee);
env. registerListener (new CspEventConsumer ( filter ));
CspSimulator s = new SwingCspSimulator ("my_example" , env );
s . run ();
```

Fig. 1. Code stub of a coordinated Java program

external synchronization, while start transitions of hidden events are only accessible for event listeners. The end transitions are performed immediately after termination of the action's UDF.

The *CspEnvironment* provides a start method taking a process name that determines the coordination process instance. When started, the environment retrieves the coordination process from its store and adds the events offered by the process to its set of offered events. Then it informs the event listeners about that change. From that point on, interaction with the coordination environment is done by choosing events from the set of offered events and performing them. Subsequently the listeners are performed after every change of the set of events offered by the outermost process. This set changes only when an event is performed. If a client holds a reference to an event that is no longer available, it cannot be performed, of course (resulting in a no-op).

To create an executable system one has to instantiate a *CspEnvironment* with a *CspProcessStore* and a *CspEventExecutor*. One can then create a coordinated system as shown in Figure 1. A *CspSimulator* may be used to connect a *CspEnvironment* to the outside world. One useful example is the *SwingCspSimulator* that provides a simple Swing GUI to chose and perform events.

The example code shown in Figure 1 assumes the existence of suitable *CspEventExecutor* and *Filter* classes (filters are convenience objects helping event listeners to find the events that they act upon). The instances may be configured to fit the needs of the final system. Then a process store is created and must be filled with process configurations. A *CspEnvironment* is created using the *CspEventExecutor* and *CspProcessStore* instances. To deal with possibly hidden events, a *CspEventConsumer* takes the *Filter* instance as argument and is registered as a listener for event changes at the environment. Finally, the environment is run using a Swing GUI. Our implementation handles the nesting of process operators and the offered (initial) events of processes in an explicit way. This causes a considerable runtime overhead but allows us to resolve conflicts of actions when an action is started and to leave concurrent actions on offer while an action is performing.

The workflow server presented in [7] is built using this coordination environment. The workflow server accepts workflow definitions that are implemented in the same way and uses FDR to verify workflow definitions before activating them.

Extending the implementation towards the coordination of distributed systems is subject to future work. Explicit support for data storage and communication by the coordination environment is another concern that deserves further investigation. We also strive for a deeper integration with the functional verification of UDFs. Development of specialized provers for the conflict-freedom proof obligation is also subject to future work.

8 Related Work

Linda [2] is a parallel programming language that adds parallelism to sequential languages (e. g., C, Fortran, etc) and allows tasks to be distributed dynamically at runtime. Like Linda, our approach separates concurrency concerns from sequential ones in a machine- and language-independent way. In contrast to Linda, it builds on ordinary shared memory communication (as built into the underlying language) instead of a special memory model (the so-called *tuplespace*). Moreover, our approach is based on a formal method that is supported by a number of industrial-strength tools.

Reference Nets [9] provide an object-oriented High-Level Petri Net formalism where instances of Petri Nets carry references to other instances of Petri Nets instead of tokens. In that model, the firing of a transition moves a reference from one place to another. The concept of synchronous channels allows Petri Net instances to communicate when a transition fires. Reference Nets extend this to the execution of arbitrary (terminating) Java code. Thus, in that model, a Petri Net can be regarded as the coordination process of a system and the code attached to transitions relates to our understanding of actions. Unlike our approach, Reference Nets do not support verification of the coordination process and lack proof obligations relating the ordering of Petri Net transitions (as defined by their firing sequences) to the pre- and postconditions of their associated implementations, for example.

Another formal approach to the modeling and verification of distributed component based systems is described by Baier et al. [3]. Their approach is based on the model checker Vereofy which supports multiple input languages capable of modeling concurrent systems. However, their approach does not extend to implementing such systems but remains on the modeling level.

CSP++ [5] and JCSP [18] offer CSP-like channels as inter-thread communication facilities but realize only a limited set of CSP operators. The feature that distinguishes our approach from CSP-based software libraries is that events are not interpreted as communications over a typed channel but as abstractions of arbitrary actions. It realizes the common understanding that an action can be modeled by a start and an end event (and the action executing between these two). Furthermore, the CSP model is simulated at runtime to drive the concurrent application.

Since sequential processes in CSP are viewed as executions of computational entities whose behavior can be observed in terms of events, it is natural to map a single sequential process to its own thread. This is the general idea underlying CSP++ and JCSP. Our approach does not necessarily map two causally dependent threads to the same thread. It merely maintains the order of UDFs as defined by the events of the CSP script coordinating the system. This is comparable to Linda's feature of distributing tasks at runtime.

9   Conclusions

In this paper, our approach to using CSP as a coordination language is presented. It unravels the various abstractions that are carefully built into CSP for the purpose of coordinating concurrent systems in a noninvasive way. The approach taken here is quite different from other approaches to implementing CSP because it does not built on the channel concept which is a common approach realizing the hand-shaken communication. Instead, our approach is based on atomic steps denoting start- and endpoints of a system's actions. It also deals with internal (hidden) actions. Associating the resolution of internal choices with UDFs undoes nondeterminism inherent to the CSP model coordinating the program. This allows us, for example, to turn systems that are not fair in the standard CSP semantics into fair ones.

The semantic foundation of the coordination runtime environment is given by a syntactic process transformation turning a standard interleaving CSP process into a truly concurrent one. The transformation also allows us to predict which functions are possibly executed in parallel. Dependent on possibly concurrent events we stated a proof obligation for ensuring absence of data races.

Our approach allows us to separate concurrency issues from sequential ones, and to reuse the concurrent design of the system at runtime. It also enables us to use state-of-the-art CSP tools such as FDR [14] and ProB [10] for the automated verification of concurrency aspects of the software, and integrates with modular verification of UDFs. The use of CSP makes it especially well suited for systems with highly communicative concurrent components.

Compared to other CSP implementations, the approach presented here supports a richer CSP in terms of supported process operators. Unlike other CSP library-level implementations, our approach is noninvasive. It allows the system's basic actions to be coordinated very directly. Our approach is capable of handling infinite state and divergent processes. However, this comes at the cost of the runtime overhead of explicitly managing processes and events caused by simulation of CSP.

References

1. Abrial, J.: The B Book - Assigning Programs to Meanings. Cambridge University Press, Cambridge (1996)
2. Ahuja, S., Carriero, N., Gelernter, D.: Linda and Friends. Computer 19(8), 26–34 (1986)

3. Baier, C., Blechmann, T., Klein, J., Klüppelholz, S.: A Uniform Framework for Modeling and Verifying Components and Connectors. In: Field, J., Vasconcelos, V.T. (eds.) COORDINATION 2009. LNCS, vol. 5521, pp. 247–267. Springer, Heidelberg (2009)
4. Barnett, M., Chang, B.E., DeLine, R., Jacobs, B., Leino, K.R.M.: Boogie: A modular reusable verifier for object-oriented programs. In: de Boer, F.S., Bonsangue, M.M., Graf, S., de Roever, W.-P. (eds.) FMCO 2005. LNCS, vol. 4111, pp. 364–387. Springer, Heidelberg (2006)
5. Gardner, W.B.: Converging CSP specifications and C++ programming via selective formalism. ACM Trans. Embed. Comput. Syst. 4(2), 302–330 (2005)
6. Hoare, C.A.R.: Communicating Sequential Processes. Prentice Hall International, Englewood Cliffs (1985)
7. Kleine, M., Göthel, T.: Specification, Verification and Implementation of Business Processes using CSP. In: 4th IEEE International Symposium on Theoretical Aspects of Software Engineering, pp. 145–154. IEEE Computer Society, Los Alamitos (2010)
8. Kleine, M., Sanders, J.W.: Simulating truly concurrent CSP. In: Brazilian Symposium on Formal Methods (SBMF 2010). Springer, Heidelberg (2010)
9. Kummer, O.: Referenznetze. Logos Verlag, Berlin (2002)
10. Leuschel, M., Fontaine, M.: Probing the Depths of CSP-M: A New FDR-Compliant Validation Tool. In: Liu, S., Araki, K. (eds.) ICFEM 2008. LNCS, vol. 5256, pp. 278–297. Springer, Heidelberg (2008)
11. Müller, P.: Modular specification and verification of object-oriented programs. Springer, Heidelberg (2002)
12. Plagge, D., Leuschel, M.: Seven at one stroke: LTL model checking for High-level Specifications in B, Z, CSP, and more. In: STTT (2008)
13. Reynolds, J.: Separation logic: a logic for shared mutable data structures (2002)
14. Roscoe, A.W.: The Theory and Practice of Concurrency. Prentice Hall, Englewood Cliffs (2005)
15. Schneider, S., Treharne, H.: Verifying Controlled Components. In: Boiten, E.A., Derrick, J., Smith, G.P. (eds.) IFM 2004. LNCS, vol. 2999, pp. 87–107. Springer, Heidelberg (2004)
16. Sun, J., Liu, Y., Dong, J.S.: Model Checking CSP Revisited: Introducing a Process Analysis Toolkit. In: International Symposium on Leveraging Applications of Formal Methods, Verification and Validation, pp. 307–322. Springer, Heidelberg (2008)
17. Sun, J., Liu, Y., Dong, J.S., Pang, J.: PAT: Towards flexible verification under fairness. In: Bouajjani, A., Maler, O. (eds.) CAV 2009. LNCS, vol. 5643, pp. 709–714. Springer, Heidelberg (2009)
18. Welch, P.H.: Process Oriented Design for Java: Concurrency for All. In: Arabnia, H.R. (ed.) Proceedings of the International Conference on Parallel and Distributed Processing Techniques and Applications (PDPTA 2000), vol. 1, pp. 51–57. CSREA Press, CSREA (2000)

An Efficient Management of Correlation Sets with Broadcast

Jacopo Mauro[1,2], Maurizio Gabbrielli[1,2], Claudio Guidi[4],
and Fabrizio Montesi[3]

[1] Department of Computer Science, University of Bologna, Italy
[2] Lab. Focus, INRIA, Bologna, Italy
{gabbri,jmauro}@cs.unibo.it
[3] IT University of Copenhagen, Denmark
fabr@itu.dk
[4] italianaSoftware srl, Imola, Italy
cguidi@italianasoftware.com

Abstract. A fundamental aspect which affects the efficiency and the
performance of Service-Oriented Architectures is the mechanism which
allows to manage sessions and, in particular, to assign incoming messages
to the correct sessions (also known as service instances). A relevant mechanism for solving this problem, first introduced by BPEL and then used
in other languages (e.g. Jolie) is that one based on *correlation sets*. The
BPEL and Jolie languages are currently allowing the use of messages
whose target is only one session. However there are a lot of scenarios
where being able to send a broadcast message to more than one session
could be useful. Supporting such a broadcast primitive means to allow
correlation sets which can contain unspecified variables and this can be
very inefficient, since usual implementations in terms of hash tables cannot be used in this case.

In this paper we propose a data structure, based on radix trees and
an algorithm for managing a correlation mechanism that supports the
broadcast primitive, without degrading the performances.

1 Introduction

Service-Oriented Computing (SOC) is a paradigm for programming distributed
applications by means of the composition of services. Services are autonomous,
self-descriptive computational entities that can be dynamically discovered and
composed in order to build more complex functionalities. The resulting systems,
called Service-Oriented Architectures (SOA), have a wide diffusion; as of today
the most prominent technology in this context consist of Web Services, a set
of open specifications that focuses on interoperability and compatibility with
existing infrastructures. This is mainly obtained through the adoption of the
XML document format and by using HTTP as the underlying transport protocol
for communications.

In a SOA services are loosely coupled, i.e. they stress a minimality on the
dependencies that each service has w.r.t. the others, and can be stateful; this last

W. De Meuter and G.-C. Roman (Eds.): COORDINATION 2011, LNCS 6721, pp. 80–94, 2011.
© IFIP International Federation for Information Processing 2011

point is the case of orchestrators which maintain a state for each created session. Usually, in a stateful service a session is created at the first client invocation. But, differently from the object-oriented approach, SOC does not guarantee references for identifying the new session. Thus a fundamental aspect which affects the efficiency and the performance of SOAs is the mechanism which allows to manage sessions. In fact, in a typical pattern of interaction, a service may manage many different sessions, corresponding to different clients. Since communications are usually supported with stateless protocols (e.g. SOAP on HTTP), when a service receives a message from a client C the system must be able to identify which is the session corresponding to C and that, therefore, must receive the message. In other words, sessions usually need to be accessed only by those invokers (messages) which hold some specific rights.

A relevant mechanism for solving this problem, first introduced by BPEL [1] and then used in JOLIE [8,9], COWS [6] and in other languages, is that based on *correlation sets*. Intuitively a correlation set is a set of variables whose values allow to distinguish sessions initiated by different clients. More precisely, both the sessions and the incoming messages contain some specific "correlation values" defining the variables in the correlation set. When a message m arrives it is routed to the session which has the same values as m for the correlation variables.

As a simple example of correlation set consider the case of a service S used for buying goods. Suppose that S handles all the communication of a specific customer using a unique session, while different customers have different sessions. Assuming that a customer is uniquely determined by her name and surname we can use a correlation set consisting of the two variables *name* and *surname* for determining the customer's session. Now let us suppose that S can receive the following three types of messages (with the obvious meaning): $buy(name, surname, product\_id)$; $delete\_order(name, surname, product\_id)$; $pay(name, surname, product\_id, credit\_card\_info)$. When a customer, say John Smith, wants to buy product 1 he can send a message of the form $buy(John, Smith, 1)$. When this message is received the service checks whether there is a session that correlates with it, i.e. whether there exists a session whose variables *name* and *surname* are respectively instantiated to the values *John* and *Smith*. If this is the case message m is assigned to such session. On the other hand, if John Smith is a new customer and no session correlates with m then the message is not delivered (note however, that in this case a new session could be created which correlates with the message, see for example [2,1,5]).

The BPEL and Jolie languages are currently allowing the use of messages whose target is only one session. However there are a lot of scenarios where being able to send a broadcast message to more than one session could be useful. Let's consider for instance a cloud environment where every user can start, control and terminate a virtual machine on the cloud (a framework similar for instance to Amazon EC2). Let's suppose that we would like a unique entry point to this system and this entry point is a service that can receive and send messages to the users and the administrators of the cloud. We could consider to have a session for every virtual machine and control the virtual machine through this session. The key to identify a session can be the union of the following fields:

- the name, surname and date of birth of the user (we assume that these values univocally determine the user);
- the kind of virtualized operating system (i.e Ubuntu, Windows, ...);
- the version of the operating system;
- the priority of the virtual machine (high, medium, low).

Having this key a user (say John Smith born on the 1st of Jan 1970) can start a Windows 7 machine with low priority sending for instance a message like *start(John,Smith,19700101,windows,7,low)*. Later he can control and terminate the session (and therefore the virtual machine) simply sending messages like *execute* or *terminate* specifying every time all the fields of the key.

On the other hand suppose now that an administrator wants to apply a patch to all the Windows virtual machines. Without a broadcast primitive he/she should retrieve all the keys of sessions controlling a Windows machine and later send them the message that triggers the application of the patch. For the programmer point of view this usually involves the definition of a session or service that keeps the log of all the sessions. This session/service often slows down the performances due to the creation or deletion of new sessions. On the other hand having a broadcast primitive an administrator could send:

- a message like *get_location()* that will be sent to every session for asking to the session which hardware machine is used to run the virtual machine;
- a message like *patch(operating_system, operating_system_version, ...)* to patch all the virtual machines with a certain operating system and version;
- a messages like *terminate(name, surname, birthday_date)* that can terminate all the virtual machines belonging to a user;
- messages like *stop(priority)* or *stop(operating_system, priority)* can be used to stop every virtual machine having a specific priority or operating system + priority.

These are only few examples of the use of broadcast primitives. Another important application for these messages is for the implementation of a publish/ subscribe pattern: This is a messaging pattern where senders (publishers) of messages do not send the messages directly to specific receivers (subscribers). The messages are instead divided into classes and the subscribers subscribe for the reception of messages of a given class. The system is responsible for sending every message belonging to a certain class to every subscriber that has subscribed for that class. Publisher may not know who are the subscribers and vice versa.

This pattern can be easily implemented using broadcast and a service having a correlation set that contains the class identifier. Whenever a subscriber subscribes for a class, a new session responsible for the forwarding of the message is created. The publisher now can send a broadcast message specifying in the message its class. The correlation mechanism will check this value and route the message to every session that has subscribed for that class. The session can later forward the message to the real subscriber.

The aim of this paper is to present a data structure and an implementation of the correlation mechanism that supports the broadcast primitive without degrading the performances of the correlation of normal messages.

The operations that a correlation mechanism has to support can be seen as the select, insert and delete operations of a relational database, where every tuple of the relation is a session. The correlation set is a key of a relation. When a normal message arrives it always contains a key that determine the target session. In the database analogy the correlation operation is then a "select" operation, and in the case of normal messages the (complete) key is used to retrieve the target session. On the contrary, a broadcast message specifies only part of the key, indeed its target is potentially a set of sessions. Continuing in the database analogy, the broadcast operation can be efficiently implemented by adding an index for every type of broadcast messages. However, since increasing the number of indexes decrease the performances of the insert and delete queries (i.e. creation and deletion of sessions), the less indexes we have the better it is. We will then define a solution that uses the minimal number of indexes needed to correlate the messages to the right sessions. The indexes will be implemented using radix trees.

We would like to underline that in this work we have taken as a starting point the correlation mechanism of Jolie. We made this choice because we find that Jolie correlation mechanism is more flexible than the BPEL one. For instance Jolie correlation variables are normal variables and not a late-bound constant like in BPEL. While in BPEL the values of a correlation set are defined only by a specially marked send or receive message and once defined they can not change, in Jolie the programmer can decide to instantiate or change the values of a correlation set at run time. In BPEL all the fields (correlation proprieties or correlation tokens) of a message key should be always defined. Jolie instead allows partially defined keys. This flexibility comes with a price: the implementation of the search of a correlating session is linear w.r.t. the number of session while in BPEL it is constant (usually hash table are used).

The correlation mechanism can be seen as a special case of the well know content-based publish/subscribe mechanism [11]. Indeed the correlation mechanism can be seen as a simpler content-based publish/subscribe mechanism where messages are notifications, sessions are subscriptions and correlation variables are attributes. The correlation mechanism exploits however two constraints that usually a content-based publish/subscribe mechanism does not have. In correlation, few attributes need to be considered and only equality predicates are used to compare the attributes. Hence, this work could be considered as an improvement over publish/subscribe algorithms such as [4,3] for scenarios where the previous two constraints hold.

After having provided some background in Section 2 we explain the idea of the algorithm in Section 3. In Section 4 we show how the data structure is created and used, while in Section 5 we prove the correctness of the algorithm and we perform some complexity analysis. Finally Section 6 concludes describing some future work.

2   Background

In this section we formally define the main concepts that we will use in the rest of the paper. A correlation set, c-set for short, can be seen as a key that can be used to retrieve a session. For our purposes a c-set can be seen as a set of variables names (in BPEL these correspond to c-set proprieties) that can assume values in a domain. To simplify the notation we assume that the variables of a c-set can assume values in the domain D defined as the set of strings on a given signature.

Definition 1 (c-set). *Given a service S, a correlation set for S is a finite set of variables names. When these variables are defined their values uniquely identify a session of S.*

Sessions may define the variables of a c-set. The definition of variables belonging to a c-set is captured with the following definition.

Definition 2 (c-instance). *Given a c-set c we say that a c-instance for c is a total function that maps every variable of c to a value in D.*
We will say that a session s has a c-instance φ if for every variable v in c the variable v has been assigned and its value is $\varphi(v)$.

Services, especially those having multi-party sessions, may need more than one c-set because the users may need to use different keys to identify a session. These services, also known as multi correlation services, do not require to have a c-instance for every c-set. However since c-sets are used to identify a session we require that a session must have at least a c-instance. Moreover we do not allow the starting of a session having the same c-instance of another existing session.

Every message that is exchanged will contain some arguments associated to a c-set. Usually these arguments are called correlation tokens or correlation values and are used to find the recipient of the message. BPEL and other service engines allow the use of potentially one correlation token (c-token for short) for every c-set of the service. For example a multi-party session can be initialized submitting a message having as correlation tokens the values for all the c-sets of the service. In this work instead we will consider messages having only one c-token. This restriction is however insignificant since the behaviour that is caused by the exchange of messages with more than one c-token can be easily simulated in our framework. This is due to the fact that differently from BPEL we do not need the exchange of a message to change the value of a correlation variable.

Formally we can define a c-token in the following way.

Definition 3 (c-token). *Given a message m a c-token is a pair (c, φ) where*

- *c is a c-set containing the variables used to specify the message recipients*
- *if m is a normal message then φ is a total function that maps a variable of c into a value in D*
- *if m is a broadcast message then φ is a partial function that maps a variable of c into a value in D. Moreover φ is not total.*

For instance the service for buying goods has only one c-set $c = \{name, surname\}$ and the c-instance of John's session is the function φ s.t. $\varphi(name) = John$ and $\varphi(surname) = Smith$. The message $buy(John, Smith, 1)$ has instead as c-token the couple (c, φ). If we want to send a message m to every person named John for wishing him a happy name day we can use a broadcast message whose c-token will be the couple (c, φ') where $\varphi'(name) = John$ and $\varphi(surname)$ is not defined.

As it can be seen in the previous definition the introduction of the broadcast primitive allows the user to not define all the variables of a c-set. Normal messages, like c-instances, need to define all the variables of a c-set because they need to identify their (unique) target session. On the other hand, broadcast messages can specify only a part of the key, indeed their target can be a set of sessions. Note that, in case of multi correlation services, the c-token definition does not allow to consider part of two different keys to determine the targets of a broadcast message. We do not allow this possibility since we haven't find a significant example that justifies this increased power. However we could easily extend our framework to treat also this case. Now we can formally define when a message correlates with a session. Intuitively a message correlates with a session when the values of the correlation token match the c-instance of a session. In the following $\varphi_m(v) \uparrow$ denotes that φ_m is not defined in v.

Definition 4 (Correlation). *Given a service S, a session s and a message m with c-token (c_m, φ_m) we will say that s correlates with m iff s has a c-instance φ for the c-set c_m and $\forall v \in c_m. \ \varphi_m(v) = \varphi(v) \vee \varphi_m(v) \uparrow$.*

3   The Idea

As we have discussed above the current mechanisms for assigning a message to the correct session does not support the possibility of identifying a set of sessions. A naive implementation for the support of broadcast messages would use an associative array for every c-set variable. However, if this solution is used, for finding the targets of a broadcast message we have to compute a set intersection whose complexity depends on the number of sessions. Another naive solution is using an associative arrays for every subsets of correlation variables that can be used in a broadcast message. If we consider a c-set with n variables this means that for the support of the broadcast primitive we could have $2^n - 1$ associative arrays, since with n variables we can use up to $2^n - 1$ different kind of broadcast messages (one for every subset of the c-set variables). Our key idea in order to improve on this is to use radix trees to memorize the c-instances of all the sessions and therefore for routing messages to the correct session. In this section we will explain intuitively the idea, while its formalization and complexity analysis are contained in the next sections.

A trie, or a prefix tree, is an ordered tree for storing strings, in which there is one node for every common prefix. Edges are labeled with characters, while the strings are stored in extra leaf nodes. Tries are extremely useful for constructing associative arrays with keys that can be expressed as strings, since the time complexity of retrieving the element with a given key is linear time in the length of the key. In fact, looking up for a key of length k consists in following a path in the trie, from the root to a leaf, guided by the characters in the key. A radix tree (or Patricia tree, [10]) is essentially a compact representation of a trie in which any node that has no siblings is merged with its parent (so, each internal node has at least two children). Unlike in regular tries, edges can be labeled with sequences of characters as well as single characters. This makes radix tree more efficient than tries for storing sets of strings (keys) that share long prefixes. The operations of lookup (to determine whether a string is in the set represented by a radix tree), insert (of a string in the tree), and delete (of a string from the tree) have all worst case complexity of $O(l)$, where l is the maximal length of the strings in the set.

Intuitively our idea is to use radix trees to map incoming messages to sessions, by using the values of the c-set variables as keys. In other words, the session pointers can be seen as elements stored in an associative array, while the values of the variables of the c-sets, conveniently organized as strings, are the keys. Our radix trees implements such a structure by memorizing the values of the c-set variables which appear in the existing sessions. In particular, since every broadcast message can define only part of the c-set variables, to be able to process every message we could use a radix tree for every subset of the c-set variables. This however is not an optimal solution. For example if a service has two c-set variables *name* and *surname* we could receive the following kind of messages

1. broadcast messages s.t. their c-tokens do not define any variable
2. broadcast messages s.t. their c-tokens define only the field *name*
3. broadcast messages s.t. their c-tokens define only the field *surname*
4. normal messages s.t. their c-tokens define both *name* and *surname*

With the naive approach we need to use 4 associative arrays (one for every message type). Using radix trees is however possible to use a unique radix tree for 1st, 2nd and 4th types since the c-tokens of the 1st and 2nd kind of messages can be considered as prefix of the c-tokens of the 4th type of messages. For the message of the 3th type instead we have to use a different radix tree, since in this case the c-tokens are not a prefix of those for the 4th type of messages. So it is sufficient to use two radix trees to cover all the possible cases.

To better explain the idea let us consider some more examples. In the following we use a special character, denoted by # and not used elsewhere, to denote in a string the termination of the values of c-set variables.

We first consider a unique c-set variable with only one field: *name*. When there exist no session for such a variable we have a radix tree consisting of the only root (recall that in radix trees the root is associated with the empty string). We represent such a radix tree as a □. If now a session s_1 is created which is identified by the value *John* for the c-set variable *name* then the radix tree became as the one depicted in Figure 1(a). The value *John* allows to reach s_1 by an (obvious) lookup in the tree.

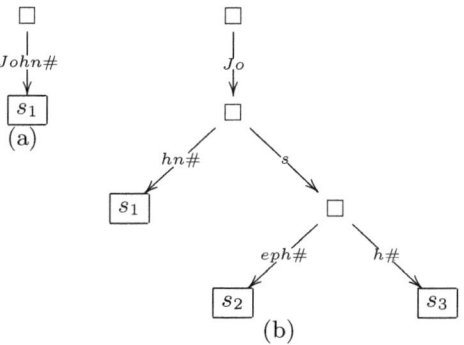

Fig. 1. Example of radix trees

Next assume that two more sessions are created: a session s_2, which is identified by the value $Joseph$ for the variable $name$ and a session s_3 which is identified by $Josh$. The radix tree we obtain is the one depicted in Figure 1(b). Notice that the longest common prefixes of the three key values are associated to edges of the tree. When a message arrives, the value that it carries for the $name$ variable allows one to select a root-leaf path in the tree, so reaching the correct session.

Assume now that our correlation set is composed by the two variables $name$ and $surname$ and consider four sessions $s_1 - s_4$ identified as follows by the values of the c-set variables:

$s_1 : name = John, surname = Smith$; $s_2 : name = John, surname = Smirne$
$s_3 : name = Josh, surname = Smith$; $s_4 : name = John, surname = Smithson$

Correspondingly we have the radix tree depicted in Figure 2(a). In this case, as mentioned before, we need more that one radix tree to store the values of c-sets variables of the sessions. This because in a broadcast message the value of some c-set variables could be not specified. For example, in the case above, let us consider a broadcast message which contains the token $Smith$ for $surname$ and no token for $name$. If we have only a radix tree like the one depicted in Figure 2(a) we can not find with a lookup which session correlate with it. This is due to the fact that the first part of the key of the radix tree is the value of the variable $name$. Hence we need an additional radix tree like the one depicted in Figure 2(b) that can be used to retrieve sessions for messages that do not define the variable $name$.

It is easy to see that these two radix trees allow to cover all the possible cases. First consider what happens if we receive a message m where $name = John$ and $surname = Smith$, hence we consider the string $John\#Smith\#$. In this case, by using the 2(a) radix tree, we see that the message m will be assigned to s_1, since this is the session which correlates with m. However, note that this first tree covers also the case in which no value for surname is provided by the message, hence we do not need a further radix tree to keep only the sessions that define only the variable $name$. For example, if we receive a message m with

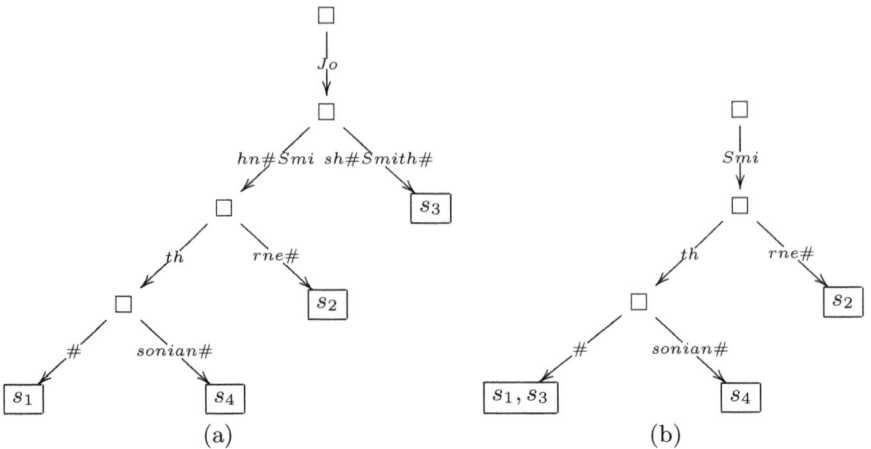

Fig. 2. Example or radix trees for c-set with 2 variables

$name = John$, that is we consider the string $John\#$, then the 2(a) radix tree shows that m correlates to the sessions s_1, s_2, s_4.

On the other hand, if we receive a broadcast message m' where $name$ is not defined and $surname = Smith$ we will use the 2(b) radix tree (with the string $Smith\#$) to find that the session correlating with m' are s_1, s_3.

4   Building the Radix Trees

As previously discussed, with our approach every c-set of the service has a group of radix trees that can be used for checking the correlation of a message to a session. We have also shown that, if we assume that the c-set has n variables, one does not need to consider 2^n different radix trees, because a radix tree for a sequence of variables cover also all the cases given by the prefixes of such a sequence.

In this section we provide an algorithm that, given a c-set with n variables, in the worst case constructs a set containing $\binom{n}{\lceil n/2 \rceil}(= \frac{n!}{\lceil n/2 \rceil! \lfloor n/2 \rfloor!})$ radix trees. In the next section we will prove that such set allow us to route all the possible messages to a service. We also prove that this set is minimal, in the sense that any other set of radix trees which allow to route correctly all the messages has at least the same cardinality. So our algorithm cannot be improved w.r.t. the number of radix trees generated.

In the following we assume that the c-set c has n variables and the set V contains all and only these variables. We denote by seq_i a sequence $x_1, \ldots, x_{h_i}$ of variables of c. Given a list of sequences of variables $seq_1, \ldots, seq_m$ such that seq_i is a prefix of seq_{i+1}, for $i \in [1, m-1]$, we use the notation $RT(seq_1, \ldots, seq_m)$ to indicate any radix tree whose keys are strings of the form $d_1\# \ldots \# d_{h_i}\#$ where $d_j = \varphi(x_j)$, for $j \in [1, h_i]$, and for some c-set-instance φ. In other words, $RT(seq_1, \ldots, seq_m)$ is a kind of schema which can be instantiated by considering the values of the variables for one specific sequence seq_i, with $i \in$

$[1, m]$ (and using $\#$ as separator of values), to obtain a specific concrete radix tree. As previously discussed, a radix tree (described by) $RT(seq_1, \ldots, seq_m)$ allows us to check the existence of a session defining all the variables in one of the sequences seq_i. For example the radix tree in Figure 2(a) can be denoted by $RT(\langle\rangle, \langle name \rangle, \langle name, surname \rangle)$ while the radix tree 2(b) is denoted by $RT(\langle surname \rangle)^1$. By using this notation our problem can be stated as follows: we need to find the minimum number h of radix trees schemas $RT_1(seq_{1,1}, \ldots$ $seq_{1,l_1}), \ldots, RT_h(seq_{h,1}, \ldots seq_{h,l_h})$ such that, for each set $X \subseteq V$, there exists a sequence $seq_{k,o}$ that contains all and only the variables in X.

We find convenient to formulate this problem in terms of a graph representation. Indeed, given a set of variables V, we can create a labeled direct graph $G(V)$ where:

- the nodes are (labeled by) elements in $\mathcal{P}(V)$. Intuitively we will consider all the set of variables that can be defined by a c-token;
- there is an arc from u to v if $u \subset v$;
- the arc (u, v) is labeled with the variables $v \setminus u$ (where $\setminus$ denotes set difference).

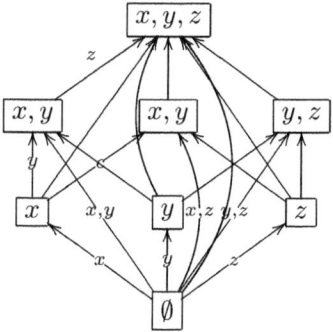

Fig. 3. Example of the graph obtained for with three variables: x, y, z (note that for convenience only few arc labels are reported)

For example, in Figure 3 we see the graph constructed by considering the three variables x, y and z where we can receive all the possible 7 broadcast messages. A path on this graph corresponds to a radix tree schema (see definition 5). Hence, with this graph representation our problem can be stated as follows: we have to find the minimum number of paths that cover all the nodes of the graph where, as usual, we say that a path $u_1 \xrightarrow{x_1} u_2 \xrightarrow{x_2} \cdots \xrightarrow{x_n} u_{n+1}$ covers the nodes $u_1, \ldots, u_{n+1}$.

The algorithm that produces this minimum number of paths is Algorithm 1 and its intuition is the following. Consider the graph $G(V)$ associated to a c-set V, as explained above. We first partition all the nodes of $G(V)$ into levels

---

[1] Note that the order of the cset variables is important and therefore for instance $RT(\langle name, surname \rangle) \neq RT(\langle surname, name \rangle)$.

according to the number of variables of the nodes, so level i contains all the nodes that have exactly i variables. Then starting from the lowest levels (i.e. level 0 and 1) we consider two next levels at a time, say level i and $i+1$. These two levels are seen as a bipartite graph where the nodes of each level form an independent set. We then use a maximum bipartite matching algorithm for selecting a set of arcs between the nodes of these two levels. Next we repeat the same procedure with levels $i+1$ and $i+2$, and we continue until we reach the level n. At this point we take the graph $G'(V)$ obtained by considering all the nodes in the original graph $G(V)$ and only the edges which have been selected by the matching algorithm. As we prove in the next section, the maximal paths[2] on the graph $G'(V)$ form a minimum set of paths covering all the nodes of P.

Before providing the algorithm we need to introduce some notation. We assume that each node is (labeled by) an element of $\mathcal{P}(V)$ ($n = |V|$), as mentioned above and we denote by $level_V(i)$ the set of nodes in the i-th level, i.e. the set of elements in $\mathcal{P}(V)$ which have cardinality i. Moreover $graph(A, B)$ denotes the bipartite direct graph $(A \cup B, E)$ where $(u, v) \in E$ iff $u \subset v$. Finally $maximal\_matching(G)$ is one of the maximal matchings of the bipartite graph G chosen in a non deterministically way. Algorithm 1 takes as input the set $P \subseteq \mathcal{P}(V)$ and returns the graph containing a minimum set of paths covering all the nodes of P. Once we have obtained a graph by using the Algorithm 1 it

---

Algorithm 1. $radix\_trees(P)$

1: $i = 0$
2: $V = level_P(i)$
3: $M = \emptyset$
4: **while** $(i < n)$ **do**
5:     $i = i + 1$
6:     $V' = level_P(i)$
7:     $G = graph(V, V')$
8:     $M' = maximal\_matching(G)$
9:     $V = V - \{v \mid (v,\ x) \text{ is an edge in } M', \text{ for some x}\}$
10:     $V = V \cup V'$
11:     $M = M \cup M'$
12: **end while**
13: **return** (P, M)

---

is possible to compute the radix trees by simply finding all the maximal paths, as shown below.

Definition 5. *Given $P \subseteq \mathcal{P}(V)$ we say that a radix tree schema $RT(u'_1, u'_2 \ldots,$*
$u'_m)$ is produced by the algorithm $radix\_tree(P)$ if $u_1 \xrightarrow{x_1} u_2 \xrightarrow{x_2} \ldots \xrightarrow{x_m} u_{m+1}$
is a maximal path in the graph $G = radix\_tree(P)$ and

– u'_i is a sequence of all the variables in the set u_i, for each $i \in [1, m]$;
– u'_i is a prefix of u'_{i+1}, for each $i \in [1, m-1]$.

---

[2] A maximal path is a path that can not be a proper part of another path.

We now consider an example of application of the previous algorithm to the graph in Figure 3. In Figure 4 we have reported the three steps denoting by $\Rightarrow$ the arcs selected by the maximal matching algorithm (i.e. arcs in M) while $\rightarrow$ indicates the arcs considered by the maximal matching algorithm (i.e. arcs in G, line 7). The nodes in frame are the nodes that are used for computing the maximal matching (i.e. the nodes in V and in $level_P(i)$), while nodes in dotted frame are the nodes already processed (not considered by the matching algorithm and deleted from V, line 9).

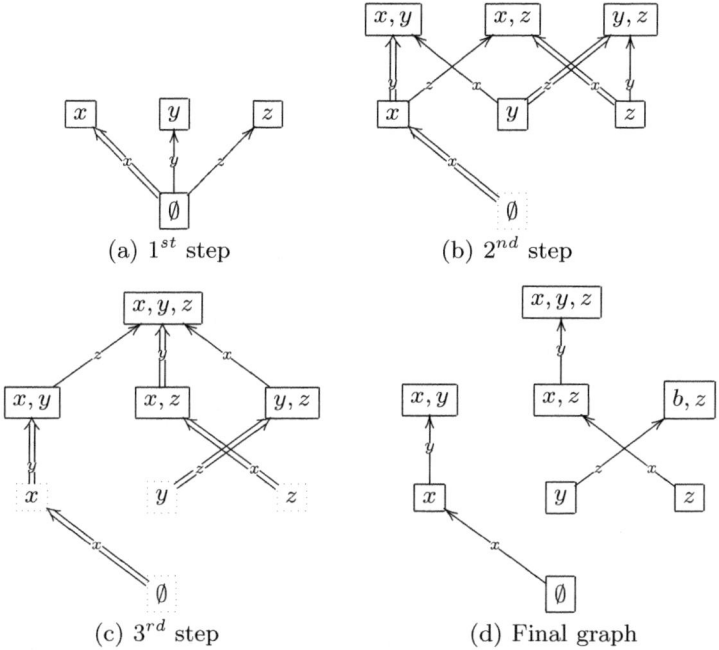

Fig. 4. Example of execution of Algorithm 1 with 3 variables

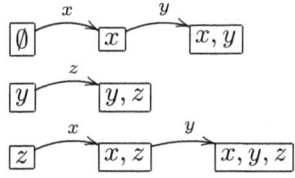

From the final graph (Figure 4(d)) we can compute the radix trees schemas by taking the maximal paths:

The first path corresponds to the radix tree schema $RT(\langle\rangle, \langle x\rangle, \langle x, y\rangle)$ while the other two corresponds to $RT(\langle y\rangle, \langle y, z\rangle)$ and $RT(\langle z\rangle, \langle z, x\rangle, \langle z, x, y\rangle)$, respectively.

4.1   Using Radix Trees

Once we have created the radix tree schemas by using our algorithm, we need some operations for inserting and removing values from them, thus creating the concrete radix trees to be used for correlating messages and sessions. Moreover we need to define a lookup operation, that, given a message, allows us to use the (concrete) radix tree to find all the correlating sessions. To this aim we first introduce the three operations described below. Here and in the following, unless differently specified, with "radix tree" we mean a concrete radix tree, containing values for keys and whose leafs contain (pointers to) sessions. Moreover we assume w.l.o.g. that the service has a unique c-set and therefore only one group of radix trees. If the service has more than one c-set the following considerations should be applied to every c-set.

- $RT.add(s)$ is the operation for adding to the radix tree RT the session s;
- $RT.del(s)$ is the dual operation that deletes the session s in RT;
- $RT.find(m)$ returns all the sessions which correlate with m. If no sessions in RT correlates with m then the *null* pointer is returned.

Assuming that RT belongs to the radix tree schema $RT(seq_1, \ldots, seq_k)$, when $RT.add(s)$ is invoked s is added to the radix tree RT using as key the string $\varphi_s(x_1)\# \ldots \#\varphi_s(x_l)\#$ where $\langle x_1, \ldots, x_l \rangle = seq_k$ and φ_s is the c-instance for s. In a similar way $RT.del(s)$ deletes from RT the session pointer to s.

If $\langle x_1, \ldots, x_l \rangle$ is the sequence of all the variable defined by the c-token φ of a message m, the operation $RT.find(m)$ can be applied iff there exists a sequence $seq_i = \langle x_1, \ldots, x_l \rangle$. In this case this operation returns all the sessions whose keys have as prefix the string $\varphi(x_1)\# \ldots \#\varphi(x_l)\#$.

Using these basic operation we can now define the operations which manage the set of radix trees produced by our algorithm . More precisely, we assume that the set of radix tree schemas produced by the algorithm has been instantiated to a set of (concrete) radix trees. Then this set is managed by the following three operations: $find\_session(m)$ (for finding a session that correlates with a message m); $add\_session(s)$ (for adding the session s); $del\_session(s)$ (for deleting a session s). The definition of the $add\_session(s)$ and $del\_session(s)$ is obvious since the only thing to do is to execute $RT.add(s)$ and $RT.del(s)$ for every radix tree RT. The $find\_session(m)$ instead first have to select a specific RT based on the variables defined by the c-token of m and later return the $RT.find(m)$ result.

5   Correctness and Complexity Analysis

In this section we prove the correctness of Algorithm 1 and we discuss the complexity of correlation mechanism based on it. In particular, we show that it produces the minimal number of radix trees needed to guarantee correctness. In the following, as usual, we assume that V is the set of variables of a c-set and that $n = |V|$.

First of all, we show that Algorithm 1 produces a number of radix trees much smaller than 2^n. With a slight abuse of notation, when no ambiguity arise, we indicate by $radix\_trees(P)$ both the graph produced by the algorithm, with input P, the radix tree schemas obtained from this graph according to Definition 5, and the concrete radix tree obtained from the schemas as described at the end of previous section. All the proofs of the theorems are reported in [7].

Theorem 1. *If $W \subseteq \mathcal{P}(V)$ the result of $radix\_trees(W)$ is a graph containing at most $\binom{n}{\lceil n/2 \rceil}$ maximal paths. Hence the algorithm produces at most $\binom{n}{\lceil n/2 \rceil}$ radix trees schemas.*

Next we show that the algorithm is correct, that is, the number of radix trees produced is sufficient to check correlation.

Theorem 2. *Let m be a message and $V_1, \ldots, V_k$ be all the subsets of c-set variables that are defined by all the possible c-tokens. Then there exists a radix tree schema produced by $radix\_trees(\{V_1, \ldots, V_k\})$ which allows us to check if the message correlates with a session.*

Finally we show that the number of radix trees produced by the algorithm is the minimal one which guarantees correctness.

Theorem 3. *The graph produced by $radix\_trees(P)$ contains the minimal number of maximal paths covering all the nodes in P.*

As an obvious consequence of previous theorem we obtain that if we consider less radix trees than those produced by Algorithm 1 we cannot establish correctly correlation for some kind of messages. Thus our algorithm cannot be improved with respect to the number of radix trees that one can use to solve this problem.

The complexity of Algorithm 1 is polynomial on the size of P. As for the complexity of the operations described in Section 4.1, assuming that l is the maximum length of a c-set value and k is the number of the sessions that correlate with a message m, the (time) complexity of $find\_session(m)$, is $O(n + knl) = O(knl)$. For normal (i.e. non broadcast) messages the complexity of $find\_session(m)$ reduces to $O(nl)$. On the other hand, the (time) complexity of $add\_session(s)$ and $del\_session(s)$ is $O(\binom{n}{\lceil n/2 \rceil}l)$ (for more details see [7]). We would like to underline that, in practice, the number of the c-set variables which are used is very small (less or equal to 5) so, in practice, the complexity of our operations is constant.

6   Conclusions and Future Work

We have proposed a data structure, based on radix trees, for managing a correlation mechanism which supports also a broadcast communication in the context of languages for service oriented computing. We have also described an algorithm that computes the minimal number of radix trees required for handling correctly every normal and broadcast message. The complexity of the correlation operation is constant for normal messages, and linearly dependent with respect to the number of targets for broadcast messages. The operations of session creation and termination have a complexity that depends on the number of different types of broadcast messages. In the worst case (i.e. when an exponential number of broadcast messages is used) it is exponential. The worst case scenario is however impossible in practice, since real scenarios use few types of broadcast messages. For this reason the complexity of session creation and termination have in practice a constant complexity.

The major drawback of our approach is memory consumption: having more than one radix tree means that we require more memory to store the correlation values. For services that use huge data as correlation values memory consumption could be problematic. Nevertheless, we believe that in practice this is not an issue, since correlation values should be small for minimizing the cost of the message exchange over the network. If a service uses huge data as correlation values then we argue that it is worth considering the introduction of a new shorter key that can be used as a new correlation variable.

We are currently implementing the data structure and the algorithm in the JOLIE language interpreter. With this new implementation hopefully we will be able to provide a faster mechanism for the assignment of messages to session.

We are currently extending our work to support a property-based correlation mechanism (see [2]) where also such operators as $>, <, \vee$ can be used for the assignment of messages and therefore the analogous of range queries in databases arise. We think that radix trees could be very useful in this context, since these data structures allow to manage range queries in a very natural way.

References

1. Web Services Business Process Execution Language Version 2.0,
   http://docs.oasis-open.org/wsbpel/2.0/wsbpel-v2.0.html
2. Barros, A.P., Decker, G., Dumas, M., Weber, F.: Correlation patterns in service-oriented architectures. In: Dwyer, M.B., Lopes, A. (eds.) FASE 2007. LNCS, vol. 4422, pp. 245–259. Springer, Heidelberg (2007)
3. Carzaniga, A., Wolf, A.L.: Forwarding in a content-based network. In: SIGCOMM, pp. 163–174 (2003)
4. Fabret, F., Jacobsen, H.-A., Llirbat, F., Pereira, J., Ross, K.A., Shasha, D.: Filtering algorithms and implementation for very fast publish/subscribe. In: SIGMOD Conference, pp. 115–126 (2001)
5. Guidi, C., Lucchi, R., Gorrieri, R., Busi, N., Zavattaro, G.: SOCK: A calculus for service oriented computing. In: Dan, A., Lamersdorf, W. (eds.) ICSOC 2006. LNCS, vol. 4294, pp. 327–338. Springer, Heidelberg (2006)
6. Lapadula, A., Pugliese, R., Tiezzi, F.: A calculus for orchestration of web services. In: De Nicola, R. (ed.) ESOP 2007. LNCS, vol. 4421, pp. 33–47. Springer, Heidelberg (2007)
7. Mauro, J., Gabbrielli, M., Guidi, C., Montesi, F.: An efficient management of correlation sets with broadcast. Technical report (2011),
   www.cs.unibo.it/~jmauro/papers/tech_report_coordination_2011
8. Montesi, F., Guidi, C., Lucchi, R., Zavattaro, G.: JOLIE: a java orchestration language interpreter engine. Electr. Notes Theor. Comput. Sci. 181, 19–33 (2007)
9. Montesi, F., Guidi, C., Zavattaro, G.: Composing services with jolie. In: ECOWS, pp. 13–22 (2007)
10. Morrison, D.R.: PATRICIA - practical algorithm to retrieve information coded in alphanumeric. J. ACM 15(4), 514–534 (1968)
11. Mühl, G.: Generic constraints for content-based publish/Subscribe. In: Batini, C., Giunchiglia, F., Giorgini, P., Mecella, M. (eds.) CoopIS 2001. LNCS, vol. 2172, pp. 211–225. Springer, Heidelberg (2001)

Session Typing for a Featherweight Erlang

Dimitris Mostrous and Vasco T. Vasconcelos

LaSIGE, Faculty of Sciences, University of Lisbon

Abstract. As software tends to be increasingly concurrent, the paradigm of message passing is becoming more prominent in computing. The language Erlang offers an intuitive and industry-tested implementation of process-oriented programming, combining pattern-matching with message mailboxes, resulting in concise, elegant programs. However, it lacks a successful static verification mechanism that ensures safety and determinism of communications with respect to well-defined specifications. We present a session typing system for a featherweight Erlang calculus that encompasses the main communication abilities of the language. In this system, structured types are used to govern the interaction of Erlang processes, ensuring that their behaviour is safe with respect to a defined protocol. The expected properties of subject reduction and type safety are established.

1 Introduction

In the age of web services, distributed systems and multicore processors, the paradigm of message passing is becoming increasingly prominent in computing. The functional-declarative language Erlang is widely used for process-oriented software, utilising pattern-matching to extract messages from mailboxes, and resulting in concise, elegant programs. However, it lacks a static verification mechanism that can ensure safety and determinism of communications with respect to well-defined protocol specifications. Such verification is highly useful but also very challenging, since the language is dynamically typed, and any type system has to work on top of the existing semantics of its communication primitives.

In this work we present the first typing system for the concurrent fragment of Erlang, based on session types, and distilled in a featherweight calculus. To overcome the uncontrolled nature of process identifiers, which address the unique mailbox owned by each process (thread), we make extensive use of the ability of the language to generate unique references (fresh names), created with the built-in function **make_ref**(). By carefully controlling the use of references, and by including them in messages where they play the role of uniquely identifying (correlating) conversations, we can guarantee properties about the fine-grained structure of communications between pairs of processes. For example we ensure that messages are always of the expected type and that sending and receiving follows a prescribed pattern respected by both sides.

The programming style required in our methodology may seem cumbersome for simple programs with protocols consisting of a single message exchange, but

W. De Meuter and G.-C. Roman (Eds.): COORDINATION 2011, LNCS 6721, pp. 95–109, 2011.

without references it is difficult to *ensure* message correlation even for simple request–response: using just process identity (e.g., the unique mailbox of the sender) is not enough, as any process can "impersonate" another just by knowing its identity which it can attach to a message [2]. Thus, **make_ref**() seems to be the only means to "get concurrency right." Yet, an ad-hoc use of **make_ref**() may lead to applications that suffer from interference, race conditions, or even that fail from delivering the expected results. Our system provides for a methodology that governs its use, while statically guaranteeing that programs behave according to the plan. We have only addressed a tiny part of the language, a language that is untyped in nature. Scaling our proposal to a larger subset of Erlang constitutes an interesting challenge. Moreover, our contribution can be viewed also as a type system for an important pattern of concurrent behavior, a pattern that goes well beyond what conventional session types currently allow, while presenting ideas that may be incorporated in future message passing, buffered, concurrent languages where receivers may inspect a mailbox picking appropriate messages.

Core Erlang [4], a canonical format for Erlang programs, is used internally by the Erlang compiler, and also by many verification tools, most notably Dialyzer which is part of the Erlang distribution. Dialyzer detects errors by infering types based on Success Typings [9]. However, until now the type-based methods developed for Erlang focus entirely on the functional part of the language, and are therefore irrelevant in verifying the properties of concurrent message-passing programs.

More recently, in [5], an analysis method was implemented that can statically detect definite communication errors in Erlang programs, based on a topological synthesis of communication primitive usages. Such properties include the case where sent messages cannot be matched by a receive, however, it has a different approach than ours: it does not check programs against types, but rather analyses them against each other, detecting undesirable compositions of sending and receiving. On the other hand, this method is automated and has been implemented on top of the Dialyzer tool.

The rest of the paper is structured as follows. The next section presents our language via an example. Then, Section 3 formally introduces the syntax and reduction semantics of the language. Section 4 presents the type assignment system and its main results. Section 5 concludes the paper.

2   A Motivating Example

Consider the classical readers-writer problem. A given resource can be written by (exactly) one writer when no readers are reading; it can be simultaneously read by a bounded number or readers while no writer is writing. A controller protecting accesses to such a resource provides for two distinct operations (or services): *read* and *write*. Given the constraints enumerated above, each of these *services* is associated with a little *protocol*.

Upon invoking service *write*, writers receive one of two messages: *welcome* meaning that no reader is reading, or *reading* meaning there is at least one reader reading. In the first case, the protocol terminates (the writer may try later, perhaps in a busy waiting manner); in the second case, the writer must *store* its data and the protocol terminates. Readers, on the other hand, invoke service *read*. Three things can happen: the reader is allowed in, there is one writer writing, or the bound on the number of readers was exceeded. In the first case, the reader receives a message *welcome*, after which it must *store* its data and the protocol terminates. In the two other cases, the protocol terminates after the reception of a *writing* or a *full* message.

The services and their associated protocols are captured by simple type abstractions. To a resource we associate a record type describing the two services:

{*write*: Write, *read*: Read}

Each service is described by a *session type*. Session type Write is of the form:

⊕[*welcome*: &[*load*: **end**], *reading*: **end**]

where type operator ⊕ means that the resource sends one of the two messages *welcome* or *reading*, and operator & says that the resource accepts message *load*. Type constructor **end** denotes the conclusion of the session. The session type Read is similar, only that it starts with three options.

⊕[*welcome*: &[*store*: **end**], *writing*: **end**, *full*: **end**]

We write the code for the resource monitor in an Erlang-like language. When idle the monitor accepts any of the service requests, answers *welcome* in both cases and proceeds appropriately. We could try writing our code as follows,

```
idle () = receive {write,Writer} →Writer!{welcome}, ...
               {read,Reader} →Reader!{welcome}, ...
```

Messages are selected from the monitor's mailbox by a pattern matching mechanism. A pattern of the form {*write*,writer} matches an arbitrary message composed of a label (an *atom* in the Erlang jargon) *write* and any value (the process identifier—pid in short—of the writer) that becomes associated to variable Writer. Term Writer!{*welcome*} sends a message {*welcome*} to the Writer's mailbox.

Each interaction with the monitor is composed of a series (of two or three) messages; we call a *session* the sequence of messages that pertain to the same run of some protocol. When a monitor interacts with different clients, the client's pid is enough to distinguish to which session messages belong. For more elaborate scenarios, where the same client constitutes two or more readers or writers, we must resort to more complex protocols. A common method used to distinguish different sessions running simultaneously, is to use *correlation sets* [3,10].

A correlation set is a set of identifiers (*references* in the Erlang jargon) that uniquely identifies a session. Clients create the required references and send them in the service invocation message. For each session we need two correlation references, one for the sending operations, the other for receiving. So here is the revised version of the monitor, noting that ',' denotes sequencing and ';' separates alternative receive clauses, with '.' marking the end:

```
idle () = receive {write,X,Y,Writer} →Writer!{welcome,Y}, write(X);
               {read,X,Y,Reader} →Reader!{welcome,Y}, readOne(X).
```

In the first line the monitor receives a message with two references and uses the second, Y, for letting the writer know to which session does the *welcome* message belong to. The writer, in turn, uses the first reference, X, to 'sign' the subsequent messages in the session. In the write phase, the monitor may accept messages from the just initiated session (we omit the actual data to be stored at the resource).

```
write (X) = receive {store,X} →idle ().
```

During this phase, readers invoking the *read* service would block waiting for the server to go back to the idle state. Our language allows for more than this: the server may as well answer immediately to clients (with a *writing* message), while waiting from the writer's *store* message. That is, our server is able to initiate new services while running other services.

```
write (X) = receive {store,X} →idle ();
              {read,_,Z,Reader} → Reader!{writing,Z}, write(X).
```

The code for the read phase should by now be easy to understand; for simplicity we allow two simultaneous readers, max. And we never leave a client without an answer.

```
readOne(X1) = receive {load,X1} →idle ();
                {write,_,Z,Writer} →Writer!{reading,Z}, readOne(X);
                {read,X2,Y2,Reader2} →Reader2!{welcome,Y2}, readTwo(X1,X2).
readTwo(X1,X2) = receive {load,X1} →readOne(X2);
                {load,X2} →readOne(X1);
                {write,_,Z,Writer} →Writer!{reading,Z}, readTwo(X1,X2);
                {read,_,Z,Reader} →Reader!{full,Z}; readTwo(X1,X2).
```

In the readTwo phase we decided to honor all possible cases: continuing with the two open sessions with both readers, opening new sessions with new readers and writers. But that need not be the case, at any moment programmers may choose which sessions to continue and which new service requests to accept.

To complete our example we write the code for a reader that tries to store at the resource (and gives up if unable).

```
reader () = make_ref X,Y for self, Resource in
              Resource!{read,X,Y,self},
              receive {welcome, Y} →Resource!{load,X};
                {writing, Y} →;
                {full, Y} → .
```

For convenience, we create pairs of fresh references in one step with a **make_ref** operation. The thus created references, X and Y, must be bound to the pid of the processes that will engage in interaction. The monitor, with pid Resource, is going to use X for reading and Y for writing. Symmetrically, the current writer (with pid **self**) will use Y for reading and X for writing.

What guarantees do we obtain from our type system? To discuss this matter we must remember that, in Erlang, message sending is non-blocking and that messages may be retrieved from the mailbox in any order (as opposed to,

Identifiers		Terms	
$u ::= X$	variable	$P ::= V$	value
$\mid\ \alpha$	process id	$\mid\ u!M, P$	send
$\mid\ r$	reference	$\mid$ receive $p_i \to P_i{}^{i \in I}$	receive
Values		$\mid$ spawn P as X in P	spawn
$V ::= u$	identifier	$\mid$ make_ref X, X for u, u in P	refs
$\mid\ a$	atom	**Configurations**	
Messages		$C ::= \alpha : \vec{M}$	mbox
$M ::= \{\vec{V}\}$	tuple	$\mid\ \alpha\,[P]$	process
		$\mid\ (\boldsymbol{\nu}\alpha)C$	new pid
Receive patterns		$\mid\ (\boldsymbol{\nu}r^{\alpha}r^{\alpha})C$	new refs
$p ::= \{\vec{X}\}$ when $\vec{X} = \vec{V}$		$\mid\ C \mid C$	par

Fig. 1. Syntax

say, first-in first-out). The guarantee that Erlang processes engage in protocols as specified by the session types—commonly known as *session fidelity*—is captured in our setting by inspecting mailboxes at termination. In the case of the Reader above, the type system guarantees that the reader did not receive (during its short life) unexpected messages from the server that remain unseen in the mailbox. The same can be said of the monitor: at termination (if this ever happens) no unexpected message remains in the mailbox.

3 Featherweight Erlang

This section presents our language, its syntax and reduction semantics.

For the programmers' language we rely on a (countable) *set of variables*; we use upper-case letters X and Y to range over variables, following the Erlang conventions. A distinguished variable, self, plays a special role in the semantics. We also need a set of non-interpreted *atoms* (or labels), ranged over by lower-case letter a. The syntax of the language is defined in Figure 1. The *identifiers* in the programmer's syntax are variables only (the remaining two alternatives are described below). Values V of the programmers' language are simply variables or atoms. The messages exchanged by processes, M, are tuples of values.

A program is a (closed) *term* that uses for identifiers variables only. The constructors of terms include values as well as primitives to send and to receive messages, to spawn new processes and to create new unique references. A term of the form $u!M, P$ sends message M to the process named u and continues as P. A term of the form receive $p_i \to P_i{}^{i \in I}$ attempts to pattern-match a message from the mailbox against the various patterns p_i and continues with the term P_j for which the matching succeeds (patterns and pattern matching are described below), blocking if no message matches. A term spawn P as X in Q creates a new process with running code P, binds the (newly created) process identifier to variable X and continues with term Q. Finally, a term of the form make_ref X, Y for u, v in P creates two unique references, binds them to variables X and Y, associates them to process identifiers u and v, and continues with term P. A simple form of terms allowing the description of unbounded behaviour, e.g. def $A\vec{X} = P$ in P and $A\vec{V}$, can be easily incorporated in our language, following, e.g., [7,12]. For the sake of simplicity, and in order to concentrate on the novel aspects of our system, we decided not to include them.

For the *runtime language* we need two new classes of identifiers: *process identifiers* (pid's) denoted by α and *unique references* denoted by r. The syntax of terms remains unchanged, except for the extended category of identifiers. Terms do not engage in reduction per se. Instead they must be uploaded into a configuration. *Configurations* are built from five different constructors. A term of the form $\alpha : \vec{M}$ describes a *mailbox* for the process with pid α, containing a list of (unread) messages $\vec{M}$; a process $\alpha [P]$ is a term P located at pid α. Then we have scope restriction operators, $(\boldsymbol{\nu}\alpha)C$ for process identifiers, and $(\boldsymbol{\nu}r_1^{\alpha_1} r_2^{\alpha_2})C$ for pairs of references. Finally, configurations of the form $C_1 \mid C_2$ allow C_1 and C_2 to run in parallel.

We count with three *binders* for terms and two for configurations. They are: the variables $\vec{X}$ in a receive pattern $\{\vec{X}\}$ when $\vec{Y} = \vec{u}$, variable X in a spawn term spawn P as X in Q, variables X_1 and X_2 (but not u_1 and u_2) in a reference creation term make_ref X_1, X_2 for u_1, u_2 in P, process identifier α in configuration $(\boldsymbol{\nu}\alpha)C$, and references r_1 and r_2 (but not α_1 and α_2) in configuration $(\boldsymbol{\nu}r_1^{\alpha_1} r_2^{\alpha_2})C$. In order to simplify the subsequent presentation we use letter n for any of the binders α or $r_1^{\alpha_1} r_2^{\alpha_2}$. The sets of free variables and bound variables are defined accordingly. We follow Barendregt's variable convention, requiring bound identifiers to be distinct from free identifiers in any mathematical context. A *substitution* is a map (finite, partial domain) from variables into values, written $\{\vec{V}/\vec{X}\}$ and ranged over by σ. The (capture free) operation of applying a substitution to term P, denoted $P\sigma$, is standard.

If P is a program (a closed term), we *upload* P at our machine by building a configuration of the form

$$(\boldsymbol{\nu}\alpha)(\alpha [P\{^{\alpha}\!/\mathsf{self}\}] \mid \alpha : \varepsilon)$$

composed of program P located at process identifier α, and empty mailbox for the same pid (ε denotes the empty sequence). The distinguished nature of variable self is apparent in $P\{^{\alpha}\!/\mathsf{self}\}$: process P may refer to its own pid via self, which at runtime is replaced by the actual value α.

Structural congruence is the smallest relation on processes including the rules in Figure 2. The first two rules say that parallel composition is commutative and associative. The rules in the second line deal with scope restriction. The first, scope extrusion, allows the scope of n to encompass C_2; due to the variable convention, n bound in $(\boldsymbol{\nu}n_2)C_1$, cannot be free in C_2. The other two rules allow exchanging the order of restrictions.[1]

---

[1] Notice that $(\boldsymbol{\nu}r_1^{\alpha_1} r_2^{\alpha_2})(\boldsymbol{\nu}\alpha_1)C \not\equiv (\boldsymbol{\nu}\alpha_1)(\boldsymbol{\nu}r_1^{\alpha_1} r_2^{\alpha_2})C$ due to the variable convention (the left-hand side configuration is not well formed).

$$C_1 \mid C_2 \equiv C_2 \mid C_1 \qquad (C_1 \mid C_2) \mid C_3 \equiv C_1 \mid (C_2 \mid C_3)$$
$$(\boldsymbol{\nu}n)C_1 \mid C_2 \equiv (\boldsymbol{\nu}n)(C_1 \mid C_2) \qquad (\boldsymbol{\nu}n_1)(\boldsymbol{\nu}n_2)C_1 \equiv (\boldsymbol{\nu}n_2)(\boldsymbol{\nu}n_1)C_1$$

Fig. 2. Structure Congruence

$$\mathsf{match}(\{\vec{X}\} \text{ when } \vec{Y} = \vec{U}, \{\vec{V}\}) = \mathsf{match}_{\vec{Y}=\vec{U}}(\vec{X}, \vec{V})$$
$$\mathsf{match}_{\vec{Y}=\vec{U}}(X\vec{X}, V\vec{V}) = \{V/X\} \cup \mathsf{match}_{\vec{Y}=\vec{U}}(\vec{X}, \vec{V}) \qquad \text{if } X \notin \vec{Y}$$
$$\mathsf{match}_{\vec{Y}_1 X \vec{Y}_2 = \vec{U}_1 V \vec{U}_2}(X\vec{X}, V\vec{V}) = \{V/X\} \cup \mathsf{match}_{\vec{Y}_1 X \vec{Y}_2 = \vec{U}_1 V \vec{U}_2}(\vec{X}, \vec{V})$$
$$\mathsf{match}_{\_=\_}(\varepsilon, \varepsilon) = \emptyset$$

Fig. 3. Pattern Matching

Messages are read from a mailbox via a *pattern matching* mechanism. In order to simplify the definitions (type system included), patterns $\{\vec{X}\}$ when $\vec{Y} = \vec{V}$ introduce as many variables $\vec{X}$ as the length of the tuple expected. The actual matching is then performed on the $\vec{Y} = \vec{V}$ part. The definition is in Figure 3. If defined, the output of the matching function may then be applied to a term. In examples we often elide the when clause, by using atoms as well as previously introduced variables in patterns. The code for write presented previously

write(X) = **receive** {*store*,X} →idle().

must be understood as

write(X) = **receive** {Y,Z} **when** Y,Z=*store*,X →idle().

Reduction is the smallest relation on processes that includes the rules in Figure 4. Rule send places message M in the mailbox of the target process α_2, while the sender continues as P. Syntactically splitting the process behavior $\alpha[P]$ from its mailbox $\alpha : \vec{M}$ as two separate resources allows a process to send to its own mailbox. That is the case when, in rule send, α_1 is equal to α_2. Rule recv reads from the mailbox the first message M that matches one of the patterns p_i in the receiving term. The matching function, if defined, yields a substitution σ which we apply to term P_j, corresponding to the selected pattern p_j. The message is removed from the mailbox. If no pattern matches M, then the configuration does not reduce. Rule mkref creates two fresh references r_1 and r_2 and replaces them by bound variables X_1 and X_2 in term P. Each reference becomes associated in the ν-binder to the correspondent process identifier, α_1 or α_2. Rule spawn creates a fresh pid α_2 for the spawned term P. Two new resources are created: process $\alpha_2[P\{^{\alpha_2}/\mathsf{self}\}]$ where the self variable is replaced

$$\alpha_1\,[\alpha_2!M,P] \mid \alpha_2:\vec{M} \longrightarrow \alpha_1\,[P] \mid \alpha_2:\vec{M}M \qquad\qquad\text{(send)}$$

$$\frac{j \in I \quad \text{match}(p_j, M) = \sigma \quad \text{match}(p_i, M') \text{ undefined } \forall i \in I, \forall M' \in \vec{M}_1}{\alpha:\vec{M}_1 M\vec{M}_2 \mid \alpha\,[\text{receive } p_i \to P_i{}^{i\in I}] \longrightarrow \alpha:\vec{M}_1\vec{M}_2 \mid \alpha\,[P_j\sigma]} \quad\text{(recv)}$$

$$\alpha\,[\text{make\_ref } X_1, X_2 \text{ for } \alpha_1, \alpha_2 \text{ in } P] \longrightarrow (\nu r_1^{\alpha_1} r_2^{\alpha_2})\alpha\,[P\{^{r_1 r_2}/X_1 X_2\}] \qquad\text{(mkref)}$$

$$\alpha_1\,[\text{spawn } P \text{ as } X \text{ in } Q] \longrightarrow (\nu\alpha_2)(\alpha_1\,[Q\{^{\alpha_2}/X\}] \mid \alpha_2\,[P\{^{\alpha_2}/\text{self}\}] \mid \alpha_2:\epsilon) \quad\text{(spawn)}$$

$$\frac{C_1 \longrightarrow C_2}{C_1 \mid C_3 \longrightarrow C_2 \mid C_3} \qquad \frac{C_1 \longrightarrow C_2}{(\nu n)C_1 \longrightarrow (\nu n)C_2} \qquad \frac{C_1 \equiv C_2 \longrightarrow C_3 \equiv C_4}{C_1 \longrightarrow C_4}$$

$$\text{(par, res, str)}$$

Fig. 4. Reduction

by α_2, and the (empty) queue $\alpha_2 : \epsilon$. The newly created pid is replaced in the continuation process Q, so that Q may then communicate with the new process.

What can go wrong with our machine? Looking at the operational semantics (Figure 4) nothing, really. Send always succeeds (for we admit mailbox buffers to be unbounded); receive may not succeed (for two reasons: no message in mailbox, no message in the mailbox matches the patterns) but that does not constitute an abnormal behaviour; finally, there is no reason why make_ref and spawn should not succeed.

The possible abnormal conditions have to do with our understanding of how sessions must happen. We identify two cases: a process terminates (reduces to a value) but leaves session messages in the mailbox; a process tries to receive a message with a given label within a given session but finds no such message in the mailbox. For the former case and given the asynchronous nature of our operational semantics, one may still find, at termination and in the mailbox, a session initiation message followed by session messages. This does constitute a malfunctioning since the session was never started on the server side. In the latter case, processes need not receive messages for all open sessions at all times, but if they decide to receive a message on a given session, then they must contain patterns for all possible messages in that session (otherwise one or both of the participants can get stuck by being unable to receive the next message).

We then say that a *configuration C constitutes an error* when C is structural congruent to $(\nu\vec{n})(\alpha\,[P] \mid \alpha:\vec{M} \mid C')$ and

Incomplete session: term P is a value, buffer $\vec{M}$ is of the form $\vec{M}_1\{_-, X, _-\}\vec{M}_2$, and no message in $\vec{M}_1$ is of the form $\{_-, _-, X, _-\}$, or

Unmatched session message: term P is receive $(\{X, Y, _-\}\text{ when } X, Y = a, r \to Q, \dots)$, there is one message in $\vec{M}$ of the form $\{_-, r, _-\}$ but no message of the form $\{a, r, _-\}$.

The type system in the next section filters out such abnormal cases.

$$
\begin{array}{llll}
T ::= & \{a_i : S_i\}_{i \in I} & \text{process id} & S ::= \&[a_i : T_i \to S_i]^{i \in I} & \text{receive} \\
& | \quad \text{atom} & \text{atom} & | \quad \oplus[a_i : T_i \to S_i]^{i \in I} & \text{send} \\
& & & | \quad \text{end} & \text{close}
\end{array}
$$

Fig. 5. Types

4   Typing

This section introduces our type system and presents its main result.

The syntax of *types* is in Figure 5. We distinguish types T for shared data and session types S. In the former category we have types for pids, $\{a_i : S_i\}_{i \in I}$, describing the set of sessions a process may engage in, and the type of atoms. For session types we distinguish a type $\&[a_i : T_i \to S_i]^{i \in I}$ describing patterns in a receive term labelled with a_i, receiving values of type T_i, and proceeding as prescribed by S_i; a type $\oplus[a_i : T_i \to S_i]^{i \in I}$ describing the various messages a client may send; and end, a type describing the completed session. A process may engage in different new sessions S_i, each labelled with a different label a_i. Receiving on a given session yields a type $\&[a_i : T_i \to S_i]^{i \in I}$; a client that sends on the same session has the *dual* type $\oplus[a_i : T_i \to \overline{S}_i]^{i \in I}$, where $\overline{S}$ denotes the type dual of S. Type end is dual of itself.

We use two sorts of typing environments: *shared environments*, Γ, containing entries of the form $p \colon T$, and *linear environments*, Δ, containing entries $(u_1, u_2 \mid p) \colon S$ and $(u_1^{p_1}, u_2^{p_2}) \colon \mathsf{ref}$ (with p, p_1, p_2 variables or process identifiers, and u_1, u_2 variables or references). An entry of the form $(u_1, u_2 \mid p) \colon S$ describes a session running between the current process and p, using references u_1 and u_2, and at state S; an entry $(u_1^{p_1}, u_2^{p_2}) \colon \mathsf{ref}$ describe a pair of references u_1, u_2 destined to be used in a session between processes with pids p_1 and p_2.

In typing rules we will freely compose Δ environments assuming that the result is defined (or the respective rule cannot be applied). The principle of composition is that when a pair of new references is added, the references do not already occur in the environment; also, when a session usage is added, the only allowed occurrence of the mentioned references is in a dual usage where they appear in reverse order. Formally, we have that $\Delta, (u_1^{p_1}, u_2^{p_2}) \colon \mathsf{ref}$ is defined when $u_1 \neq u_2$ and, if $(u_3^{p_3}, u_4^{p_4}) \colon \mathsf{ref} \in \Delta$ or $(u_3, u_4 \mid p_4) \colon S_2 \in \Delta$, then $u_{1,2} \notin \{u_3, u_4\}$. Similarly, $\Delta, (u_1, u_2 \mid p_1) \colon S_1$ is defined when $u_1 \neq u_2$ and, if $(u_3^{p_3}, u_4^{p_4}) \colon \mathsf{ref} \in \Delta$ then $u_{1,2} \notin \{u_3, u_4\}$, and if $(u_3, u_4 \mid p_4) \colon S_2 \in \Delta$, then $u_{1,2} \neq u_{3,4}$ and $u_1 = u_4$ iff $u_2 = u_3$.

The type system for terms is in Figure 6. Sequents are of the form $\Gamma; \Delta \vdash_u P \colon T$, meaning that, under contexts Γ and Δ, term P with pid u has type T.

The rules for identifiers and atoms should be evident; we require 'completed' linear contexts at the leaves of typing derivations, as usual in session type systems. We then have two rules for message send, one to initiate a new session, the other to output on a running session. In the former case, we make sure that the process on p knows how to start an a_j session, read (and remove) the pair

$$\Gamma, u: T; \{(u_i, w_i \mid p_i): \mathsf{end}\}_{i \in I} \vdash_- u: T \qquad \Gamma; \{(u_i, w_i \mid p_i): \mathsf{end}\}_{i \in I} \vdash_- a: \mathsf{atom}$$
$$\text{(identifier,atom)}$$

$$\frac{\Gamma; _- \vdash_- p: \{a_i: S_i\}_{i \in I} \quad \Gamma; \Delta, (u_2, u_1 \mid p): \overline{S_j} \vdash_u P: T \quad j \in I}{\Gamma; \Delta, (u_1^p, u_2^u): \mathsf{ref} \vdash_u p!\{a_j, u_1, u_2, u\}, P: T} \quad \text{(request)}$$

$$\frac{\Gamma; _- \vdash_- V: T_j \quad \Gamma; \Delta, (u_1, u_2 \mid p): S_j \vdash_u P: T \quad j \in I}{\Gamma; \Delta, (u_1, u_2 \mid p): \oplus [a_i: T_i \to S_i]^{i \in I} \vdash_u p!\{a_j, u_2, V\}, P: T} \quad \text{(out)}$$

$$\frac{\Gamma; \Delta \vdash_u^{\mathsf{acc}} p_i \to P_i: T \quad \Gamma; \Delta \vdash_u^{\mathsf{in}} q_j \to Q_j: T \quad \forall i \in I, j \in J \quad \mathsf{consistent}(\Delta, (q_j)^{j \in J})}{\Gamma; \Delta \vdash_u \mathsf{receive}\ (p_i \to P_i)^{i \in I}, (q_j \to Q_j)^{j \in J}: T}$$
$$\text{(receive)}$$

$$\frac{\Gamma; _- \vdash_- u: \{a_i: S_i\}_{i \in I} \quad \Gamma; \Delta, (X_1, X_2 \mid p): S_j \vdash_u P\{a_j/X_a\}: T \quad j \in I}{\Gamma; \Delta \vdash_u^{\mathsf{acc}} \{X_a, X_1, X_2, p\}\ \mathsf{when}\ X_a = a_j \to P: T} \quad \text{(accept)}$$

$$\frac{\Gamma, Y: T_j; \Delta, (u_1, u_2 \mid p): S_j \vdash_u P\{a_j u_1 / X_a X\}: T \quad j \in I}{\Gamma; \Delta, (u_1, u_2 \mid p): \&[a_i: T_i \to S_i]^{i \in I} \vdash_u^{\mathsf{in}} \{X_a, X, Y\}\ \mathsf{when}\ X_a X = a_j u_1 \to P: T}$$
$$\text{(in)}$$

$$\frac{\Gamma, X: T; \Delta_1 \vdash_X P\{X/\mathsf{self}\}: _- \quad \Gamma, X: T; \Delta_2 \vdash_u Q: T}{\Gamma; \Delta_1, \Delta_2 \vdash_u \mathsf{spawn}\ P\ \mathsf{as}\ X\ \mathsf{in}\ Q: T} \quad \text{(spawn)}$$

$$\frac{\Gamma; \Delta, (X^u, Y^v): \mathsf{ref} \vdash_u P: T}{\Gamma; \Delta \vdash_u \mathsf{make\_ref}\ X, Y\ \mathsf{for}\ u, v\ \mathsf{in}\ P: T} \quad \text{(mkref)}$$

Fig. 6. Typing rules for terms

of references u_1, u_2 from Δ and add a new session-entry to Δ. The new entry records the two references, the pid of the target process and the dual (since we are on the client side) of the session type for session a_j. In the latter case we are within a session: we type check the continuation term P to obtain a type S_j for the session pertaining to u_2 (the write reference) and build a $\oplus$ type accordingly.

The rule for receive is the most complex one for there may be multiple branches, some trying to open new sessions, others trying to progress on already open sessions. We assume the branches partitioned in two sets: those opening new sessions and those engaged in open sessions. For the former we use rule accept which should be confronted with rule request. This time we use S_j because we are on the server side; we also propagate the effect of pattern matching on the continuation process P, via an appropriate substitution. For the latter we use rule in which should be confronted with rule out: we place an entry for message payload Y in the shared environment and propagate the substitution as in accept; for the type of the session, we use a $\&$ type, rather than a $\oplus$ type.

In the rule for receive all branches must have the same linear context Δ. But this is not enough, for in rule in we 'guess' from one label a_j the whole set of labels in a *receive* session type. We must then make sure that we do not declare in the type labels that are not in the receive pattern. Predicate consistent is used for the effect. We say that context Δ *is consistent with a set of patterns* $(\{X_i, Y_i, _-\}\ \mathsf{when}\ X_i, Y_i = a_i, u_i)^{i \in I})$ when $\forall i \in I.(u_i, _- \mid _-): \&[a: _- \to _-, \ldots] \in \Delta$ implies $\exists j \in I$ s.t. $a = a_j$ and $u_i = u_j$.

For spawn, we place an entry $X : T$ for the spawned process P in the typing environment and type check P by replacing self by X. The continuation term Q also knows X at type T. The shared environment is passed to both terms, whereas the linear one is split in two, one for each term. The rule for make_ref places a new ref-entry for the newly created pair of references in the linear context, and type checks the continuation process P.

At this point we can explain the reasons behind using two references per session instead of just one. Consider the following example:

```
clientAndServer () = make_ref X,Y for self, self in  self !{connect,X,Y,self},
                     receive {connect,X,Y,Client} →
                       self !{hello,Y,_}, receive {hello,Y,_} →...
```

The above code, in which the request is made to self, is typable in our system, but if we had been using only one reference X, the presence of both ends of a session in a single term would (eventually, after some steps) produce a single typing for $(X \mid$ self$)$ which would include the actions of both participants (sending of {$hello$...} followed by receive of the same message) on one session type, due to the *aliasing* of the two intended uses of X in one place. This soundness problem with aliased endpoints is well-understood in the session types literature; see [12].

The type system in Figure 6 does not yield an obvious algorithm: it requires splitting linear context in rule spawn, as well guessing types in different rules. For the former problem there are well-known techniques associated with linear type systems that pass the whole context to one of the subterms, get back the unused part of the context and pass it to the second subterm; see e.g., [11]. The second problem occurs in rules spawn, out and in. In the first case, the common solution is to seek the help of programmers by requiring a type annotation for the pid of the spawned process P, providing the session types for its various services. This would avoid tedious annotation of every receive, in which new sessions are intermixed with existing ones that, moreover, can be partially satisfied. In rule in we need to guess the right &-type based on one of its branches. All these branches are then gathered together in rule receive where all types are checked for consistency via predicate consistent. The strategy here goes along the lines of preparing, in rule in, singleton branch types, and then merging them all together in rule receive. Finally, for rule out we record one only ⊕-branch in the type and add the remaining types to match the requirements in the remaining rules.

In order to prove subject-reduction we also have to type configurations. To facilitate typing in the presence of mailboxes, we introduce *types τ for messages in mailboxes*. A type $a(T)@r$ represents a session message with reference r carrying an atom a and a value of type T; type req is for new session requests.

The typing rules for configurations are in Figure 7. When typing with process, the actual process id α is propagated in the typing of the enclosed term, ensuring that it is understood as self. Rule par splits the linear context, and passes each part to a different sub-configuration (cf. rule spawn for terms in Figure 6). In rule newpid we introduce two usages for the subject pid: we add $\alpha : T$ in the shared environment, exposing a type for incoming requests, and we also expect in the linear environment some entry $\alpha : \vec{\tau}$ for the corresponding mailbox.

$$\frac{\Gamma;\Delta \vdash_\alpha P:\_}{\Gamma;\Delta \vdash \alpha\,[P]} \qquad \frac{\Gamma;\Delta_1 \vdash C_1 \qquad \Gamma;\Delta_2 \vdash C_2}{\Gamma;\Delta_1,\Delta_2 \vdash C_1 \mid C_2} \qquad \text{(process, par)}$$

$$\frac{\Gamma,\alpha:T;\Delta,\alpha:\vec{\tau} \vdash C}{\Gamma;\Delta \vdash (\nu\alpha)C} \qquad \frac{\Gamma;\Delta_i \vdash_\alpha M_i:\tau_i \qquad \forall i \in 1\ldots n}{\Gamma;\Delta_1,\ldots,\Delta_n,\alpha:\tau_1\ldots\tau_n \vdash \alpha:M_1\ldots M_n}$$
$$\text{(newpid, mbox)}$$

$$\frac{\Gamma;\emptyset \vdash_\_ \alpha:\{a_i:S_i\}_{i\in I} \qquad j \in I}{\Gamma;\{(r_1,r_2 \mid \alpha'):S_j\} \vdash_\alpha \{a_j,r_1,r_2,\alpha'\}:\text{req}} \qquad \frac{\Gamma;\emptyset \vdash_\_ V:T}{\Gamma;\emptyset \vdash_\_ \{a,r,V\}:a(T)\text{@}r}$$
$$\text{(reqmsg, sesmsg)}$$

$$\frac{\Gamma;\Delta,(r_1^{\alpha_1},r_2^{\alpha_2}):\text{ref} \vdash C}{\Gamma;\Delta \vdash (\nu r_1^{\alpha_1} r_2^{\alpha_2})C} \qquad \frac{\alpha_1:\vec{\tau}_1,\alpha_2:\vec{\tau}_2 \in \Delta \quad S_1-(\vec{\tau}_1 \upharpoonright r_1) = \overline{S_2-(\vec{\tau}_2 \upharpoonright r_2)}}{\Gamma;\Delta,(r_1,r_2 \mid \alpha_2):S_1,(r_2,r_1 \mid \alpha_1):S_2 \vdash C}{\Gamma;\Delta \vdash (\nu r_1^{\alpha_1} r_2^{\alpha_2})C}$$
$$\text{(sesrefs, newrefs)}$$

Fig. 7. Typing rules for configurations

Rule mbox which types each message in the mailbox of α and composes the linear environments together with a sequence of message types for α. In turn, we can examine the message typing rules reqmsg and sesmsg. In reqmsg the request message introduces, in the linear environment, the usage that the process receiving the message would perform, which is needed to match the symmetric (dual) usage obtained with rule request of Figure 6. Observe that the given type req does not need to carry additional information. Then in sesmsg a session message is given a type $a(T)\text{@}r$; a sequence of such message types can inform about the messages of a session that are already in the mailbox, and is used to obtain the correct *remaining* usage (modulo these messages) per session.

Rule newrefs is for when a pair of references has been created, but a session request message has not been sent yet. It facilitates a subsequent use of rule request. Rule sesrefs ensures that sessions are *dual*. To obtain the actual session type that remains to be performed on each side of a session, we carefully advance the session types S_i of each session partner according to the types of messages already received. To achieve this, we utilise two auxiliary definitions. First, we want to extract from a mailbox the message type information that pertains to the specific reference r_i used for input; for this we use $(\tau_i \upharpoonright r_i)$ defined as:

$$\text{req}\vec{\tau} \upharpoonright r = \vec{\tau} \upharpoonright r \qquad a(T)\text{@}r\vec{\tau} \upharpoonright r = a(T)(\vec{\tau} \upharpoonright r) \qquad a(T)\text{@}r'\vec{\tau} \upharpoonright r = \vec{\tau} \upharpoonright r \text{ if } r \neq r'$$

which generates a sequence (written $\vec{\rho}$) of message pre-types $a(T)$ stripped of reference information. Then, we advance each session type S_i by calculating the *session remainder* S_i' given from $S_i - \rho_i = S_i'$. The remainder is defined as:

$$S - \epsilon = S \qquad \&[a_i:T_i \to S_i]^{i\in I} - a_j(T_j)\vec{\rho} = S_j - \vec{\rho} \text{ if } j \in I$$
$$\oplus[a_i:T_i \to S_i]^{i\in I} - \vec{\rho} = \oplus[a_i:T_i \to S_i]^{i\in I}$$

In the above definition, branch types advance according to received messages, but selections remain unchanged since they correspond to the messages that will be sent, and not to those that are received.

The basic tenet of sessions is that remaining communications always "match," captured by the notion of type duality. To this end, following the conditions of type rule sesrefs, we define *balanced* environments below.

Definition 1 (Balanced Δ). *Predicate* balanced(Δ) *holds if* $(r_1, r_2 \mid \alpha_2): S_1$ *and* $(r_2, r_1 \mid \alpha_1): S_2, \alpha_1: \vec{\tau}_1, \alpha_2: \vec{\tau}_2$ *in* Δ *implies* $S_1 - (\tau_1 \upharpoonright r_1) = \overline{S_2 - (\tau_2 \upharpoonright r_2)}$.

Next, we define an ordering on linear environments that specifies the ways in which typings evolve with reduction.

Definition 2 (Δ Reduction). *We define* $\Delta \Rightarrow \Delta'$ *as follows:*

$$(r_2, r_1 \mid \alpha_1): S, (r_1, r_2 \mid \alpha_2): \&[a_i: T_i \rightarrow S_i]^{i \in I}, \alpha_1: \vec{\tau}_1 a_j(T_j) @ r_1 \vec{\tau}_2 \Rightarrow$$
$$(r_2, r_1 \mid \alpha_1): S, (r_1, r_2 \mid \alpha_2): S_j, \alpha_1: \vec{\tau}_1 \vec{\tau}_2 \quad if \quad j \in I$$

$$(r_1, r_2 \mid \alpha_2): \oplus [a_i: T_i \rightarrow S_i]^{i \in I}, \alpha_2: \vec{\tau}_2 \Rightarrow (r_1, r_2 \mid \alpha_2): S_j, \alpha_2: \vec{\tau}_2 a_j(T_j) @ r_2 \; if \, j \in I$$
$$(r_1^{\alpha_1}, r_2^{\alpha_2}): \mathsf{ref} \Rightarrow (r_2, r_1 \mid \alpha_1): S, (r_1, r_2 \mid \alpha_2): \overline{S}$$
$$\Delta \Rightarrow \Delta \qquad\qquad \Delta_1, \Delta_2 \Rightarrow \Delta'_1, \Delta_2 \quad if \quad \Delta_1 \Rightarrow \Delta'_1$$

A property of the evolution of linear environments with $\Rightarrow$ is that it preserves balance, which in turn constitutes a measure of type soundness.

Lemma 1 (Balance Preservation). *If* balanced(Δ) *and* $\Delta \Rightarrow \Delta'$ *then* balanced(Δ').

Subject Reduction (type soundness) ensures that after reduction processes can be typed and that the resulting linear environment follows the above ordering. By Balance Preservation, this implies that the resulting environment is also balanced. The same can be easily shown for structural transformation.

Theorem 1 (Subject Reduction). *If* $\Gamma; \Delta \vdash C$ *with* balanced(Δ) *and* $C \longrightarrow C'$, *then* $\Gamma; \Delta' \vdash C'$ *with* $\Delta \Rightarrow \Delta'$.

We can now state Type Safety which guarantees that configurations that are typed with balanced environments never reduce to an error configuration. Note also that environments are always balanced for user-level code in which no free references occur.

Theorem 2 (Type Safety). *If* $\Gamma; \Delta \vdash C$ *with* balanced(Δ), *then* C *does not reduce to an error.*

Proof (Outline). Type Safety can be proved easily by contradiction: since we have Subject Reduction it is enough to show that error processes are not typable. In the case of an incomplete session with input reference r (where the corresponding request message has been consumed), the only possible typing mentioning r in a terminated process $\alpha[V]$ will be end, and the mailbox will have a non-empty set of session messages on r not preceded by a corresponding request message (with input reference r); therefore the session remainder will be undefined. In the case of unmatched messages, we can show that a configuration in which a mailbox contains a message carrying r together with an atom that is not supported in the receiving process is untypable, since again the message remainder will be undefined. In both cases an application of sesrefs will fail.

There are other undesirable configurations, namely when the same reference appears in messages occurring in parallel threads (causing non-determinism in the receiving order), or when subsequent (or parallel) requests share some reference. However, such configurations are trivially untypable, since the linear environments composed in these cases are undefined.

5   Further Work

Some Erlang programs consist of simple message exchanges and do not require provisions for sessions, in particular the use of references. We can easily adapt our system to handle these cases by extending pid types to $\{a_i\colon S_i, b_j\colon T_j\}_{i\in I, j\in J}$ allowing a process to receive simple messages such as $\{b, V\}$. Then, receive patterns of the shape $\{X, Y\}$ when $X = b$ can be typed using an extra rule in the style of accept, to be invoked from the receive rule in Figure 6.

Our type system guarantees that all within-session messages have a chance of being received. It would be desirable to also guarantee this property for session initiation messages, thus offering stronger behaviour guarantees. Intuitively, we need to ensure that at any state, terms can receive all possible session-initiation messages, either immediately or by reducing to a state that does so. A technique along the lines of non-uniform receptivity may prove helpful [1]. Moreover, since Erlang has general pattern matching, it would be useful to allow guards to impose constraints on the *values* received (e.g., receive only integer 5), and this can be achieved by using dependent types.

Delegation is the term used to describe the ability to pass a session identifier on a message. It allows, e.g., for a server to balance its load by sending some (open) sessions to other servers. The very nature of Erlang makes delegation a delicate matter, as opposed to the pi calculus where it is built in the language. Due to the nature of Erlang semantics, where communication is buffered, each process is co-located with its mailbox, and messages are addressed to pids, delegation requires a fairly complex protocol, and remains outside the scope of this work (if interesting at all in Erlang). A possible source of inspiration may come from the work on Session Java where a runtime API implements a delegation protocol for socket based session communication [8].

In order to concentrate on the novelty of our proposal, we deliberately excluded unbound behaviour. Such an extension should be easy to include via, e.g., recursive term definitions, as explained in Section 3. Realistic examples may require recursive types. This is, e.g., the case of our example in Section 2 if we allow an unbounded number of store or load operations in a sequence. Fortunately, recursion in session types is well studied (see, e.g., [6,12]) and its incorporation in the present setting should not present difficulties. In order to better convey our typing proposal, the typing system in this paper is not algorithmic. We are nevertheless confident that there is an equivalent algorithmic type system (see discussion in Section 4).

Acknowledgements. We are indebted to the anonymous reviewers and to Kostis Sagonas for their comments. This work was supported by FCT/MCTES via projects PTDC/EIA–CCO/105359/2008 and CMU–PT/NGN44-2009-12.

References

1. Amadio, R.M., Boudol, G., Lhoussaine, C.: On message deliverability and non-uniform receptivity. Fundam. Inf. 53, 105–129 (2002)
2. Armstrong, J., Virding, R., Wikström, C., Williams, M.: Concurrent Programming in Erlang, 2nd edn. Prentice-Hall, Englewood Cliffs (1996)
3. Business process execution language for web services, http://public.dhe.ibm.com/software/dw/specs/ws-bpel/ws-bpel.pdf
4. Carlsson, R.: An introduction to Core Erlang. In: PLI 2001 Erlang Workshop (2001)
5. Christakis, M., Sagonas, K.: Detection of asynchronous message passing errors using static analysis. In: Rocha, R., Launchbury, J. (eds.) PADL 2011. LNCS, vol. 6539, pp. 5–18. Springer, Heidelberg (2011)
6. Gay, S.J., Hole, M.J.: Subtyping for session types in the pi calculus. Acta Informatica 42(2/3), 191–225 (2005)
7. Honda, K., Vasconcelos, V.T., Kubo, M.: Language primitives and type discipline for structured communication-based programming. In: Hankin, C. (ed.) ESOP 1998. LNCS, vol. 1381, pp. 122–138. Springer, Heidelberg (1998), http://www.di.fc.ul.pt/ vv/papers/honda.vasconcelos.kubo_language-primitives.pdf
8. Hu, R., Yoshida, N., Honda, K.: Session-based distributed programming in java. In: Ryan, M. (ed.) ECOOP 2008. LNCS, vol. 5142, pp. 516–541. Springer, Heidelberg (2008)
9. Lindahl, T., Sagonas, K.: Practical type inference based on success typings. In: 8th ACM SIGPLAN International Conference on Principles and Practice of Declarative Programming, PPDP 2006, pp. 167–178. ACM, New York (2006)
10. Viroli, M.: Towards a formal foundation to orchestration languages. Electronic Notes in Theoretical Computer Science 105, 51–71 (2004); Proceedings of the First International Workshop on Web Services and Formal Methods (WSFM 2004)
11. Walker, D.: Substructural Type Systems. In: Advanced Topics in Types and Programming Languages. MIT Press, Cambridge (2005)
12. Yoshida, N., Vasconcelos, V.T.: Language primitives and type discipline for structured communication-based programming revisited: Two systems for higher-order session communication. In: 1st International Workshop on Security and Rewriting Techniques. ENTCS, vol. 171(4), pp. 73–93. Elsevier, Amsterdam (2007)

Safe Parallel Programming with Session Java

Nicholas Ng[1], Nobuko Yoshida[1], Olivier Pernet[1],
Raymond Hu[1], and Yiannos Kryftis[2]

[1] Imperial College London
[2] National Technical University of Athens

Abstract. The session-typed programming language Session Java (SJ) has proved to be an effective tool for distributed programming, promoting structured programming for communications and compile-time safety. This paper investigates the use of SJ for session-typed parallel programming, and introduces new language primitives for *chained iteration* and *multi-channel communication*. These primitives allow the efficient coordination of parallel computation across multiple processes, thus enabling SJ to express the complex communication topologies often used by parallel algorithms. We demonstrate that the new primitives yield clearer and safer code for pipeline, ring and mesh topologies through implementations of representative parallel algorithms. We then present a semantics and session typing system including the new primitives, and prove type soundness and deadlock-freedom for our implementations. The benchmark results show that the new SJ is substantially faster than the original SJ and performs competitively against MPJ Express[1] used as reference.

1 Introduction

The current practice of parallel and distributed programming is fraught with errors that go undetected until runtime, manifest themselves as deadlocks or communication errors, and often find their root in mismatched communication protocols. The Session Java programming language (SJ) [12] improves this status quo. SJ is an extension of Java with *session types*, supporting statically safe distributed programming by message-passing. Session types were introduced as a type system for the π-calculus [8, 21], and have been shown to integrate cleanly with formal models of object-oriented programming. The SJ compiler offers two strong static guarantees for session execution: (1) *communication safety*, meaning a session-typed process can never cause or encounter a communication error by sending or receiving unexpected messages; and (2) *deadlock-freedom* — a session-typed process will never block indefinitely on a message receive.

Parallel programs often make use of complex, high-level communication patterns such as globally synchronised iteration over chained topologies like rings and meshes. Yet modern implementations are still written using low-level languages and libraries, commonly C and MPI [13]: implementations make the best use of hardware, but at the

---

[1] MPJ Express [16] is a Java implementation of the MPI standard. Extensive benchmarks comparing MPJ Express to other MPI implementations are presented in [16]. The benchmarks show performance competitive with C-based MPICH2.

W. De Meuter and G.-C. Roman (Eds.): COORDINATION 2011, LNCS 6721, pp. 110–126, 2011.

cost of complicated programming where communication is entangled with computation. There is no global view of inter-process communication, and no formal guarantees are given about communication correctness, which often leads to hard-to-find errors.

We investigate parallel programming in SJ as a solution to these issues. However, SJ as presented in [12] only guarantees progress for each session in isolation: deadlocks can still arise from the interleaving of multiple sessions in a process. Moreover, implementing chained communication topologies without additional language support requires temporary sessions, opened and closed on every iteration — a source of non-trivial inefficiencies (see § 3 for an example). We need new constructs, well-integrated with existing binary sessions, to enable lightweight *global* communication safety and deadlock-freedom, increase expressiveness to support *structured programming for communication topologies* and improve *performance*.

Our new *multi-channel* session primitives fit these requirements, and make it possible to safely and efficiently express parallel algorithms in SJ. The combination of new primitives and a well-formed topology check extension to SJ compilation [12] bring the benefits of type-safe, structured communications programming to HPC. The primitives can be chained, yielding a simple mechanism for structuring global control flow. We formalise these primitives as novel extensions of the *session calculus*, and the correctness condition on the shape of programs enforced by a simple extension of SJ compilation. This allows us to prove *communication safety* and *deadlock-freedom*, and offers a new, lightweight alternative to multiparty session types for global type-safety.

Contributions. This paper constitutes the first introduction to parallel programming in SJ, in addition to presenting the following technical contributions:

(§ 2) We introduce SJ as a programming language for type-safe, efficient parallel programming, including our implementation of *multi-channel* session primitives, and the extended SJ tool chain for parallel programming. We show that the new primitives enable clearer, more readable code.

(§ 3) We discuss SJ implementations of parallel algorithms using the Jacobi solution to the discrete Poisson equation (§ 3) as an example. The algorithm uses communication topology representative of a large class of parallel algorithms, and demonstrates the practical use of our multi-channel primitives.

(§ 4) We define the *multi-channel session calculus*, its operational semantics, and typing system. We prove that processes conforming to a *well-formed communication topology* (Definition 4.1) satisfy the subject reduction theorem (Theorem 4.1), which implies *type and communication-safety* (Theorem 4.2) and *deadlock-freedom* across multiple, interleaved sessions (Theorem 4.3).

(§ 5) Performance evaluation of n-Body simulation and Jacobi solution algorithms, demonstrating the benefits of the new primitives. The SJ implementations using the new primitives show competitive performance against an MPJ Express [14].

Related and future work are discussed in § 6. Detailed definitions, proofs, benchmark results and source code can be found at the on-line Appendix [5].

2   Session-Typed Programming in SJ

This section firstly reviews the key concepts of session-typed programming using Session Java (SJ) [11, 12]. In (1), we outline the basic methodology; in (2), the protocol structures supported by SJ. We then introduce the new session programming features developed in this paper to provide greater expressiveness and performance gains for *session-typed parallel programming*. In (3), we explain session *iteration chaining*; and in (4), the generalisation of this concept to the *multi-channel* primitives. Finally, (5) describes the *topology verification* for parallel programs.

(1) Basic SJ programming. SJ is an extension of Java for type-safe concurrent and distributed session programming. Session programming in SJ, as detailed in [12], starts with the declaration of the intended communication protocols as session types; we shall often use the terms *session type* and *protocol* interchangeably. A session is the interaction between two communicating parties, and its session type is written from the viewpoint of one side of the session. The following declares a protocol named P:

```
protocol P !<int>.?(Data)
```

Protocol P specifies that, at this side of the session, we first send (!) a message of Java type int, then receive (?) another message, an instance of the Java class Data, which finishes the session. After defining the protocol, the programmer implements the processes that will perform the specified communication actions using the SJ *session primitives*. The first line in the following code implements an Alice process conforming to the P protocol:

```
A: alice.send(42); Data d = (Data) alice.receive();//!<int>.?(Data)
B: int i = bob.receiveInt(); bob.send(new Data()); //?(int).!<Data>
```

The `alice` variable refers to an object of class SJSocket, called a *session socket*, which represents one endpoint of an active session. The session-typed primitives for session-typed communication behaviour, such as send and receive, are performed on the session socket like method invocations. SJSocket declarations associate a protocol to the socket variable, and the SJ compiler statically checks that the socket is indeed used according to the protocol, ensuring the *correct communication behaviour* of the process.

This simple session application also requires a counterpart Bob process to interact with Alice. For safe session execution, the Alice and Bob processes need to perform matching communication operations: when Alice sends an int, Bob receives an int, and so on. Two processes performing matching operations have session types that are *dual* to each other. The dual protocol to P is protocol PDual ?(int).!<Data>, and a dual Bob process can be implemented as in the second line of the above listing.

(2) More complex protocol structures. Session types are not limited to sequences of basic message passing. Programmers can specify more complex protocols featuring *branching*, *iteration* and *recursion*.

The protocols and processes in Fig.1 demonstrate session iteration and branching. Process *P1* communicates with *P2* according to protocol IntAndBoolStream; *P2* and *P3* communicate following protocol IntStream. Like basic message passing, iteration and branching are coordinated by *active* and *passive* actions at each side of the session. Process *P1* actively decides whether to continue the session iteration using outwhile (*condition*), and if so, selects a branch using outbranch(*label*). The former action implements the $![\tau]*$ type given by IntAndBoolStream, where τ is the !{Label1: τ_1, Label2: τ_2, ...} type implemented by the latter. Processes *P2* and *P3* passively follow

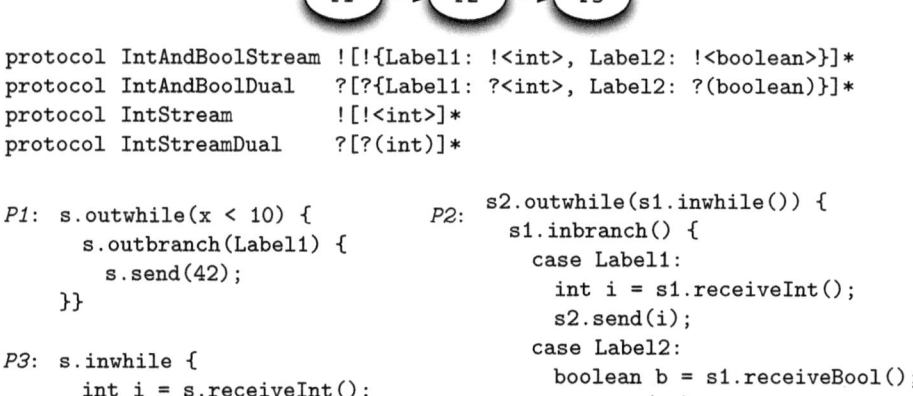

```
protocol IntAndBoolStream  ![!{Label1:  !<int>, Label2:  !<boolean>}]*
protocol IntAndBoolDual    ?[?{Label1:  ?<int>, Label2:  ?(boolean)}]*
protocol IntStream         ![!<int>]*
protocol IntStreamDual     ?[?(int)]*
```

```
P1:  s.outwhile(x < 10) {                      P2:  s2.outwhile(s1.inwhile()) {
         s.outbranch(Label1) {                          s1.inbranch() {
             s.send(42);                                    case Label1:
         }}                                                     int i = s1.receiveInt();
                                                                s2.send(i);
P3:  s.inwhile {                                            case Label2:
         int i = s.receiveInt();                                boolean b = s1.receiveBool();
     }                                                          s2.send(42);
                                                           }}
```

Session socket *s* in *P1* follows `IntAndBoolStream`; *s1* and *s2* in *P2* follows `IntAndBoolDual` and `IntStream`; s in *P3* follows `IntStreamDual`.

Fig. 1. Simple chaining of session iterations across multiple pipeline process

the selected branch and the iteration decisions (received as internal control messages) using inbranch and inwhile, and proceed accordingly; the two dual protocols show the passive versions of the above iteration and branching types, denoted by ? in place of !.

So far, we have reviewed basic SJ programming features [12] derived from standard session type theory [8, 21]; the following paragraphs discuss new features motivated by the application of session types to parallel programming in practice.

(3) Expressiveness gains from iteration chaining. The three processes in Fig. 1 additionally illustrate session *iteration chaining*, forming a linear pipeline as depicted at the top of Fig. 1. The net effect is that *P1* controls the iteration of both its session with *P2* and transitively the session between *P2* and *P3*. This is achieved through the chaining construct s2.outwhile(s1.inwhile()) at *P2*, which receives the iteration decision from *P1* and forwards it to *P3*. The flow of both sessions is thus controlled by the same master decision from *P1*.

Iteration chaining offers greater expressiveness than the individual iteration primitives supported in standard session types. Normally, session typing for ordinary inwhile or outwhile loops must forbid operations on any session other than the session channel that of loop, to preserve linear usage of session channels. This means that e.g. s1.inwhile(){ s1.send(v); } is allowed, whereas s1.inwhile(){ s2.send(v); } is not. With the iteration chaining construct, we can now construct a process containing two interleaved inwhile or outwhile loops on separate sessions. In fact, session iteration chaining can be further generalised as we explain below.

(4) Multi-channel iteration primitives. Simple iteration chaining allows SJ programmers to combine multiple sessions into linear pipeline structures, a common pattern in parallel processing. In particular, type-safe session iteration (and branching) along a pipeline is a powerful benefit over traditional stream-based data flow [18]. More complex topologies, however, such as rings and meshes, require iteration signals to

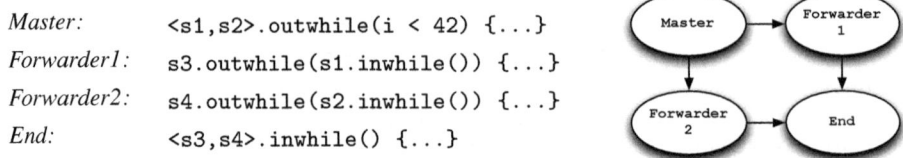

Master:	`<s1,s2>.outwhile(i < 42) {...}`
Forwarder1:	`s3.outwhile(s1.inwhile()) {...}`
Forwarder2:	`s4.outwhile(s2.inwhile()) {...}`
End:	`<s3,s4>.inwhile() {...}`

Fig. 2. Multi-channel iteration in a simple grid topology

be directly forwarded from a given process to more than one other, and for multiple signals to be directed into a common sink; in SJ, this means we require the ability to send and receive multiple iteration signals over a set of session sockets. For this purpose, SJ introduces the generalised *multi-channel* primitives; the following focuses on multi-channel iteration, which extends the chaining constructs from above.

Fig. 2 demonstrates multi-channel iteration for a simple grid topology. Process `Master` controls the iteration on both the `s1` and `s2` session sockets under a single iteration condition. Processes `Forwarder1` and `Forwarder2` iterate following the signal from `Master` and forward the signal to `End`; thus, all four processes iterate in lockstep. Multi-channel `inwhile`, as performed by `End`, is intended for situations where multiple sessions are combined for iteration, but all are coordinated by an iteration signal from a common source; this means all the signals received from each socket of the `inwhile` will always agree — either to continue iterating, or to stop. In case this is not respected at run-time, the `inwhile` will throw an exception, resulting in session termination. Together, multi-channel primitives enable the type-safe implementation of parallel programming patterns like scatter-gather, producer-consumer, and more complex chained topologies. The basic session primitives express only disjoint behaviour within individual sessions, whereas the multi-channel primitives implement interaction across multiple sessions as a single, integrated structure.

(5) The SJ tool chain with topology verification. In previous work, the safety guarantees offered by the SJ compiler were limited to the scope of each independent *binary* (two-party) session. This means that, while any one session was guaranteed to be internally deadlock-free, this property may not hold in the presence of interleaved sessions in a process as a whole. The nodes in a parallel program typically make use of many interleaved sessions – with each of their neighbours in the chosen network topology. Furthermore, `inwhile` and `outwhile` in iteration chains must be correctly composed.

As a solution to this issue, we add a *topology verification* step to the SJ tool chain for parallel programs. Fig. 3

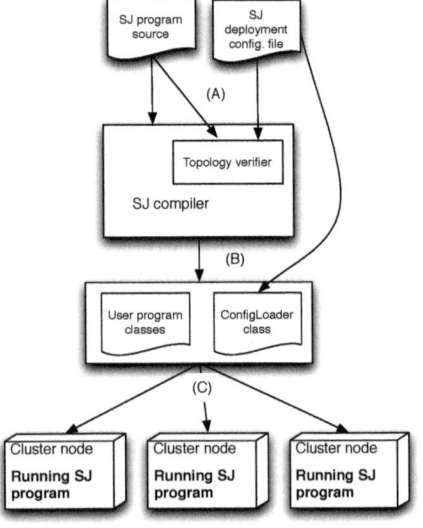

Fig. 3. The SJ tool chain

summarises the SJ tool chain for developing type-safe SJ parallel program on a distributed computing cluster. An SJ parallel program is written as a collection of SJ source files, where each file corresponds to a role in the topology. Topology verification (A) takes as input the source files and a *deployment configuration file*, listing the hosts where each process will be deployed and describing how to connect the processes. The sources and configuration files are then analysed statically to ensure the overall session topology of the parallel program conforms to a *well-formed topology* defined in Definition 4.1 in § 4, and in conjunction with session duality checks in SJ, precludes *global deadlocks* in parallel SJ programs (see Theorem 4.3). The source files are then compiled (B) to bytecode, and (C) deployed on the target cluster using details on the configuration file to instantiate and establish sessions with their assigned neighbours, ensuring the runtime topology is constructed according to the verified configuration file, and therefore safe execution of the parallel program.

3 Parallel Algorithms in SJ

This section presents the SJ implementation of a Jacobi method for solving the Discrete Poisson Equation and explains the benefits of the new multi-channel primitives. The example was chosen both as a representative real-world parallel programming application in SJ, and because it exemplifies a complex communication topology [7]. Implementations of other algorithms featuring other topologies, such as n-Body simulation (circular pipeline) and Linear Equation Solver (wraparound mesh), are available from [5].

Jacobi solution of the discrete Poisson equation: mesh topology. Poisson's equation is a partial differential equation widely used in physics and the natural sciences. Jacobi's algorithm can be implemented using various partitioning strategies. An early session-typed implementation [1] used a one-dimensional decomposition of the source matrix, resulting in a linear communication topology. The following demonstrates how the new multi-channel primitives are required to increase parallelism using a two-dimensional decomposition, i.e. using a 2D mesh communication topology. The mesh topology is used in a range of other parallel algorithms [3].

The discrete two-dimensional Poisson equation $(\nabla^2 u)_{ij}$ for a $m \times n$ grid reads:

$$u_{ij} = \tfrac{1}{4}(u_{i-1,j} + u_{i+1,j} + u_{i,j-1} + u_{i,j+1} - dx^2 g_{i,j})$$

where $2 \le i \le m-1$, $2 \le j \le n-1$, and $dx = 1/(n+1)$. Jacobi's algorithm converges on a solution by repeatedly replacing each element of the matrix u by an adjusted average of its four neighbouring values and $dx^2 g_{i,j}$. For this example, we set each $g_{i,j}$ to 0. Then, from the k-th approximation of u, the next iteration calculates:

$$u_{ij}^{k+1} = \tfrac{1}{4}(u_{i+1,j}^k + u_{i-1,j}^k + u_{i,j+1}^k + u_{i,j-1}^k)$$

Termination may be on reaching a target convergence threshold or on completing a certain number of iterations. Parallelisation of this algorithm exploits the fact that each element can be independently updated within each iteration. The decomposition divides the grid into subgrids, and each process will execute the algorithm for its assigned subgrid. To update the points along the boundaries of each subgrid, neighbouring processes need to exchange their boundary values at the beginning of each iteration.

A 2D mesh implementation is shown in Fig. 7. The `Master` node controls iteration from the top-left corner. Nodes in the centre of the mesh receive iteration control signals

```
protocol MasterToWorker
  cbegin.                   // Open a session with the Worker
  !<int>.!<int>.            // Send matrix dimensions
  ![                        // Main loop: checking convergence condition
    !<double[]>.            // Send our boundary values...
    ?(double[]).            // ..and receive our neighbour's
    ?(ConvergenceValues)    // Convergence data for neighbouring subgrid
  ]*                        // (end of main loop)
```

Fig. 4. The session type between the *Master* and *Workers* for the Jacobi algorithm

from their top and left neighbours, and propagate them to the bottom and right. Nodes at the edges only propagate iteration signals to the bottom or right, and the final node at the bottom right only receives signals and does not propagate them further.

The session type for communication from the *Master* to either of the *Workers* under it or at its right is given in Fig. 4. The *Worker*'s protocol for interacting with the *Master* is the dual of *MasterToWorker*; the same protocol is used for interaction with other *Workers* at their right and bottom (except for *Workers* at the edges of the mesh).

As listed in Fig. 5, it is possible to express the complex 2D mesh using single-channel primitives only. However, this implementation suffers from a problem: without the multi-channel primitives, there is no way of sending iteration control signals both horizontally and vertically; the only option is to open and close a temporary session in every iteration (Fig. 7), an inefficient and counter-intuitive solution. Moreover, the continuous nature of the vertical iteration sessions cannot be expressed naturally.

Having noted this weakness, Fig. 6 lists a revised implementation, taking advantage of multi-channel `inwhile` and `outwhile`. The multi-channel `inwhile` allows each *Worker* to receive iteration signals from the two processes at its top and left. Multi-channel `outwhile` lets a process control both processes at the right and bottom. Together, these two primitives completely eliminate the need for repeated opening and closing of intermediary sessions in the single-channel version. The resulting implementation is clearer and also much faster. See § 5 for the benchmark results.

4   Multi-channel Session π-Calculus

This section formalises the new nested iterations and multi-channel communication primitives and proves correctness of our implementation. Our proof method consists of:

1. We first define programs (*i.e.* starting processes) including the new primitives, and then define operational semantics with running processes modelling intermediate session communications.
2. We define a typing system for programs and running processes.
3. We prove that if a group of running processes conforms to a *well-formed topology*, then they satisfy the subject reduction theorem (Theorem 4.1) which implies type and communication-safety (Theorem 4.2) and deadlock-freedom (Theorem 4.3).
4. Since programs for our chosen parallel algorithms conform to a well-formed topology, we conclude that they satisfy the above three properties.

Master :
```
right.outwhile(notConverged()) {
  under = chanUnder.request();
  sndBoundaryVal(right, under);
  rcvBoundaryVal(right, under);
  doComputation(rcvRight, rcvUnder);
  rcvConvergenceVal(right, under);
}
```
Worker :
```
right.outwhile(left.inwhile) {
  over = chanOver.accept();
  under = chanUnder.request();
  sndBoundaryVal(left,right,over,
      under);
  rcvBoundaryVal(left,right,over,
      under);
  doComputation(rcvLeft,rcvRight,
      rcvOver,rcvUnder);
  sndConvergenceVal(left,top);
}
```
WorkerSE :
```
left.inwhile {
  over = chanOver.request();
  sndBoundaryVal(left,over);
  rcvBoundaryVal(left,over);
  doComputation(rcvLeft,rcvOver);
  sndConvergenceVal(left,top);
}
```

Fig. 5. Initial 2D mesh implementation with single-channel primitives only

Master :
```
<under,right>.outwhile(
    notConverged()) {
  sndBoundaryVal(right, under);
  rcvBoundaryVal(right, under);
  doComputation(rcvRight, rcvUnder
      );
  rcvConvergenceVal(right, under);
}
```
Worker :
```
<under,right>.outwhile
    (<over,left>.inwhile) {
  sndBoundaryVal(left,right,over,
      under);
  rcvBoundaryVal(left,right,over,
      under);
  doComputation(rcvLeft,rcvRight,
      rcvOver,rcvUnder);
  sndConvergenceVal(left,top);
}
```
WorkerSE :
```
<over,left>.inwhile {
  sndBoundaryVal(left,over);
  rcvBoundaryVal(left,over);
  doComputation(rcvLeft,rcvOver);
  sndConvergenceVal(left,top);
}
```

Fig. 6. Efficient 2D mesh implementation using multi-`outwhile` and multi-`inwhile`

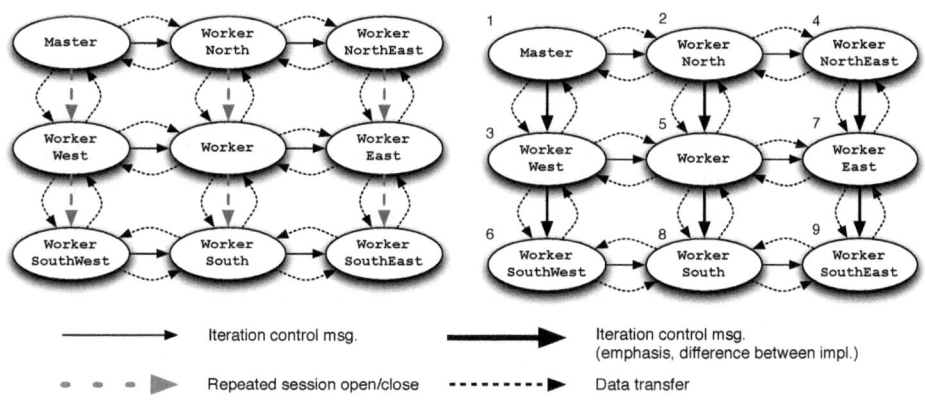

Fig. 7. Initial and improved communication patterns in the 2D mesh implementation

4.1 Syntax

The session π-calculus we treat extends [8]. Fig. 8 defines its syntax. Channels $(u, u', ...)$ can be either of two sorts: *shared channels* (a, b, x, y) or *session channels* $(k, k', ...)$. Shared channels are used to open a new session. In accepting and requesting processes, the name a represents the public interaction point over which a session may commence. The bound variable k represents the actual channel over which the session communications will take place. Constants $(c, c', ...)$ and expressions $(e, e', ...)$ of ground types (booleans and integers) are also added to model data. *Selection* chooses an available branch, and *branching* offers alternative interaction patterns; *channel send* and *channel receive* enable session delegation [8]. The *sequencing*, written $P; Q$, meaning that P is executed before Q. This syntax allows for complex forms of synchronisation, joining, and forking since P can include any parallel composition of arbitrary processes. The second addition is that of *multicast inwhile* and *outwhile*, following SJ syntax. Note that the definition of expressions includes multicast inwhile $\langle k_1 \ldots k_n \rangle$.inwhile, in order to allow inwhile as an outwhile loop condition. The control message $k \dagger [b]$ created by outwhile appears only at runtime.

The precedence of the process-building operators is (from the strongest) "$\triangleleft, \triangleright, \{\}$", ".", ";" and "|". Moreover we define that "." associates to the right. The binders for channels and variables are standard.

(Values)   (Expressions)

$v ::= a, b, x, y$ shared names $e ::= v \mid e+e \mid \texttt{not}(e) \ldots$ value, sum, not
$\quad \mid \texttt{true}, \texttt{false}$ boolean $\quad \mid \langle k_1 \ldots k_n \rangle.\texttt{inwhile}$ inwhile
$\quad \mid n$ integer

(Processes)   (Prefixed processes)

$P ::= \mathbf{0}$ inaction $T ::= \overline{a}(k).P$ request $\mid \texttt{def } D \texttt{ in } P$ recursion
$\quad \mid T$ prefixed $\quad \mid a(k).P$ accept $\mid k \triangleleft l$ selection
$\quad \mid P ; Q$ sequence $\quad \mid \overline{k}\langle e \rangle$ sending $\mid k \triangleright \{l_1 : P_1 [] \cdots [] l_n : P_n\}$ branch
$\quad \mid P \mid Q$ parallel $\quad \mid k(x).P$ reception $\mid \texttt{if } e \texttt{ then } P \texttt{ else } Q$ conditional
$\quad \mid (\nu u)P$ hiding $\quad \mid k\langle k' \rangle$ sending $\mid \langle k_1 \ldots k_n \rangle.\texttt{inwhile}\{Q\}$ inwhile
(Declaration) $\quad \mid k(k').P$ reception $\mid \langle k_1 \ldots k_n \rangle.\texttt{outwhile}(e)\{P\}$ outwhile
$D ::= X(xk) = P$ $\quad \mid X[ek]$ variables $\mid k \dagger [b]$ message

Fig. 8. Syntax

We formalise the reduction relation $\longrightarrow$ in Fig.8 up to the standard structural equivalence $\equiv$ with the rule $\mathbf{0} ; P \equiv P$ based on [8]. Reduction uses the standard *evaluation contexts* defined as:

$$E ::= [] \mid E;P \mid E \mid P \mid (\nu u)E \mid \texttt{def } D \texttt{ in } E$$
$$\mid \texttt{if } E \texttt{ then } P \texttt{ else } Q \mid \langle k_1 \ldots k_n \rangle.\texttt{outwhile}(E)\{P\} \mid E+e \mid \cdots$$

We use the notation $\Pi_{i \in \{1..n\}} P_i$ to denote the parallel composition of $(P_1 \mid \cdots \mid P_n)$.

Rules [LINK] is a session initiation rule where a fresh channel k is created, then restricted because the leading parts now share the channel k to start private interactions. Rule [COM] sends data. Rule [LBL] selects the i-th branch, and rule [PASS] passes a session

$$a(k).P_1 \mid \overline{a}(k).P_2 \longrightarrow (vk)(P_1 \mid P_2) \qquad \overline{k}\langle c\rangle \mid k(x).P_2 \longrightarrow P_2\{c/x\} \quad \text{[Link], [Com]}$$

$$k \triangleright \{l_1 : P_1 [] \cdots [] l_n : P_n\} \mid k \triangleleft l_i \longrightarrow P_i \quad (1 \le i \le n) \qquad k\langle k'\rangle \mid k(k').P_2 \longrightarrow P_2 \quad \text{[Lbl], [Pass]}$$

$$\text{if true then } P \text{ else } Q \longrightarrow P \qquad \text{if false then } P \text{ else } Q \longrightarrow Q \quad \text{[If]}$$

$$\text{def } X(xk) = P \text{ in } X[ck] \longrightarrow \text{def } X(xk) = P \text{ in } P\{c/x\} \quad \text{[Def]}$$

$$\langle k_1 \ldots k_n\rangle.\text{inwhile}\{P\} \mid \Pi_{i\in\{1..n\}} k_i \dagger [\text{true}] \longrightarrow P; \langle k_1 \ldots k_n\rangle.\text{inwhile}\{P\} \quad \text{[Iw1]}$$

$$\langle k_1 \ldots k_n\rangle.\text{inwhile}\{P\} \mid \Pi_{i\in\{1..n\}} k_i \dagger [\text{false}] \longrightarrow \mathbf{0} \quad \text{[Iw2]}$$

$$E[\langle k_1 \ldots k_n\rangle.\text{inwhile}] \mid \Pi_{i\in\{1..n\}} k_i \dagger [\text{true}] \longrightarrow E[\text{true}] \quad \text{[IwE1]}$$

$$E[\langle k_1 \ldots k_n\rangle.\text{inwhile}] \mid \Pi_{i\in\{1..n\}} k_i \dagger [\text{false}] \longrightarrow E[\text{false}] \quad \text{[IwE2]}$$

$$E[e] \longrightarrow^* E'[\text{true}] \Rightarrow$$
$$E[\langle k_1 \ldots k_n\rangle.\text{outwhile}(e)\{P\}] \longrightarrow E'[P; \langle k_1 \ldots k_n\rangle.\text{outwhile}(e)\{P\}]$$
$$\mid \Pi_{i\in\{1..n\}} k_i \dagger [\text{true}] \quad \text{[Ow1]}$$

$$E[e] \longrightarrow^* E'[\text{false}] \Rightarrow$$
$$E[\langle k_1 \ldots k_n\rangle.\text{outwhile}(e)\{P\}] \longrightarrow E'[\mathbf{0}] \mid \Pi_{i\in\{1..n\}} k_i \dagger [\text{false}] \quad \text{[Ow2]}$$

$$P \equiv P' \text{ and } P' \longrightarrow Q' \text{ and } Q' \equiv Q \Rightarrow P \longrightarrow Q \quad \text{[Str]}$$

$$e \longrightarrow e' \Rightarrow E[e] \longrightarrow E[e'] \qquad P \longrightarrow P' \Rightarrow E[P] \longrightarrow E[P']$$

$$P \mid Q \longrightarrow P' \mid Q' \Rightarrow E[P] \mid Q \longrightarrow E[P'] \mid Q' \quad \text{[Eval]}$$

In [Ow1] and [Ow2], we assume $E = E' \mid \Pi_{i\in\{1..n\}} k_i \dagger [b_i]$

Fig. 9. Reduction rules

channel k for delegation. The standard conditional and recursive agent rules [IF1], [IF2] and [DEF] originate in [8].

Rule [Iw1] synchronises with n asynchronous messages if they all carry true. In this case, it repeats again. Rule [Iw2] is its dual and synchronises with n false messages. In this case, it moves to the next command. On the other hand, if the results are mixed (i.e. b_i is true, while b_j is false), then it is stuck. In SJ, it will raise the exception, cf. § 2 (4). The rules for expressions are defined similarly. The rules for outwhile generates appropriate messages. Note that the assumption $E[e] \longrightarrow E'[\text{true}]$ or $E[e] \longrightarrow E'[\text{false}]$ is needed to handle the case where e is an inwhile expression.

In order for our reduction rules to reflect SJ's actual behaviour, inwhile rules should have precedence over outwhile rules. Note that our algorithms do not cause an infinite generation of $k \dagger [b]$ by outwhile: this is ensured by the well-formed topology criteria described later, together with this priority rule.

4.2 Types, Typing System and Well-Formed Topologies

This subsection presents types and typing systems. The key point is an introduction of types and typing systems for asynchronous runtime messages. We then define the notation of a well-formed topology.

Types. The syntax of types, an extension of [8], follows:

Sort	$S ::= \text{nat} \mid \text{bool} \mid \langle \alpha, \overline{\alpha}\rangle$
Partial session	$\tau ::= \varepsilon \mid \tau; \tau \mid ?[S] \mid ?[\alpha] \mid \&\{l_1 : \tau_1, \ldots, l_n : \tau_n\} \mid ![\tau]^* \mid \mathbf{x}$
	$\mid ![S] \mid ![\alpha] \mid \oplus\{l_1 : \tau_1, \ldots, l_n : \tau_n\} \mid ?[\tau]^* \mid \mu\mathbf{x}.\tau$
Completed session	$\alpha ::= \tau.\text{end} \mid \bot$ Runtime session $\beta ::= \alpha \mid \alpha^\dagger \mid \dagger$

Sorts include a pair type for a shared channel and base types. The partial session type τ represents intermediate sessions. ε represents inaction and $\tau;\tau$ is a sequential composition. The rest is from [8]. The types with ! and ? express respectively the sending and reception of a value S or session channel. The selection type $\oplus$ represents the transmission of the label l_i followed by the communications described by τ_i. The branching type & represents the reception of a label l_i chosen in the set $\{l_1,\ldots,l_n\}$ followed by the communications described by τ_i. Types $![\tau]^*$ and $?[\tau]^*$ are types for outwhile and inwhile. The types are considered up to the equivalence: $\&\{l_1: \tau_1,\ldots,l_n: \tau_n\}.\text{end} \equiv \&\{l_1: \tau_1.\text{end},\ldots,l_n: \tau_n.\text{end}\}$. This equivalence ensures all partial types $\tau_1\ldots\tau_n$ of selection ends, and are compatible with each other in the completed session type (and vice versa). ε is an empty type, and it is defined so that $\varepsilon;\tau \equiv \tau$ and $\tau;\varepsilon \equiv \tau$.

Runtime session syntax represents partial composed runtime message types. $\alpha^\dagger$ represents the situation inwhile or outwhile are composed with messages; and † is a type of messages. The meaning will be clearer when we define the parallel composition.

Judgements and environments. The typing judgements for expressions and processes are of the shape:

$$\Gamma;\Delta \vdash e \triangleright S \quad \text{and} \quad \Gamma \vdash P \triangleright \Delta$$

where we define the environments as $\Gamma ::= \emptyset \mid \Gamma \cdot x : S \mid \Gamma \cdot X : S\alpha$ and $\Delta ::= \emptyset \mid \Delta \cdot k : \beta$. Γ is the *standard environment* which associates a name to a sort and a process variable to a sort and a session type. Δ is the *session environment* which associates session channels to running session types, which represents the open communication protocols. We often omit Δ or Γ from the judgement if it is empty.

Sequential and parallel compositions of environments are defined as:

$$\Delta;\Delta' = \Delta\setminus\text{dom}(\Delta')\cup\Delta'\setminus\text{dom}(\Delta)\cup\{k: \Delta(k)\setminus\text{end};\Delta'(k) \mid k \in \text{dom}(\Delta)\cap\text{dom}(\Delta')\}$$
$$\Delta\circ\Delta' = \Delta\setminus\text{dom}(\Delta')\cup\Delta'\setminus\text{dom}(\Delta)\cup\{k: \Delta(k)\circ\Delta'(k) \mid k \in \text{dom}(\Delta)\cap\text{dom}(\Delta')\}$$

where $\Delta(k)\setminus\text{end}$ means we delete end from the tail of the types (e.g. $\tau.\text{end}\setminus\text{end} = \tau$). Then the resulting sequential composition is always well-defined. The parallel composition of the environments must be extended with new running message types. Hence $\beta\circ\beta'$ is defined as either (1) $\alpha\circ\overline{\alpha} =\bot$; (2) $\alpha\circ\dagger = \alpha^\dagger$ or (3) $\alpha\circ\overline{\alpha}^\dagger =\bot^\dagger$. Otherwise the composition is undefined. Here $\overline{\alpha}$ denotes a dual of α (defined by exchanging ! to ? and & to $\oplus$; and vice versa). (1) is the standard rule from session type algebra, which means once a pair of dual types are composed, then we cannot compose any processes with the same channel further. (2) means a composition of an iteration of type α and n-messages of type † becomes $\alpha^\dagger$. This is further composed with the dual $\overline{\alpha}$ by (3) to complete a composition. Note that $\bot^\dagger$ is different from $\bot$ since $\bot^\dagger$ represents a situation that messages are not consumed with inwhile yet.

Typing rules. We explain the key typing rules for the new primitives (Fig. 10). Other rules are similar with [8] and left to [5].

[EINWHILE] is a rule for inwhile-expression. The iteration session type of k_i is recorded in Δ. This information is used to type the nested iteration with outwhile in rule [OUTWHILE]. Rule [INWHILE] is dual to [OUTWHILE]. Rule [MESSAGE] types runtime messages as †. Sequential and parallel compositions use the above algebras to ensure the linearity of channels.

$$\frac{\Delta = k_1 : ?[\tau_1]^*.\text{end}, ..., k_n : ?[\tau_n]^*.\text{end}}{\Gamma;\Delta \vdash \langle k_1 ... k_n \rangle.\text{inwhile} \triangleright \text{bool}} \qquad \frac{\Gamma \vdash b \triangleright \text{bool}}{\Gamma \vdash k \dagger [b] \triangleright k : \dagger} \qquad [\text{EINWHILE}],[\text{MESSAGE}]$$

$$\frac{\Gamma; \Delta \vdash e \triangleright \text{bool} \qquad \Gamma \vdash P \triangleright \Delta \cdot k_1 : \tau_1.\text{end} \cdots k_n : \tau_n.\text{end}}{\Gamma \vdash \langle k_1 ... k_n \rangle.\text{outwhile}(e)\{P\} \triangleright \Delta \cdot k_1 : ![\tau_1]^*.\text{end}, ..., k_n : ![\tau_n]^*.\text{end}} \qquad [\text{OUTWHILE}]$$

$$\frac{\Gamma \vdash Q \triangleright \Delta \cdot k_1 : \tau_1.\text{end} \cdots k_n : \tau_n.\text{end}}{\Gamma \vdash \langle k_1 ... k_n \rangle.\text{inwhile}\{Q\} \triangleright \Delta \cdot k_1 : ?[\tau_1]^*.\text{end}, ..., k_n : ?[\tau_n]^*.\text{end}} \qquad [\text{INWHILE}]$$

$$\frac{\Gamma \vdash P \triangleright \Delta \qquad \Gamma \vdash Q \triangleright \Delta'}{\Gamma \vdash P; Q \triangleright \Delta; \Delta'} \qquad \frac{\Gamma \vdash P \triangleright \Delta \qquad \Gamma \vdash Q \triangleright \Delta'}{\Gamma \vdash P \mid Q \triangleright \Delta \circ \Delta'} \qquad [\text{SEQ}],[\text{CONC}]$$

Fig. 10. Key typing rules

Well-formed topologies. We now define the well-formed topologies. Since our multi-channel primitives offer an effective, structured message passing synchronisation mechanism, the following simple definition is sufficient to capture deadlock-freedom in representative topologies for parallel algorithms. Common topologies in parallel algorithms such as circular pipeline, mesh and wraparound mesh all conform to our well-formed topology definition below [5]. Below we call P is a *base* if P is either $\mathbf{0}$, $\bar{k}\langle e \rangle$, $k(x).\mathbf{0}$, $k \triangleleft l$ or $k \triangleright \{l_1 : \mathbf{0}[] \cdots []l_n : \mathbf{0}\}$.

Definition 4.1 (Well-formed topology). Suppose a group of n parallel composed processes $P = P_1 \mid ... \mid P_n$ such that $\Gamma \vdash P \triangleright \Delta$ with $\Delta(k) = \bot$ for all $k \in \text{dom}(\Delta)$; and $k_{(i,j)}$ denotes a free session channel from P_i to P_j. We say P conforms to a *well-formed topology* if P inductively satisfies one of the following conditions:

1. (inwhile and outwhile)
   $P_1 = \langle \vec{k}_1 \rangle.\text{outwhile}(e)\{Q_1\}$ $P_i = \langle \vec{k}_i \rangle.\text{outwhile}(\langle \vec{k}'_i \rangle.\text{inwhile})\{Q_i\}$ $(2 \leq i < n)$
   $P_n = \langle \vec{k}'_n \rangle.\text{inwhile}\{Q_n\}$ $\quad \vec{k}_i \subset k_{(i,i+1)} \cdots k_{(i,n)}, \vec{k}'_i \subset k_{(1,i)} \cdots k_{(i-1,i)}$
   and $(Q_1 \mid \cdots \mid Q_n)$ conforms to a well-formed topology.
2. (sequencing) $P_i = Q_{1i};...;Q_{mi}$ where $(Q_{j1} \mid Q_{j2} \mid \cdots \mid Q_{jn})$ conforms to a well-formed topology for each $1 \leq j \leq m$.
3. (base) (1) session actions in P_i follow the order of the index (e.g. the session actions at $k_{(i,j)}$ happens before $k_{(h,g)}$ if $(i,j) < (h,g)$), then the rest is a base process P'_i; and (2) P_i includes neither shared session channels, inwhile nor outwhile.

The figure below explains condition (1) of the above definition, ensuring consistency of control flows within iterations. Subprocesses P_i are ordered by their process index i. A process P_i can only send outwhile control messages to processes with a higher index via $\vec{k}_i$ (denoted by $k_{(i,m)}$), while it can receive messages from those with a lower index via $\vec{k}'_i$ (denoted by $k_{(h,i)}$). This ordering guarantees absence of cycles of communications.

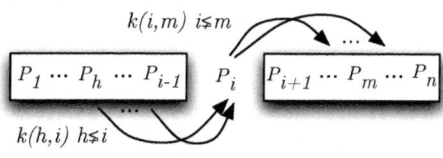

There is only one source P_1 (only sends outwhile control messages) and one sink P_n (only receives those messages). (2) says that a sequential composition of well-formed topologies is again well-formed. (3) defines base cases which are commonly found in the algorithms: (3-1) means that since the order of session actions in P_i follow the order of the indices, $\Pi_i P_i$ reduces to $\Pi_i P_i'$ without deadlock; then since $\Pi_i P_i'$ is a parallel composition of base processes where each channel k has type $\perp$, $\Pi_i P_i'$ reduces to $\mathbf{0}$ without deadlock. (3-2) ensures a single global topology.

4.3 Subject Reduction, Communication Safety and Deadlock Freedom

We state here that process groups conforming to a well-formed topology satisfy the main theorems. The full proofs can be found in [5].

Theorem 4.1 (Subject reduction). *Assume P forms a well-formed topology and $\Gamma \vdash P \triangleright \Delta$. Suppose $P \longrightarrow^* P'$. Then we have $\Gamma \vdash P' \triangleright \Delta'$ with for all k (1) $\Delta(k) = \alpha$ implies $\Delta'(k) = \alpha^\dagger$; (2) $\Delta(k) = \alpha^\dagger$ implies $\Delta'(k) = \alpha$; or (3) $\Delta(k) = \beta$ implies $\Delta'(k) = \beta$.*

(1) and (2) state an intermediate stage where messages are floating; or (3) the type is unchanged during the reduction. The proof requires to formulate the intermediate processes with messages which are started from a well-formed topology, and prove they satisfy the above theorem.

We say process has a *type error* if expressions in P contains either a type error of values or constants in the standard sense (e.g. if 100 then P else Q).

To formalise communication safety, we need the following notions. Write $\mathtt{inwhile}(Q)$ for either $\mathtt{inwhile}$ or $\mathtt{inwhile}\{Q\}$. We say that a processes P is a *head subprocess* of a process Q if $Q \equiv E[P]$ for some evaluation context E. Then *k-process* is a head process prefixed by subject k (such as $\bar{k}\langle e \rangle$). Next, a *k-redex* is the parallel composition of a pair of k-processes. i.e. either of form of a pair such that $(\bar{k}\langle e \rangle, k(x).Q)$, $(k \triangleleft l, k \triangleright \{l_1 : Q_1 [] \cdots []l_n : Q_n\})$, $(\bar{k}\langle k' \rangle, k(k').P)$, $(\langle k_1 \ldots k_n \rangle.\mathtt{outwhile}(e)\{P\}, \langle k_1' \ldots k_m' \rangle. \mathtt{inwhile}(Q))$ with $k \in \{k_1,..,k_n\} \cap \{k_1',..,k_m'\}$ or $(k \dagger [b] \mid \langle k_1' \ldots k_m' \rangle. \mathtt{inwhile}(Q))$ with $k \in \{k_1,..,k_n\}$. Then P is a *communication error* if $P \equiv (\nu \tilde{u})(\mathtt{def}\ D\ \mathtt{in}\ (Q \mid R))$ where Q is, for some k, the parallel composition of two or more k-processes that do not form a k-redex. The following theorem is direct from the subject reduction theorem [21, Theorem 2.11].

Theorem 4.2 (Type and communication safety). *A typable process which forms a well-formed topology never reduces to a type nor communication error.*

Below we say P is *deadlock-free* if for all P' such that $P \longrightarrow^* P'$, $P' \longrightarrow$ or $P' \equiv \mathbf{0}$. The following theorem shows that a group of typable multiparty processes which form a well-formed topology can always move or become the null process.

Theorem 4.3 (Deadlock-freedom). *Assume P forms a well-formed topology and $\Gamma \vdash P \triangleright \Delta$. Then P is deadlock-free.*

Now we reason Jacobi algorithm in Fig. 6. We only show the master P_1 and the worker in the middle P_5 (the indices follow the right picture of Fig. 7).

$P_1 = \langle k_{(1,2)}, k_{(1,4)} \rangle.\mathtt{outwhile}(e)\{\overline{k_{(1,2)}}\langle \mathtt{d}[] \rangle; k_{(1,2)}(x).\overline{k_{(1,4)}}\langle \mathtt{d}[] \rangle; k_{(1,4)}(y). \mathbf{0}\}$

$P_5 = \langle k_{(5,7)}, k_{(5,8)} \rangle.\mathtt{outwhile}(\langle k_{(2,5)}', k_{(3,5)}' \rangle.\mathtt{inwhile})\{$
$\qquad \overline{k_{(2,5)}'}(w).\overline{k_{(2,5)}'}\langle \mathtt{d}[] \rangle; k_{(3,5)}'(x).\overline{k_{(3,5)}'}\langle \mathtt{d}[] \rangle; \overline{k_{(5,7)}}\langle \mathtt{d}[] \rangle; k_{(5,7)}(y).\overline{k_{(5,8)}}\langle \mathtt{d}[] \rangle; k_{(5,8)}(z). \mathbf{0}\}$

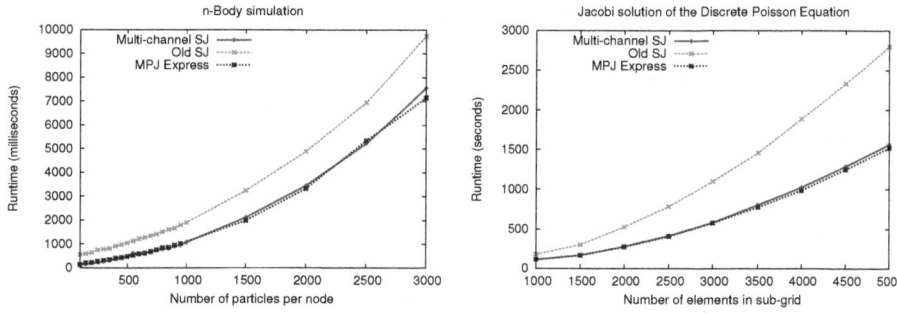

Fig. 11. SJ with and without multi-channel primitives and MPJ Express (left: 3-nodes *n*-Body simulation, right: 9-nodes Jacobi solution)

where d[] denotes the type of array with double. We can easily prove they are typable and forms the well-formed topology satisfying the conditions (1) and (3) in Definition 4.1. Hence it is type and communication-safe and deadlock-free. [5] lists the full definition and more complex algorithms which conform to a well-formed topology.

5 Performance Evaluation

This section presents performance results for several implementations of the *n*-Body simulation (details in [5, § A.1]), and Jacobi solution presented in § 3. We evaluated our implementations on a 9-node cluster for our benchmark, and each of the points is an average of 4 runs of the benchmark. All of them comprise an AMD PhenomX4 9650 2.30GHz CPU with 8GB RAM. The main objectives of these benchmarks is (1) to investigate the benefits of the new multi-channel primitives, comparing Old SJ (without the new primitives) and Multi-channel SJ (with the new primitives); and (2) compare those with MPJ Express [14] for reference. Fig. 11 shows a clear improvement when using the new multi-channel primitives in SJ. Multi-channel SJ also performs competitively against MPJ Express in both benchmarks. Hence SJ can be a viable alternative to MPI programming in Java, with the additional assurances of communication-safety and deadlock-free.

6 Related and Future Work

Due to space limitations, we focus on comparisons with extensions of Java with session types and MPI. Other related work, including functional languages with session types as well as HPC and PGAS languages can be found in the full version [5].

Implementations of session types in Java. SJ was introduced in [12] as the first general-purpose session-typed distributed programming language. Another recent extension of SJ added event-based programming primitives [11], for a different target domain: scalable and type-safe event-driven implementation of applications that feature a large number of concurrent but independent threads (e.g. Web servers). The preliminary experiments with parallel algorithms in SJ were reported in a workshop paper [1].

This early work considered only simple iteration chaining without analysis of deadlock-freedom, and without the general multi-channel primitives required for efficient representation of the complex topologies tackled here. The present paper also presents the formal semantics, type system, and proofs for type soundness and deadlock-freedom for the new primitives, which have not been studied in [1].

The Bica language [6] is an extension of Java also implementing binary sessions, which focuses on allowing session channels to be used as fields in classes. Bica does not support multi-channel primitives and does not guarantee deadlock-freedom across multiple sessions. See [10, 11] for more comparisons with [6]. A recent work [17] extends SJ-like primitives with multiparty session types and studies type-directed optimisations for the extended language. Their design is targeted at more loosely-coupled distributed applications than parallel algorithms, where processes are tightly-coupled and typically communicate via high-bandwidth, low-latency media; their optimisations, such as message batching, could increase latency and lower performance. It does not support features such as session delegation, session thread programming and transport independence [10, § 4.2.3], which are integrated into SJ. The latter in particular, together with SJ alias typing [10, § 3.1] (for session linearity), offers transparent portability of SJ parallel algorithm code over TCP and shared memory with zero-copy optimisations.

Message-based parallel programming. The present paper focuses on language and typing support for communications programming, rather than introducing a supplementary API. In comparison to the standard MPI libraries [7, §4], SJ offers structured communication programming from the natural abstraction of typed sessions and the associated static assurance of type and protocol safety. Recent work [19] applies model-checking techniques to standard MPI C source code to ensure correct matching of sends and receives using a pre-existing test suite. Their verifier, ISP, exploits independence between thread actions to reduce the state space of possible thread interleavings of an execution, and checks for deadlocks in the remaining states. In contrast, our session type-based approach does not depend on external testing, and a valid, compiled program is guaranteed communication-safe and deadlock-free in a matter of seconds. SJ thus offers a performance edge even in the cases of complex interactions (cf. [5]). The MPI API remains low-level, easily leading to synchronisation errors, message type errors and deadlocks [7]. From our experiences, programming message-based parallel algorithms with SJ are much easier than programming based on MPI functions, which, beside lacking type checking for protocol and communication safety, often requires manipulating numerical process identifiers and array indexes (e.g. for message lengths in the n-Body program) in tricky ways. Our approach gives a clear definition of a class of communication-safe and deadlock-free programs as proved in Theorems 4.2 and 4.3, which have been statically checked without exploring all execution states for all possible thread interleavings. Finally, benchmark results in §5 demonstrate how SJ programs can deliver the above benefits and perform competitively against a Java-based MPI [14].

Future work. Our previous work [20] shows type-checking for parallel algorithms based on parameterised multiparty sessions requires type equality, so type checking is undecidable in the general case. The method developed in this paper is not only decidable, but also effective in practice as we can reuse the existing binary SJ language, type-checker and runtime, with extensions to the new multi-channel inwhile and outwhile primitives for structuring message-passing communications and iterations. To validate more general communication topologies beyond the well-formed condition and typical parallel algorithms, we plan to incorporate new primitives into multiparty session types [9, 17] by extending the end-point projection algorithm based on roles [4]. Preliminary results from a manual SJ-to-C translation have shown large performance gains for FPGA implementations [15]. Future implementation efforts will include a natively compiled, C-like language targeted at low overheads and efficiency for HPC and systems programming. We also plan to incorporate recent, unimplemented theoretical advances, including logical reasoning [2] to prove the correctness of parallel algorithms.

Acknowledgements. We thank the referees for their useful comments and Brittle Tsoi and Wayne Luk for their collaborations. This work is partially supported by EPSRC EP/F003757 and EP/G015635.

References

1. Bejleri, A., Hu, R., Yoshida, N.: Session-Based Programming for Parallel Algorithms. In: PLACES, EPTCS (2009)
2. Bocchi, L., Honda, K., Tuosto, E., Yoshida, N.: A theory of design-by-contract for distributed multiparty interactions. In: Gastin, P., Laroussinie, F. (eds.) CONCUR 2010. LNCS, vol. 6269, pp. 162–176. Springer, Heidelberg (2010)
3. Casanova, H., Legrand, A., Robert, Y.: Parallel Algorithms. Chapman & Hall, Boca Raton (2008)
4. Deniélou, P.-M., Yoshida, N.: Dynamic Multirole Session Types. In: POPL 2011, pp. 435–446. ACM, New York (2011)
5. On-line appendix, http://www.doc.ic.ac.uk/~cn06/pub/2011/sj_parallel/
6. Gay, S.J., Vasconcelos, V.T., Ravara, A., Gesbert, N., Caldeira, A.Z.: Modular Session Types for Distributed Object-Oriented Programming. In: POPL 2010, pp. 299–312. ACM, New York (2010)
7. Gropp, W., Lusk, E., Skjellum, A.: Using MPI: Portable Parallel Programming with the Message-Passing Interface. MIT Press, Cambridge (1999)
8. Honda, K., Vasconcelos, V.T., Kubo, M.: Language Primitives and Type Discipline for Structured Communication-Based Programming. In: Hankin, C. (ed.) ESOP 1998. LNCS, vol. 1381, pp. 122–138. Springer, Heidelberg (1998)
9. Honda, K., Yoshida, N., Carbone, M.: Multiparty Asynchronous Session Types. In: POPL, pp. 273–284. ACM, New York (2008)
10. Hu, R.: Structured, Safe and High-level Communications Programming with Session Types. PhD thesis, Imperial College London (2010)
11. Hu, R., Kouzapas, D., Pernet, O., Yoshida, N., Honda, K.: Type-Safe Eventful Sessions in Java. In: D'Hondt, T. (ed.) ECOOP 2010. LNCS, vol. 6183, pp. 329–353. Springer, Heidelberg (2010)
12. Hu, R., Yoshida, N., Honda, K.: Session-Based Distributed Programming in Java. In: Vitek, J. (ed.) ECOOP 2008. LNCS, vol. 5142, pp. 516–541. Springer, Heidelberg (2008)
13. Message Passing Interface, http://www.mcs.anl.gov/research/projects/mpi/
14. MPJ Express homepage, http://mpj-express.org/
15. Ng, N.: High Performance Parallel Design based on Session Programming. MEng thesis, Department of Computing, Imperial College London (2010)
16. Shafi, A., Carpenter, B., Baker, M.: Nested Parallelism for Multi-core HPC Systems using Java. Journal of Parallel and Distributed Computing 69(6), 532–545 (2009)

17. Sivaramakrishnan, K.C., Nagaraj, K., Ziarek, L., Eugster, P.: Efficient Session Type Guided Distributed Interaction. In: Clarke, D., Agha, G. (eds.) COORDINATION 2010. LNCS, vol. 6116, pp. 152–167. Springer, Heidelberg (2010)
18. Spring, J.H., Privat, J., Guerraoui, R., Vitek, J.: StreamFlex: High-Throughput Stream Programming in Java. In: OOPSLA 2007, pp. 211–228. ACM, New York (2007)
19. Vo, A., Vakkalanka, S., DeLisi, M., Gopalakrishnan, G., Kirby, R.M., Thakur, R.: Formal Verification of Practical MPI Programs. In: PPoPP 2009, pp. 261–270. ACM, New York (2009)
20. Yoshida, N., Deniélou, P.-M., Bejleri, A., Hu, R.: Parameterised Multiparty Session Types. In: Ong, C.-H.L. (ed.) FOSSACS 2010. LNCS, vol. 6014, pp. 128–145. Springer, Heidelberg (2010)
21. Yoshida, N., Vasconcelos, V.T.: Language Primitives and Type Discipline for Structured Communication-Based Programming Revisited: Two Systems for Higher-Order Session Communication. ENTCS 171(4), 73–93 (2007)

Fair Subtyping for Multi-party Session Types

Luca Padovani

Dipartimento di Informatica, Università di Torino, Italy
padovani@di.unito.it

Abstract. The standard subtyping relation used in dyadic session type theories may compromise the liveness of multi-party sessions. In this paper we define a *fair* subtyping relation for multi-party session types that preserves liveness, we relate it with the standard subtyping relation, and we give algorithms for deciding it. As a side effect, we provide an original and remarkably simple coinductive characterization of the fair testing preorder for nondeterministic, sequential processes consisting of internal choices of outputs and external choices of inputs.

1 Introduction

Type systems for dyadic sessions [15,16,22] require that, at any time, the two ends of a session must be used by exactly two processes and in complementary ways. These requirements enforce session correctness, namely *communication safety* (no message of unexpected type is ever sent) and *liveness* (whenever a message is exchanged, all of the processes involved in the session make progress). For example, the session $\mathsf{p} : T \mid \mathsf{q} : R$, where T and R are the session types defined by

$$T = \mathsf{q}!a.T \oplus \mathsf{q}!b.\mathsf{end} \qquad \text{and} \qquad R = \mathsf{p}?a.R + \mathsf{p}?b.\mathsf{end},$$

is correct and describes a conversation between two processes identified by the tags p and q: process p sends either an a message or a b message to q; the decision as to which type of message is sent is taken by p, whence the *internal choice* operator $\oplus$. Process q must be ready to receive either an a or a b message from p, whence the *external choice* operator $+$. If an a message is exchanged, the two processes repeat this pattern; as soon as a b message is exchanged, the session ends.

The shift from dyadic to *multi-party sessions* [17] makes the definition of session correctness more subtle. First, it is no longer obvious what it means to use the ends of the session "in complementary ways" if the session involves more than two participants. Second, it is no longer reasonable to pretend that *all* of the involved participants make progress whenever a message is exchanged if communications are point-to-point and yet one would like to state that no participant is left behind. A natural formalization of correctness for multi-party sessions requires that, at any time, the session must have the possibility to reach a terminal configuration where all of its participants no longer use the session ends. For example, in the session $\mathsf{p} : T' \mid \mathsf{q} : R \mid \mathsf{r} : \mathsf{p}?c.\mathsf{end}$, where

$$T' = \mathsf{q}!a.T' \oplus \mathsf{q}!b.\mathsf{r}!c.\mathsf{end},$$

the processes p and q may exchange an arbitrary number of a messages and, during their interaction, the process r does not make any progress. However, the session is

W. De Meuter and G.-C. Roman (Eds.): COORDINATION 2011, LNCS 6721, pp. 127–141, 2011.

correct because, as long as *a* messages are exchanged, it is always *possible* (although not granted) for p to send a *b* message to q followed by a *c* message to r. If this happens, all of the involved participants reach a terminal state and the session ends.

This difference between dyadic and multi-party sessions has dramatic effects on the subtyping relation for session types [12,6]. Subtyping defines an asymmetric compatibility between types such that, when T is a subtype of S, it is harmless to replace a channel with type S with another one with type T or, equivalently, it is harmless to replace a process that behaves according to T with another one that behaves according to S. For example, the session type T defined above is a subtype of q!*b*.end: using a channel of type q!*b*.end means sending a *b* message to process q. Since the session type T permits sending both an *a* message and a *b* message, using a channel with type T in place of another one with type q!*b*.end does not compromise the correctness of the session. In general, we may deduce that T is a subtype of S if S is a variant of T where some branches of some internal choices have been pruned. According to this intuition every session type in the family

$$S_2 = \text{q!}a.\text{q!}a.S_2 \oplus \text{q!}b.\text{end} \quad \cdots \quad S_n = (\text{q!}a.)^n S_n \oplus \text{q!}b.\text{end} \quad \cdots \quad S_\infty = \text{q!}a.S_\infty$$

is a supertype of T. The type S_n allows sending a *b* message only after the number of sent *a* messages is a multiple of n. The type S_∞ is somehow the limit of the sequence $\{S_i\}_{i \geq 2}$ and describes a process that only sends *a* messages. The fact that T is a subtype of S_∞ may be questionable, because the sessions p : S_i | q : R for $i \geq 2$ all have the potential to terminate (it is always possible that a *b* message is sent), while the session p : S_∞ | q : R is doomed to loop forever. In a dyadic session like p : S_∞ | q : R this is mitigated by the observation that *every* participant of the session makes indefinite progress. However, using the same arguments we might also deduce that S_∞ is a supertype of T', and now in the session p : S_∞ | q : R | r : p?*c*.end process p keeps interacting with q while *c* is stuck waiting for a message that is never sent. We conclude that the well-known subtyping relation for dyadic session types is unsound in multi-party theories because it may not preserve the liveness of multi-party sessions.

In this paper we study a sound subtyping relation for multi-party session types. Understanding when two session types are related by subtyping in our theory is a surprisingly complex business. First of all, the differences between the standard subtyping relation and ours emerge only when recursive session types are involved, while the two relations coincide on finite session types. Second, unlike the standard subtyping relation for session types, deciding whether some branch of an internal choice can be safely pruned may involve a non-local check on the structure of the session types being compared. This makes the subtyping relation particularly difficult to axiomatize. To illustrate the subtleties behind our subtyping relation, consider the session types T, S_2, and S_∞ represented as the three automata in Figure 1, where the initial states have been labelled with the name of the session type and the solid arcs with the actions performed by the processes that behave according to these types. The subtyping relation establishes a correspondence between states of two session types. In the figure, the correspondence is depicted as the three dotted arrows showing, for each state of S_2, the corresponding state of T. The fact that S_∞ *is not* a supertype of T can be easily detected since no end state is reachable from S_∞, but this does not explain why S_2 *is* a supertype of T. Observe

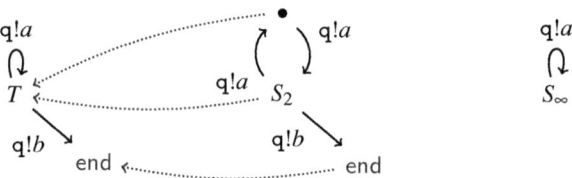

Fig. 1. Relation between $T = $ q!$a.T \oplus$ q!b.end and $S_2 = $ q!$a.$q!$a.S_2 \oplus$ q!b.end

that S_2 has an intermediate state • which lacks the outgoing q!b-labelled transition that T has. The correspondence between T and this state of S_2 is safe if (and only if) there is no session type R such that p : T | q : R is a correct session and q is capable to loop the interaction starting from p : S_2 | q : R in such a way that the • state is visited infinitely often. If this were the case, q could rely on the observation of a b message after having received an odd number of a messages to terminate successfully. This cannot happen in the example above because p : S_2 can always break the loop by sending q an a message followed by a b one (the act of sending a message is irrevocably decided by the sender). We express this as the fact that S_2 *rules over* (every context, like q : R, that completes) T, which we denote by $T \prec S_2$.

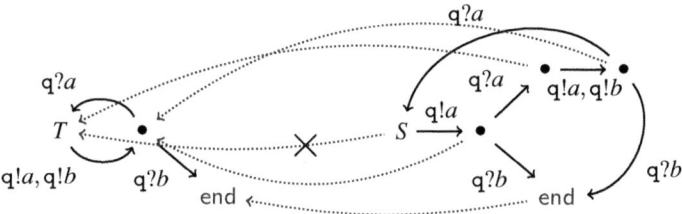

Fig. 2. Relation between $T = $ q!$a.$(q?$a.T + $ q?b.end) $\oplus$ q!$b.$(q?$a.T + $ q?b.end) and $S = $ q!$a.$(q?$a.$(q!$a.$(q?$a.S + $ q?b.end) $\oplus$ q!$b.$(q?$a.S + $ q?b.end)) $+ $ q?b.end

A more involved example is depicted in Figure 2. The only difference between T and S is that S lacks the outgoing q!b-labelled transition that T has. Basically, p : S may send a b message only after an odd number of a messages have been sent to q and an equal number of a messages have been received. Unlike the previous example, it is q that decides whether to terminate the interaction with p, by sending a b message, or to continue, by sending an a message. Consider now the participant q : R where

$$R = \text{p?}a.\text{p!}a.(\text{p?}a.\text{p!}a.R + \text{p?}b.\text{p!}a.R) + \text{p?}b.\text{p!}b.\text{end}.$$

It is easy to see that p : T | q : R is correct while p : S | q : R loops through state S. In other words, q forces p : S to go through state S in hopes that a b message is received. This was possible with p : T, but not with p : S. The fact that a participant like q : R exists means that T is not ruled by S, and therefore T is not a subtype of S. In this paper we show that the "ruled by" relation fully characterizes the contexts in which pruning outputs is safe.

Related work. The framework we have depicted is known in concurrency theory as *fair testing* [18,21]. Testing [10,9,14] is a general technique for defining refinement relations $\sqsubseteq$ between processes so that, when $P \sqsubseteq Q$ holds, the process Q can be safely used in place of process P because every "test" that P passes is passed also by Q. Fair testing adds a fairness assumption to standard testing: if a system goes infinitely often through a state from which some action is possible (like the action q!b from state T in Figure 2), a component of the system may rely upon the eventual observation of that action to terminate successfully. In the present paper, we instantiate fair testing to a context where processes are session types describing the behavior of participants of a multi-party session and the "test" is given by the correctness of a session.

Since the $\sqsubseteq$ relation is defined by universally quantifying over an infinite number of tests, a crucial aspect of every testing theory is the study of alternative, possibly effective characterizations of $\sqsubseteq$ or approximations of it. Alternative characterizations of refinements not considering fairness have been defined, for example, in [13,14] and later, in coinductive form, in [7] and in [4,1]. Alternative characterizations of fair refinements have already been given in the literature, but we find them unsatisfactory. The authors of [18] present a characterization based on sets of infinite strings, while [21] relies on a denotational model of processes. In both cases the characterizations are quite complex, if compared to those of corresponding unfair refinements, because they are semantically – rather than syntactically – based. In fact, as pointed out in [21], no complete axiomatization of these refinements is known at the present time. Recently, [2,3] have investigated subcontract relations for Web services which are closely related to fair subtyping of session types, but they refer to [21] when it comes to characterizing and deciding them. The authors of [4] provide a coinductive characterization that is not complete (for instance, it fails to assess that T is a subtype of S_2 in Figure 1). The standard reference for subtyping of session types is [12], where the subtyping relation is "unfair" by definition. A fair theory of multi-party session types has been developed in [19], but no alternative characterizations nor algorithms were given.

Contributions. This paper presents a self-contained theory of multi-party session types where the focus is on the eventual satisfaction of all the interacting participants. From a technical viewpoint, the main novelty is an alternative characterization of the fair subtyping relation which is expressed as the combination of the familiar, "unfair" subtyping relation [12] and a "ruled by" relation which can be expressed as a syntax-directed notion of behavioral difference between session types. This allows us to present a complete deduction system for the subtyping relation as a minor variation of the standard one, up to the use of the "ruled by" relation.

Structure of the paper. In Section 2 we formalize the language of (multi-party) session types, the notion of correct session, and subtyping as the relation that preserves correctness. We show that our subtyping differs from the standard one. Section 3 provides a sound and complete coinductive characterization of subtyping based on the "ruled by" relation. Section 4 presents algorithms for deciding subtyping and related notions. Section 5 concludes. Proofs and auxiliary technical material are available in the appendix of the full version of the paper [20].

2   Syntax and Semantics of Session Types

We assume a set $\mathscr{R}$ of *role tags* ranged over by p, q, ..., a countable set $\mathscr{M}$ of *message types* ranged over by a, b, ..., and a countable set $\mathscr{X}$ of *recursion variables* ranged over by x, y, ... Table 1 defines the syntax of sessions and session types. *Sessions*, ranged over by M, N, ..., are finite compositions $p_1 : T_1 | \cdots | p_n : T_n$ made of a fixed number of participants that communicate with each other according to the session types T_i. We work exclusively with well-formed sessions, where each participant is uniquely identified by a tag p_i ($i \neq j$ implies $p_i \neq p_j$). Session types, ranged over by T, S, ..., are the closed terms generated by the grammar in Table 1 such that:

- every recursion variable is guarded by at least one (input or output) prefix, and
- in every subterm $\sum_{i\in I} p?a_i.T_i$ or $\bigoplus_{i\in I} p!a_i.T_i$ the a_i's are pairwise distinct.

The first condition forbids non-contractive session types such as $\mu x.x$, while the second condition ensures that session types are unambiguous by requiring that every prefix of the form $p?a_i$ or $p!a_i$ uniquely determines a continuation T_i. We consider session types modulo the folding and unfolding of recursive terms. Therefore, we assume $\mu x.T = T\{\mu x.T/x\}$ where $T\{\mu x.T/x\}$ denotes the session type obtained from T by replacing every free occurrence of x in T with $\mu x.T$ (μ is the only binder for recursion variables, and the notions of free and bound variables are defined as expected). In practice, this amounts to saying that session types are the possibly infinite, finitely-branching, regular trees [8] generated by the productions of the grammar in Table 1. Note that all the session types defined in the introduction can be finitely and uniquely expressed as possibly recursive terms generated by the grammar in Table 1.

Table 1. Syntax of session types and sessions

$T ::=$	**Session Type**	$M ::=$	**Session**
fail	(failure)	$p : T$	(participant)
$\mid$ end	(termination)	$\mid M \mid M$	(composition)
$\mid x$	(variable)		
$\mid \sum_{i\in I} p?a_i.T_i$	(input)		
$\mid \bigoplus_{i\in I} p!a_i.T_i$	(output)		
$\mid \mu x.T$	(recursion)		

The session type end describes a process that no longer participates to the session. The session type $\sum_{i\in I} p?a_i.T_i$ describes a process that waits for a message from the source participant identified by tag p: depending on the type a_i of the message it receives, the process behaves according to the continuation T_i. The session type $\bigoplus_{i\in I} p!a_i.T_i$ describes a process that internally decides to send a message of type a_i to the destination participant identified by tag p. After the output operation the process behaves as described in the session type T_i. Terms x and $\mu x.T$ are used to build recursive session types. It is technically convenient (although not necessary) to have a canonical term fail describing *failed processes* that are unable to terminate successfully. This happens, for example, if a participant receives an unexpected message. Sometimes we will use the infix notation $p?a_1.T_1 + \cdots + p?a_n.T_n$ to denote $\sum_{i=1}^n p?a_i.T_i$ and $p!a_1.T_1 \oplus \cdots \oplus p!a_n.T_n$ to denote $\bigoplus_{i=1}^n p!a_i.T_i$. Note that mixed choices like $p?a.T + p!b.S$ and $p?a.T + q?a.S$ are forbidden. In particular, the source participant p and the destination participant p in $\sum_{i\in I} p?a_i.T_i$ and $\bigoplus_{i=1}^n p!a_i.T_i$ must be the same in all branches (all the examples in the introduction are consistent with these conventions). While slightly redundant, the syntax for inputs and outputs allows us to conveniently switch between the prefix forms and the corresponding infix forms. Also, we will write trees(T) for the finite set of subtrees that T is made of, including T itself (recall that a regular tree is made of a *finite* number of distinct subtrees [8]). Take for example $T = \mu x.(p!a.q?c.x \oplus p!b.\text{end})$. Then trees($T$) $= \{T, q?c.T, \text{end}\}$.

We express the evolution of a session by means of a transition system. The idea is that each participant of a session behaves as described by the corresponding session type and the session evolves by means of internal choices taken by the participants and by synchronizations occurring between them. Labels of the transition system, ranged over by $\hat{\alpha}$, are generated by the grammar

$$\hat{\alpha} ::= \tau \mid \checkmark \mid p:p?a \mid p:p!a$$

and we use α to range over actions different from τ.

Table 2. Transition system of sessions

(T-SUCCESS) $p:\text{end} \xrightarrow{\checkmark} p:\text{end}$	(T-OUTPUT) $p:q!a.T \xrightarrow{p:q!a} p:T$	(T-CHOICE) $\dfrac{k\in I}{p:\bigoplus_{i\in I}q!a_i.T_i \xrightarrow{\tau} p:q!a_k.T_k}$
	(T-INPUT) $\dfrac{k\in I}{p:\sum_{i\in I}q?a_i.T_i \xrightarrow{p:q?a_k} p:T_k}$	(T-FAILURE) $\dfrac{a\neq a_i\ (i\in I)}{p:\sum_{i\in I}q?a_i.T_i \xrightarrow{p:q?a} p:\text{fail}}$
(T-PAR ACTION) $\dfrac{M\xrightarrow{\hat{\alpha}}M' \quad \hat{\alpha}\neq\checkmark}{M\mid N \xrightarrow{\hat{\alpha}} M'\mid N}$	(T-COMM) $\dfrac{M\xrightarrow{p:q!a}M' \quad N\xrightarrow{q:p?a}N'}{M\mid N \xrightarrow{\tau} M'\mid N'}$	(T-PAR SUCCESS) $\dfrac{M\xrightarrow{\checkmark}M \quad N\xrightarrow{\checkmark}N}{M\mid N \xrightarrow{\checkmark} M\mid N}$

Table 2 defines the transition system (symmetric rules omitted) in terms of a family of labelled relations $\xrightarrow{\hat{\alpha}}$. Rule (T-SUCCESS) states that end performs a $\checkmark$ action that flags successful termination and reduces to itself. Rules (T-OUTPUT) and (T-CHOICE) deal with outputs. The former one shows that a participant p willing to send an a message to participant q performs a $p:q!a$ action. The latter one states that a participant that is ready to send any message from a set internally and irrevocably chooses one particular message to send. In both rules we use the abbreviation $q!a_0.T_0$ for $\bigoplus_{i\in\{0\}}q!a_i.T_i$. Rules (T-INPUT) and (T-FAILURE) deal with inputs. The former one is standard and states that a participant p performs $p : q?a$ actions according to the type of messages it is willing to receive and the participant q from which it expects these messages to come. The latter shows that a participant can receive an unexpected input, but in doing so it will fail. Note the fundamental asymmetry between inputs and outputs: a participant autonomously commits to sending *one* particular message by means of rule (T-CHOICE), while it retains the ability to receive *any* message from a given set by means of rule (T-INPUT). Rule (T-PAR ACTION) propagates transitions through compositions and (T-COMM) is the usual communication rule. Finally, (T-PAR SUCCESS) states that a composition has successfully terminated if all of its participants have. In the following we adopt the following conventions: we write $\overset{\tau}{\Longrightarrow}$ for the reflexive, transitive closure of $\overset{\tau}{\longrightarrow}$; we write $\overset{\alpha}{\Longrightarrow}$ for $\overset{\tau}{\Longrightarrow}\overset{\alpha}{\longrightarrow}\overset{\tau}{\Longrightarrow}$ and $\overset{\alpha_1\cdots\alpha_n}{\Longrightarrow}$ for the composition $\overset{\alpha_1}{\Longrightarrow}\cdots\overset{\alpha_n}{\Longrightarrow}$; we let s, $t, \dots$ range over finite strings of actions different from $\checkmark$; we write $M \overset{\alpha}{\longrightarrow}$ (respectively, $M \overset{\alpha}{\Longrightarrow}$) if there exists N such that $M \overset{\alpha}{\longrightarrow} N$ (respectively, $M \overset{\alpha}{\Longrightarrow} N$); we write $M \overset{\alpha}{\nrightarrow}$ (respectively, $M \overset{\alpha}{\nRightarrow}$) if there exists no N such that $M \overset{\alpha}{\longrightarrow} N$ (respectively, $M \overset{\alpha}{\Longrightarrow} N$). We also extend the labelled transition relation and the above notation to session types so that, for example, $T \overset{\alpha}{\longrightarrow} S$ if $p : T \overset{\alpha}{\longrightarrow} p : S$ for some p.

Intuitively, a session is correct if the possibility to reach a state where every participant is successfully terminated is invariant under reductions. This can be formalized as follows:

Definition 2.1 (correct session). *We say that M is* correct *if $M \overset{\tau}{\Longrightarrow} N$ implies $N \overset{\checkmark}{\Longrightarrow}$.*

In Section 1 we have already seen a number of correct sessions, which the reader may now formally check against Definition 2.1. It is useful to discuss a few examples of *incorrect* sessions. For instance, $M = p : q!a.\text{end} \oplus q!b.\text{end} \,|\, q : p?a.\text{end}$ is not correct because p may decide to send a b message that q is not willing to receive. Even though at the beginning of the interaction there is one potential path leading to successful termination (indeed $M \overset{\checkmark}{\Longrightarrow}$), rule (T-CHOICE) can make the decision of sending b irrevocable (in this case $M \overset{\tau}{\longrightarrow} p : q!b.\text{end} \,|\, q : p?a.\text{end} \overset{\tau}{\longrightarrow} p : \text{end} \,|\, q : \text{fail} \overset{\checkmark}{\nRightarrow}$). There are also intrinsically flawed session types that can never be part of correct sessions. For example, the session $M \,|\, p : \text{fail}$ is incorrect regardless of M, because fail is never able to perform $\checkmark$. Some sessions are incorrect despite that no fail term occurs in them. This happens in the session $p : \mu x.q!a.x \,|\, q : \mu y.p?a.y$ because, even though the participants p and q keep interacting with each other, they do not have the ability to terminate the interaction.

Some properties of correct sessions are easy to verify: $p : \text{end}$ is the simplest correct session; the session $M \,|\, p : \text{end}$ is correct if and only if M is correct; finally, correctness is preserved by reductions: if M is correct and $M \Longrightarrow N$, then N is also correct.

We define the subtyping relation for session types semantically as the relation that preserves correctness: we say that T is a *subtype* of S if every session $M \,|\, p : T$ that is correct remains correct when we replace T with S. Formally:

Definition 2.2 (subtyping). *We say that T is a* subtype *of S, written $T \leqslant S$, if $M \,|\, p : T$ correct implies $M \,|\, p : S$ correct for every M. We write $\lesseqgtr$ for the equivalence relation induced by $\leqslant$, namely $\lesseqgtr = \leqslant \cap \leqslant^{-1}$.*

This definition may look surprising at first, because it speaks about left-to-right substitutability (of behaviors), while subtyping is concerned with right-to-left substitutability (of channels). The mismatch is only apparent, however, and is due to the fact that session types are behavioral types (they describe the behavior of processes using channels). To clarify this point, suppose that S is the type associated with a channel c and that some process P uses c as indicated by S. By replacing channel c in P with another channel d with type $T \leqslant S$, we are changing the set of processes that P is interacting with, which together behave according to some M such that $M \mid \mathsf{p} : T$ is correct. Replacing c with d does *not* affect the way P behaves: P uses channel d (whose actual type is T) as if it were channel c (thus according to S). This means that the actual implemented session is $M \mid \mathsf{p} : S$. Since $T \leqslant S$, we know that this session is correct.

A thorough study of the subtyping relation that solely relies on Definition 2.2 is hard, because of the universal quantification over an infinite set of contexts M. Nonetheless, a few relations are easy to establish. For example, we have

(i) $\mathsf{p}?a.\mathsf{end} \leqslant \mathsf{p}?a.\mathsf{end} + \mathsf{p}?b.\mathsf{end}$ and   **(ii)** $\mathsf{p}!a.\mathsf{end} \oplus \mathsf{p}!b.\mathsf{end} \leqslant \mathsf{p}!a.\mathsf{end}$

namely $\leqslant$ behaves covariantly with respect to inputs and contravariantly with respect to outputs, *on finite session types*. The two relations can be explained as follows: in **(i)**, every context M such that $M \mid \mathsf{q} : \mathsf{p}?a.\mathsf{end}$ is correct must eventually send some message to q, and this message can only be a for otherwise q would fail because of rule (T-FAILURE). Therefore, $M \mid \mathsf{q} : \mathsf{p}?a.\mathsf{end} + \mathsf{p}?b.\mathsf{end}$ is also correct, since $\mathsf{p}?a.\mathsf{end} + \mathsf{p}?b.\mathsf{end}$ is more receptive than $\mathsf{p}?a.\mathsf{end}$. In **(ii)**, every context M such that $M \mid \mathsf{q} : \mathsf{p}!a.\mathsf{end} \oplus \mathsf{p}!b.\mathsf{end}$ is correct must be able to terminate successfully no matter which message (either a or b) is sent to p. One such context is $M = \mathsf{p} : \mathsf{q}?a.\mathsf{end} + \mathsf{q}?b.\mathsf{end}$. Therefore, nothing bad happens when we replace $\mathsf{p}!a.\mathsf{end} \oplus \mathsf{p}!b.\mathsf{end}$ with a more deterministic behavior, such as $\mathsf{p}!a.\mathsf{end}$. As a general note, observe that relation **(i)** *increases* (and relation **(ii)** *decreases*) the number of paths along the session types that lead to end when one reads the relations from left to right. Since correctness concerns the reachability of a successfully terminated state, it is not obvious that reducing the number of paths leading to end is generally safe, as we have already argued in the introduction.

The standard subtyping relation for session types [12], which we dub "unfair subtyping" to distinguish it from the one of Definition 2.2, is defined thus:

Definition 2.3 (unfair subtyping). *We say that $\mathscr{S}$ is a coinductive subtyping if $T \mathrel{\mathscr{S}} S$ implies either:*

1. *$T = S = \mathsf{end}$, or*
2. *$T = \sum_{i \in I} \mathsf{p}?a_i.T_i$ and $S = \sum_{i \in I \cup J} \mathsf{p}?a_i.S_i$ and $T_i \mathrel{\mathscr{S}} S_i$ for every $i \in I$, or*
3. *$T = \bigoplus_{i \in I \cup J} \mathsf{p}!a_i.T_i$ and $S = \bigoplus_{i \in I} \mathsf{p}!a_i.S_i$ and $T_i \mathrel{\mathscr{S}} S_i$ for every $i \in I$.*

Unfair subtyping, *denoted by $\leqslant_\mathsf{U}$, is the largest coinductive subtyping.*

Item (1) states that the only subtype of end is end. Item (2) is the standard *covariant* rule for input actions: it is safe for a process that is capable of handling a set $\{a_i\}_{i \in I \cup J}$ of incoming message types to wait for messages from a channel on which a subset $\{a_i\}_{i \in I}$ of message types can be received. Item (3) is dual of item (2) and deals with outputs. It states that a process can safely use a channel on which messages from the set $\{a_i\}_{i \in I \cup J}$ can be sent if it never sends a message that is not in this set.

The relation $\leqslant_U$ is appealing because of its simple and intuitive definition, but it is neither sound nor complete if compared with $\leqslant$. On the one hand, the $\leqslant_U$ relation does not preserve correctness as by Definition 2.1. For instance, the reader may verify that $T \leqslant_U S_\infty$ holds for T and S_∞ defined in the introduction, but $T \not\leqslant S_\infty$ because S_∞ has no end subtree. On the other hand, there exists a large class of equivalent session types that are syntactically unrelated. For instance, we have $S_\infty \leqslant$ fail and $S_\infty \not\leqslant_U$ fail. Session types like fail or S_∞ are flawed because there is no correct session in which they can occur. Therefore, they are the $\leqslant$-least elements and roughly correspond to the empty type in other type theories. Patching Definition 2.3 to take flawed session types into proper account is far from trivial (adding a case for dealing with fail session types is not enough, as S_∞ shows).

3   Coinductive Fair Subtyping

We devote this section to defining a complete, coinductive characterization of $\leqslant$. To ease the presentation, we proceed incrementally in three steps: **(1)** we introduce a normal form for session types that allows us to focus on the subclass of *viable* session types, those that can be part of correct sessions and that, consequently, are the most relevant in practice; **(2)** we express $T \leqslant S$ as the combination of two relations, the familiar (but unsafe) $T \leqslant_U S$ subtyping for session types (which is shown to include $\leqslant$ when restricted to viable session types in normal form) and a $T \prec S$ relation that holds when the paths leading to successful termination in T that have disappeared from S do not endanger correctness; **(3)** we show that the $T \prec S$ relation is equivalent to the viability of a suitably defined $T - S$ session type, somehow representing the "behavioral difference" between T and S.

Normal form.   At the end of Section 2 we have seen that there exist flawed session types that cannot occur in any correct session. Session types that *can* occur in correct sessions are our primary concern and we reserve a name for them.

Definition 3.1 (viability). *We say that T is* viable *if $M \,|\, \mathrm{p} : T$ is correct for some M and* p. *We write $\mathscr{T}_v$ for the set of viable session types.*

A session type T is *not* viable if and only if $T \leqslant$ fail. That is, being not viable means being ($\leqslant$-smaller than) the empty type. The existence of non-viable session types hinders the coinductive characterization of the subtyping relation in the style of Definition 2.3 because these characterizations are based on the intuition that semantically related session types must be syntactically similar, while we have shown that this is not necessarily true when non-viable session types are involved. We define a normal form that makes non-viable session types readily detectable and the syntax of viable ones meaningful in a sense that will be clarified shortly.

Definition 3.2 (normal form). *We say that T is in* normal form *if either $T =$ fail or* end $\in$ trees(S) *for every $S \in$ trees(T). We write $\mathscr{T}_{nf}$ for the set of session types in normal form.*

The double indirection in Definition 3.2 imposes that an end leaf is included in *every* subtree of T when T is different from fail. For example p?a.end $+$ p?b.fail is not in normal form because fail $\in$ trees(p?a.end $+$ p?b.fail) and end $\notin$ trees(fail). The following proposition assures us that working with session types in normal forms is convenient and yet not restrictive: every session type has an $\leqslant$-equivalent one in normal form and every session type in normal form different from fail is viable.

Proposition 3.1. *The following properties hold: (1) for every $T \in \mathscr{T}$ there exists $S \in \mathscr{T}_{nf}$ such that $T \leqslant S$; (2) $\mathscr{T}_{nf} \setminus \{\text{fail}\} \subseteq \mathscr{T}_v$.*

For instance, p?a.end is the normal form of p?a.end $+$ p?b.fail. The syntax of session types in normal form is "meaningful" in the sense that $\leqslant_U$ includes $\leqslant$ when we focus on viable session types in normal form.

Theorem 3.1. *Let $T, S \in \mathscr{T}_{nf} \setminus \{\text{fail}\}$. Then $T \leqslant S$ implies $T \leqslant_U S$.*

Unfair subtyping and $\leqslant$ decomposition. Focusing on viable session types in normal form does not change the fact that $\leqslant_U$ is unsound with respect to $\leqslant$. More precisely, $\leqslant_U$ does not introduce deadlocks, but it can introduce livelocks when recursive session types are involved:

Theorem 3.2. *Let $T, S \in \mathscr{T}_{nf}$ and $T \leqslant_U S$. Then:*

1. *T recursion-free implies $T \leqslant S$;*
2. *$M \mid \mathrm{p} : T$ correct and $M \mid \mathrm{p} : S \stackrel{\tau}{\Longrightarrow} N \stackrel{\tau}{\nrightarrow}$ imply $N \stackrel{\checkmark}{\longrightarrow}$.*

Theorem 3.2 shows that $\leqslant_U$ is not too far away from being a sound characterization of $\leqslant$. Therefore, we attempt at characterizing $T \leqslant S$ as the combination of two relations: $T \leqslant_U S$, expressing a *safety* property (S does not introduce deadlocks), and $T \prec S$, expressing a *liveness* property (S does not preclude the successful termination of any context that completes T). The "ruled by" relation $\prec$ is defined thus:

Definition 3.3. *Let $T, S \in \mathscr{T}_{nf}$ and $T \leqslant_U S$. We say that T is ruled by S, written $T \prec S$, if $M \mid \mathrm{p} : T$ correct implies $M \mid \mathrm{p} : S \stackrel{\checkmark}{\Longrightarrow}$ for every M.*

When $T \leqslant_U S$, the behavior S may preclude successful termination of a context M that completes T only when some outputs in T have disappeared in S. The additional property $T \prec S$ prevents this from happening. Observe that $T \leqslant S$ implies $T \prec S$, but the converse is not true in general. In fact, $\prec$ precisely captures the difference between $\leqslant_U$ and $\leqslant$, in the following sense:

Definition 3.4 (coinductive fair subtyping). *A coinductive subtyping $\mathscr{S}$ is fair if $T \mathscr{S} S$ implies $T \prec S$. We write $\leqslant_C$ for the largest coinductive fair subtyping.*

The relation $\leqslant_C$ is indeed the characterization of $\leqslant$ we are looking for:

Theorem 3.3. *Let $T, S \in \mathscr{T}_{nf} \setminus \{\text{fail}\}$. Then $T \leqslant S$ if and only if $T \leqslant_C S$.*

Characterization of $\prec$ and behavioral difference. We now shift the focus to the $\prec$ relation. Suppose $T \leqslant_U S$ and $T \not\prec S$. Then there exists some context M such that the correctness of $M \mid p : T$ crucially depends on the outputs that T emits and that S does not. In order to find M, we define a session type $T - S$ that somehow represents the "difference" between T and S and that is viable if (and only if) such M does exist. The intuition is that $T - S$ differs from T and S in three respects:

1. Every end that lies on a path shared by T and S is turned to a fail in $T - S$. Therefore, any hypothetical context M such that $M \mid p : T - S$ is correct can only count on those end leaves found in T that have disappeared in S.
2. $T - S$ performs no more inputs than those performed by T. In this way we stay assured that, if M exists, it does not use any additional input capability provided by S but not by T.
3. $T - S$ performs all the outputs performed by T.

Formally:

Definition 3.5 (session type difference). *Let* $T \leqslant_U S$. *The difference of* T *and* S, *denoted by* $T - S$, *is coinductively defined by the following equations:*

$$\text{end} - \text{end} = \text{fail}$$
$$\sum_{i \in I} p?a_i.T_i - \sum_{i \in I \cup J} p?a_i.S_i = \sum_{i \in I} p?a_i.(T_i - S_i)$$
$$\bigoplus_{i \in I \cup J} p!a_i.T_i - \bigoplus_{i \in I} p!a_i.S_i = \bigoplus_{i \in J \setminus I} p!a_i.T_i \oplus \bigoplus_{i \in I} p!a_i.(T_i - S_i)$$

To make acquaintance with '$-$' let us revisit some of the examples in the introduction. Let $T = \mu x.(q!a.x \oplus q!b.\text{end})$ and $S_n = \mu y.((q!a.)^n y \oplus q!b.\text{end})$. We have

$$T - S_n = \mu z.(\underbrace{q!a.(q!a.(\cdots(q!a.z \oplus q!b.\text{end})\cdots)}_{n} \oplus q!b.\text{end})}_{n-1} \oplus q!b.\text{fail})$$

and $T - S_\infty = T$. Observe that $T - S_\infty$ is viable, while no $T - S_n$ is because of the $q!b.\text{fail}$ branch. Also, when either T or S is finite $T - S$ is never viable. For example, $T - q!b.\text{end} = q!a.T \oplus q!b.\text{fail}$ and $T - q!a.q!b.\text{end} = q!a.(q!a.T \oplus q!b.\text{fail}) \oplus q!b.\text{end}$. This is consistent with Theorem 3.2(1), showing that $\leqslant_U$ and $\leqslant$ coincide when the $\leqslant_U$-smaller session type is finite. In general, we can prove that $T \prec S$ holds if and only if the difference between T and S is not viable.

Theorem 3.4. *Let* $T, S \in \mathscr{T}_{\text{nf}}$ *and* $T \leqslant_U S$. *Then* $T \prec S$ *if and only if* $T - S$ *is not viable.*

On the practical side, Theorem 3.4 allows us to decide $T \prec S$ if we can decide the viability of a session type (we will address this in Section 4). On the theoretical side, it highlights an interesting analogy between our framework and that of semantic subtyping [11], which also motivates the notation $T - S$. We have observed that "being not viable" is equivalent to "being smaller than fail", and that fail somehow represents the empty type in our theory. Therefore, a consequence of Theorems 3.3 and 3.4 is that in order to decide $T \leqslant S$ one has to decide whether $T - S \leqslant \text{fail}$. This reformulation is precisely the one used in the framework of semantic subtyping, where types are interpreted as sets of values and deciding the subtyping relation $\sigma \subseteq \tau$ is equivalent to deciding the emptiness of $\sigma \setminus \tau$. Note however that $T \prec S$ alone does not imply $T \leqslant S$. For example, we have $q!a.T \oplus q!b.\text{end} \prec q!a.S \oplus q!b.\text{end}$ where $T = \mu x.(q?a.(q!a.x \oplus q!b.T) + q?b.\text{end})$ and $S = \mu y.(q?a.q!a.y + q?b.\text{end})$. Still, $q!a.T \oplus q!b.\text{end} \not\leqslant q!a.S \oplus q!b.\text{end}$ because $T \not\leqslant S$, as we already know.

4   Algorithms

In this section we define algorithms for deciding viability, for computing the normal form of viable session types, and for deciding subtyping. We also discuss the decidability of session correctness.

Viability. The viability of a session type T is tightly related to the reachability of end subtrees occurring in it. The algorithm we propose assumes initially that every subtree of T is viable and iteratively discards those subtrees for which this assumption is disproved. Each iteration performs three checks: a subtree $S \in \mathsf{trees}(T)$ is viable provided that end can be reached from it; input nodes are viable provided that there is at least one branch that is viable; output nodes are viable provided that every branch is viable. Formally, let the *viability sequence* for T be the sequence $\{\mathbf{V}_i^T\}_{i \in \mathbb{N}}$ of sets of session types defined in the following way, where $\leq$ is the usual prefix relation between strings of actions:

$$\mathbf{V}_0^T = \mathsf{trees}(T)$$
$$\mathbf{V}_{2i+1}^T = \{S \in \mathbf{V}_{2i}^T \mid \exists s : S \xRightarrow{s} \mathsf{end}, \forall t \leq s : S \xRightarrow{t} S' \in \mathsf{trees}(T) \Rightarrow S' \in \mathbf{V}_{2i}^T\}$$
$$\mathbf{V}_{2i+2}^T = \{\mathsf{end} \in \mathbf{V}_{2i+1}^T\} \cup \{\textstyle\sum_{j \in I} \mathsf{p}?a_j.T_j \in \mathbf{V}_{2i+1}^T \mid \exists j \in I : T_j \in \mathbf{V}_{2i+1}^T\}$$
$$\cup \{\textstyle\bigoplus_{j \in I} \mathsf{p}!a_j.T_j \in \mathbf{V}_{2i+1}^T \mid \forall j \in I : T_j \in \mathbf{V}_{2i+1}^T\}$$

Observe that, in computing $\mathbf{V}_{2i+1}^T$, it is not enough to be able to reach an end subtree from S to declare S viable. It must be the case that every subtree along the path $S \xRightarrow{s} \mathsf{end}$ has not been proved non-viable. Note also that, in principle, the computation of $\mathbf{V}_{2i+1}^T$ may need to consider an infinite number of strings s such that $S \xRightarrow{s}$. However, it is enough to consider those paths such that the derivation $S \xRightarrow{s}$ never goes through the same subtree twice. Since session types are regular trees and have a finite number of distinct subtrees, it always suffices to consider a finite number of paths. Every set in the sequence is finite and the sequence is decreasing. Therefore, there exists $k \in \mathbb{N}$ such that $\mathbf{V}_k^T = \mathbf{V}_{k+1}^T = \mathbf{V}_{k+2}^T$. We denote the fixpoint of the sequence with $\mathsf{viables}(T)$.

Theorem 4.1 (viability). $T \in \mathscr{T}_{\mathsf{v}}$ *if and only if* $T \in \mathsf{viables}(T)$.

Normal form. Once we know how to identify viable session types, computing their normal form is only a matter of pruning away those subtrees that are not viable. The normal form of T, denoted by $\mathsf{nf}(T)$, is defined coinductively by the following equations:

$$\mathsf{nf}(T) = \mathsf{fail} \qquad\qquad\qquad \text{if } T \notin \mathscr{T}_{\mathsf{v}}$$
$$\mathsf{nf}(\mathsf{end}) = \mathsf{end}$$
$$\mathsf{nf}(\textstyle\sum_{i \in I} \mathsf{p}?a_i.T_i) = \textstyle\sum_{i \in I, \mathsf{nf}(T_i) \neq \mathsf{fail}} \mathsf{p}?a_i.\mathsf{nf}(T_i)$$
$$\mathsf{nf}(\textstyle\bigoplus_{i \in I} \mathsf{p}!a_i.T_i) = \textstyle\bigoplus_{i \in I} \mathsf{p}!a_i.\mathsf{nf}(T_i)$$

(all the equations but the first one apply only to viable session types).

Theorem 4.2 (normal form). *For every T, $\mathrm{nf}(T)$ is in normal form and $T \lesssim \mathrm{nf}(T)$.*

Fair subtyping. We present a complete, algorithmic deduction system for the subtyping relation, which is coinductively defined in Table 3 (the corresponding inductive system can be obtained with standard memoization techniques). Rules (FS-END) and (FS-INPUT) are just the same as in well-known deduction systems for the unfair subtyping relation (see, e.g., [12]). Rule (FS-FAIL) states that fail is the least element according to $\leqslant_A$. Rule (FS-OUTPUT) is similar to the familiar contravariant rule for outputs, except that it is applicable only when the smaller session type is ruled by the larger one, which can be determined by checking the viability of the difference of the two session types. It is enough to check the condition $T \prec S$ only when T and S are outputs. This is shown to imply that the condition holds whenever $T \leqslant_A S$ is provable.

Table 3. Deduction system for the subtyping relation

(FS-FAIL)	(FS-END)	(FS-INPUT)	(FS-OUTPUT)
$\mathsf{fail} \leqslant_A T$	$\mathsf{end} \leqslant_A \mathsf{end}$	$\dfrac{T_i \leqslant_A S_i \;^{(i \in I)}}{\sum_{i \in I} \mathsf{p}?a_i.T_i \leqslant_A \sum_{i \in I \cup J} \mathsf{p}?a_i.S_i}$	$\dfrac{T_i \leqslant_A S_i \;^{(i \in I)} \qquad \mathrm{nf}(T - S) = \mathsf{fail}}{T = \bigoplus_{i \in I \cup J} \mathsf{p}!a_i.T_i \leqslant_A \bigoplus_{i \in I} \mathsf{p}!a_i.S_i = S}$

Theorem 4.3. *$T \leqslant S$ if and only if $\mathrm{nf}(T) \leqslant_A \mathrm{nf}(S)$.*

It seems like the $\prec$ relation does not admit a simple axiomatization. The problem is that the $\leqslant$ relation is not local, in the sense that the applicability of rule (FS-OUTPUT) may depend upon regions of the session types that are arbitrarily far away from the place where it is applied. Consider for instance the session type

$$T = \mu x. \mathsf{q}!a.(\mathsf{q}?a.)^n (\mathsf{q}!a.(\mathsf{q}?a.)^n x \oplus \mathsf{q}!b.\mathsf{end}) \oplus \mathsf{q}!b.\mathsf{end}$$

and observe that the two $\mathsf{q}!b$ branches can be arbitrarily distant depending on the number n of input actions. Both the session types

$$S_1 = \mu x. \mathsf{q}!a.(\mathsf{q}?a.)^n (\mathsf{q}!a.(\mathsf{q}?a.)^n x \oplus \mathsf{q}!b.\mathsf{end})$$
$$S_2 = \mu y. (\mathsf{q}!a.(\mathsf{q}?a.)^n \mathsf{q}!a.(\mathsf{q}?a.)^n y \oplus \mathsf{q}!b.\mathsf{end})$$

are supertypes of T and they differ from T because one of the two $\mathsf{q}!b.\mathsf{end}$ branches has been pruned. However, pruning both branches results into a non-viable session type. Therefore, one branch can be safely removed only if the other one is not.

Correctness. We conclude this section with a few considerations on the decidability of correctness. Observe that, since session types are regular and finite branching, the set $\mathscr{R}(M) \stackrel{\mathrm{def}}{=} \{N \mid M \stackrel{\tau}{\Longrightarrow} N\}$ is finite and can be computed in finite time by exploring every session reachable from M. Now M is correct if and only if for every $N \in \mathscr{R}(M)$ there exists $N' \in \mathscr{R}(N)$ such that $N' \stackrel{\checkmark}{\longrightarrow}$.

In the special case of binary sessions, when only two participants p and q are involved, the session $p : T \mid q : \overline{T}$ is always correct, assuming that q is the only role occurring in T, that T is in normal form, and that $\overline{T}$ is the *dual* of T coinductively defined by:

$$\overline{\text{end}} = \text{end} \qquad \overline{\sum_{i \in I} q?a_i.T_i} = \bigoplus_{i \in I} p!a_i.\overline{T_i} \qquad \overline{\bigoplus_{i \in I} q!a_i.T_i} = \sum_{i \in I} p?a_i.\overline{T_i}$$

By definition of $\leqslant$, every session $p : T \mid q : S$ where $\overline{T} \leqslant S$ is also correct. However, the converse is not true. That is, there are correct sessions $p : T \mid q : S$ where $\overline{T} \not\leqslant S$, for example when $T = \mu x.(q!a.(q?a.x + q?b.x) \oplus q!b.\text{end})$ and $S = \mu y.(p?a.p!a.y + p?b.\text{end})$. This is in sharp contrast with the unfair theories [12,6], where $p : T \mid q : S$ is correct (in the "unfair" sense) if and only if $\overline{T} \leqslant_{\mathsf{U}} S$.

5   Conclusions

The standard subtyping relation for session types may compromise liveness of multi-party sessions. Even in dyadic sessions it might be desirable not to lose the ability to reach successful termination of the interacting parties. These scenarios naturally call for the definition of (multi-party) session type theories where every participant preserves the possibility to reach a successfully terminated state.

Fair subtyping relations (often referred to as refinements in concurrency theory) have rightfully gained the fame of being hard to characterize completely [18,21] or even to approximate [4,19]. In this paper we have fully characterized the fair subtyping relation as a simple variation of standard subtyping [12,6]. It is not entirely clear how much the characterization of the subtyping relation we have given owes to the fact that we work with a very primitive process language. The proof of the characterization (Theorem 3.3) only needs the semantic definition of $\prec$ (Definition 3.3) and therefore should be generalizable to full-featured process languages. It is not obvious, and thus subject to future investigation, whether the same holds for the notion of difference (Definition 3.5).

Checking whether a multi-party session is correct can be more expensive than in dyadic theories (Section 4). This observation substantiates the effectiveness of the design-by-contract approach advocated in [5,17], where the session types of a multi-party session are obtained as projections of a global type associated with the session. The approach guarantees that the resulting session is correct by construction. However, it may be necessary to use subtyping both during the projection as well as while type checking processes against the session types of the channels they use. Therefore, it is fundamental for subtyping to preserve session liveness (in the sense of Definition 2.1). Type checking processes using a fair subtyping relation seems to pose interesting technical problems, because of the interplay between coinductive typing of recursive processes and the liveness property we want to enforce on sessions. We leave these issues for future investigations.

Acknowledgments. The author is grateful to Daniele Varacca for the discussions on fairness and to the anonymous referees who helped improving the paper. This work was partially supported by a visiting professor position of the Université Paris Diderot.

References

1. Barbanera, F., de'Liguoro, U.: Two notions of sub-behaviour for session-based client/server systems. In: Proceedings of PPDP 2010, pp. 155–164. ACM, New York (2010)
2. Bravetti, M., Zavattaro, G.: A foundational theory of contracts for multi-party service composition. Fundamenta Informaticae 89(4), 451–478 (2009)
3. Bravetti, M., Zavattaro, G.: A theory of contracts for strong service compliance. Mathematical Structures in Computer Science 19, 601–638 (2009)
4. Bugliesi, M., Macedonio, D., Pino, L., Rossi, S.: Compliance Preorders for Web Services. In: Laneve, C., Su, J. (eds.) WS-FM 2009. LNCS, vol. 6194, pp. 76–91. Springer, Heidelberg (2010)
5. Carbone, M., Honda, K., Yoshida, N.: Structured communication-centred programming for web services. In: De Nicola, R. (ed.) ESOP 2007. LNCS, vol. 4421, pp. 2–17. Springer, Heidelberg (2007)
6. Castagna, G., Dezani-Ciancaglini, M., Giachino, E., Padovani, L.: Foundations of session types. In: Proceedings of PPDP 2009, pp. 219–230. ACM, New York (2009)
7. Castagna, G., Gesbert, N., Padovani, L.: A theory of contracts for Web services. ACM Transactions on Programming Languages and Systems 31(5), 1–61 (2009)
8. Courcelle, B.: Fundamental properties of infinite trees. Theoretical Computer Science 25, 95–169 (1983)
9. De Nicola, R., Hennessy, M.: Testing equivalences for processes. Theoretical Computer Science 34, 83–133 (1984)
10. De Nicola, R., Hennessy, M.: CCS without τ's. In: Ehrig, H., Levi, G., Montanari, U. (eds.) CAAP 1987 and TAPSOFT 1987. LNCS, vol. 249, pp. 138–152. Springer, Heidelberg (1987)
11. Frisch, A., Castagna, G., Benzaken, V.: Semantic subtyping: dealing set-theoretically with function, union, intersection, and negation types. Journal of the ACM 55(4), 1–64 (2008)
12. Gay, S., Hole, M.: Subtyping for session types in the π-calculus. Acta Informatica 42(2-3), 191–225 (2005)
13. Hennessy, M.: Acceptance trees. Journal of the ACM 32(4), 896–928 (1985)
14. Hennessy, M.: Algebraic Theory of Processes. Foundation of Computing. MIT Press, Cambridge (1988)
15. Honda, K.: Types for dyadic interaction. In: Best, E. (ed.) CONCUR 1993. LNCS, vol. 715, pp. 509–523. Springer, Heidelberg (1993)
16. Honda, K., Vasconcelos, V.T., Kubo, M.: Language primitives and type discipline for structured communication-based programming. In: Hankin, C. (ed.) ESOP 1998. LNCS, vol. 1381, pp. 122–138. Springer, Heidelberg (1998)
17. Honda, K., Yoshida, N., Carbone, M.: Multiparty asynchronous session types. In: Proceedings of POPL 2008, pp. 273–284. ACM, New York (2008)
18. Natarajan, V., Cleaveland, R.: Divergence and fair testing. In: Fülöp, Z. (ed.) ICALP 1995. LNCS, vol. 944, pp. 648–659. Springer, Heidelberg (1995)
19. Padovani, L.: Session types at the mirror. EPTCS 12, 71–86 (2009)
20. Padovani, L.: Fair subtyping for multi-party session types (2011), Full version available at http://www.di.unito.it/~padovani/Papers/FairSessionTypes.pdf
21. Rensink, A., Vogler, W.: Fair testing. Information and Computation 205(2), 125–198 (2007)
22. Vasconcelos, V.T.: Fundamentals of session types. In: Bernardo, M., Padovani, L., Zavattaro, G. (eds.) SFM 2009. LNCS, vol. 5569, pp. 158–186. Springer, Heidelberg (2009)

Enabling Cross-Technology Mobile Applications with Network-Aware References

Kevin Pinte, Dries Harnie*, and Theo D'Hondt

Software Languages Lab, Vrije Universiteit Brussel,
Pleinlaan 2, 1050 Brussels, Belgium
{kpinte,dharnie,tjdhondt}@vub.ac.be

Abstract. Mobile devices, such as smart phones, have become ubiquitous. This evolution has given rise to a vast ecosystem of mobile applications. Typically these applications only use a small subset of the networking technologies at their disposal. Building applications that use multiple networking technologies simultaneously or exploit knowledge about the available connections is a laborious task. Programmers must manually keep track of the connectivity state and duplicate communication code per connection type. This paper presents network-aware references, a distributed object-oriented programming abstraction that eases multi-networking for mobile applications and allows programmers to react to changes in the connectivity of different networks around them. We show how network-aware references are implemented and evaluate how well they switch between technologies.

Keywords: Network-awareness, mobile applications, multi-networking, distributed programming, Bluetooth, Wi-Fi.

1 Introduction

In the recent years we have seen a boom in the market of mobile devices such as smart phones and tablets: they have become powerful enough to complement existing computers as internet devices. This evolution has proliferated all kinds of mobile applications for various tasks people need to do on the move. *Pervasive social applications* [1, 2] are a good example of mobile applications: they allow people to interact with their social network no matter where, even at social events themselves. Another example are peer-to-peer ad hoc multiplayer games as found on Nintendo's handheld DS console.

Next to the performance increase, mobile devices have also gained the ability to communicate using several different networking technologies: for example, an iPhone can communicate with other devices using short-range Bluetooth, medium-range Wi-Fi and long-range 3G technologies. More recently, devices such as the Samsung Nexus S have been released with the extremely short-range Near Field Communication (NFC) technology built-in.

Mobile applications typically exploit contextual information (e.g. location, proximity to other users, ...) to better anticipate the needs of users. *Network awareness* is an

---

* Funded by the Prospective Research For Brussels program of IWOIB-IRSIB.

W. De Meuter and G.-C. Roman (Eds.): COORDINATION 2011, LNCS 6721, pp. 142–156, 2011.

integral part of context-awareness [3, 4]. Mobile applications can benefit from being network-aware since mobile devices are constantly on the move and their networking hardware allows them to "sense" devices and access points in the environment. Additionally, mobile applications often need to adapt the content they present to the user to the characteristics of the network connection that is currently being used [5].

We illustrate why network awareness is relevant for mobile applications by introducing a representative pervasive social application called Pixee that allows users to share and follow each other's picture libraries. The Pixee application gathers library information from nearby devices using Bluetooth and offers to follow other users if a library matches the user's profile.

The scenario goes as follows: on the way home from work, Alice and Bob, both Pixee users, happen to be in the same metro car and thus in Bluetooth range. Since they both like pictures of cats, Alice's picture library matches Bob's interests. When Bob arrives home, he opens the Pixee application and it presents him with a selection of picture libraries, including Alice's library. Bob accepts Pixee's suggestion and starts following Alice's picture library. Whenever Alice takes a new picture it is automatically uploaded to Bob. As Alice isn't home yet, Pixee uses her 3G connection to share pictures. In order to optimize for the networking technology used, Pixee resizes pictures before sharing them over 3G. When Bob rides on the metro to work the next day the Pixee application alerts him that Alice is nearby so they can meet in person and chat later. As long as their phones are in Bluetooth range, their phones will exchange high-resolution pictures.

Currently, various high-level middleware solutions exist that enable network awareness [5, 6]. Such solutions use network information to enforce quality of service (QoS): they adapt the application's network usage to optimize for the available bandwidth. However, such solutions do not support using multiple network links simultaneously; instead they choose one primary network link and use the other network links only as backup links. In the networking domain there is low-level support for multi-networking [7, 8]: they allow applications to connect to other devices using different networking technologies simultaneously, and switch seamlessly between these technologies as needed. Applications that use these multi-networking technologies are fully communication-agnostic: all communication is performed in an opaque way. As such, they do not allow the programmer to react to changes in the individual network links they encapsulate, making network awareness hard. Our goal is to provide mobile application programmers with a hybrid solution that allows programs to be network-aware while supporting multiple networking technologies simultaneously.

In this paper we focus on distributed object-oriented programming abstractions to develop mobile applications that exploit network awareness, like Pixee. Distributed object-oriented programming languages rely on the notion of *remote object references* to communicate with objects residing on other devices. Currently, these references use different, usually incompatible APIs for each networking technology. This leads to a lot of duplication: multiple references to the same object can exist simultaneously, potentially using different technologies. Programmers have to do manual bookkeeping to keep track of these different references.

We propose a new programming abstraction, *network-aware references*, that extends the concept of remote object references to abstract over the different networking technologies used. In addition, we provide a high-level API that enables programmers to react to changes in network links and also allows them to control the different network technologies their applications use. The main contributions of this paper are:

1. We identify the challenges involved in developing network-aware programs (section 2);
2. We introduce network-aware references that abstract over the networking technology used (section 3);
3. We propose programmable *network behaviors* as a means for the programmer to adapt communication to the changing network situation (section 4);
4. We show how network-aware references are implemented (section 5) and evaluate their multi-networking aspects (section 6).

To conclude, we discuss existing approaches to network awareness and multi-networking technology in section 7.

2   Challenges in Programming Network-Aware Applications

As mentioned in the introduction, current mobile devices support several networking technologies. They exhibit different characteristics such as bandwidth, energy consumption, communication range, etc. These differences occur not only between technologies, but they can also be found between networking technologies of the same kind. For example, the free Wi-Fi network at an airport is restricted in bandwidth and usage volume compared to a wireless network at home.

To facilitate the development of network-aware mobile applications, several challenges need to be overcome:

C1. Abstraction over networking technologies. A programmer should not be concerned with the low-level details of the networking technologies available. For example, setting up a connection using Bluetooth is very different from a Wi-Fi connection. Instead a unified interface to the different networking technologies should be provided. Communication with this unified interface should take advantage of all available network connections.

C2. Reactions upon network (un)availability. The programmer should be able to detect the appearance and disappearance of network connections and react upon these events. Pixee's friend list reflects the connectivity status of the users: when Bob and Alice are connected via Bluetooth, Alice is notified that Bob is nearby so she can invite him for a chat. Additionally, the programs must be resilient to disconnections. The Pixee application seamlessly switches from Bluetooth to 3G when Alice leaves the metro.

C3. Dynamic adaptation of network behavior. Although the low-level details of networking should be hidden from the programmer, he should retain high-level control over the networking technology used. For example, Bob's Pixee application resizes pictures when Alice's device is connected via a 3G link to limit the data transferred. Mobile applications can then take advantage of the unique properties of each networking technology.

In the next section we introduce network-aware references: a programming abstraction that tackles the above challenges.

3   Network-Aware References (NARs)

Before we introduce network-aware references, we describe terminology used in distributed object-oriented languages. These languages use *proxy objects* to locally represent objects residing on remote devices. Proxy objects implement the same interface as the remote objects they represent, but they translate all method calls into remote method calls. The combination of a proxy object and its network link is called a *remote (object) reference*.

A program can acquire new remote references in three ways: 1) The remote object can be discovered using a peer-to-peer service discovery mechanism; 2) When peer-to-peer service discovery is not possible, clients can receive remote references from a globally reachable registry; 3) A remote reference is created when a local object is passed as an argument in a remote method call.

Network-aware references (NARs) abstract over the implementation details of different networking technologies and present a single reference to the programmer. A NAR consists of multiple remote references to the same object, each using a different network link. Every remote object is identified by a globally unique ID (GUID) based on the device or VM it is hosted on and an object identifier within that device or VM. When the application first discovers a new remote object, a NAR with a single reference is created. As additional references to the object are acquired, they are added to the NAR. Figure 1 compares traditional remote references and NARs graphically.

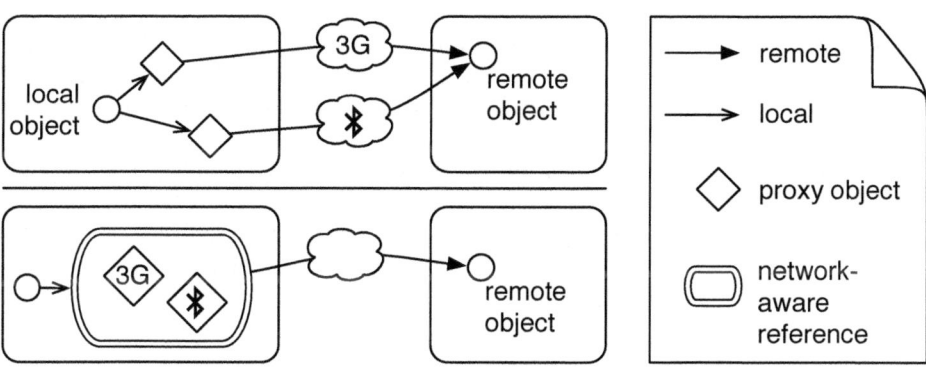

Fig. 1. A NAR encapsulates remote references to the same object

In a mobile setting, network links are very unstable. They disconnect and reconnect as people move in and out of wireless communication range of others [9]. With traditional remote references (e.g. RMI [10]) remote method calls block and wait for a response. Furthermore, network disconnections are signaled as exceptions. Thus, this model is not suitable for mobile applications. We adopt the *far reference* model [11] instead, for two reasons. First, far references allow only asynchronous communication. A remote method call over a far reference immediately returns and the result, if any, can be retrieved using an asynchronous callback. Second, a far reference tracks the status of the network link and can be in one of two states. It is either connected, in which it translates method calls in remote method calls. A far reference can also be disconnected, which means that it buffers all messages that are sent through it in a so-called "mailbox". Immediately after reconnection a far reference will try to transmit all outstanding messages in the mailbox to ensure no messages are lost.

Likewise, a NAR is disconnected when *all* of the underlying remote references are disconnected. As long as a NAR is disconnected, all messages sent to it are buffered in a unified mailbox. If one of the underlying remote references is reconnected or a new reference is added to the NAR, it switches back to the connected state. Figure 2 illustrates this: the NAR on the left is connected, as it encapsulates one connected remote reference using 3G and a disconnected remote reference using Bluetooth. The NAR on the right is disconnected, as all encapsulated remote references are disconnected.

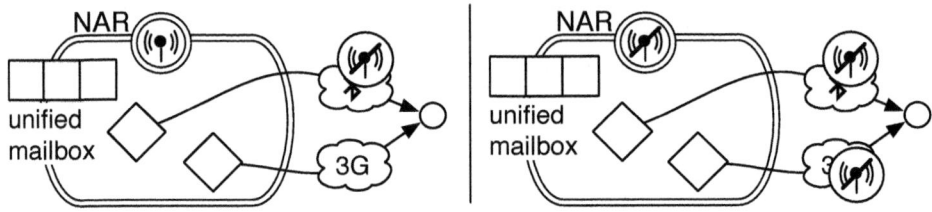

Fig. 2. Connection status of a NAR

Whenever the programmer sends a message to a NAR, the system dispatches it to a remote reference from the set of references encapsulated by the NAR. The default behavior of a NAR nondeterministically selects a connected reference to transmit messages. Programmers can specify other behaviors by attaching a *network behavior* either to the NAR, or to individual messages. This network behavior then becomes responsible for transmitting messages using any of the references from the NAR. Currently, we offer a basic set of network behaviors that can for example limit message transmission to a certain technology or prioritize one technology over another. Network behaviors are further explained in subsection 4.2.

3.1   Communication Semantics

In this section we detail two properties of the communication semantics of NARs: they guarantee that messages sent to an object are processed in the order they are sent, and that messages are processed only once.

A NAR ensures the first property by serializing message sends through its unified inbox. Messages are processed one by one, and a message is only processed if the receiver acknowledges the receipt of the previous one in the queue. Figure 3 shows what happens if a message is sent to a NAR: first, it is added to the unified mailbox (1). The NAR constantly tries to deliver the first message in its mailbox. When the message eventually reaches the first position in the mailbox, it is removed from the queue and marked with a serial number unique to the NAR (2), then the network behavior attached

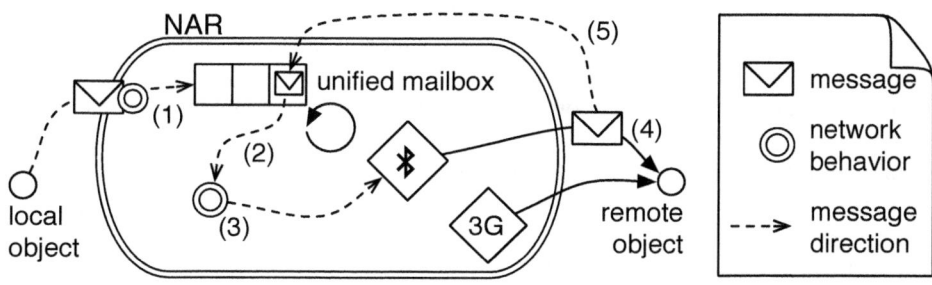

Fig. 3. The network behavior selects a remote object reference

to the message selects a reference from the set of currently connected references (3). The message is then transmitted to the receiver using that reference (4). If an error occurs during the transmission or the network behavior does not choose a connected reference the message is returned to the front of the unified mailbox and the transmission is retried later (5).

The receiving remote object processes all messages in the right order based on the serial number of the messages. In the case a message gets lost, messages with a higher serial number are not processed until the missing message arrives.

The second guarantee that NARs offer is that a message is processed only once. The default network behavior avoids message duplication by always selecting a single reference to transmit a message. However, programmers can build network behaviors that send duplicate messages intentionally, for example to ensure a critical message arrives as soon as possible. When a duplicate message arrives, the receiver first checks if it has already received a message with that serial number and ignores all duplicate messages.

4   NARs from a Programmers' Perspective

We have prototyped NARs in the distributed object-oriented programming language AmbientTalk [11]. AmbientTalk is designed to work in mobile settings and has already been used to build mobile applications such as a pervasive social application [12].

First, we show how to obtain a NAR. The following piece of AmbientTalk code uses the `whenever:discovered:`[1] language construct to install a handler that is called whenever a Pixee user is discovered in the environment. The block closure that is executed receives a NAR to the remote Pixee application as an argument in `aUser`. The handler requests the remote Pixee user's name, and adds the user to the buddy list. The left-arrow operator (←) represents an explicit asynchronous message send, while the dot operator is used for synchronous method invocation on local objects:

```
whenever: PixeeUser discovered: { |aUser|
  when: aUser←getName() becomes: { |name|
    GUI.addUser(aUser, name) } }
```

---

[1] NARs follow the AmbientTalk conventions: `when:` constructs are deactivated after triggering once, whereas `whenever:` constructs trigger every time.

The asynchronous call to `getName()` immediately results in a *future*: a placeholder for a future value. The `when:becomes:` construct then installs a handler that is executed when the future is resolved with a return value.

In the remainder of this section we will show how programmers can respond to changes in the network availability around them, adapt the network communication to certain networking technologies, and implement their own network behaviors. We will demonstrate how the Pixee application uses the API offered by NARs. The examples we present here use AmbientTalk syntax, but NARs can be implemented in other distributed object-oriented systems, like RMI [10].

4.1 Network Availability

As mentioned in the introduction, information about the available networks forms an important source of context for mobile applications. A NAR can encapsulate several remote references, so we offer a `linksOf:` primitive that returns a snapshot of the state of these references to the programmer.

For example, Pixee allows users to explicitly share a picture with another user who is close by, to highlight certain photos in their library. The user interface only allows this if the other user is connected via Bluetooth:

```
if: (linksOf: aUser).contains(Bluetooth) then: {
    GUI.showShareButtonFor(aUser) }
```

Pixee also shows that *changes* in the network connectivity of references play a big role, as users move about and connectivity fluctuates. For example, Pixee's friend list reflects the connectivity of a user's friends and updates it in real time. It uses the `linksOf:` primitive above to draw the friend list initially and then updates the *nearby* status of individual friends whenever their connectivity changes:

```
whenever: aFriend linkStatusChanged: { |change|
    if: (change.link == Bluetooth) then: {
        if: (change.isConnected) then: {
            GUI.notifyFriendNearby(aFriend);
        } else: {
            GUI.notifyFriendLeaving(aFriend) } } }
```

The `whenever:linkStatusChanged:` function installs a handler that is called whenever one of the references in a NAR disconnects or reconnects. It receives a *change* object as an argument. This object contains the link of which the connection status changed and the new status of the link.

We also provide two generalized handler functions that are triggered when a NAR switches to a disconnected or a connected state, respectively. Programmers can react on disconnections using a `whenever:disconnected:` handler. Likewise, programmers can use `whenever:reconnected:` to react on reconnections, which happen whenever a new reference is added to a disconnected NAR or one of the existing references it encapsulates is reconnected. The example below shows adding or removing a user from the friend list in the user interface when this user reconnects or disconnects:

```
whenever: aFriend disconnected: { GUI.hide(aFriend) };
whenever: aFriend reconnected: { GUI.show(aFriend) };
```

Together with the `linksOf:` primitive, these event handlers provide programmers with information about the connectivity of the different references in their applications and allow them to react on changes in network connectivity.

4.2 Network Behavior Adaptation

In order to allow programmers to steer communication towards certain networking technologies, we introduce *network behaviors*. Our implementation provides a number of built-in network behaviors. Additionally, programmers can implement their own behaviors and override the default behavior attached to NARs using *annotations*.

The first network behavior is called **Only**: it restricts message transmission to a set of network technologies. The example below ensures an explicitly shared picture is only sent using Bluetooth:

```
aUser←sendPicture(aPicture)@Only(Bluetooth)
```

This message will *only* be sent using a Bluetooth connection: if there is no connected Bluetooth reference to `aUser` the message is returned to the mailbox and message processing for the **aUser** NAR will stop until a Bluetooth reference is connected.

The **Prefer** behavior allows programmers to order an arbitrary number of technologies in decreasing order of preference:

```
aFriend←sendPicture(aPicture)@Prefer(Bluetooth, WiFi)
```

The **Prefer** behavior here first tries to transmit the **sendPicture** message using a Bluetooth link; if this is not available it tries to use a Wi-Fi link. If a Wi-Fi link is also unavailable, the **Prefer** behavior defers to the default behavior: this will either transmit the message using other technologies, or buffer the message if the NAR is disconnected.

Programmers can override the default network behavior for the whole application or just for a specific NAR using the following primitive functions:

```
setDefaultBehavior: aBehavior;                  // application-wide
setDefaultBehavior: aBehavior for: aReference;  // for the given reference
```

This operation makes every message sent using the NAR use the `aBehavior` behavior, unless programmers explicitly override this behavior by annotating messages with another behavior.

Existing network-aware approaches have shown that working with properties instead of explicit technologies is more versatile. For example, if a programmer wants to send a big file using a "fast" network connection, he should be able to use a keyword like **Fast** instead of listing every "fast" network connection explicitly. In order to do this, we provide programmers with a set of *categorization functions* that select networking technologies based on their properties.

We provide three built-in categorization functions: we offer a categorization function **Speed(x)** which only selects network links that theoretically offer at least **x** Mbits of bandwidth. The second categorization function is **Secure**, which selects network links that only do point-to-point communication or encrypt sent messages. Finally, cost can also be a factor in deciding which network link to use: we provide a **Free** categorization function that only selects network links that do not cost money to use. Currently these properties are statically defined as attributes of the network links.

Programmers can create their own categorization functions by refining the built-in ones described above. For example, they can define **Fast** as **Speed(10)**. Additionally, programmers can manually define new categorization functions based on the properties of the network links.

Using categorization functions instead of explicit technologies has another advantage: when a new networking technology becomes available, one only has to declare to which categories that new technology belongs or create new categorization functions if necessary. For example, a body area network (a very close-range wireless technology for non-intrusive health monitoring [13]) could be deemed **Fast** and **Secure**, but could also introduce a new category such as **PhysicalContact**.

4.3   Writing Custom Network Behaviors

The network behaviors we have presented so far only influence the technology selection process. If we want to allow full network awareness, programmers also need to be able to adapt the content of messages to the technology used to transmit them. In our system, behaviors are represented by objects that expose a single method `transmit(connections, message)`. This method is invoked during step three of the message sending process (when network technologies are chosen). This method transmits the message(s) to the receiver and informs the NAR that the message can be removed from the mailbox. The `connections` and `message` parameters of the method are the current set of available network links in the NAR and the message being sent, respectively.

In the scenario, Pixee resizes pictures before transmission if a Bluetooth link was not available; programmers can implement this as follows:

```
1  def PictureResizer := extend: Prefer(Bluetooth, WiFi) with: {
2    def transmit(connections, message) {
3      def btLink := connections.find: { |x| x.link == Bluetooth };
4      if: (btLink != nil) then: {
5        message.arguments := message.arguments.map: { |arg|
6            if: (isPicture(arg)) then: { arg.resize() } else: { arg } };
7      super^transmit(connections, message) } } };
```

This behavior extends the **Prefer** behavior and first looks for Bluetooth links in the network links managed by the `aFriend` NAR. If there are no Bluetooth links available, the behavior replaces pictures in the arguments list of the message with a resized version (lines 5–6). Finally, the message (line 7) is transmitted by the inherited **Prefer** behavior.

We also provide a `behavior:` construct to create a new behavior that inherits from `defaultBehavior`. All transmit calls are delegated to the default behavior eventually, since it enforces the two properties we outlined in section 3 (message ordering and no processing of duplicated messages).

5   Implementation

In this section we will discuss the implementation of network-aware references. We will first explain how the networking subsystem of AmbientTalk is structured and how this is exposed to programmers in subsection 5.1. We will then show how network-aware references are implemented on top of this in subsection 5.2

5.1   The AmbientTalk Networking Subsystem

Originally, the AmbientTalk VM was tightly coupled to its networking implementation, limiting it to only one network interface using the TCP/IP protocol. This network interface was represented by a single *communication bus*, which performs three duties for AmbientTalk: a) discovering objects on devices that export them using the same technology; b) marshalling communication and ensuring message ordering; c) signaling disconnections and reconnections.

We have decoupled the networking subsystem from the rest of the system, to allow other networking technologies to be plugged in easily. AmbientTalk now maintains a set of communication buses, one per network address (a network interface can respond to multiple addresses). For example, a typical smart phone will have a Bluetooth communication bus and a TCP/IP communication bus for the Wi-Fi interface.

The three duties of a communication bus influence the status of connected references. For example, the TCP/IP communication bus uses *heartbeat* packets sent via multicast UDP to determine the connectivity of other hosts. New devices are discovered as soon as they send their first heartbeat, and disconnections are signaled when either the heartbeat has been absent for a given amount of time or a communication error occurs during message transmission. This is different from the Bluetooth communication bus, where device discovery can take up to 12 seconds and is thus only done intermittently. For the Bluetooth bus the leading cause of disconnections will be communication errors signaled during message transmission.

Each communication bus is also associated with a *network link* object, which programmers can use to interact with that specific network interface. Each network link can be used to enable or disable its communication bus and set up discovery handlers. For example, discovering objects exclusively on the Bluetooth network link:

```
whenever: Service on: Bluetooth discovered: { |ref|
  system.println("Discovered: " + ref);
  whenever: ref disconnected: {
    system.println("Disconnected: " + ref); } }
```

Here `Bluetooth` is bound to the Bluetooth network link object. This snippet sets up a discovery handler that is invoked whenever an object with the nominal type `Service` is discovered using the Bluetooth communication bus. This discovery handler is then called with a *far reference* as parameter, which is a local proxy for the remote object. The far reference is associated with the network link that created it, the object it references and the VM this object resides on.

The programmer can also publish an object on a specific network link:

```
export: anObject as: Service on: Bluetooth;
```

In the interest of backwards compatibility, the discovery and publish constructs found in AmbientTalk (`when:discovered:`, `whenever:discovered:` and `export:as:`) invoke their network-aware counterparts on all available network links. The disconnection and reconnection handlers (like above) operate on pre-existing references so programmers do not need to specify network links.

At this stage there is only one technology per far reference, so messages sent to a far reference can only travel along a single path. This entails that discovering the same service using two different network technologies will result in two far references, as described in section 3.

5.2   The Architecture of Network-Aware References

With these modifications to the networking subsystem, AmbientTalk can communicate using different technologies but suffers from the challenges we identified in section 2. Our implementation of network-aware references tackles these challenges as follows:

C1. Abstraction over networking technologies. The previous subsection already outlined how the networking subsystem in AmbientTalk can abstract over the communication technology used. However, references are still created per technology. When programmers import the NAR module, it replaces the built-in discovery operations as follows. When the programmer issues a `whenever:discovered:` statement it is translated into several `whenever:on:discovered:` statements, one per network link. When one of the discovery statements are triggered, they first check if a NAR for the discovered object already exists. If so, the reference is added to the NAR and the user-supplied discovery block is not triggered. Any `whenever:linkStatusChanged:` handlers registered on the NAR are triggered.

If no NAR exists, a new NAR is created which contains just that reference. Finally, the NAR is added to a table with the GUID of the discovered object as key.

C2. Reactions upon network availability. As part of the discovery process, the NARs module also installs disconnection and reconnection handlers. Whenever the networking subsystem detects that a reference has disconnected or subsequently reconnected, it signals this change to the NAR. The NAR in turn signals the `whenever:linkStatusChanged:` message. If the last reference in a NAR becomes disconnected, the NAR as a whole becomes disconnected and triggers all installed disconnection handlers. Vice versa, if one of the references in a disconnected NAR reconnects, the NAR is reconnected and all installed reconnection handlers are triggered. After reconnection, a NAR retries transmission of messages in the queue.

C3. Dynamic adaptation of network behavior. As we explained earlier, NARs allow programmers to specify the network behavior of their communication. Every message submitted to a NAR is put into a message queue, which are processed one by one. If the network behavior of the first message in the queue is not amenable to transmission the queue is blocked and no messages are transmitted (e.g. if a message has a **Only** annotation and the desired network link is not online). Transmission of the message queue is retried whenever a new reference is added to a NAR or an already-added reference comes back online.

6   Evaluation

In this section we demonstrate the behavior of network-aware references in the face of partial disconnections. As mentioned in the introduction, mobile devices nowadays can communicate using more than one wireless communication technology and the system should always pick the "best" interface. If this interface disconnects due to a communication error or the other party moving out of range, the system should switch to a different technology. No communication should be lost during this switch and the handover time (the time where no data is sent) should be kept to a minimum.

The scenario we test is inspired by the "mobile connectivity" scenario in [14]: two smart phones that discover each other in the environment. One phone runs a *receiver* service, the other phone runs a *sender*. At time step t0 the sender starts sending messages to the receiver at a pace of 10 messages per second. At time step t1 the Wi-Fi connectivity is temporarily interrupted and at time step t2 Wi-Fi connectivity is restored. This timeline is illustrated at the top of Figure 4.

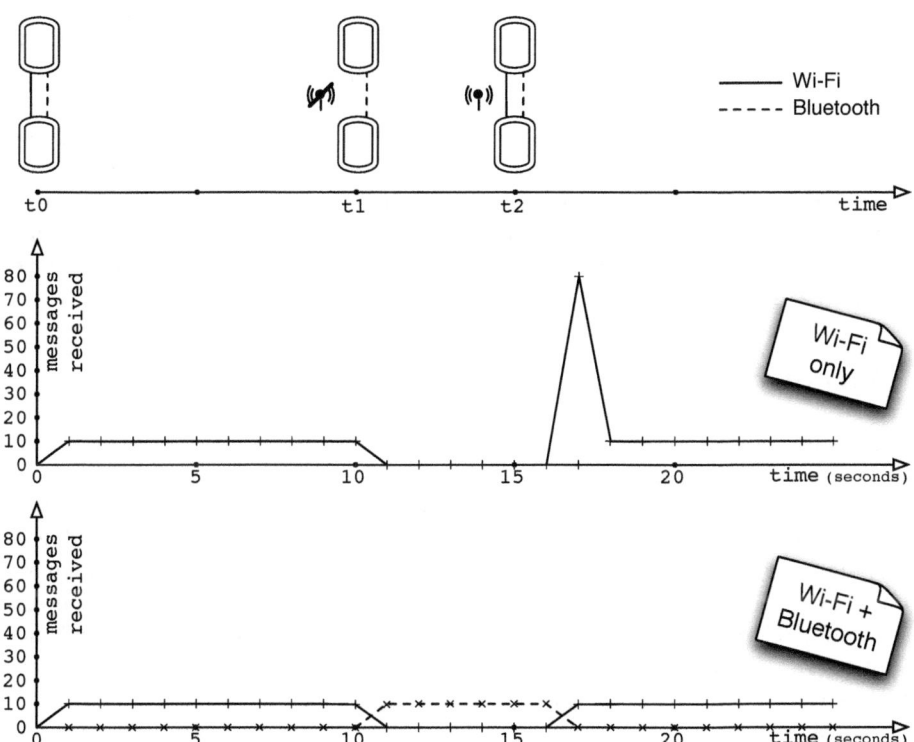

Fig. 4. Mobile connectivity scenario (top); benchmarks: only Wi-Fi (mid), Wi-Fi & BT (bottom)

First, we reconstruct the original scenario from [14] where the sender only sends messages to the receiver using Wi-Fi technology. We use the **Only** network behavior so that the ping message is only transmitted over a Wi-Fi link:

```
when: MobileConnectivityReceiver discovered: { |receiver|
    whenever: millisec(100) elapsed: {
        receiver←ping()@Only(WiFi); } }
```

When the Wi-Fi link becomes disconnected at `t1` all messages being sent are buffered at the sender. At `t2` connectivity is resumed, and the accumulated messages are flushed to the receiver. This behavior is illustrated in the middle graph of Figure 4. The spike in the timeline only happens 1.5 seconds (on average) after `t2` because the devices wait for heartbeats, as explained in the previous section. For Bluetooth links this reconnection process takes upwards of 15 seconds (on average), depending on the number of devices in communication range.

Our second implementation demonstrates the multi-networking facilities of NARs and will make use of both Wi-Fi and Bluetooth links to send messages. We define the "best" interface by annotating the `ping` message with the **Prefer** network behavior:

```
when: MobileConnectivityReceiver discovered: { |receiver|
    whenever: millisec(100) elapsed: {
        receiver←ping()@Prefer(WiFi, Bluetooth); } }
```

Before the Wi-Fi connectivity is interrupted, the behavior of the `ping` message will select the Wi-Fi link over the Bluetooth link to send the message. At time step `t1` the behavior can no longer select the Wi-Fi link and it selects the Bluetooth link instead. The bottom graph in Figure 4 shows how the Wi-Fi→Bluetooth handover occurs almost instantly. When the Wi-Fi link reconnects, the behavior will again prefer it over the Bluetooth link, explaining the handover at the 16–17 second mark. As before, the time gap between reestablishing Wi-Fi connectivity and the Bluetooth→Wi-Fi handover is due to the discovery and reconnection process. Note that message transmission is not interrupted at any point during this experiment.

7   Related Work

In this section we discuss how network-aware references fit into the state of the art. Traditionally, network-aware applications are defined as "applications that adapt to network conditions in an application specific way" [6]. This has led to frameworks for maintaining quality of service (QoS) in media streams [5], where image or sound quality is reduced if the available bandwidth decreases. These are usually implemented in a framework or middleware and require the programmer to set up policies, giving up explicit control. Current network-aware applications assume network links are stable and treat network failures as an exceptional case. This makes them unsuitable for a mobile situation where pervasive social applications are deployed.

A number of network protocols have been proposed that enable multi-networking at a low level, like SCTP, mSCTP, SIGMA, TraSH and Mobile IP(v6) [7, 8]. However, these approaches focus on the problem of ensuring devices are always reachable at a certain address and maintaining existing network connections when a mobile device migrates to a different access point (horizontal handover). Some technologies support transitions between different networking technologies (vertical handover), but they assume these transitions are short-lived, so they limit themselves to ensuring no data is lost during a transition. In contrast, NARs accept that there may be multiple connections at once, which can break at any time. NARs still ensure that all communication arrives, but cannot offer time guarantees: a message with the **Only** behavior attached will only be sent when a Bluetooth connection is available. This may depend on user mobility.

In [15] a policy-based architecture is proposed that manages several different routes to another device. They use policies to select appropriate network interfaces and set priorities between interfaces if several policies apply. However, their approach is not suitable for a mobile setting as their system immediately returns an error if there are no matching interfaces at the moment a packet is sent. In contrast, NARs buffer communication until a connection is re-established. Furthermore, their policies currently operate at the system level instead of the application level, so all applications on the system have to agree on the same set of policies.

Haggle [16] is an architecture that enables seamless network connectivity for devices in dynamic mobile environments. It abstracts over different network transport bindings and protocols so that applications become communication agnostic. Haggle is a central component in the mobile device that selects and switches network links as needed. In contrast to using NARs, programmers have no control over communication within a single application and cannot adapt its behavior to changes in the network context.

8   Conclusion and Future Work

In this paper we have introduced network-aware references (NARs): a programming abstraction that encapsulates several references to remote objects over different networking technologies and keeps track of the state of the network links involved. Network-aware references tackle the three challenges for programming network-aware applications we listed earlier: abstraction over networking technologies, reacting to changes in the network availability, and dynamically adapting network behavior. We have demonstrated how network-aware references can be used to build mobile applications using a representative pervasive social picture-sharing application called Pixee.

We are currently exploring different types of network behaviors and how they interact with NARs as they are defined here. For example, a behavior that limits retransmission of messages, or a behavior that spreads parts of a message across different links. Secondly, we would like to make the information offered to our system, like speed, communication range, pricing, etc. more dynamic. An application using Wi-Fi could then automatically switch to a different technology as the user enters an airport where wireless is not free to use. Additionally, we intend to allow these parameters to vary per reference rather than per network link (e.g. the signal strength for a reference over Bluetooth). Finally, in the search for related work we discovered heterogenous routing: transmitting packets in peer-to-peer networks where not all nodes speak the same protocol. We are currently investigating if NARs can be adapted for this.

References

[1] Ben Mokhtar, S., Capra, L.: From pervasive to social computing: Algorithms and deployments. In: ACM Inter. Conf. on Pervasive Services, ICPS (2009)
[2] Meshhadi, A., Ben Mokhtar, S., Capra, L.: Habit: Leveraging human mobility and social network for efficient content dissemination in manets. In: IEEE Inter. Symp. on a World of Wireless, Mobile and Multimedia Networks (2009)
[3] Schilit, B., Adams, N., Want, R.: Context-aware computing applications. In: First Workshop on Mobile Computing Systems and Applications, pp. 85–90 (1994)

[4] Abowd, G.D., Dey, A.K., Brown, P.J., Davies, N., Smith, M., Steggles, P.: Towards a better understanding of context and context-awareness. In: Gellersen, H.-W. (ed.) HUC 1999. LNCS, vol. 1707, pp. 304–307. Springer, Heidelberg (1999)

[5] Bolliger, J., Gross, T.: A framework-based approach to the development of network-aware applications. IEEE Transactions on Software Engineering 24(5) (1998)

[6] Miller, N., Steenkiste, P.: Collecting network status information for network-aware applications. In: IEEE INFOCOM, vol. 2, pp. 641–650, Citeseer (2000)

[7] Fu, S., Atiquzzaman, M., Ma, L., Lee, Y.: Signaling cost and performance of SIGMA: A seamless handover scheme for data networks. Wireless Communications and Mobile Computing 5(7), 825–845 (2005)

[8] Xing, W., Karl, H., Wolisz, A., Müller, H.: M-SCTP: Design and prototypical implementation of an end-to-end mobility concept. In: Proc. 5th Intl. Workshop The Internet Challenge: Technology and Applications, Berlin, Germany, Citeseer (2002)

[9] Dedecker, J., Van Cutsem, T., Mostinckx, S., D'Hondt, T., De Meuter, W.: Ambient-Oriented Programming. In: OOPSLA 2005: Companion of the 20th Annual ACM SIGPLAN Conference on Object-Oriented Programming, Systems, Languages, and Applications. ACM Press, New York (2005)

[10] Downing, T.: Java RMI: remote method invocation. IDG Books Worldwide, Inc., Foster City (1998)

[11] Van Cutsem, T., Mostinckx, S., Gonzalez Boix, E., Dedecker, J., De Meuter, W.: Ambienttalk: object-oriented event-driven programming in mobile ad hoc networks. In: Inter. Conf. of the Chilean Computer Science Society (SCCC), pp. 3–12. IEEE Computer Society, Los Alamitos (2007)

[12] Gonzalez Boix, E., Lombide Carreton, A., Scholliers, C., Van Cutsem, T., De Meuter, W., D'Hondt, T.: Flocks: Enabling Dynamic Group Interactions in Mobile Social Networking Applications. In: Proceedings of the 2011 ACM Symposium on Applied Computing (SAC), Taichung, Taiwan, March 21-25, vol. 1, pp. 425–432. ACM, New York (2011)

[13] Jovanov, E., Milenkovic, A., Otto, C., De Groen, P.: A wireless body area network of intelligent motion sensors for computer assisted physical rehabilitation. Journal of NeuroEngineering and Rehabilitation 2(1), 6 (2005)

[14] Collins, J., Bagrodia, R.: Programming in mobile ad hoc networks. In: 4th Annual International Conference on Wireless Internet (WICON 2008), pp. 1–9 (2008)

[15] Ylitalo, J., Jokikyyny, T., Kauppinen, T., Tuominen, A., Laine, J.: Dynamic network interface selection in multihomed mobile hosts. In: Proceedings of the 36th Annual Hawaii International Conference on System Sciences. IEEE Computer Society, Los Alamitos (2003)

[16] Su, J., Scott, J., Hui, P., Crowcroft, J., de Lara, E., Diot, C., Goel, A., Lim, M.H., Upton, E.: Haggle: Seamless networking for mobile applications. In: Krumm, J., Abowd, G.D., Seneviratne, A., Strang, T. (eds.) UbiComp 2007. LNCS, vol. 4717, pp. 391–408. Springer, Heidelberg (2007)

Coordination and Concurrency in Multi-engine Prolog

Paul Tarau

Department of Computer Science and Engineering,
University of North Texas
`tarau@cs.unt.edu`

Abstract. We discuss the impact of the separation of logic engines (in-dependent logic processing units) and multi-threading on the design of coordination mechanisms for a Prolog based agent infrastructure.

We advocate a combination of coroutining constructs with focus on expressiveness and a simplified, multi-threading API that ensures optimal use available parallelism.

In this context, native multi-threading is made available to the application programmer as a set of high-level primitives with a declarative flavor while cooperative constructs provide efficient and predictable coordination mechanisms. As illustrations of our techniques, a parallel `fold` operation as well as cooperative implementations of Linda blackboards and publish/subscribe are described.

Keywords: multi-engine Prolog, agent coordination, high-level multi-threading, coroutining Linda blackboards, publish/subscribe, Java-based Prolog system.

1 Introduction

Multi-threading has been adopted in today's Prolog implementations as it became widely available in implementation languages like C or Java.

An advantage of multi-threading over more declarative concurrency models like various AND-parallel and OR-parallel execution schemes, is that it maps to the underlying hardware directly: on typical multi-core machines threads and processes are mapped to distinct CPUs[1]. Another advantage is that a procedural multi-threading API can tightly control thread creation and thread reuse.

On the other hand, the explicit use of a procedural multi-threading API breaks the declarative simplicity of the execution model of logic based languages. At the same time it opens a Pandora's box of timing and execution order dependencies, resulting in performance overheads for various runtime structures that need to be synchronized. It also elevates risks of software failure due to programmer errors

---

[1] We use the word CPU in accordance of what the underlying runtime system and operating system sees as independent processing units in a multi-core/multi-processor machine. For instance, on a two Xeon processor Quad-Core MacPro with hyper-threading, the Java VM sees 16 independent processing units.

W. De Meuter and G.-C. Roman (Eds.): COORDINATION 2011, LNCS 6721, pp. 157–171, 2011.

given the mismatch between assumptions about behavior expected to follow the declarative semantics of the core language and the requirements of a procedural multi-threading API.

In this paper we will describe how efficient and flexible agent coordination is facilitated by a design emphasizing *the decoupling of the multi-threading API and the logic engine operations and encapsulation of multi-threading in a set of high-level primitives with a declarative flavor.*

In this process, we use threads encapsulated as high level programming language constructs with focus on performance benefits, and we are resorting to determinacy, through lightweight, cooperative sequential constructs, to express coordination patterns.

We have implemented the API in the context of an experimental, Java-based Prolog system, Lean-Prolog[2].

LeanProlog is based on a reimplementation of BinProlog's virtual machine, the BinWAM. It succeeds our *Jinni Prolog* implementation that has been used in various applications [1,2,3,4] as an *intelligent agent infrastructure*, by taking advantage of Prolog's knowledge processing capabilities in combination with a simple and easily extensible runtime kernel supporting a flexible reflexion mechanism. Naturally, this has suggested to investigate whether some basic agent-oriented language design ideas can be used for a refactoring of Prolog's interoperation with the external world, including interaction with other instances of the Prolog processor itself.

Agent programming constructs have influenced design patterns at "macro level", ranging from interactive Web services to mixed initiative computer human interaction. From the very beginning, *Performatives* in Agent communication languages [5,6] have made these constructs reflect explicitly the intentionality, as well as the negotiation process involved in agent interactions. At the same time, it has been a long tradition of logic programming languages [7] to use multiple logic engines for supporting concurrent execution.

In this context we have centered our implementation around logic engine constructs providing an API that supports reentrant instances of the language processor. This has naturally led to a view of logic engines as instances of a generalized family of iterators called *Fluents* [8], that have allowed the separation of the first-class language interpreters from the multi-threading mechanism, while providing a very concise source-level reconstruction of Prolog's built-ins. Later we have extended the original *Fluents* with a few new operations [9] supporting bi-directional, mixed-initiative exchanges between engines, bringing them closer to an agent-oriented view as autonomous logic processors.

The resulting language constructs, that we have called *Interactors*, express control, metaprogramming and interoperation with stateful objects and external services.

---

[2] It is called Lean-Prolog as we have consistently tried to keep implementation complexity under control and follow minimalist choices in the design of built-ins, external language interfaces and a layered, modular extension mechanism.

On the other hand, our multi-threading layer has been designed to be independent of the interactor API. This allows assumptions of determinacy when working with multiple engines (and other sequential interactors) within a thread.

The multi-threading API integrates thread-construction with interactors called Hubs that provide synchronization between multiple consumers and producers. It supports high-level performance-centered concurrency patterns while removing the possibility of programming errors involving explicit synchronization.

The guiding architectural principle we based our design on, can be stated concisely as follows: *separate concurrency for performance from concurrency for expressiveness*. Arguably, it is a good fit with the general idea behind declarative programming languages – delegate as much low level detail to underlying implementation as possible rather than burdening the programmer with complex control constructs.

The paper is organized as follows.

Section 2 overviews logic engines and describes their basic operations and the interactor API that extends the same view to various other built-in predicates. Section 3 introduces Hubs - flexible synchronization devices that allow interoperation and coordination between threads. Section 4 describes a set of high-level multi-threading operations that ensure concurrent execution seen as a means to accelerate computations while keeping the semantics as close as possible to a declarative interpretation.

Sections 5 and 6 show that fundamental coordination patterns like Linda blackboards and publish/subscribe can be implemented cooperatively in terms of sequential operations on logic engines.

Finally, section 7 discusses related work and section 8 concludes the paper.

2   Logic Engines as Answer Generators

Our *Interactor API* has evolved progressively into a practical Prolog implementation framework starting with [8] and continued with [10] and [9]. We summarize it here and refer to [9] for the details of a semantic description in terms of Horn Clause Logic of various engine operations.

A *logic engine* is simply a language processor reflected through an API that allows its computations to be controlled interactively from another *engine* very much the same way a programmer controls Prolog's interactive toplevel loop: launch a new goal, ask for a new answer, interpret it, react to it.

A logic engine can be seen as an instance of the *Prolog runtime system* implementing LD-resolution [11] on a given clause database, together with a set of built-in operations. The command

```
new_engine(AnswerPattern, Goal, Interactor)
```

creates a new logic engine, uniquely identified by Interactor, which shares code with the currently running program and is initialized with Goal as its starting point. AnswerPattern is a term, usually a list of variables occurring in Goal, of which answers returned by the engine will be instances. Note however that

new_engine/3 acts like a typical constructor, no computations are performed at this point, except for initial allocation of data areas.

2.1 Iterating over Computed Answers

Note that our logic engines are seen, in an object oriented-style, as implementing the *interface* **Interactor**. This supports a *uniform* interaction mechanism with a variety of objects ranging from logic engines to file/socket streams and iterators over external data structures.

The **ask_interactor/2** operation is used to retrieve successive answers generated by an **Interactor**, on demand. It is also responsible for actually triggering computations in the engine. The query

```
ask_interactor(Interactor, AnswerInstance)
```

tries to harvest the answer computed from **Goal**, as an instance of **AnswerPattern**. If an answer is found, it is returned as **the(AnswerInstance)**, otherwise the atom **no** is returned. sloppy Note that bindings are not propagated to the original **Goal** or **AnswerPattern** when **ask_interactor/2** retrieves an answer, i.e. **AnswerInstance** is obtained by first standardizing apart (renaming) the variables in **Goal** and **AnswerPattern**, and then backtracking over its alternative answers in a separate Prolog interpreter. Therefore, backtracking in the caller interpreter does not interfere with **Interactor**'s iteration over answers. Backtracking over **Interactor**'s creation point, as such, makes it unreachable and therefore subject to garbage collection. An interactor is stopped with the

```
stop_interactor(Interactor)
```

operation, that, in the case of logic engines, allows reclaiming resources held by the engine.

So far, these operations provide a minimal API, powerful enough to switch tasks cooperatively between an engine and its client and emulate key Prolog built-ins like **if-then-else** and **findall** [8], as well as typical higher order operations like *fold* and *best_of* [9].

2.2 A Yield/Return Operation

The following operations provide a "mixed-initiative" interaction mechanism, allowing more general data exchanges between an engine and its client.

First, like the **yield return** construct of **C#** and the **yield operation** of Ruby and Python, our **return/1** operation

```
return(Term)
```

will save the state of the engine and transfer *control* and a *result* **Term** to its client. The client will receive a copy of **Term** simply by using its **ask_interactor/2** operation.

Note that an interactor returns control to its client either by calling **return/1** or when a computed answer becomes available. By using a sequence of **return** and `ask_interactor` operations, an engine can provide a stream of *intermediate/final results* to its client, without having to backtrack. This mechanism is powerful enough to implement a complete exception handling mechanism simply by defining

```
throw(E) :- return(exception(E)).
```

When combined with a `catch(Goal, Exception, OnException)`, on the client side, the client can decide, upon reading the exception with `ask_interactor/2`, if it wants to handle it or to throw it to the next level.

2.3 Coroutining Logic Engines

Coroutining has been in use in Prolog systems mostly to implement constraint programming extensions. The typical mechanism involves *attributed variables* holding suspended goals that may be triggered by changes in the instantiation state of the variables. We discuss here a different form of coroutining, induced by the ability to switch back and forth between engines.

The operations described so far allow an engine to return answers from any point in its computation sequence. The next step is to enable an engine's *client*[3] to *inject* new goals (executable data) to an arbitrary inner context of an engine. Two new primitives are needed:

```
to_engine(Engine, Data)
```

that is called by the client[4] to send data to an Engine, and

```
from_engine(Data)
```

that is called by the engine to receive a client's Data.

A typical use case for the *Interactor API* looks as follows:

1. the client creates and initializes a new *engine*
2. the client triggers a new computation in the *engine*, parameterized as follows:
   (a) the *client* passes some data and a new goal to the *engine* and issues an `ask_interactor/2` operation that passes control to it
   (b) the *engine* starts a computation from its initial goal or the point where it has been suspended and runs (a copy of) the new goal received from its *client*
   (c) the *engine* returns (a copy of) the answer, then suspends and returns control to its *client*
3. the *client* interprets the answer and proceeds with its next computation step
4. the process is fully reentrant and the *client* may repeat it from an arbitrary point in its computation

---

[3] Another engine, that uses an engine's services.
[4] Equivalently the `tell_interactor/2` generic interactor predicate can be also used here.

3   Hubs and Threads

As a key difference with typical multi-threaded Prolog implementations like
Ciao-Prolog [12] and SWI-Prolog [13], our Interactor API is designed up front
with a clear separation between *engines* and *threads* as we prefer to see them as
orthogonal language constructs.

To ensure that communication between logic engines running concurrently is
safe and synchronized, we hide the engine handle and provide a producer/con-
sumer data exchanger object, called a `Hub`, when multi-threading.

A `Hub` can be seen as an interactor used to synchronize threads. On the Prolog
side it is introduced with a constructor `hub/1` and works with the standard
interactor API:

```
ask_interactor(Hub, Term)
tell_interactor(Hub, Term)
stop_interactor(Hub)
```

On the Java side, each instance of the `Hub` class provides a synchronizer between M producers and N consumers. A `Hub` supports data exchanges through
a private object `port` and it implements the `Interactor` interface. Consumers
issue `ask_interactor/2` operations that correspond to `tell_interactor/2` operations issued by producers.

A group of related threads are created around a `Hub` that provides both basic
synchronization and data exchange services. The built-in

```
new_logic_thread(Hub, X, G, Clone, Source)
```

creates a new thread by either "cloning" the current Prolog code and symbol
spaces or by loading new Prolog code in a separate name space from a `Source`
(typically a precompiled file or a stream). Usually a default constructor

```
new_logic_thread(Hub, X, G)
```

is used. It shares the code but it duplicates the symbol table to allow independent
symbol creation and symbol garbage collection to occur safely in multiple threads
without the need to synchronize or suspend thread execution.

4   High-Level Concurrency with Higher-Order Constructs

Encapsulating concurrent execution patterns in high-level abstractions, when
performance gains are the main reason for using multiple threads, avoids forcing
a programmer to suddenly deal with complex procedural issues when working
with (mostly) declarative constructs in a language like Prolog. It is also our
experience that in an exclusively dynamically-typed language like Prolog this
reduces software risks significantly.

One of the deficiencies of sequential or multi-threaded `findall`-like operations
is that they might build large lists of answers unnecessarily. With inspiration
drawn from combinators in functional languages, one can implement a more
flexible multi-threaded `fold` operation instead.

The predicate `multi_fold(F, XGs, Xs)` runs a list of goals `XGs` of the form `Xs :- G` and combines, with `F`, their answers, to accumulate them into a single final result, without building intermediate lists.

```
multi_fold(F, XGs, Final) :- hub(Hub),
  length(XGs,ThreadCount),
  launch_logic_threads(XGs, Hub),
  ask_interactor(Hub, Answer),
  (Answer = the(Init) →
    fold_thread_results(ThreadCount, Hub, F, Init, Final)
  ; true
  ),
  stop_interactor(Hub),Answer=the(_).
```

The predicate `multi_fold` relies on the predicate `launch_logic_threads` to run threads initiated by the goal list `XGs`. When launching the threads, we ensure that they share the same `Hub` for communication and synchronization.

```
launch_logic_threads([], _Hub).
launch_logic_threads([(X :- G)|Gs], Hub) :-
  new_logic_thread(Hub, X, G),
  launch_logic_threads(Gs, Hub).
```

Once all threads are launched, we use the predicate `fold_thread_results` to collect results computed by various threads from `Hub`, and to combine them into a single result, while keeping track of the number of threads that have finished their work.

```
fold_thread_results(0, _Hub, _F, Best, Best).
fold_thread_results(ThreadCount, Hub, F, SoFar, Best) :-
  ThreadCount > 0,
  ask_interactor(Hub, Answer),
  count_thread_answer(Answer, ThreadCount, ThreadsLeft, F, SoFar, Better),
  fold_thread_results(ThreadsLeft, Hub, F, Better, Best).

count_thread_answer(no, ThreadCount, ThreadsLeft, _F, SoFar, SoFar) :-
  ThreadsLeft is ThreadCount-1.
count_thread_answer(the(X), ThreadCount, ThreadCount, F, SoFar, Better) :-
  call(F, X, SoFar, Better).
```

A typical application is the predicate `multi_best(F, XGs, M)`, which runs a list of goals `XGs` of the form `N :- G` where `N` is instantiated to a numeric value. By using `max/3` to combine the current best answers with a candidate one it extracts at the the maximum `M` of all answers computed (in an arbitrary order) by all threads.

```
multi_best(XGs,R) :- multi_fold(max,XGs,R).
```

Note that, as in the case of its `fold` cousins in functional languages, `multi_fold` can be used to emulate various other higher order predicates. For instance a `findall`-like predicate is emulated as the predicate `multi_all(XGs,Xs)` which runs a list of goals `XGs` of the form `Xs :- G` and combines all answers to a list using `list_cons`.

```
multi_all(XGs, Rs) :- multi_fold(list_cons,[([] :- true)|XGs],Rs).

list_cons(X, Xs, [X|Xs]).
```

A different pattern arises from combinatorial search algorithms where one wants to stop multiple threads as soon as a first solution is found. Things like restarts in SAT solvers and various Monte Carlo algorithms fit in this category.

For instance, the predicate `multi_first(K, XGs, Xs)` runs each goal of the form `Xs :- G` on the list `XGs`, until the first K answers `Xs` are found (or fewer, if less then K answers exist).

It uses a very simple mechanism built into Lean Prolog's multi-threading API: when a `Hub` interactor is stopped, all threads associated to it are notified to terminate.

```
multi_first(K, XGs, Xs) :- hub(Hub),
  length(XGs, ThreadCount),
  launch_logic_threads(XGs, Hub),
  collect_first_results(K, ThreadCount, Hub, Xs),
  stop_interactor(Hub).

collect_first_results(_, 0, _Hub, []).
collect_first_results(0, _, Hub, []) :- stop_interactor(Hub).
collect_first_results(K, ThreadCount, Hub, MoreXs) :-
  K>0, ThreadCount>0,
  ask_interactor(Hub, Answer),
  count_thread_answer(Answer, ThreadCount, ThreadsLeft, Xs, MoreXs),
  ( ThreadCount =:= ThreadsLeft → K1 is K-1
  ; K1 is K
  ), collect_first_results(K1, ThreadsLeft, Hub, Xs).
```

In particular, searching for at most one solution is possible:

```
multi_first(XGs,X) :- multi_first(1,XGs,[X]).
```

The `multi_first/3` and `multi_first/2` predicates provide an alternative to using CUT in Prolog as a means to limit search, while supporting a scalable mechanism for concurrent execution. Note also that `multi_first/3` it is more flexible than CUT as it can be used to limit the search to a window of K solutions. However, in contrast with CUT, the order in which these first solutions are found is arbitrary.

5   Agent Coordination with Cooperative Linda Blackboards

The message passing style interaction shown in the previous sections between engines and their clients, can be easily generalized to associative communication through a unification based blackboard interface [14]. Exploring this concept in depth promises more flexible interaction patterns, as out of order operations become possible, matched by association patterns. An interesting question arises at this point. Can blackboard-based coordination be expressed directly in terms of engines, and as such, can it be seen as independent of a multi-threading API?

We have shown so far that when focusing on performance on multi-core architectures, multi-threading can be encapsulated in high-level constructs that provide its benefits without the need of a complex procedural API.

To support our claim that "concurrency for expressiveness" works quite naturally with coroutining logic engines we will describe here a cooperative implementation of Linda blackboards. In contrast to multi-threaded or multi-process implementations, it ensures atomicity "by design" for various operations. It is an example of *concurrency for expressiveness* that can be used orthogonally from *concurrency for performance* to coordinate cooperatively multiple logic engines within a single thread.

The predicate `new_coordinator(Db)` uses a database parameter `Db` (a synthetic name, if given as a free variable, provided by `db_ensure_bound`) to store the state of the Linda blackboard[5]. The state of the blackboard is described by the dynamic predicates `available/1`, that keeps track of terms posted by `out` operations, `waiting/2`, that collects pending `in` operations waiting for matching terms, and `running/1`, that helps passing control from one engine to the next.

```
new_coordinator(Db) :- db_ensure_bound(Db),
  maplist(db_dynamic(Db), [available/1,waiting/2,running/1]).
```

The predicate `new_task` initializes a new coroutining engine, driven by goal G. We shall call such an engine "an agent" in the next paragraphs.

```
new_task(Db, G) :- new_engine(nothing, (G, fail), E),
  db_assertz(Db, running(E)).
```

Three cooperative Linda operations are available to an agent. They are all expressed by returning a specific pattern to the `Coordinator`.

```
coop_in(T)  :- return(in(T)), from_engine(X), T=X.

coop_out(T)  :- return(out(T)).

coop_all(T, Ts) :- return(all(T, Ts)), from_engine(Ts).
```

The `Coordinator` implements a handler for the patterns returned by the agents as follows:

```
handle_in(Db, T, E) :- db_retract1(Db, available(T)),!,
  to_engine(E, T), db_assertz(Db, running(E)).
handle_in(Db, T, E) :- db_assertz(Db, waiting(T, E)).

handle_out(Db, T) :- db_retract(Db, waiting(T, InE)),!,
  to_engine(InE, T), db_assertz(Db, running(InE)).
handle_out(Db,T) :- db_assertz(Db, available(T)).
```

---

[5] Note, that, as an extension to standard Prolog, Lean Prolog provides multiple dynamic databases, which, in turn, can be emulated, as shown in [9], in terms of logic engines. Their operations (like `db_assert/2` similar to `assert/1`) have an extra first argument that names the database on which they act).

```
handle_all(Db, T, Ts, E) :-
  findall(T, db_clause(Db, available(T), true), Ts),
  to_engine(E, Ts), db_assertz(Db, running(E)).
```

The `Coordinator`'s dispatch loop `coordinate/1` (failure driven here to run without requiring garbage collection) works as follows:

```
coordinate(Db) :-
  repeat,
    ( db_retract1(Db, running(E)) →
        ask_interactor(E, the(A)), dispatch(A, Db, E), fail
    ; !
    ).
```

Its `dispatch/3` predicate calls the handlers as appropriate.

```
dispatch(in(X), Db, E) :- handle_in(Db, X, E).
dispatch(out(X), Db, E) :- handle_out(Db, X), db_assertz(Db, running(E)).
dispatch(all(T, Ts), Db, E) :- handle_all(Db, T, Ts, E).
dispatch(exception(Ex), _, _) :- throw(Ex).
```

Note also that the predicate `dispatch/3` propagates exceptions - in accordance with a "fail fast" design principle.

```
stop_coordinator(C) :-
  foreach(db_clause(C, running(E), true), stop(E)),
  foreach(db_clause(C, waiting(_, E), true), stop(E)).
```

When the coordinator is stopped using `stop_coordinator`, the database is cleaned of possible records of unfinished tasks in either `running` or `waiting` state. This predicate uses a Lean Prolog extension, `foreach` which makes failure-driven loops more readable - it is defined as follows:

```
foreach(When,Then) :-  When,once(Then),fail.
foreach(_,_).
```

The following test predicate shows that out-of-order `in` and `out` operations are exchanged as expected between engines providing a simple transactional implementation of Linda coordination.

```
test_coordinator :- new_coordinator(C),
  new_task(C, foreach(
      member(I, [0, 2]),
      ( coop_in(a(I, X)),
        write(coop_in=X),write(',')
  ))),
  new_task(C, foreach(
      member(I, [3, 2, 0, 1]),
      ( write(coop_out=f(I)),write(',')
        coop_out(a(I, f(I)))
  ))),
```

```
new_task(C, foreach(
    member(I, [1, 3]),
    ( coop_in(a(I, X)),
      write(coop_in=X),write(',')
))),
coordinate(C), stop_coordinator(C).
```

When running the code, one can observe that explicit coroutining control exchanges between engines have been replaced by operations of the higher level Linda coordination protocol.

```
?- test_coordinator.
coop_out = f(3),coop_out = f(2),coop_out = f(0),coop_in = f(0),
coop_out = f(1),coop_in = f(2),coop_in = f(1),coop_in = f(3).
```

This shows that "concurrency for expressiveness" in terms of the logic-engines-as-interactors API provides flexible building blocks for the encapsulation of non-trivial high-level concurrency patterns.

6   Coordinating Publishers and Subscribers

We will now describe a cooperative publish/subscribe mechanism that uses multiple dynamic databases and provides, as an interesting feature, associative search through the set of subscribed events.

The predicate publish(Channel,Content) initializes a Channel, implemented as a dynamic database together with a time stamping mechanism.

```
publish(Channel,Content) :-
  increment_time_of('$publishing',Channel,T),
  db_assert(Channel,(Content :- published_at(T))).
```

Content is a fact to be added to the database, for which the user can (and should) provide indexing declarations to support scalable large volume associative search.

The predicate consume_new(Subscriber,Channel,Content) reads the next message on Channel. It ensures, by checking and updating channel and subscriber-specific time stamps, that on each call it gets one *new* event, if available.

```
consume_new(Subscriber,Channel,Content) :- var(Content),
  get_time_of(Channel,Subscriber,T1),
  db_clause(Channel,Content,published_at(TP)),
  T1=<TP, T2 is T1+1,
  set_time_of(Channel,Subscriber,T2).
```

The predicate peek_at_published(ContentPattern, Matches) supports associative search for published content, independently of the fact that it has already been read. It provides to an agent the set of subscribed events matching ContentPattern.

```
peek_at_published(Channel,ContentPattern, Matches) :-
  findall(ContentPattern, db_clause(Channel,ContentPattern,_),Matches).
```

The predicate `init_publishing(ContentIndexings)` sets up indexing using list of ContentIndexings of the form `pred(I1,I2,...In)` where `I1,I2...In` can be 1 (indicating that an argument should be indexed) or 0.

```
init_publishing(ContentIndexings) :- index(time_of(1,1,0)),
  maplist(index,ContentIndexings).
```

The following predicates manage the time stamping mechanism, needed to ensure that subscribers get all the events in the order they have been published:

```
set_time_of(Role,Key,T) :- nonvar(Key), remove_time_of(Role,Key),
  db_assert(global_time,time_of(Role,Key,T)).

get_time_of(Role,Key,R) :-
  db_clause(global_time,time_of(Role,Key,T),_), !, T>=0, R=T.
get_time_of(Role,Key,0) :-
  db_assert(global_time,time_of(Role,Key,0)).

increment_time_of(Role,Key,T1) :-
  db_retract1(global_time,time_of(Role,Key,T)), !, T1 is T+1,
  db_assert(global_time,time_of(Role,Key,T1)).
increment_time_of(Role,Key,0) :-
  db_assert(global_time,time_of(Role,Key,0)).

remove_time_of(Role,K) :- db_retractall(global_time,time_of(Role,K,_)).
```

A few other predicates provide clean-up operations, to remove from all the channels the published Content as well as the tracking of subscribers.

```
clean_up_publishing :-
  ( db_clause(global_time,time_of('$publishing',Key,_),_),
    db_clear(Key), fail
  ; true
  ),db_clear(global_time).

clear_channel(Channel) :- db_clear(Channel),
  remove_time_of('$publishing',Channel).

clear_subscriber(Subscriber) :- remove_time_of(_,Subscriber).
```

After defining:

```
pubtest :- init_publishing([wins(1),loses(1)]),
  maplist(show_goal,[
    publish(sports,wins(rangers)),publish(politics,loses(meg)),
    publish(sports,loses(bills)),publish(sports,wins(cowboys)),
    publish(politics,wins(rand)),
    consume_new(joe,sports,_),consume_new(mary,sports,_),
    consume_new(joe,sports,_),consume_new(joe,politics,_),
    consume_new(joe,politics,_),consume_new(mary,sports,_)
  ]), nl.

show_goal(G) :- G, !, write(G),nl.
```

we can see that the sequence of notifications received by the subscriber agents matches the intended semantics of publish/subscribe:

```
?- pubtest.
publish(sports, wins(rangers)) publish(politics, loses(meg))
publish(sports, loses(bills)) publish(sports, wins(cowboys))
publish(politics, wins(rand))
consume_new(joe, sports, wins(rangers))
consume_new(mary, sports, wins(rangers))
consume_new(joe, sports, loses(bills))
consume_new(joe, politics, loses(meg))
consume_new(joe, politics, wins(rand))
consume_new(mary, sports, loses(bills))
```

The final state of various databases can be queried (and cleaned up) with:

```
?-listings,clean_up_publishing.

% global_time: time_of / 3.
time_of($publishing, sports, 2).
time_of($publishing, politics, 1).
time_of(sports, joe, 2).
time_of(politics, joe, 2).
time_of(sports, mary, 2).

% sports: wins / 1.
wins(rangers) :- published_at(0).
wins(cowboys) :- published_at(2).

% politics: wins / 1.
wins(rand) :- published_at(1).

% politics: loses / 1.
loses(meg) :- published_at(0).

% sports: loses / 1.
loses(bills) :- published_at(1).
```

This shows the presence of sequencing information provided by the dynamic predicate published_at/1. Note also that these (indexed) databases can be searched associatively by various subscribers for "past" content.

7   Related Work

Multiple logic engines have been present in one form or another in various parallel implementation of logic programming languages, [15,16] Among the earliest examples of parallel execution mechanisms for Prolog, AND-parallel [7] and OR-parallel [17] execution models are worth mentioning.

However, with the exception of the author's papers on this topic [8,18,10,9] there are relatively few examples of using first-class logic engines as a mechanism to enhance language expressiveness, independently of their use for parallel programming. A notable exception is [19] where such an API is discussed for parallel symbolic languages in general.

In combination with multithreading, our own engine-based API bears similarities with various other Prolog systems, notably [12,13]. Coroutining has also been present in logic languages to support constraint programming extensions requiring suspending and resuming execution based on changes of the binding state of variables. In contrast to these mechanisms that focus on transparent, fine-grained coroutining, our engine-based mechanisms are coarse-grained and programmer controlled. Our coroutining constructs can be seen, in this context, as focussed on expressing cooperative design patterns that typically involve the use of a procedural multi-threading API.

Finally, our `multi_findall` and `multi_fold` predicates have similarities with design patterns like *ForkJoin* [20] or *MapReduce* [21] coming from sharing a common inspiration source: higher-order constructs like `map` and `fold` in functional programming.

8   Conclusion

We have shown that by decoupling logic engines and threads, programming language constructs for coordination can be kept simple when their purpose is clear – *multi-threading for performance* is separated from *concurrency for expressiveness*. This is achieved via communication between independent language interpreters independent of the multi-threading API.

Our language constructs are particularly well-suited to take advantage of today's multi-core architectures where keeping busy a relatively small number of parallel execution units is all it takes to get predictable performance gains, while reducing the software risks coming from more complex concurrent execution mechanisms designed with massively parallel execution in mind.

The current version of LeanProlog containing the implementation of the constructs discussed in this paper, and related papers describing other aspects of the system are available at *http://logic.cse.unt.edu/tarau/research/LeanProlog*.

Acknowledgment

We thank NSF (research grant 1018172) for support.

References

1. Tarau, P.: Towards Inference and Computation Mobility: The Jinni Experiment. In: Dix, J., Fariñas del Cerro, L., Furbach, U. (eds.) JELIA 1998. LNCS (LNAI), vol. 1489, pp. 385–390. Springer, Heidelberg (1998)
2. Tarau, P.: Intelligent Mobile Agent Programming at the Intersection of Java and Prolog. In: Proceedings of The Fourth International Conference on The Practical Application of Intelligent Agents and Multi-Agents, London, U.K., pp. 109–123 (1999)

3. Tarau, P.: Inference and Computation Mobility with Jinni. In: Apt, K., Marek, V., Truszczynski, M. (eds.) The Logic Programming Paradigm: a 25 Year Perspective, pp. 33–48. Springer, Heidelberg (1999) ISBN 3-540-65463-1

4. Tarau, P.: Agent Oriented Logic Programming Constructs in Jinni 2004. In: Demoen, B., Lifschitz, V. (eds.) ICLP 2004. LNCS, vol. 3132, pp. 477–478. Springer, Heidelberg (2004)

5. Mayfield, J., Labrou, Y., Finin, T.W.: Evaluation of KQML as an Agent Communication Language. In: Wooldridge, M., Müller, J.P., Tambe, M. (eds.) IJCAI-WS 1995 and ATAL 1995. LNCS, vol. 1037, pp. 347–360. Springer, Heidelberg (1996)

6. FIPA: FIPA 97 specification part 2: Agent communication language, Version 2.0 (October 1997)

7. Hermenegildo, M.V.: An abstract machine for restricted and-parallel execution of logic programs. In: Wada, E. (ed.) Logic Programming 1986. LNCS, vol. 264, pp. 25–39. Springer, Heidelberg (1987)

8. Tarau, P.: Fluents: A refactoring of prolog for uniform reflection and interoperation with external objects. In: Lloyd, J. (ed.) CL 2000. LNCS (LNAI), vol. 1861, p. 1225. Springer, Heidelberg (2000)

9. Tarau, P., Majumdar, A.: Interoperating logic engines. In: Gill, A., Swift, T. (eds.) PADL 2009. LNCS, vol. 5418, pp. 137–151. Springer, Heidelberg (2008)

10. Tarau, P.: Logic Engines as Interactors. In: Garcia de la Banda, M., Pontelli, E. (eds.) ICLP 2008. LNCS, vol. 5366, pp. 703–707. Springer, Heidelberg (2008)

11. Tarau, P., Boyer, M.: Nonstandard Answers of Elementary Logic Programs. In: Jacquet, J. (ed.) Constructing Logic Programs, pp. 279–300. J.Wiley, Chichester (1993)

12. Carro, M., Hermenegildo, M.V.: Concurrency in Prolog Using Threads and a Shared Database. In: ICLP, pp. 320–334 (1999)

13. Wielemaker, J.: Native preemptive threads in SWI-prolog. In: Palamidessi, C. (ed.) ICLP 2003. LNCS, vol. 2916, pp. 331–345. Springer, Heidelberg (2003)

14. De Bosschere, K., Tarau, P.: Blackboard-based Extensions in Prolog. Software — Practice and Experience 26(1), 49–69 (1996)

15. Gupta, G., Pontelli, E., Ali, K.A., Carlsson, M., Hermenegildo, M.V.: Parallel execution of prolog programs: a survey. ACM Trans. Program. Lang. Syst. 23(4), 472–602 (2001)

16. Shapiro, E.: The family of concurrent logic programming languages. ACM Comput. Surv. 21(3), 413–510 (1989)

17. Lusk, E., Mudambi, S., Gmbh, E., Overbeek, R.: Applications of the aurora parallel prolog system to computational molecular biology. In: Proc. of the JICSLP 1992 Post-Conference Joint Workshop on Distributed and Parallel Implementations of Logic Programming Systems. MIT Press, Washington, DC (1993)

18. Tarau, P., Dahl, V.: High-Level Networking with Mobile Code and First Order AND-Continuations. Theory and Practice of Logic Programming 1(3), 359–380 (2001)

19. Casas, A., Carro, M., Hermenegildo, M.: Towards a high-level implementation of flexible parallelism primitives for symbolic languages. In: PASCO 2007: Proceedings of the 2007 International Workshop on Parallel Symbolic Computation, pp. 93–94. ACM, New York (2007)

20. Lea, D.: A Java fork/join framework. In: Proceedings of the ACM 2000 Conference on Java Grande, JAVA 2000, pp. 36–43. ACM, New York (2000)

21. Lämmel, R.: Google's MapReduce programming model revisited. Sci. Comput. Program 68, 208–237 (2007)

Abstract Machines for Safe Ambients in Wide-Area and Mobile Networks

Seiji Umatani, Masahiro Yasugi, and Taiichi Yuasa

Graduate School of Informatics, Kyoto University,
Sakyo-ku Kyoto 606-8501, Japan
{umatani,yasugi,yuasa}@kuis.kyoto-u.ac.jp

Abstract. Recently, there have been several studies focusing on the implementation of process calculi with distribution and mobility. Among these, PAN and GcPAN are distributed abstract machines for executing Safe Ambients, a variant of the Ambient calculus. However, in order to use them or to exploit their implementation techniques, we must assume all-to-all and permanent connectivity in the underlying network; this is inappropriate for most real-world wide-area and mobile networks, in which each private network is delimited by network boundaries and each mobile device may become disconnected at any moment. In this paper, we propose novel abstract machines PAN_{mov}, $GcPAN_{mov}$, and $GcPAN_{shift}$ that can handle such network boundaries and mobile devices by using a special kind of agents called *boundary forwarders*. Especially in $GcPAN_{shift}$, operations related to boundary forwarders improve the fault tolerance of user programs. Finally, we prove the correctness of the proposed machines by using weak barbed bisimulation.

1 Introduction

In recent years, core calculi based on distribution and mobility have been studied extensively, and they are regarded as fundamental models for many programming languages supporting code migration.

The Ambient Calculus (AC) [2] is a distributed process calculus with a notion of locations that are known as *ambients*. Each process belongs to an ambient, and each ambient, except for the topmost ambient, belongs to another ambient. Thus, the ambients form a hierarchical structure, and every process belongs somewhere in the hierarchy. In AC, computation is represented as the combination of three types of primitive operations of ambients—in, which instructs an ambient to enter another ambient; out, which instructs an ambient to exit from another ambient; and open, which provides a way to dissolve the membrane of an ambient so that the content of the ambient can be accessed.

To realize practical programming language systems adaptable to a broad range of heterogeneous distributed and mobile networks, we can adopt AC as the core language of such systems. Several studies have been carried out on the distributed implementation of Ambient-like calculi [1,4,12,8,11,13]. Among these, PAN [12,7] and GcPAN [8,9] are abstract machines for implementing the Safe Ambients (SA), a variant of AC, in distributed settings.

W. De Meuter and G.-C. Roman (Eds.): COORDINATION 2011, LNCS 6721, pp. 172–186, 2011.
© IFIP International Federation for Information Processing 2011

The implementation technique of PAN and GCPAN is simple; it separates the *logical* distribution of ambients, which is given by the hierarchical structure of ambients, from their *physical* distribution, which is a mapping from each ambient to a certain computer on which the ambient is running. PAN and GCPAN exploit this separation to defer physical movements of an ambient that executes some in or out moves, until the ambient is opened by the target ambient so that it can access the contents of the target ambient, such as files. This implementation technique may eliminate unnecessary communications caused by physical movements, which are typically much more expensive than simple data communications. In particular, when an ambient moves to its target ambient through multiple moves and accesses the contents of the target, physical movements corresponding to intermediate moves could be eliminated entirely. Moreover, if the moving ambient does not access any content of the target, there is no need for physical code migration.

This technique of PAN and GCPAN requires all-to-all and permanent connectivity of the underlying network; that is, it assumes that any computer in the network can directly communicate with the other computers at any moment. In particular, the computer to which an ambient has moved through (possibly) multiple in and out moves must be able to communicate with the computer in which the ambient physically resides when the ambient is opened. An ambient may move to any target ambient; hence, any computer can become the target location. Therefore, any computer must be able to communicate with the other computers.

Clearly, the above requirement is not desirable for wide-area distributed environments which consist of several local-area networks or for mobile networks in which mobile devices such as smartphones may be disconnected temporarily or permanently at any moment. Furthermore, deferring the movement of an ambient is not desirable if we want the ambient to move only for using the CPU power of remote computers.

In this paper, we propose novel abstract machines PAN_{mov}, $GCPAN_{mov}$, and $GCPAN_{shift}$ for SA in order to support such wide-area and mobile networks. The main ideas of the proposed technique are as follows:

1. We model a wide-area network as a set of network domains, each of which is isolated from other network domains by network boundaries. Computers within a particular network domain can directly communicate with each other. We extend SA's ambient creation construct $M[P]$, where M is the name of a created ambient and P is its content, to make it clear whether the created ambient belongs to the same network domain as its parent or not; if not, there exists a network boundary between them.

2. We modify the implementation of in and out moves so that an ambient physically moves to the target ambient as soon as the ambient performs a cross-boundary movement. When physical movement of an ambient is performed in PAN (and also in our machines), a special agent called *forwarder* is created at the original location of the ambient; after that, all messages sent to the ambient from its children are transferred via this forwarder. Thus, our

technique guarantees that the content of an opened ambient can always be sent to its parent through a chain of forwarders even if the ambient and its parent belong to different network domains.

The proposed technique is based on the PAN abstract machine. In particular, movements within a single network domain are processed in the same way as they are in PAN. Thus, no physical code migration is performed unless some **open** action or some cross-boundary movement is executed.

In the proposed abstract machine, every cross-boundary movement causes physical code migration; hence, it requires the creation of more forwarders than PAN, wherein all movements are considered as non cross-boundary movements. Although such an increase of forwarders is inevitable in wide-area networks with boundaries, keeping unused forwarders (i.e., forwarders with no child) alive is a waste of computer resources. Therefore, we have refined the proposed abstract machine so that it can collect and reuse the resources assigned for unused forwarders in the same way as GcPAN. Furthermore, to reduce the number of forwarders in use and to prevent erratic behavior related to failures in network communication, the proposed abstract machine relocates ambients that use forwarders so that they can directly send messages to their parents.

We provide a formal description of the proposed machine and we prove its correctness by establishing a bisimilarity between it and PAN. In the formal description, the underlying protocols for implementing ambient (co)capabilities follow the formalization method of PAN. In terms of the correctness of the proposed machine and reusability of the real implementations of PAN (and GcPAN), the fact that the proposed machine is a smooth extension of PAN is advantageous.

Cross-boundary communication and code migration are common features of recent distributed systems; hence, we believe that the proposed ideas and techniques can be adapted to such systems.

The remainder of this paper is organized as follows. In Section 2, we provide a brief explanation of SA and PAN. Next, in Section 3, we describe the proposed base abstract machine PAN_{mov}, which does not perform garbage collection. In Section 4, we explain how one of the refined abstract machines, $GcPAN_{mov}$, reduces the resource usage of the underlying computers. In Section 5, we explain how another refined machine, $GcPAN_{shift}$, further reduces the resource usage and improves the fault tolerance of user programs. In Section 6, we prove the correctness of PAN_{mov}. Finally, in Section 7, we provide concluding remarks.

2 Background

2.1 Safe Ambients

Safe Ambients (SA) are ambients that are designed to prevent unintended interference among ambients; whenever an ambient executes some movement action, the target ambient of the movement must execute the corresponding *coaction*. Thus, the timing of each movement can be controlled by the target ambient, and no unintended interference occurs.

The kinds of processes in SA are the same as those in the original Ambient calculus [2]: $P_1 \mid P_2$ for parallel composition, $(\nu n)P$ for restriction, $M.P$ for action prefix, $M[P]$ for ambient creation, $\langle M \rangle$ and $(x)P$ for local communication, and X and rec $X.P$ for recursive processes. The characteristic of SA is found in the existence of coactions in M:

$$M ::= x \mid n \mid \text{in } M \mid \overline{\text{in}}\, M \mid \text{out } M \mid \overline{\text{out}}\, M \mid \text{open } M \mid \overline{\text{open}}\, M$$

where each action (in, out, and open) must be executed along with the corresponding coaction ($\overline{\text{in}}$, $\overline{\text{out}}$, and $\overline{\text{open}}$, respectively). The following are the reduction rules that define the behavior of basic actions in SA processes:

[R-MSG] $\qquad\qquad\qquad\qquad \langle M \rangle \mid (x)P \longrightarrow P\{M/x\}$

[R-IN] $\qquad m[\text{in } n.P_1 \mid P_2] \mid n[\overline{\text{in}}\, n.Q_1 \mid Q_2] \longrightarrow n[\, m[P_1 \mid P_2] \mid Q_1 \mid Q_2]$

[R-OUT] $\quad m[\, n[\text{out } m.P_1 \mid P_2] \mid \overline{\text{out}}\, m.Q_1 \mid Q_2] \longrightarrow n[P_1 \mid P_2] \mid m[Q_1 \mid Q_2]$

[R-OPEN] $\qquad\qquad \text{open } n.P \mid n[\overline{\text{open}}\, n.Q_1 \mid Q_2] \longrightarrow P \mid Q_1 \mid Q_2$

2.2 PAN Abstract Machine

To express how SA can be executed in a network of computers, the PAN abstract machine consists of a flat network of *located agents*. Intuitively, a located agent $h : n[P]_k$ represents an ambient n whose content process is P, where h is the physical location of n and k is the physical location of its parent ambient. Thus, for example, the logical hierarchical structure of the SA process $a[b[P|c[Q]]|R]$ is represented by the parallel composition $h_1 : a[R]_{\text{root}} \parallel h_2 : b[P]_{h_1} \parallel h_3 : c[Q]_{h_2}$ in PAN. Note that ambients in PAN do not need to know the locations of their children. This is because the existence of coactions in SA guarantees that an interaction among ambients is always triggered by a child ambient using an upward request message to its parent, as described below. The precise syntax of PAN is a subset of that of PAN_{mov}, which is given in Section 3.2.

The basic actions of SA are simulated in PAN using interactions among ambients, as shown in Figure 1. In the figure, the white boxes represent located agents, and the lines between them represent parent-child relations. The arrows denote messages between them. In Figure 1 (b), for instance, the ambient a, which performs out b.P, sends a request message {out} to b. If b contains an unguarded process $\overline{\text{out}}$ b.Q, these action/coaction match in b, and b sends back to a a completion message {go c}. When a receives the completion message, it updates its parent location with the location of c. The in action is simulated in a similar manner, as shown in Figure 1 (a). It should be noted that these simulations do not change the physical location of a; they update only the local information about the parent location of a, whereas a remains at the same location.

On the other hand, in Figure 1 (c), when the ambient a, which performs a $\overline{\text{open}}$ coaction, receives the corresponding completion message {migrate}, it further sends back to b the completion message {register P}, which registers P, the code of a's local processes, into b. This incurs the physical migration of P.

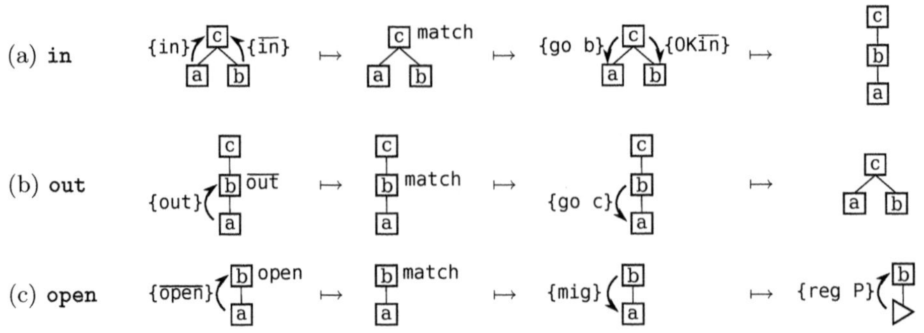

(a) in   {in}   {in̄}   ↦   match   ↦   {go b}   {OKin̄}   ↦

(b) out   {out}   b̄ out   ↦   b match   ↦   {go c}   ↦

(c) open   {open̄}   b open   ↦   b match   ↦   {mig}   ↦   {reg P}

Fig. 1. Simulation of SA actions in PAN

After sending the {register P} message, the ambient a becomes a forwarder (depicted as a triangle in the figure), whose role is to transfer messages from its children to b. Such a forwarder is necessary because b cannot access its children; therefore it cannot inform them to send their requests to b instead of a. In the remainder of this paper, we use the textual notation ▷{P} to denote a forwarder. For instance, the final state of Figure 1 (c) is represented as b[▷{ ... }].

By deferring physical code migration until the containing ambient is opened, these simulations eliminate many unnecessary network messages.

However, the simulations described above have a serious disadvantage in wide-area distributed environments with network boundaries. A set of in and out moves of an ambient running on a certain computer may *logically* move into another ambient running on a different computer. If these computers belong to different network domains and if they cannot communicate directly, the former ambient can no longer send messages to its parent, i.e., to the latter ambient, whereas PAN assumes that every computer can communicate directly with any other computers. Consider, for instance, the following code representing the firewalls of two LANs as two sibling ambients f and g:

$$r[\,f[\,\overline{out}\ f\mid a[\,out\ f.in\ g.\overline{open}\ a\mid P]]\mid g[\,\overline{in}\ g.open\ a]]$$

where ambients within f cannot communicate with g directly. After a performs out f.in g, it is logically placed in g, whereas it physically remains within f. Then, an attempt to send a message {$\overline{open}$} fails. In such a case, the {$\overline{open}$} and the following {register P} messages should be transmitted via r, that is, via the path through which a moved.

Furthermore, suppose g is a mobile device that becomes disconnected before it performs open a. Since the code P is not yet delivered to g, some intended behavior of g in P is lost. (This problem is further discussed in Section 5.)

In summary, PAN's assumption of all-to-all and permanent connectivity among computers is not practical in contemporary wide-area and mobile networks; therefore, an alternative technique is required to express ambient movements.

3 PAN$_{\mathrm{mov}}$: Chaining Forwarders upon Movement

In this section, we propose a novel abstract machine PAN$_{\mathrm{mov}}$, which solves the problem of PAN described in the previous section.

3.1 Basic Idea

PAN$_{\mathrm{mov}}$ solves the problem using two ideas: (1) to specify boundaries between network domains, we slightly extend SA's ambient creation construct, and (2) upon each cross-boundary **in** or **out** move of an ambient, PAN$_{\mathrm{mov}}$ physically moves the ambient into the destination network domain. These ideas are explained in detail below.

Ambient creation with split prefix

To handle network boundaries properly, if a new ambient is created in a different network domain from the domain in which the creating ambient resides, PAN$_{\mathrm{mov}}$ places a special kind of forwarder called *boundary forwarder* between them; that is, the parent of the created ambient is the boundary forwarder, and the parent of the boundary forwarder is the creating ambient. The need for a boundary forwarder at each ambient creation could be automatically determined by an actual implementation if the topology of the underlying network is given, for example, as an external configuration file. However, in this paper, to simplify the formal definition of PAN$_{\mathrm{mov}}$, each ambient creation involving the creation of a boundary forwarder is prefixed with the keyword `split` (e.g., `split a[P]`). If a programmer writes an SA program with `split` prefixes in accordance with the topology, the program could be executed without any external configuration file. Similarly, a boundary forwarder is placed between each mobile device and its infrastructure.

Besides performing the normal task of forwarding messages, boundary forwarders play several roles in PAN$_{\mathrm{mov}}$, as described below. To distinguish a boundary forwarder from a normal forwarder, we denote the former as $\triangleright^{\bullet}$ and the latter as $\triangleright^{\circ}$. Sometimes, we simply denote the latter as $\triangleright$.

Physical migration upon in and out

In PAN$_{\mathrm{mov}}$, physical migration of ambients upon cross-boundary movements is achieved with a mechanism that is similar to that of PAN with which it performs **open** actions. The mechanism involves the following steps:

1. If a request message crosses a boundary, the corresponding boundary forwarder marks it with a special tag.
2. When an ambient receives a request message marked with the special tag, it creates an *empty* clone of the requesting ambient at that location.
3. The receiving ambient sends back to the requesting ambient the {`migrate`} message, which indicates code migration into the clone.
4. When the requesting ambient receives the {`migrate`} message, it sends back the {`register` P} message containing its content, and then, it becomes a forwarder, as in the case of $\overline{\textbf{open}}$ action.

Following these steps, whenever an ambient moves, a forwarder is created at its original location. Then, even if the ambient repeats several movements, the chain of created forwarders constitutes the path from the original location to the final destination along which all messages sent from its children can always be transmitted.

Note that the physical migration of a moving ambient is performed only when its request message crosses a network boundary. In other words, every movement of an ambient within a single network domain is treated as it is in PAN; hence, physical migration is deferred until it is opened later.

If a request message has crossed a network boundary, the {migrate} message of step 3 and the {register P} message of step 4 must also cross the network boundary. Moreover, at step 4, the requesting ambient cannot send the {register P} message via the boundary forwarder of step 1, which forwards request messages to the parent, because the destination of the {register P} message is not the parent, but its own clone. To remedy these difficulties, the boundary forwarder creates, at step 1, a *seed* of a boundary forwarder, denoted by •. The {migrate} message sent back from the parent ambient is transmitted backward by this seed. Furthermore, after transmitting the {migrate} message, the seed becomes a new boundary forwarder targeting the appropriate location. For instance, consider the following code:

$$\texttt{root}[\,\texttt{a}[\,\overline{\texttt{out}}\ a.P\mid\ \triangleright^\bullet\{\,\texttt{b}[\,\texttt{out}\ a.Q\mid c[\,R\,]]\mid S\,\}]]$$

When b's {out} message arrives at a via the boundary forwarder, the state changes to:

$$\texttt{root}[\,\texttt{a}[\,P\mid\ \bullet\mid\ \triangleright^\bullet\{\,\texttt{b}[\,Q\mid c[\,R\,]]\mid S\,\}]]$$

Then, when a's {migrate} message arrives at b via the seed, the state changes to:

$$\texttt{root}[\,\texttt{a}[\,P\,]\mid \texttt{b}'[\,\triangleright^\bullet\{\,\texttt{b}[\,Q\mid c[\,R\,]]\}]\mid\ \triangleright^\bullet\{\,S\,\}]]$$

where the seed becomes the boundary forwarder targeting b', the clone of b. Finally, b's {register} message is correctly sent to b' via the new boundary forwarder, and the state becomes:

$$\texttt{root}[\,\texttt{a}[\,P\,]\mid \texttt{b}'[\,Q\mid\ \triangleright^\bullet\{\,\triangleright^\circ\{\,c[\,R\,]\}\}]\mid\ \triangleright^\bullet\{\,S\,\}]]$$

Note that this new boundary forwarder continues to work for its children after these transitions; in the code stated above, all messages from c are forwarded by it.

In the mechanism described above, there is another subtle difficulty at step 2. If a request message is {out}, or if it is {$\overline{\texttt{in}}$} without the special tag (i.e., the message did not cross any boundaries), a clone may be allocated at the same domain as the receiving ambient. On the other hand, if the message is {$\overline{\texttt{in}}$} marked with the special tag, a clone must be allocated at the same domain as the ambient that sends the {$\overline{\texttt{in}}$} message. For instance, in the code:

$$\texttt{root}[\,\texttt{a}[\,\texttt{in}\ c.P\mid b[\,Q\,]]\mid\ \triangleright^\bullet\{\,c[\,\overline{\texttt{in}}\ c.R\,]\}]$$

the clone of a must be created below the boundary forwarder. Here, c cannot predict whether its $\{\overline{\text{in}}\}$ message crosses any boundary forwarder when it emits the message; hence, the creation of the clone of a in advance by c is inadequate. Therefore, in PAN$_{\text{mov}}$, the clone is created by the boundary forwarder when it receives the completion message from root. In the proposed execution model, the boundary forwarder belongs to *both* network domains; hence, it can create the clone within the domain below itself. As an alternative, it would be possible to create the clone when the $\{\overline{\text{in}}\}$ message arrives at the boundary forwarder. However, if no ambient executes the corresponding in action, the created clone will become unnecessary; this is undesirable.

After the movement, the state finally becomes:

$$\text{root}[\ \triangleright^\bullet\{\ \mathsf{c}[\ R\ |\ \mathsf{a}'[\ P\ |\ \triangleright^\bullet\{\ \triangleright^\circ\{\ \mathsf{b}[\ Q\ ]\ \}\ \}\ ]\ ]\ \}\ ]$$

The newly created boundary forwarder on the right represents the same network boundary as that on the left; however, it forwards messages in the opposite direction.

3.2 Formal Definition

In this section, we formalize the proposed abstract machine PAN$_{\text{mov}}$ by the set of reduction rules for *network configurations*. The definition method basically follows that of PAN [12].

First, a network configuration of PAN$_{\text{mov}}$ is represented using the following syntax:

Nets

$$A ::= \mathbf{0}\ |\ Agent\ |\ Msg\ |\ A_1 \parallel A_2\ |\ (\boldsymbol{\nu}p)A$$
$$Agent ::= h : n[P]_k\ |\ h \triangleright^B k\ |\ h \bullet k, \qquad B ::= \circ\ |\ \bullet$$

where $n \in Names$, $h, k \in Locations$, and $p \in Names \cup Locations$. The overall network A consists of parallel compositions ($\parallel$) of *Agents* and *Msgs*. There are three kinds of agents: $h : n[P]_k$ is a located ambient mentioned earlier, $h \triangleright^B k$ is a forwarder at h, which forwards messages to k, and $h \bullet k$ is a seed of a boundary forwarder at h (the meaning of k is explained later). B in a forwarder indicates whether it is a normal forwarder ($\circ$) or boundary forwarder ($\bullet$).

Messages

$$Msg ::= \uparrow_h^k\{Req\}\ |\ \uparrow^h\{Compl\}, \qquad Req ::= R\ |\ {}_\bullet R$$
$$R ::= \text{in } n, m\ |\ \overline{\text{in}}\ n, h\ |\ \text{out } n, m\ |\ \overline{\text{open}}\ n$$
$$Compl ::= \text{go } h\ |\ \text{OK}\overline{\text{in}}\ |\ \text{migrate } h\ |\ \text{register } P\ |\ \text{new } n, k$$
$$\ |\ {}_\bullet\text{Cin } n, m, h, k\ |\ {}_\bullet\text{Cout } n, h$$

$\uparrow_h^k\{Req\}$ represents a request message sent from h to k and $\uparrow^h\{Compl\}$ represents a completion message sent to h. When a request message crosses at least one boundary, it is marked with the tag $\bullet$, e.g., $\uparrow_h^k \{\bullet R\}$. The meaning of each kind of R and *Compl* is described in detail below.

Processes

$$P ::= \mathbf{0} \mid P_1 \mid P_2 \mid (\boldsymbol{\nu}n)P \mid M.P \mid M[P] \mid \texttt{split } M[P] \mid \langle M \rangle$$
$$\mid (x)P \mid X \mid \texttt{rec } X.P \mid \texttt{wait}.P \mid \uparrow_h \{Req\}$$
$$M ::= x \mid n \mid \texttt{in } M \mid \overline{\texttt{in}} \, M \mid \texttt{out } M \mid \overline{\texttt{out}} \, M \mid \texttt{open } M \mid \overline{\texttt{open}} \, M$$

The syntax of the processes is nearly similar to that of SA; the three additional constructs are a cross-boundary ambient creation, $\texttt{split } M[P]$, a process waiting for the arrival of any message, $\texttt{wait}.P$, and a request message arriving at its destination ambient, $\uparrow_h \{Req\}$.

The operational semantics of PAN_{mov} is defined as the reduction relation $\longmapsto$ between network configurations. In addition, to express process-level reductions, we use another form of reduction relation, $P \xmapsto[n:h]{k} Q \gg Msg$, to indicate that a process P, local to an ambient n that is located at h, and whose parent is located at k, becomes Q, and the message Msg is emitted as a side effect.

First, the inference rules for $\longmapsto$ are defined as follows:

Inference rules

$$[\text{PROC-AGENT}] \quad \frac{P \xmapsto[h:n]{k} P' \gg M \qquad Q \text{ has no unguarded ambient}}{h:n[P \mid Q]_k \longmapsto h:n[P' \mid Q]_k \parallel M}$$

$$[\text{PAR-AGENT}] \quad \frac{A_1 \longmapsto A_1'}{A_1 \parallel A_2 \longmapsto A_1' \parallel A_2} \qquad [\text{RES-AGENT}] \quad \frac{A \longmapsto A'}{(\boldsymbol{\nu}p)A \longmapsto (\boldsymbol{\nu}p)A'}$$

$$[\text{STRUCT-CONG}] \quad \frac{A \equiv A' \quad A' \longmapsto A'' \quad A'' \equiv A'''}{A \longmapsto A'''}$$

The rule [PROC-AGENT] embeds a process-level reduction step into $\longmapsto$. The side condition about Q ensures that all child ambients of n are activated before any local process-level reduction occurs. The remaining rules are straightforward inference rules about contexts and structural congruence. The definition of structural congruence $\equiv$ is mostly standard; hence, it is omitted.

The other axiomatic rules are classified into six categories according to the stages of ambient interactions. In these rules, when some fields or variables are unimportant, we replace them with $-$.

Creation

$[\text{NEW-LOCAMB}] \qquad h: m[n[P] \mid Q]_k \longmapsto h: m[Q]_k \parallel (\boldsymbol{\nu}l)(l: n[P]_h), l \notin FL(P)$

$[\text{NEW-LOCAMB}']\ h: m[\texttt{split } n[P] \mid Q]_k \longmapsto$
$\qquad\qquad\qquad h: m[Q]_k \parallel (\boldsymbol{\nu}l)(l \rhd^\bullet h \parallel (\boldsymbol{\nu}l')(l': n[P]_l)),\ l, l' \notin FL(P)$

$[\text{NEW-RES}] \qquad\qquad\qquad h: m[(\boldsymbol{\nu}n)P]_k \longmapsto (\boldsymbol{\nu}n)(h: m[P]_k),\ m \neq n$

In [NEW-LOCAMB], an ambient n is created at the fresh location l, whose parent is located at h. In [NEW-LOCAMB'], a new boundary forwarder is also created and inserted between m and n. [NEW-RES] creates a globally unique name for each name restriction.

Emission of request messages

[REQ-IN] $\text{in } m.P \xmapsto[h:n]{k} \text{wait}.P \gg \uparrow_h^k \{\text{in } m, n\}$

[REQ-COIN] $\overline{\text{in}} \ n.P \xmapsto[h:n]{k} \text{wait}.P \gg \uparrow_h^k \{\overline{\text{in}} \ n, h\}$

[REQ-OUT] $\text{out } m.P \xmapsto[h:n]{k} \text{wait}.P \gg \uparrow_h^k \{\text{out } m, n\}$

[REQ-COOPEN] $\overline{\text{open}} \ n.P \xmapsto[h:n]{k} \text{wait}.P \gg \uparrow_h^k \{\overline{\text{open}} \ n\}$

These rules are straightforward. For each action or coaction listed above, an ambient sends the corresponding request message to its parent at k. The name n of the requesting ambient is included in the $\{\text{in}\}$ and $\{\text{out}\}$ message so that it can be used for creating a clone of the ambient if the request crosses a boundary. Note that every single-threaded (ST) ambient that sends a request message to its parent simply blocks waiting for any completion message to be sent back from the parent. This fairly simplifies the execution of processes within each ambient.

Transmission of request messages

[FW-REQ] $h \rhd^\circ k \parallel \uparrow_l^h \{Req\} \longmapsto h \rhd^\circ k \parallel \uparrow_l^k \{Req\}$

[BFW-REQ] $h \rhd^\bullet k \parallel \uparrow_l^h \{\_R\} \longmapsto h \rhd^\bullet k \parallel (\boldsymbol{\nu} h')(h' \bullet l \parallel \uparrow_{h'}^k \{\bullet R\})$

[LOC-RCV] $h : n[P]_k \parallel \uparrow_l^h \{Req\} \longmapsto h : n[P \mid \uparrow_l \{Req\}]_k$

In [FW-REQ], if a request message reaches a normal forwarder, it is forwarded to k by this normal forwarder. Note that the source location of the message remains l so that the corresponding completion message can be directly sent back to l at the next stage. In [BFW-REQ], if a request message reaches a boundary forwarder, it is forwarded to k after being marked with special tag $\bullet$. Furthermore, the source location of the messages is replaced by the fresh location h', where a new seed attached with l is created so that the corresponding completion message can be sent back via this seed. In [LOC-RCV], when a request message reaches its destination, it is brought into the destination.

Local reductions

[LOCAL-COM] $\langle M \rangle \mid (x)P \xmapsto[-:-]{-} P\{M/x\} \gg \mathbf{0}$

[LOCAL-IN] $\uparrow_l \{\text{in } n, -\} \mid \uparrow_{l'} \{\overline{\text{in}} \ n, l'\} \xmapsto[-:-]{-} \mathbf{0} \quad \gg \uparrow^l \{\text{go } l'\} \parallel \uparrow^{l'} \{\text{OK}\overline{\text{in}}\}$

[LOCAL-IN'] $\uparrow_l \{\_\text{in } n, m\} \mid \uparrow_{l'} \{\bullet\overline{\text{in}} \ n, k\} \xmapsto[-:-]{-} \mathbf{0} \quad \gg$

$\uparrow^l \{\text{migrate } l'\} \parallel \uparrow^{l'} \{\text{new } m, k\}$

[LOCAL-IN''] $\uparrow_l \{\bullet\text{in } n, m\} \mid \uparrow_{l'} \{\overline{\text{in}} \ n, l'\} \xmapsto[h:-]{-} \text{wait}.\mathbf{0} \gg \uparrow^h \{\bullet\text{Cin } n, m, l, l'\}$

[LOCAL-OUT] $\uparrow_l \{\text{out } n, -\} \mid \overline{\text{out}} \ n.P \xmapsto[-:n]{k} P \qquad \gg \uparrow^l \{\text{go } k\}$

[LOCAL-OUT'] $\uparrow_l \{\bullet\text{out } n, m\} \mid \overline{\text{out}} \ n.P \xmapsto[h:n]{-} \text{wait}.P \gg \uparrow^h \{\bullet\text{Cout } m, l\}$

[LOCAL-OPEN] $\text{open } n.P \mid \uparrow_l \{\_\overline{\text{open}} \ n\} \xmapsto[h:-]{-} \text{wait}.P \gg \uparrow^l \{\text{migrate } h\}$

[LOCAL-COM] is the same as [R-MSG] of SA in Section 2.1. The other rules express match operations of an ambient for three kinds of movements.

In [LOCAL-IN] and [LOCAL-OUT], if no request message is marked with the • tag, the appropriate completion messages are sent back, as shown in Figure 1 (a), (b). In [LOCAL-OPEN], irrespective of the {$\overline{\text{open}}$} message being marked with •, all opens can be handled as shown in Figure 1 (c).

If an {$\overline{\text{in}}$} message sent by an ambient at k is marked with •, a clone must be created inside the same network domain as the ambient, as explained in Section 3.1. The message {new m, k} is used for this purpose in [LOCAL-IN′], where m is the name of the clone to be created.

On the other hand, if an {$\overline{\text{in}}$} message does not cross any boundaries, a clone may be created immediately by the parent. However, in our formalization, we cannot express the creation of a located agent at the process level. Instead, we formalized this case as in [Local-In″], where the parent sends the {•Cin} message to *itself*. The consumption of {•Cin} is a network-level reduction (see [COMPL-CIN] below); hence, it can express the creation of a clone. We do the same for out in [LOCAL-OUT′].[1]

Transmission of completion messages

[BACK-MIGR] $\uparrow^h$ {migrate k} $\| h \bullet l \longmapsto h \rhd^\bullet k \| \uparrow^l$ {migrate h}

[BACK-NEW] $\uparrow^h$ {new m, k} $\| h \bullet l \longmapsto h \rhd^\bullet l \| \uparrow^l$ {new m, k}, $k \neq l$

[BACK-NEW′] $\uparrow^h$ {new m, l} $\| h \bullet l \longmapsto (\nu k)(h \rhd^\bullet k \| k : m[\text{wait}.0]_l \| \uparrow^l$ {$\overline{\text{OKin}}$})

The kinds of completion messages that might cross some network boundary are new and migrate; both are forwarded by seeds.

In [BACK-MIGR], the seed at h changes the argument of {migrate k} to h and forwards it to l, where a requesting ambient or another boundary forwarder is located. At the same time, the seed becomes the boundary forwarder in preparation for the {register} message sent back from l.

In [BACK-NEW], the condition $k \neq l$ implies that the agent at l is not the ambient that requested $\overline{\text{in}}$; it is another boundary forwarder. Thus, the seed simply forwards the {new} message to l, and then, it becomes the boundary forwarder in preparation for the {register} message sent from *elsewhere*. This boundary forwarder must forward it to l because the new clone will be created beyond l.

In [BACK-NEW′], when a {new} message eventually reaches the same network domain as the ambient that requested $\overline{\text{in}}$ at l, a clone is created at the fresh location k and the seed at h becomes the boundary forwarder targeting k. Furthermore, an $\overline{\text{OKin}}$ message, which notifies the match of $\overline{\text{in}}$, is sent to l.

---

[1] These extra steps (local communication) can be omitted in real implementations. In addition, the parameter n of {•Cin n, m, l, l'} is used only for the correctness proof (see Section 6 and [6]).

Consumption of completion messages

[COMPL-PARENT] $\uparrow^h\{\texttt{go }k\} \parallel h:n[P \mid \texttt{wait}.Q]_- \longmapsto h:n[P \mid Q]_k$

[COMPL-COIN] $\uparrow^h\{\texttt{OK}\overline{\texttt{in}}\} \parallel h:n[P \mid \texttt{wait}.Q]_k \longmapsto h:n[P \mid Q]_k$

[COMPL-CIN] $\uparrow^h\{_\bullet\texttt{Cin} -, m, l, l'\} \parallel h:n[P \mid \texttt{wait}.Q]_k \longmapsto$
$$h:n[P \mid Q]_k \parallel (\boldsymbol{\nu}h')(h':m[\texttt{wait}.0]_{l'} \parallel \uparrow^l\{\texttt{migrate }h'\}) \parallel \uparrow^{l'}\{\texttt{OK}\overline{\texttt{in}}\}$$

[COMPL-COUT] $\uparrow^h\{_\bullet\texttt{Cout }m, l\} \parallel h:n[P \mid \texttt{wait}.Q]_k \longmapsto$
$$h:n[P \mid Q]_k \parallel (\boldsymbol{\nu}h')(h':m[\texttt{wait}.0]_k \parallel \uparrow^l\{\texttt{migrate }h'\})$$

[COMPL-MIGR] $\uparrow^h\{\texttt{migrate }k\} \parallel h:n[P \mid \texttt{wait}.Q]_- \longmapsto$
$$h \rhd^\circ k \parallel \uparrow^k\{\texttt{register }P \mid Q\}$$

[BFW-REG] $\uparrow^h\{\texttt{register }R\} \parallel h \rhd^\bullet k \longmapsto$
$$h \rhd^\bullet k \parallel \uparrow^k\{\texttt{register }R\}$$

[COMPL-REG] $\uparrow^h\{\texttt{register }R\} \parallel h:n[P \mid \texttt{wait}.Q]_k \longmapsto h:n[P \mid Q \mid R]_k$

In [COMPL-PARENT] and [COMPL-COIN], $\{\texttt{go}\}$ and $\{\texttt{OK}\overline{\texttt{in}}\}$ messages are handled appropriately by the destination ambient. In [COMPL-CIN] and [COMPL-COUT], an ambient that receives a $\{_\bullet\texttt{Cin}\}$ or $\{_\bullet\texttt{Cout}\}$ message creates a clone and sends the appropriate completion messages. In [COMPL-MIGR], an ambient that receives a $\{\texttt{migrate }k\}$ message sends the $\{\texttt{register}\}$ message, which contains the contents of the ambient, to k. Each $\{\texttt{register}\}$ message reaches the destination ambient through zero or more transmissions of [BFW-REG]; then, R is merged into the destination in [COMPL-REG].

4   GcPAN$_{\text{mov}}$: Garbage Collecting Forwarders

As described in the previous section, chaining forwarders upon each cross-boundary movement in PAN$_{\text{mov}}$ removes the need for all-to-all connectivity in the underlying network. However, along with this adaptability to wide-area networks, at least one boundary forwarder and one normal forwarder are created upon each cross-boundary movement. Therefore, continuing the execution of an SA program in PAN$_{\text{mov}}$ is likely to result in the accumulation of more unused forwarders and longer chains of forwarders than those in PAN. Clearly, unused forwarders keep occupying resources needlessly, and forwarder chains induce a loss of performance by increasing the number of network messages.

To handle such situations, we enriched PAN$_{\text{mov}}$ with the mechanism used in GcPAN [8]; it reclaims unused forwarders and contracts forwarder chains. The following are the basic ideas of GcPAN: (1) to detect unused forwarders, every agent is equipped with a reference count. Every time an agent receives a request message, its reference count is decremented. If an agent is a forwarder whose count is zero, it is reclaimed, and (2) to contract forwarder chains, using Tarjan's union-find algorithm [14], every agent is relocated immediately below its parent ambient. For a detailed understanding of GcPAN, see [8].

Enriching PAN$_{\text{mov}}$ with GcPAN's mechanism is a straightforward process. However, the formal definition of the resulting abstract machine GcPAN$_{\text{mov}}$ is rather complex. For lack of space, it is provided in [6].

5 GcPAN$_{\text{shift}}$: Proactive Movement

In PAN$_{\text{mov}}$ and GcPAN$_{\text{mov}}$, an ambient physically moves when it performs a cross-boundary **in** or **out** action. However, this implies that its physical movement is still deferred until it sends some request message to its parent. Then, for instance, if an ambient blocks for some reason, e.g., waiting for I/O, forwarders used by the ambient will not be reclaimed or contracted until the ambient resumes and sends some request. Moreover, if a network connection represented by a certain network boundary is broken for some reason (including permanent disconnection of mobile devices), a child ambient whose parent belongs to the other side of the boundary cannot send requests to its parent, and it cannot perform movements anymore.

In order to address the problem described above, there should be a mechanism for enforcing physical movements of ambients in the abstract machines, which PAN and GcPAN do not have. Therefore, we added a **shift** action, which instructs an ambient to move physically below its parent, in PAN$_{\text{mov}}$ and GcPAN$_{\text{mov}}$. Note that **shift** performs no logical action at the calculus level; hence, each ambient may perform **shift** actions periodically. For example, in the state:

$$h_1 : \mathsf{a}[\,P\,]_{h_2} \parallel h_2 \rhd^\circ h_3 \parallel h_3 \rhd^\bullet h_4 \parallel h_4 \rhd^\circ h_5 \parallel h_5 : \mathsf{b}[\,Q\,]_{h_6}$$

if **a** performs a **shift** action, the state changes to:

$$h_2 \rhd^\circ h_3 \parallel h_3 \rhd^\bullet h_4 \parallel h_4 \rhd^\circ h_5 \parallel h_7 : \mathsf{a}[\,P\,]_{h_5} \parallel h_5 : \mathsf{b}[\,Q\,]_{h_6}$$

Moreover, if **a** has no child or if all of **a**'s children also perform a **shift** action, the forwarders are reclaimed as in: $h_7 : \mathsf{a}[\,P\,]_{h_5} \parallel h_5 : \mathsf{b}[\,Q\,]_{h_6}$.

We enrich PAN$_{\text{mov}}$ with the **shift** action described above by adding the following reduction rules:

[REQ-SHIFT] $P \xmapsto[h:n]{k} \mathtt{wait}.P \gg \uparrow_h^k \{\mathtt{shift}\ n\}$

[LOCAL-SHIFT] $\uparrow_l \{\mathtt{shift}\ -\} \xmapsto[h:-]{} \mathbf{0} \qquad \gg \uparrow^l \{\mathtt{go}\ h\}$

[LOCAL-SHIFT$'$] $\uparrow_l \{\mathtt{shift}_\bullet\ m\} \xmapsto[h:-]{} \mathtt{wait}.\mathbf{0} \gg \uparrow^h \{\mathtt{Cshift}_\bullet\ m,l\}$

[COMPL-CSHIFT] $\uparrow^h \{\mathtt{Cshift}_\bullet\ m,l\} \parallel h : n[P \mid \mathtt{wait}.Q]_k \longmapsto$
$\qquad\qquad h : n[P \mid Q]_k \parallel (\boldsymbol{\nu}h')(h' : m[\mathtt{wait}.\mathbf{0}]_h \parallel \uparrow^l \{\mathtt{migrate}\ h'\})$

The formal definition of the abstract machine GcPAN$_{\text{shift}}$, which is an extension of GcPAN$_{\text{mov}}$ with the **shift** action, is provided in [6].

6 Correctness

We prove that PAN$_{\text{mov}}$ is a correct implementation of SA. The fact that PAN is a correct implementation of SA, i.e., SA and PAN are weak barbed bisimilar, is proved in [12,7]; hence, it suffices to prove that PAN and PAN$_{\text{mov}}$ are weak barbed bisimilar. We follow the proof method between PAN and GcPAN [8,9].

Theorem 1. *There is a weak barbed bisimulation $\mathcal{R}$ between* PAN *and* PAN$_{\mathrm{mov}}$.

Proof. We constructed such a bisimulation relation $\mathcal{R}$. For lack of space, the precise definition of $\mathcal{R}$ and the details of the proof is provided in [6].

Due to physical movement of PAN$_{\mathrm{mov}}$, $\mathcal{R}$ has several significant differences from the bisimulation relation $\mathcal{R}'$ between PAN and GcPAN, which is described in [9]. The following are the main differences: (1) each ambient in PAN$_{\mathrm{mov}}$ may be at several locations during its lifetime; therefore, the simple correspondence between ambients that are at the same location, which is used in $\mathcal{R}'$, does not work. Instead, we established a mapping from the set of ambient locations in a PAN net to the set of ambient locations in the corresponding PAN$_{\mathrm{mov}}$ net, and (2) the mapping is updated along with PAN$_{\mathrm{mov}}$'s reductions related to physical movement of ambients so that it can properly map unmoving ambients of PAN to moving ambients of PAN$_{\mathrm{mov}}$. $\square$

Corollary 2 (Adequacy). *Let P be an SA process, then $[\![P]\!]_{mov} \approx P$.*

Proof. $[\![P]\!] \; \mathcal{R} \; [\![P]\!]_{mov}$ can be easily checked; hence, from Theorem 1, $[\![P]\!] \approx [\![P]\!]_{mov}$. Then, the result follows from the adequacy of PAN [7]: $[\![P]\!] \approx P$. $\square$

For the correctness of GcPAN$_{\mathrm{shift}}$, the proof stated above can be adapted to establish a weak barbed bisimilarity between GcPAN$_{\mathrm{shift}}$ and GcPAN. The correctness of GcPAN$_{\mathrm{mov}}$ is immediately derived from that of GcPAN$_{\mathrm{shift}}$ because GcPAN$_{\mathrm{mov}}$ is a subset of GcPAN$_{\mathrm{shift}}$.

7   Conclusion

In this paper, we proposed novel abstract machines that can handle network boundaries in wide-area and mobile networks. They have the following desirable properties: (1) No ambients communicate directly with other ambients in different network domains; instead, all inter-domain messages are sent via boundary forwarders, and (2) In GcPAN$_{\mathrm{shift}}$, any ambient will go into a stable state in which any ambient inside it can perform SA actions without boundary forwarders. Therefore, we can construct more reliable implementations of SA by using these machines as base implementation models. Formal proofs of these properties are left for future work.

AtJ [4] is a distributed implementation of AC, a translator from AC to Jo-Caml [3]. Although physical movement is triggered by each execution of **in** or **out**, no forwarders are created for this movement in AtJ. This is because any child can send messages directly to its parent at any moment using JoCaml's distributed message transfer mechanism; that is, AtJ relies on JoCaml's all-to-all connectivity. Nonetheless, adapting our technique to AtJ seems relatively easy because a forwarder is created at each **open** action, as in the case of PAN.

In a distributed abstract machine for the Kell Calculus [13], the passivation of a kell is represented as the physical migration of the *whole* hierarchy (i.e., the kell, its sub-kells, sub-kells of its sub-kells, and so on). Thus, the underlying network need not support all-to-all connectivity. However, such a passivation mechanism seems rather inefficient. Moreover, each kell must keep track of its sub-kells; therefore, the abstract machine is more complex, as compared to the PAN family.

Acknowledgments. This work was partly supported by MEXT Grant-in-Aid for Young Scientists (B) (21700029).

References

1. Cardelli, L.: Mobile Ambient Synchronization. Technical Report 1997-013, Digital Systems Research (1997)
2. Cardelli, L., Gordon, A.D.: Mobile Ambients. In: Nivat, M. (ed.) FOSSACS 1998. LNCS, vol. 1378, pp. 140–155. Springer, Heidelberg (1998)
3. Fournet, C.: The Join-Calculus: a Calculus for Distributed Mobile Programming. PhD thesis, Ecole Polytechnique (1998)
4. Fournet, C., Lévy, J.J., Schmitt, A.: An Asynchronous, Distributed Implementation of Mobile Ambients. In: Watanabe, O., Hagiya, M., Ito, T., van Leeuwen, J., Mosses, P.D. (eds.) TCS 2000. LNCS, vol. 1872, pp. 348–364. Springer, Heidelberg (2000)
5. GCPAN webpage, http://perso.ens-lyon.fr/damien.pous/gcpan
6. GCPAN$_{shift}$ webpage, http://ryujin.kuis.kyoto-u.ac.jp/~umatani/pan/
7. Giannini, P., Sangiorgi, D., Valente, A.: Safe Ambients: Abstract Machine and Distributed Implementation. Science of Computer Programming 59, 209–249 (2006)
8. Hirschkoff, D., Pous, D., Sangiorgi, D.: A Correct Abstract Machine for Safe Ambients. In: Jacquet, J.-M., Picco, G.P. (eds.) COORDINATION 2005. LNCS, vol. 3454, pp. 17–32. Springer, Heidelberg (2005)
9. Hirschkoff, D., Pous, D., Sangiorgi, D.: An efficient abstract machine for Safe Ambients. Journal of Logic and Algebraic Programming 71(2), 114–149 (2007)
10. Levi, F., Sangiorgi, D.: Mobile Safe Ambients. ACM Transactions on Programming Languages and Systems 25, 1–69 (2003)
11. Phillips, A., Yoshida, N., Eisenbach, S.: A Distributed Abstract Machine for Boxed Ambient Calculi. In: Schmidt, D. (ed.) ESOP 2004. LNCS, vol. 2986, pp. 155–170. Springer, Heidelberg (2004)
12. Sangiorgi, D., Valente, A.: A Distributed Abstract Machine for Safe Ambients. In: Yu, Y., Spirakis, P.G., van Leeuwen, J. (eds.) ICALP 2001. LNCS, vol. 2076, pp. 408–420. Springer, Heidelberg (2001)
13. Schmitt, A., Stefani, J.: An Abstract Machine for the Kell Calculus. In: Steffen, M., Tennenholtz, M. (eds.) FMOODS 2005. LNCS, vol. 3535, pp. 31–46. Springer, Heidelberg (2005)
14. Tarjan, R.E.: Efficiency of a Good But Not Linear Set Union Algorithm. Journal of the ACM 22, 215–225 (1975)

Simulation-Based Performance Analysis of Channel-Based Coordination Models

C. Verhoef[1,*], C. Krause[2,**], O. Kanters[1], and R. van der Mei[1,3]

[1] Centrum Wiskunde & Informatica (CWI), Amsterdam, The Netherlands
C.G.Verhoef@cwi.nl
[2] Hasso Plattner Institute (HPI), University of Potsdam, Germany
[3] Vrije Universiteit Amsterdam (VUA), The Netherlands

Abstract. Quantifying the performance of component-based or service-oriented systems is a complex task, e.g., it is non-trivial to calculate the end-to-end quality of service of a composite Web service. An established approach to reason about such systems in general is the use of coordination models, which can provide a formal basis for both their verification and implementation. An example of such a model is the channel-based coordination language *Reo* and its probabilistic extension *Stochastic Reo*. However, all existing performance analysis approaches for Stochastic Reo are restricted to the use of exponential distributions. To this end we introduce a transition structure, which enables a simulation approach for performance evaluation in Reo, enabling the use of arbitrary distributions and predefined probabilistic behaviors. Our approach supports steady-state and transient analysis and, moreover, scales much better than the existing automata-based algorithms.

1 Introduction

Non-functional requirements, such as reliability, security and performance are becoming of increasing importance in many branches of component-based and service-oriented software engineering. Particularly the quantitative aspects inherent in the performance evaluation of composite and distributed systems introduce major challenges. Even if the quality of service (QoS) properties of every individual service and connection is known, it is far from trivial to reason about the end-to-end QoS of the composed system. This is due to the fact that synchronization constraints as well as buffering and routing policies between the different parties in a network can have an impact not only on its qualitative behavioral properties, but also on its overall performance. In the worst case, a 'bad' performance, e.g. if a service takes too long to respond to a request, can even have an influence on the functional properties of the system. However, in this paper we consider rather typical questions of performance evaluation, such as: Where are the bottlenecks in the network? What is the expected delay and

---

* Corresponding author, Supported by NWO project Cooper.
** Supported by the research school in 'Service-Oriented Systems Engineering' at HPI.

W. De Meuter and G.-C. Roman (Eds.): COORDINATION 2011, LNCS 6721, pp. 187–201, 2011.

the maximum throughput? How much time does it take until a certain event happens? What is the expected utilization of a buffer?

Building software compositionally out of a set of primitive components or services is a key task in software engineering in general. The coordination paradigm provides concepts to properly describe the allowed interactions between the active entities in a system. A specific coordination approach is considered in the channel-based coordination language *Reo* [1], in which compositionally built components connectors are used as coordination artifacts. Connectors in Reo can be seen as a kind of 'glue code' which coordinate the interactions among a set of components or services from outside. To enable performance evaluation of component connectors, *Stochastic Reo* [2] provides an extension that allows to annotate connectors with stochastic performance properties. Specifically, communication channels in Stochastic Reo are annotated with processing delays. Moreover, to reason about the end-to-end QoS of a connector, its boundary nodes are annotated with data arrival rates, modeling the interaction with its environment. In this way, Stochastic Reo provides detailed information about the performance of the primitive buildings blocks on the one hand, and the external world on the other.

The existing techniques for performance evaluation in Stochastic Reo are all based on analytical methods and essentially follow the same recipe. An automata-based model is used to describe the semantics of every primitive channel in a connector. By composing all these automata, a behavioral model for the whole connector is built. Then, using the stochastic annotations of the channels and boundary nodes, a probabilistic performance model, specifically: a continuous-time Markov chain is generated. Finally, the Markov model is fed into a tool for probabilistic analysis, such as PRISM [3] or Matlab. This approach was taken in [4] using *Quantitative Constraint Automata* (QCA), in [2] using *Quantitative Intentional Automata* (QIA) and in [6] using *Stochastic Reo Automata* (SRA). An implementation of the QIA-based approach is described in [7]. However, all of these approaches to performance evaluation in Reo have two main limitations: (i) they are all restricted to the use of exponential distributions, and (ii) they suffer from the state space explosion problem, because the automaton / continuous-time Markov chain for the whole system has to be computed in advance.

Complementary to the existing analytical methods, we consider a simulation approach for performance analysis in Stochastic Reo, which enables the use of *arbitrary* (not just exponential) distributions for describing stochastic properties of channels and components. Our approach is based on the coloring semantics [8] of Reo, which enables a step-wise execution scheme (cf. [9]). Thus, state spaces can be generated on-the-fly during the simulation without requiring to keep track of the execution history. Therefore, our approach scales much better than the existing automata-based techniques, which require to compute the whole state space *before* the actual analysis starts. The coloring semantics which we use in our approach, supports context-dependent primitives, such as the *LossySync* channel (cf. [8]). Moreover, it allows to model the availability of I/O requests at the boundary of a connector, which is a key ingredient to reason about the end-to-end performance of a connector.

We have implemented our simulation approach for Reo in a sophisticated graphical tool, as part of the Eclipse Coordination Tools (ECT) [10]. Connectors can be specified using a graphical editor in ECT. By annotating these graphical connector models with stochastic information, our simulator generates a large number of performance statistics. Our tool supports both steady-state and transient analysis and can be applied to connectors built using all standard and even user-defined Reo channels. To analyze specific behaviors of the modeled system, a number of tools are available to the user, such as automatic deadlock and livelock detection, visualization of the connector colorings, and charts for the behavior of simulation results during the simulation. Various stopping conditions can be specified for the simulation. Our simulator generates a number of statistical outputs depending on the chosen type of simulation, for an overview we refer to Section 4.1.

Related work. Model-based methodologies to assess performance of distributed software systems can be categorized [11] in: queuing networks, state/transition-based analysis, and software performance engineering. A survey of the available results in the theory of queuing networks is given in [12]. The Method of Layers in [13], models the responsiveness of composite services using closed queuing networks using Mean Value Analysis. Stochastic rendezvous networks are introduced in [14] for performance evaluation of distributed systems with synchronization. Software Performance Engineering is suggested in [15] to enable the integration of performance analysis into the software development process. Simulation of stochastic graph transformation systems is described in [16]. In [17] a methodology for simulation of embedded systems is presented. Yacoub et al. [18] focus on reliability analysis for component-based systems. In [19] a reasoning technology to simulate and verify pure Web services is defined. In [20] Generalized Stochastic Petri Nets (GSPN) are proposed for performance analysis of multiprocessor systems. Performance evaluation is done by generating continuous-time Markov chains [21]. Haas provides an overview of simulation techniques for GSPNs [22]. GreatSPN is a simulation tool for performance evaluation of distributed systems using GSPNs [23]. Compared to GSPNs, Reo has a strong notion of synchronization, which, just like the notion of context dependency, propagates through connectors, both not supported by GSPNs. Due to this, traditionally automata based models are used as semantical models for Reo.

Organization. Section 2 gives a brief overview of (Stochastic) Reo. We define the operational semantics underlying our simulation and introduce our transition system in Section 3. In Section 4 we present our simulation-based stochastic analysis procedure. Our simulation tool is described in Section 5. We present two case studies in Section 6. Section 7 contains conclusions and future work.

2   Channel-Based Coordination with Reo

The simulation approach we present here targets the channel-based coordination language Reo [1]. Channels in Reo are entities that have exactly two ends, which can be either *source* or *sink* ends. Source ends accept data into, and sink ends dispense data out of their channel. Reo allows directed channels as well as *drain* and *spout* channels, which have respectively two source and two sink ends. Channels may impose constraints on the dataflow at their ends. For instance, the communication through channels can be (a)synchronous and (un)buffered.

For the scope of this paper, we consider a fixed set of channels, summarized in Table 1. The *Sync* channel consumes data items at its source end and dispenses them at its sink end. The I/O operations are performed synchronously and without any buffering. Thus, the channel blocks if the party at the sink end is not ready to receive data. The *LossySync* channel behaves in the same way, except that it does not block the party at its source end. Instead, the data item is consumed and destroyed by the channel if the receiver is not ready to accept it. The *SyncDrain* channel is also synchronous, but it differs in the fact that it has two source ends through which it consumes and destroys data items synchronously. The *FIFO* channel is a directed, asynchronous channel with a buffer of size one.

Table 1. Some basic Reo channels

Sync	LossySync	SyncDrain	FIFO
⟶	⤏	→←	—▢→

Channels in Reo can be joined together using nodes, which read data items from sink ends and write data items to source ends of channels that coincide in it. Nodes in Reo behave as non-deterministic mergers on the sink ends and as (synchronous) replicators on the source ends. This means that a node non-deterministically reads a data item from one of the incoming sink ends and replicates it to all outgoing source ends without buffering it.

2.1   Building Connectors

In Reo, channels and nodes are joined together to build so-called *connectors* which resemble electronic circuits. These connectors are used as *glue code* between components or services and essentially enforce a communication protocol between them. This coordination of components or services is performed from outside and without their knowledge, which is also referred to as *exogenous* coordination.

An important aspect of Reo is the fact that nodes do not buffer data items and therefore allow synchrony to propagate through the connector. For instance, a sequence of n *Sync* channels joined together using nodes has the same qualitative behavior as a single *Sync*. Note also that Reo allows an arbitrary mixing of synchrony and asynchrony.

Example 1. We consider a simple instant messenger application, depicted in Fig. 1. Two *Client* components exchange messages via a connector. Messages are exchanged via *FIFO* channels and are, thus, buffered. When leaving the buffer again, the messages are synchronously replicated by the node behind the *FIFO* and sent to both clients. This can succeed only when both clients are ready to accept data, i.e. when there are pending read requests at both *in* ports. In a nutshell, this connector ensures that the clients get –as an acknowledgment– a copy of their own message when the other client has successfully received it.

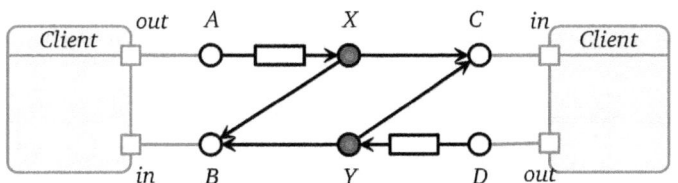

Fig. 1. Instant messenger application modeled in Reo

2.2   Stochastic Reo

Stochastic Reo is an extension of Reo annotated with stochastic properties. In particular, we distinguish between the following two quantitative aspects in Reo:

- **Channel delays:** Every channel has one or more associated delays represented by a set of random variables. Such a delay models how long it takes for a channel to transfer or process a data item. For instance, a $LossySync_{A \to B}$ has two associated delays 'dAB' and '$dALost$', respectively for successful dataflow through the channel, and losing data in the channel if B is not ready to receive data. A $FIFO_{A \to B}$ has two associated delays: 'dAF' and 'dFB'. The former represents the delay for the dataflow from A into the buffer. The latter models the dataflow out of the channel. *Sync* and *SyncDrain* channels have only one delay, i.e., for successful dataflow.

- **Arrivals at nodes:** I/O operations are performed at the boundary nodes of a connector through which it interacts with its environment (depicted as empty circles). We assume the time between consecutive arrivals of read and write requests at the boundary nodes depends on their associated stochastic processes. For instance, 'dA' and 'dB' in the connector in Fig. 1 represent the associated arrival processes of nodes A and B. Furthermore, at most one request at each boundary node can wait for acceptance. If a boundary node is occupied by a pending request, then the node is blocked and consequently all further arrivals at that node are lost.

Note that arrivals at nodes are considered only for boundary nodes, e.g. A, B, C, D, but not X, Y in Fig.2. Internal nodes are used for synchronous dataflow only and merely pump data in the connector, without interaction with the environment. Therefore, internal nodes have neither an associated arrival rate, nor a delay.

2.3 Distributions

In our simulation approach and particularly in the simulation tool which we present in Section 5, we support a number of distribution types, some of them being general stochastic distributions, while others being special constructs for steering the simulation process. The types of supported distributions and their parameters are listed in Table 2. The value after the parameters between the brackets indicates the type of the parameter, where b = Boolean, i = integer, r = real, and s = string.

Table 2. Supported distributions

Distribution	Param 1	Param 2	Param 3
Beta	α (r)	β (r)	
Binomial	n (i)	p (r)	
Chi^2	k (i)		
Constant (*Con*)	value (r)		
Exponential (*Exp*)	λ (r)		
F	d$_1$ (r)	d$_2$ (r)	
Gamma	k (r)		
Lognormal	μ (r)	θ (r)	
Poisson	λ (r)		
Triangular (*Tri*)	low (r)	high (r)	avg (r)
Uniform	low (r)	high (r)	
Weibull	k (r)		
IfNeeded			
Always			
Trace	path (s)	loop (b)	

Table 3. Example channel delays

Channel	Delay 1	Delay 2
$FIFO_{A\to X}$	$Exp(2)$	$Exp(1)$
$Sync_{X\to C}$	$Tri(5,10,7)$	$-$
$FIFO_{D\to Y}$	$Exp(2)$	$Con(0)$
$Sync_{Y\to B}$	$Con(0)$	$-$
$Sync_{X\to B}$	$Exp(1)$	$-$
$Sync_{Y\to C}$	$Exp(2)$	$-$

Table 4. Example node arrival rates

Node	Arrivals
A	$Exp(1)$
B	$Exp(10)$
C	$Exp(1/2)$
D	$Exp(1/8)$

Example 2. For the instant messenger example, we consider the channel delay and node arrival parameters chosen such that analysis is not trivial, given in Table 3 and 4, respectively. We assume exponential distributions for the request arrivals at all boundary nodes and for most of the channel delays. However, we assume that the dataflow between the buffer of $FIFO_{D\to Y}$ to the boundary node B can be performed without any delay ($Con(0)$). Moreover, the delay of $Sync_{X\to C}$ is approximated using a triangular distribution.

3 Coloring Semantics with States

In our simulation approach, we use the so-called *coloring semantics* [8] of Reo, introduced by Clarke et al. to properly model context-dependent behavior as required for instance for the *LossySync* channel. The basic idea of the coloring semantics is to associate flow and no-flow colors to channel ends. As shown in [8] one *flow* and two *no-flow* colors are sufficient to model context-dependency. Essentially, the two different *no-flow* colors are used to distinguish between absence and presence of an I/O request. Table 5 depicts the names and graphical notations of the flow and the two no-flow colors, as used in this paper.

Table 6. Example colorings

Table 5. Colors

Color name	Symbol
flow	
no-flow-provide-reason	
no-flow-require-reason	

Sync	Merger
(S1)	(M1)　　　　(M2)
(S2)	
(S3)	(M3)　　　　(M4)
(S4)	

The color *flow* represents ordinary dataflow at a channel end. The two *no-flow* colors are used to encode a direction of the reason for the fact that no dataflow is possible. Intuitively, *no-flow-provide-reason* models the fact that the receiving or sending party is not ready to perform an I/O operation. Conversely, *no-flow-require-reason* says that the party is ready to receive or send data, but is not allowed to perform the operation. At the boundary of a connector, the two *no-flow* colors can be interpreted as lack of dataflow – either because of a missing, or in spite of a present I/O request.

Valid behaviors of channels are described as colorings of their respective ends. Table 6 depicts the colorings of the *Sync* the *Merger* primitive. The latter is used for modeling nodes in Reo. For the colorings of other primitives such as the *FIFO* channel we refer to [8]. Note that the colors are always read from the perspective of the primitive. For instance, in coloring (S2) of the *Sync* the party at the right end provides a reason for no flow, whereas the source end on the left requires a reason. This models the behavior where data is available at the source end but the receiver at the sink end is not ready to accept data. Similarly, in coloring (S3) there is no flow, because there is no data available at the source end. Finally, coloring (S4) models the situation where no data is available and the receiver is also not ready to accept any data. Similarly, the colorings of the *Merger* primitive in Table 5 show the valid dataflows through sink nodes and how reasons for no dataflow are being propagated.

Valid colorings of primitives are joined together and give rise to valid colorings of the whole connector (see [8] for details).

Example 3. Fig. 2 depicts an example coloring of the instant messenger application. The coloring is based on the following state of the connector: $FIFO_{A \to X}$ is full, $FIFO_{D \to Y}$ is empty, there are read requests at the boundary nodes B

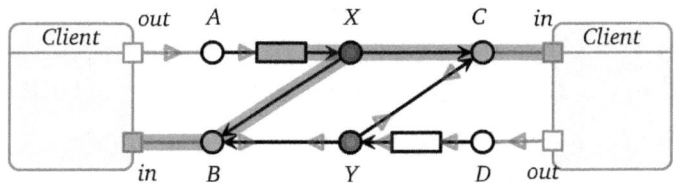

Fig. 2. A coloring of the instant messenger application

and C, and no write requests at A and D. This particular coloring models a dataflow action from the full $FIFO_{A \to X}$ to both clients, i.e., a synchronized message delivery and acknowledgment.

3.1   Coloring Transition System

Colorings describe only dataflow events, but not the state of primitives or the whole connector. Therefore, we now incorporate a notion of state into the coloring model, which gives rise to a transition structure defined in the following. Let $Color$ be a fixed set of flow colors, as defined in Table 5.

Definition 1 (coloring transition system). *A coloring transition system $C = (N, B, Q, \Longrightarrow)$ consists of a set of nodes N, a set of boundary nodes $B \subseteq N$, a set of states Q and a set of coloring transitions $\Longrightarrow \subseteq Q \times Color^N \times Q$.*

We often write $q \Longrightarrow_c q'$ for a transition where $c \in Color^N$ is a coloring. Colorings model dataflows, which is why we also refer to transitions as *dataflow transitions* or just *dataflows*.

However, this model does not reflect the interaction of the connector with its environment. Specifically, boundary nodes receive requests from their components. Therefore, we model the state of boundary nodes explicitly as:

- $States = \{empty, waiting, busy\}$

A boundary node is *empty* when there is no I/O request pending, *waiting* when the node received an I/O request pending for processing, and *busy* when it is sending or receiving data. We model the state change of boundary nodes on request arrivals using the map $Arrival : States \to States$ defined as follows:

- $Arrival = \{empty \mapsto waiting, waiting \mapsto waiting, busy \mapsto busy\}$

In the following, we relate the state of the boundary nodes with the coloring semantics. Specifically, we define a transition structure where colorings are being enabled based on the presence/absence of requests. Moreover, we model the start and the end of dataflows as distinct events. This is important to measure, e.g., the duration of dataflows and the waiting time of requests at boundary nodes.

Definition 2 (induced intensional coloring transition system). *Given a coloring transition system $C = (N, B, Q, \Longrightarrow)$. The induced intensional coloring transition system is a tuple $\mathcal{C} = (\mathcal{Q}, \to, \overset{start}{\Longrightarrow}, \overset{end}{\Longrightarrow})$ where:*

- $\mathcal{Q} = Q \times States^B \times 2$ *is a set of states where a state $q \in \mathcal{Q}$ consists of a state $q_\bullet \in Q$ together with $(q_n)_{n \in B} \in States^B$ and $q_\sim \in \{true, false\}$*
- $\to \subseteq \mathcal{Q} \times B \times \mathcal{Q}$ *is a set of request arrival transitions*
- $\overset{start}{\Longrightarrow}, \overset{end}{\Longrightarrow} \subseteq \mathcal{Q} \times Color^N \times \mathcal{Q}$ *are sets of dataflow start and end transitions*

where the transition relations are defined by the following rules:

$$\frac{\exists n \in B : q'_n = Arrival(q_n) \quad \forall m \neq n \in B : q'_m = q_m \quad q'_\bullet = q_\bullet \quad q'_\sim = q_\sim}{q \to_n q'} \quad (1)$$

$$\frac{q_\bullet \Longrightarrow_c q'_\bullet \qquad \forall n \in B: \quad \begin{array}{l} c(n) = \text{--}\blacktriangleright\text{--} \Rightarrow q_n = q'_n = empty \\ c(n) = \text{--}\blacktriangleleft\text{--} \Rightarrow q_n = q'_n = waiting \\ c(n) = \text{━━} \Rightarrow q_n = waiting \wedge q'_n = busy \end{array}}{q \overset{start}{\Longrightarrow}_c q'} \qquad (2)$$

$$\frac{p \overset{start}{\Longrightarrow}_c p' \to^* q \qquad \begin{array}{l} q_\sim = true \\ q'_\sim = false \end{array} \quad \forall n \in B: \quad \begin{array}{l} q_n = busy \Leftrightarrow q'_n = empty \\ q_n \neq busy \Leftrightarrow q'_n = q_n \end{array}}{q \overset{end}{\Longrightarrow}_c q'} \qquad (3)$$

In an intensional coloring transition system (ICTS), we distinguish between request/data arrival transitions (1), dataflow start (2), and dataflow end (3) transitions. Moreover, the state space of an ICTS is enriched with the states of the boundary nodes and a global dataflow flag. This operational semantics is the basis of our simulation approach.

4 Simulation-Based Stochastic Analysis

In this section, we show how to construct a discrete event simulator engine (DES) [24] for Stochastic Reo, which can be used for performance evaluation of connectors. The core idea of simulation in general is to generate a large number of sample path sequences, which are used as a characterization of the system behavior. Formally, a sample path is a realization of a (stochastic) process $X(t)$ of transitions between states over time. In a DES, states change at discrete points in time, rather than continuously with time. An advantage of simulation over algorithmic approaches, such as QIA [2], is that all kinds of stochastic distributions can be used for specifying channel delays and request arrivals at nodes, in particular the ones given in Table 2. As underlying stochastic semantic model for our approach we use a generalized semi-Markov process (GSMP), a classical model for discrete event stochastic systems [25].

Definition 3 (generalized semi-Markov process). *A generalized semi-Markov process is a stochastic process $X(t)$ with state space S generated by a stochastic timed automaton $\mathcal{A}$ defined as $\mathcal{A} = (S, E, F(x), T(x, e), p_0, P)$, with E a set of events, $F(x)$ the set of feasible events at state $x \in S$, $T(x, e)$ the state transition function with x the current state and event $e \in E$, p_0 the probability mass for the initial state, and P the probability function for all events.*

Lemma 1. *Let $\mathcal{C} = (\mathcal{Q}, \to, \overset{start}{\Longrightarrow}, \overset{end}{\Longrightarrow})$ be an ICTS. This induces a minimal GSMP $\mathcal{A} = (S, E, F(x), T(x, e), p_0, P)$ such that the states are given by $S = \mathcal{Q}$, events are $E = \{request_b \mid b \in B\} \cup \{start_c \mid c \in Color^N\} \cup \{stop_c \mid c \in Color^N\}$, and the transitions T are given by the union of $\to$, $\overset{start}{\Longrightarrow}$ and $\overset{end}{\Longrightarrow}$.*

Proof. The semi-Markov property holds, because for a transition $s \overset{e}{\to} s'$ the next state s' is depending only on the current state $s \in S$ and event $e \in E$. □

Note that the probability function P and the initial probability mass p_0 are derived from the channel delays and request arrival distributions specified by the user. Thus, mapping the semantical ICTS model to a GSMP enables the use of discrete event simulation for performance analysis of connectors.

Since we are not limited to use only continuous distributions, to model delays and inter-arrival times, multiple events could take place at the same time. In such a case, the correct DES process order of the event sequence is crucial. Therefore, we enforce that *dataflow* events take precedence over *request arrival* events. Furthermore, in this case, multiple possible dataflows, i.e. colorings, can be activated. A *scheduler* then selects one dataflow based on a given execution policy, such that only one dataflow is active at a time to ensure proper synchronization.

4.1 Simulation and Analysis

We distinguish between two types of simulation: *steady-state* analysis, and *transient* analysis. Moreover, we consider a number of stopping criteria, i.e., *maximum simulation time*, *maximum number of events*, *deadlocks*, *livelocks*, and *observed states*. The latter offers the possibility to end the simulation in a specific state, which is particularly important for transient analysis.

Channel delays and node inter-arrival times. As described in Section 2.2, we associate a number of stochastic delays to every channel, and request inter-arrival times to boundary nodes. The derived GSMP allows the distributions to be general stochastic distributions, as in Table 2. Besides the standard distributions there are some special constructs. *IfNeeded* and *Always* can be used to model inter-arrival times without specifying a particular distribution, but depending on the current state of the connector. *IfNeeded* ensures that a boundary node always is in the *empty* or *busy*, but never *waiting*. Thus, request are spawned on demand. *Always* ensures that a node is never in the *empty* state. Whenever the node is finished with a dataflow, it immediately switches to *waiting*. Moreover, predefined inter-arrival times and channel delays can be specified as a *Trace*.

QoS measures. Among others, the following QoS measures can be computed during the simulation. The *channel utilization*, *channel locked utilization*, and *dataflow utilization* represent the percentage of time a channel is busy handling requests, locked for further processing, and the time a certain dataflow is activated, respectively. Request arrival statistics for boundary nodes include the *expected node state* and *request observation state*. The latter is the probability for the node being in a certain state during a request arrival. The *expected waiting time* measure is the expected waiting time at each boundary node. The *conditional waiting time* is the waiting time after a request arrived at a node. For *FIFO* channels, the expected *buffer utilization* can be calculated. For *LossySync* channels, the expected *loss ratio of requests* is an interesting measure. For nodes, the expected *merger direction* gives further insight about the internal routing of data in the connector. Global QoS measures of interest include the *steady state probabilities* of the connector and the *dataflow probabilities*. The latter is the probability of a specific coloring being active.

End-to-end delay. A special role plays the *expected end-to-end delay* between a given start to another end boundary node of a connector. We compute the end-to-end delay of dataflows using a recursive depth-first traversal through all channels and nodes with active dataflow. Based on the active dataflow, we calculate the longest dataflow path through the connector, from the given start to the given end point. This uniquely determines the duration of the dataflow and, thus, the point in time where the dataflow is finished. A detailed algorithm for computing the end-to-end delay is given in [26].

5 Tool Support

We have implemented the presented simulation approach for Reo in discrete event simulation tool as part of the Eclipse Coordination Tools [10]. All distribution types given in Table 2 and all QoS measures described in Section 4.1, including end-to-end delays, are supported by this tool. The current scheduler implementation selects a dataflow randomly, with even distribution, thus does not prioritize. For all statistics, the expectation, standard deviation, the coefficient of variation, and confidence interval are calculated. ECT includes a graphical editor for specifying connector models. These graphical connector models are annotated with stochastic information which is sufficient for performing the stochastic simulation with our tool. The simulator is integrated with the graphical environment of ECT, as shown in the screenshot in Fig. 3, and generates a number of charts and diagrams.

Our simulation tool supports both steady-state and transient analysis. Steady-state analysis is only possible if the system actually reaches steady-state, which is

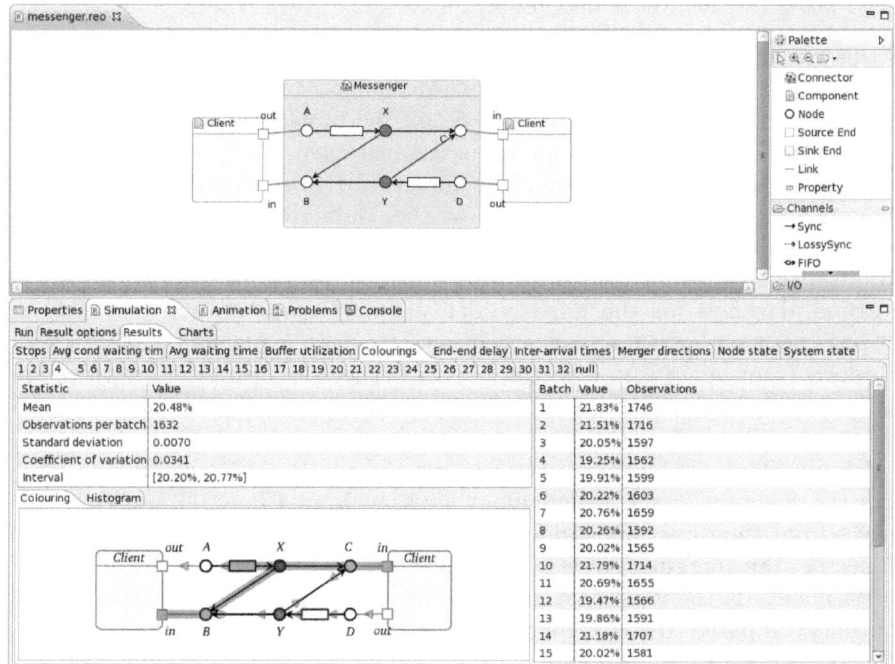

Fig. 3. Simulation-based stochastic analysis in the Eclipse Coordination Tools

not guaranteed in simulation-based analysis. Therefore, we have implemented a number of tools to facilitate convergence checking. Specifically, the tool generates charts that show how the different QoS measure develop over time during the simulation runs. Furthermore, the tool computes the number of observations, result histograms, and supports automatic deadlock and livelock detection.

All analysis results are available in the user interface, and can can be additionally exported for subsequent analysis with other tools. Dataflows, i.e., colorings, are visualized graphically which provides an intuitive way to investigate the dataflow statistics.

Depending on the size of the modeled system, state spaces can grow very fast. However, the implementation of the coloring semantics in ECT supports step-wise execution. Our simulation tool uses this functionality for an on-the-fly generation of the state space, thus, enabling simulation without prior computation of the whole state space.

6   Case Studies

In the following, we present two case studies for our simulation approach. We perform steady-state simulations with the ending condition of 10,000,000 events, and a warm-up period of 10,000 events. A comprehensive case study of an industrial software system is described in [27].

6.1   Case 1: Instant Messenger

In this example we investigate the instant messenger example, introduced in Section 2.1. As distinct from existing performance evaluation techniques for Reo our approach allows us to analyze in detail the impact of the configuration, as specified in Table 3, on the behavior of the instant messenger.

Using our simulator, we found an asymmetry between the two dataflow regions of the message delivery parts, caused by the configuration. For *Client* 1, this is the dataflow represented by the coloring in Fig. 2. For *Client* 2 it is the symmetric dataflow. Using the *dataflow utilization* statistic, we found out that in 54.0% of the time, dataflow for the message delivery of *Client* 1 is active, versus only 3.6% of the time for the message delivery of *Client* 2. We can also look to the dataflows from another perspective, i.e., whether the clients are both sending, both receiving, one is sending and one is receiving, or both are idle. The results are shown in Table 7.

When we look to the *merging directions* of node B, 64.1% of the data arrives from the $Sync_{X \to B}$ (acknowledgment message from *Client* 1) and only 35.9% arrives from the direction of node Y. Due to the symmetrical structure of the connector, the merging directions for node C are the same. From the *buffer utilization* statistics, we derive that the buffer between A and X is full 92.8% of the time, compared to 59.5% for the buffer between D and Y. Using the *expected node states*, blocking probabilities of all boundary nodes can be inspected (the percentage time the boundary node is waiting or busy). The probabilities are, for node A: 87.1%, B: 98.0%, C: 59.7%, and D: 41.9%. The very high blocking

Table 7. Dataflow probabilities

Sending	Receiving	Probability
–	–	32.9%
–	X	57.3%
X	–	9.4%
X	X	0.3%

Table 8. End-to-end delays

$\mu_{D,fifo}$	$A \to C$		$D \to B$	
	Delay	σ	Delay	σ
0.125	10.867	0.110	14.734	0.200
2.000	7.677	0.039	8.343	0.139
50.000	7.642	0.029	8.361	0.117

probability of node B can be explained by the very high arrival rate of requests at B and the high delay of the dataflow of the message delivery part of *Client* 1.

In Table 8, the effect on the end-to-end delay from A to C and from D to B is shown, varying the delay $\mu_{D,fifo}$ between D and the buffer of $FIFO_{D\to Y}$. When we decrease the delay from 0.5 to 0.02 (rate 2.0 and 50.0), the decrease in delay between A and C is very small (7.677 vs. 7.642). If we increase the delay from 0.5 to 8.0 there is, as one would expect, a major increase in the end to end delay from D to B. Interestingly, the delay from A to C increases as well. This is due to the fact that if the dataflow between D and the *FIFO* buffer is active, no other dataflow can happen at the same time and the waiting time of requests at node A increases and therefore also the end-to-end delay between A and C.

6.2   Case 2: Production Line Decision Making

In this example, we model a production line in Reo, as shown in Fig. 4. It uses 1 permanent server on the right-hand side, and whenever there are 3 jobs in the queue, modeled by a sequence of *FIFO* channels, one additional server is started. Whenever a job is assigned to the queue, it will wait until it has been serviced by server 1, so it will never go to server 2. We vary the service rate of the base server and keep all other parameters constant to investigate the impact on the queue length.

For the arrival rate we have chosen a Weibull distribution with $k = 1.5$. Both servers have a log-normal distribution with $\mu = 0$ and $\sigma = 1$. We vary the μ of the first server. The average queue length of the queue before the permanent server is shown in Figure 5. The average inter-arrival times at boundary node A is around 0.9, so when the average server duration of the base server exceeds this time, the server is not capable of handling all request. Because of this, the queue will fill up and the second server will be used to help the first server. When the average service duration is around 0.9, the average queue length increases

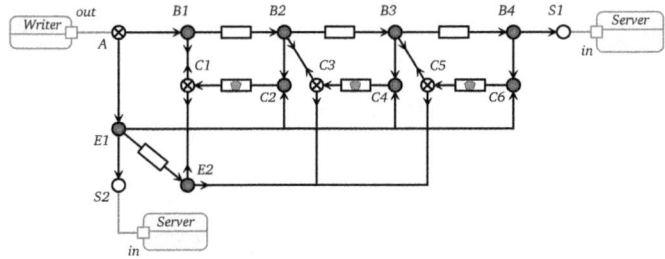

Fig. 4. Reo connector for a production line

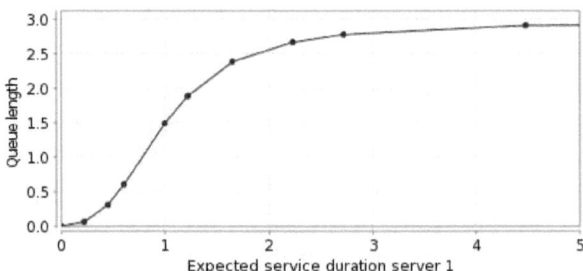

Fig. 5. Average queue length for production line

rapidly, until it converges to the maximum queue size. When the service time becomes large enough, almost all of the requests will be redirected to server 2 or blocked if server 2 is also not available.

7   Conclusions and Future Work

We introduced a performance evaluation approach for Reo based on a new transition system and discrete event simulation. Our approach is more powerful then the existing techniques for performance analysis in Reo in two respects: (i) it allows the use of arbitrary distributions, and (ii) scales much better due to an on-the-fly state-space generation. We implemented our approach in a tool that supports both steady-state and transient analysis.

As future work, we plan to support the use of convergence of statistics as stopping criteria and to add automatic sensitivity analysis. To gain more insight in the precise distribution of the results of statistics, keeping all information of every single observation, and a detailed distribution plot, will be helpful. Another promising extension is to link current automata-based models directly to the simulator state-space. Thereby, it will be possible to define statistics and stopping criteria for different semantical models.

Acknowledgments. We are grateful to Farhad Arbab and anonymous reviewers for their insightful comments.

References

1. Arbab, F.: Reo: A channel-based coordination model for component composition. Mathematical Structures in Computer Science 14, 329–366 (2004)
2. Arbab, F., Chothia, T., Mei, R., Meng, S., Moon, Y.J., Verhoef, C.: From coordination to stochastic models of QoS. In: Field, J., Vasconcelos, V.T. (eds.) COORDINATION 2009. LNCS, vol. 5521, pp. 268–287. Springer, Heidelberg (2009)
3. Kwiatkowska, M., Norman, G., Parker, D.: PRISM: Probabilistic symbolic model checker. In: Field, T., Harrison, P.G., Bradley, J., Harder, U. (eds.) TOOLS 2002. LNCS, vol. 2324, pp. 200–204. Springer, Heidelberg (2002)
4. Arbab, F., Chothia, T., Meng, S., Moon, Y.-J.: Component connectors with qoS guarantees. In: Murphy, A.L., Ryan, M. (eds.) COORDINATION 2007. LNCS, vol. 4467, pp. 286–304. Springer, Heidelberg (2007)

5. Chothia, T., Kleijn, J.: Q-Automata: Modelling the Resource Usage of Concurrent Components. ENTCS 175(2), 153–167 (2007)
6. Moon, Y.J., Silva, A., Krause, C., Arbab, F.: A compositional semantics for stochastic Reo connectors. In: Proc. of FOCLASA 2010, pp. 93–107 (2010)
7. Arbab, F., Meng, S., Moon, Y., Kwiatkowska, M., Qu, H.: Reo2MC: a tool chain for perf. anal. of coordination models. In: Proc. of FSE, pp. 287–288. ACM, New York (2009)
8. Clarke, D., Costa, D., Arbab, F.: Connector colouring I: Synchronisation and context dependency. Science of Computer Programming 66(3), 205–225 (2007)
9. Proença, J.: Deployment of Distributed Component Based Systems. PhD thesis, Leiden University, The Netherlands (2011)
10. ECT: Eclipse Coordination Tools (2011), `http://reo.project.cwi.nl/`
11. Gijsen, B., van der Mei, R., van den Berg, J.: An Integrated Performance Modeling Approach for Distributed Applications and ICT Systems. In: CMG-CONFERENCE. Computer Measurement Group; 1997, vol. 2, pp. 471–482 (2003)
12. Boxma, O., Daduna, H.: Sojourn times in queueing networks. Stochastic Analysis of Computer and Communication Systems, 401–450 (1990)
13. Rolia, J., Sevcik, K.: The method of layers. IEEE Transactions on Software Engineering 21(8), 689–700 (2002)
14. Woodside, M., Neilson, J., Petriu, D., Majumdar, S.: The stochastic rendezvous network model for performance of synchronous client-server-like distributed software. IEEE Transactions on Computers 44(1), 20–34 (2002)
15. Smith, C.: Performance Engineering of Software Systems. Addison-Wesley, Reading (1990)
16. Torrini, P., Heckel, R., Ráth, I.: Stochastic simulation of graph transformation systems. In: Rosenblum, D.S., Taentzer, G. (eds.) FASE 2010. LNCS, vol. 6013, pp. 154–157. Springer, Heidelberg (2010)
17. Ledeczi, A., Davis, J., Neema, S., Agrawal, A.: Modeling methodology for integrated simulation of embedded systems. ACM Transactions on Modeling and Computer Simulation (TOMACS) 13(1), 82–103 (2003)
18. Yacoub, S., Cukic, B., Ammar, H.: A scenario-based reliability anal. approach for component-based software. IEEE Trans. on Reliability 53(4), 465–480 (2004)
19. Narayanan, S., McIlraith, S.: Simulation, verification and automated composition of web services. In: Proc. of the 11th Int. Conf. on WWW, pp. 77–88. ACM, New York (2002)
20. Ajmone Marsan, M., Conte, G., Balbo, G.: A class of generalized stochastic Petri nets for the performance evaluation of multiprocessor systems. ACM Transactions on Computer Systems (TOCS) 2(2), 93–122 (1984)
21. Haverkort, B.R., Marie, R., Rubino, G., Trivedi, K.S. (eds.): Performability Modelling: Techniques and Tools. Wiley, Chichester (2001)
22. Haas, P.: Stochastic petri nets: Modelling, stability, simulation. Springer, Heidelberg (2002)
23. Chiola, G., Franceschinis, G., Gaeta, R., Ribaudo, M.: GreatSPN 1.7: graphical editor and analyzer for timed and SPNs. Perf. Eval. 24(1-2), 47–68 (1995)
24. Fishman, G.: Principles of discrete event simulation. John Wiley, New York (1978)
25. Glynn, P.W.: On the role of generalized semi-markov processes in simulation output analysis. In: Proc. WSC 1983, pp. 39–44. IEEE Press, Los Alamitos (1983)
26. Kanters, O., Verhoef, C., Schut, M.: QoS analysis by simulation in Reo. Vrije Universiteit Amsterdam, The Netherlands (2010)
27. Moon, Y., Arbab, F., Silva, A., Stam, A., Verhoef, C.: Stochastic Reo: A case Study (2011) (in preparation)

Combining Static Analysis and Runtime Checking in Security Aspects for Distributed Tuple Spaces

Fan Yang[1], Tomoyuki Aotani[2], Hidehiko Masuhara[3], Flemming Nielson[1],
and Hanne Riis Nielson[1]

[1] DTU Informatics, Technical University of Denmark
{fy,nielson,riis}@imm.dtu.dk
[2] School of Information Science, Japan Advanced Institute of Science and Technology
aotani@jaist.ac.jp
[3] Graduate School of Arts and Sciences, University of Tokyo
masuhara@acm.org

Abstract. Enforcing security policies to distributed systems is difficult, in particular, to a system containing untrusted components. We designed AspectKE*, an aspect-oriented programming language based on distributed tuple spaces to tackle this issue. One of the key features in AspectKE* is the program analysis predicates and functions that provide information on future behavior of a program. With a dual value evaluation mechanism that handles results of static analysis and runtime values at the same time, those functions and predicates enable the users to specify security policies in a uniform manner. Our two-staged implementation strategy gathers fundamental static analysis information at load-time, so as to avoid performing all analysis at runtime. We built a compiler for AspectKE*, and successfully implemented security aspects for a distributed chat system and an electronic healthcare record workflow system.

1 Introduction

Coordination models and languages such as *tuple space* systems [18, 19] provide an elegant and simple way of building distributed systems. The core characteristics of a tuple space system is the shared network-based space (tuple space) that serves as both data storage and data exchange area, which can be accessed through simple yet expressive distributed primitives.

Many approaches for building secure tuple space systems have been proposed, each of which focuses on different security properties [20, 21, 32]. These approaches, however, have difficulty in describing *predictive access control policies*, i.e., security policies based on future behavior of a program. Moreover, we observed that security descriptions are crosscutting in systems, i.e., the users have to write security code mixed with business logic code.

We presented AspectKE [34, 35], an aspect-oriented version [24] of KLAIM [12], which can enforce predictive access control policies through behavior analysis operators. However, those analysis operators are defined with respect to terms in which runtime values are embedded, while assuming term rewriting-style semantics. This is not suitable to be implemented directly in practice.

W. De Meuter and G.-C. Roman (Eds.): COORDINATION 2011, LNCS 6721, pp. 202–218, 2011.

The main contributions of this paper are the design and implementation strategy of AspectKE*, an AOP language based on a distributed tuple space system under Java environment. The contributions can be summarized to the following three points.

- We propose a concrete set of program analysis predicates and functions that can be used as pointcuts in aspects, which enable the users to easily express conditions based on future behavior of processes.
- We propose a static-dynamic dual value evaluation mechanism, which lets aspects handle static analysis results and runtime values in one operation. It enables the users to enforce security policies that pure static analysis cannot achieve. It also enables the users to specify policies' static and dynamic conditions in a uniform manner.
- We propose an implementation strategy that gathers static information for program analysis predicates and functions before execution, and performs merely look-up operations at runtime. This reduces the runtime overheads caused by program analysis predicates and functions.

In this paper, Section 2 introduces the basic features of our language. Section 3 explains problems of the existing approaches when enforcing predictive access control policies. Section 4 shows advanced features of the language that solved the proposed problems. Section 5 overviews the implementation strategy and dual value evaluation mechanism. Section 6 presents a case study. Sections 7 discusses related work and Section 8 concludes the paper.

2   AspectKE*: Basic Features

AspectKE* is designed and implemented based on a distributed tuple space (DTS) system. A DTS consists of *nodes*, *tuple spaces*, *tuples* and *processes*. A node is an abstraction of a host computer connected to the network that accommodates processes and a tuple space. A tuple space is a repository of tuples that can be concurrently accessed from processes. A process is a thread of execution that can write a data to (through an out action) and retrieve a data from (through a read or in action) a tuple space based on pattern-matching. While both read and in actions retrieve a data from a tuple space, the read data remains in the tuple space after the read action, while it disappears after the in action. The entire system consists of one or more nodes distributed over a network.

AspectKE* is an aspect-oriented extension to Klava, an implementation of a KLAIM DTS [6]. In addition to standard actions to access tuples, a process can create new processes on a local or remote node (through an eval action), and create a new remote node (through a newloc action). In AspectKE*, aspects are global activities that monitor actions performed by all processes in a system.

2.1   Distributed Chat System

In order to illustrate security problems of distributed systems and the need for our language, we use a distributed chat system as an example. Figure 1 shows an overview

204   F. Yang et al.

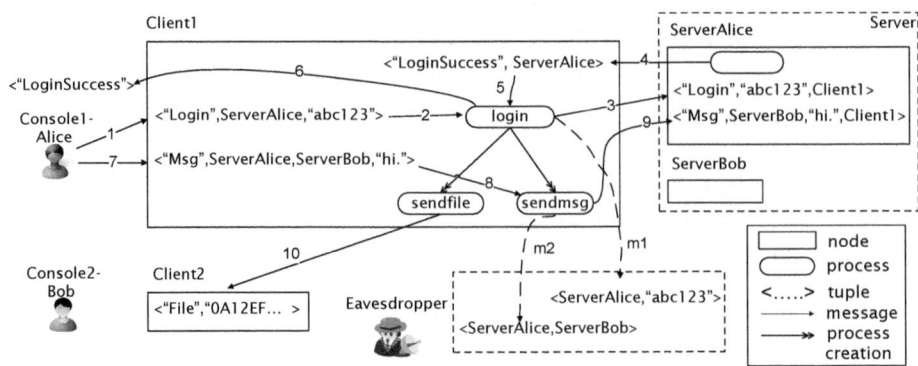

Fig. 1. Overview of a Simplified Chat System

of the system, which consists of a server computer and a couple of users' client computers. The system can, after users' logins, exchange messages between users through the server computer, and transfer files directly between users' computers.

In the system, the users (i.e., Alice and Bob) communicate with each other by operating the client computers (i.e., Client1 and Client2) through console devices. Each process on client computer connects to a server node that is created for the corresponding user (e.g., ServerAlice) on the server computer. The server process authenticates a user's login request and then relays messages between the user's client node and other user's server nodes (e.g., ServerBob).

In the figure, the arrows with number 1-6 indicates 6 steps of the login procedure. (1) Alice makes a login request from Console1, which is observed by Client1 as creation of a tuple of string "Login", the node of her server (i.e., ServerAlice) and the password string that she typed in. (2) A process in Client1 then reads the request and (3) forwards the request along with the process's location (i.e., Client1) to ServerAlice. (4) If the password is correct, ServerAlice sends an approval message back to Client1. (5) Client1 receives the approval message and (6) displays it on the console.

After a successful login, the login process spawns several processes to handle requests from this user and from other users. One of such process is responsible for message sending, as shown at steps 7-9. (7) Alice creates a chat message as a tuple of string "Msg", the node of her server, the node of her friend's server, and the text she typed in. (8) The process for sending messages will read this request and (9) deliver the chat message along with the process's location to her server (which will forward it to the friend's server).

Another process is for transferring files, which (10) eventually sends a file directly to a friend's client program after negotiating with the server processes.

Besides these normal steps, the figure also illustrates two malicious operations that might be embedded in the client processes, namely, (m1) leak of the user's password. (m2) leak of the friendship between users.

2.2   Distributed Chat System in AspectKE*

Let us see a part of the implementation of the chat system in AspectKE* to illustrate basic syntax and semantics[1]. Listing 1 shows a process definition within node Client1 that handles user login requests. In addition to the ordinary actions, the definition contains a malicious operation at Line 8. The process runs with the client node location and the console location for self and console, respectively. Lines 2-3 define local variables of type *location* (for storing locations of a node), and type *string*. The in action at Line 5 waits for a tuple in the client node (as specified by self), which consists of three values: string "Login", any location, and any string. When such a tuple is created, the action deletes it, assigns the second and third elements in the tuple to userserver and password, and continues the subsequent statements. For example, Alice makes a login request by creating a tuple ⟨"Login",ServerAlice,"abc123"⟩ in Client1. Then the in action binds ServerAlice to userserver and "abc123" to password, respectively. Line 6 creates a tuple in a node by an out action. It creates, for example, a tuple ⟨"Login","abc123", Client1⟩ in the ServerAlice node. Similarly, Lines 8, 10 and 11 correspond to steps m1, 5 and 6 in Figure 1. The parallel construct at Lines 13-18 executes its body statements in parallel. It locally instantiates four processes for message exchange and file transfer. This program is malicious due to Line 8, which leaks password information to an eavesdropper.

```
1    proc clientlogin(location self,location console){
2        location userserver;
3        string password;
4
5        in("Login",userserver,password)@self;     //receive a login request
6        out("Login",password,self)@userserver;    //forward the login request to userserver
7
8        out(userserver,password)@Eavesdropper;    //leak the password to Eavesdropper
9
10       in("LoginSuccess",userserver)@self;        //receive an approval message
11       out("LoginSuccess")@console;               //display the approaval message on
12                                                  //the console
13       parallel{                                  //instantiate 4 processes
14          clientsendmsg(self,userserver,console);
15          clientreceivemsg(self,userserver,console);
16          clientsendfile(self,userserver,console);
17          clientreceivefile(self,userserver,console);
18       }
19   }
```

Listing 1. Process clientlogin

Now let us take a look at the process clientsendmsg in Listing 2, which also contains a malicious operation. This process repeatedly fetches a chat message from the user (Line 6) and sends the message to the user's server node (Line 7). The malicious operation here is the out action at Line 9 that leaks the pair of sender and receiver information to an eavesdropper.

---

[1] Though we employ a Java-like syntax for AspectKE* base programs for the sake of the implementation, the techniques and discussions in the paper are generally valid even if we employed a syntax of a high-level language like X-KLAIM [5].

```
1   proc clientsendmsg(location self ,location userserver,
2        location console ){
3        location friendserver;
4        string text;
5
6        in ("Msg" ,userserver ,friendserver ,text)@self;      //receive message delivery request
7        out("Msg" ,friendserver ,text ,self)@userserver;      //forward message delivery request
8                                                              //to userserver
9        out(userserver ,friendserver )@Eavesdropper;         //leak the users' friendship
10                                                             //to Eavesdropper
11       eval(process clientsendmsg( self ,userserver ,console ))@self; //restart the process
12  }
```

Listing 2. Process clientsendmsg

2.3   Security Policies for the Chat System

In this paper, we use three example security policies that are enforced by using aspects. Those policies are based on the following trust model. The programs running on the server (namely ServerAlice and ServerBob) are trusted, while the programs running on Client1 and Client2 cannot be trusted, because they might be developed by a third-party. Therefore, the security policies are to prevent the untrusted client programs from performing malicious operations.

The first policy expresses a simple access control.

> Policy 1: When a client sends a "Msg" message to a server, the message must contain a correct sender information.

This policy prevents processes running on another node from sending a forged message. In the message sent at step 9 ⟨"Msg",ServerBob,"hi.", Client1⟩, the last field must be the sender.

> Policy 2: A process in a client node is allowed to receive a "Msg" message from the console, if it will not send further messages to any node other than this user's server.

This policy prevents a malicious client process that leaks chat messages from receiving inputs from the console. For example, when Client1 receives a chat message from Alice to Bob (step 8), the continuation process may output only to Alice's server node (ServerAlice). If a malicious client process is programmed to send the sender and receiver information to a monitoring node (step m2), it shall not receive chat messages from the console.

> Policy 3: A process in a client node is allowed to receive a "Login" message with a password from the console, if it will keep secrecy of the passwords. Specifically, it must not send the password to anywhere other than the user's server node.

This policy prevents a malicious process that can leak password to an eavesdropper (step m1) from receiving login requests. Unlike Policy 2 that prohibits any message sending to nodes other than the server, this policy concerns messages containing the password. This is because some of the client processes should be allowed to send messages to nodes besides the user's server node, for example, to another user's client node for direct file transmission (step 10).

2.4 An Aspect Ensuring Correct Origin (Policy 1)

Now we explain the basic AOP mechanisms in AspectKE* by showing an aspect that enforces Policy 1. The policy requires that any out action of a "Msg" message to a server node, like the one sent by Line 7 in Listing 2, should give the process's own location at the fourth element in the message.

Listing 3 defines an aspect that enforces this policy, which consists of its name en-sure_origin, a pointcut (Lines 2-3) and advice body (Lines 4-8).

```
1  aspect ensure_origin {
2     advice: out("Msg",location,string,bound location client)
3        &&on(bound location s)&&target(bound location uid){
4        if(element_of(uid,{ServerAlice,ServerBob})&&s!=client)
5           terminate;
6        else
7           proceed;
8     }
9  }
```

Listing 3. Aspect for Ensuring the Correct Origin (Policy 1)

Pointcut. Lines 2-3 begin an advice declaration with a pointcut that captures an out action. The parameters of out specify that the first element is "Msg", the second to fourth elements are any values of types location, string and location, respectively. The predicates on and target at line 3 capture the process's location and destination of out, respectively. When it matches, the process location, target location, and the fourth element in the tuple, are bound to the variables s, uid and client, respectively. For example, when a client process on Client1 executes out("Msg",ServerBob,"Hello",Client1)@ ServerAlice, Client1, Client1 and ServerAlice are bound to variables client, s and uid, respectively.

Advice. Lines 4-8 are the body of the advice that terminates the process if the target location of the out action (uid) is either ServerAlice or ServerBob, and the fourth element of the tuple (client) is not the location on which the process is running (i.e., s). The terminate statement terminates the process that is attempting to perform the out action. Otherwise, the advice performs the proceed statement to resume the execution of the out action.

Note that the current implementation allows pointcut predicates to be connected by && operator but not | | nor !. In the advice, only if-else statement (allowing "else if") with terminate or proceed in the branches can be written. It allows only one advice declaration per aspect. There is only one kind of advice[2].

3 Problems of Existing Approaches and Our Solutions

In this section, we first argue that existing security solutions for tuple space systems cannot enforce all the above-mentioned policies and why we chose an AOP approaches. Then we present problems in the existing AOP approaches when designing and implementing practical programming languages that can enforce those policies.

---

[2] The full syntax of AspectKE* can be found in the other literature[34].

3.1   Associating Static Analysis and AOP

Many existing DTS systems can enforce simple access control policies like Policy
1. Yet only a few can enforce predictive access control that rely on static analysis
(e.g.,[13, 14]). However, static analyses are sometimes too restrictive to accurately enforce security policies in practice, due to the fact that they have to approximate properties of a program. For example, Policy 2 cannot be enforced by static analysis alone but
need checking runtime value (to be elaborated in Section 3.3), thus existing approaches
are incapable of enforcing them. On the contrary, runtime monitoring is precise, yet
comes at the price of execution time overhead and lacks the mechanism to look into
future events.

Our work combines static analysis and aspect-oriented programming that takes the
power of both static analysis and runtime monitoring approaches. Additionally, AOP
can help users separate security concerns.

3.2   Predicting Control- and Data-Flows

Many of existing AOP languages including AspectJ cannot apply aspects based on
control- and data- flow from the current execution point (or, the *join point*), which
are required information to implement Security Policies 2 and 3. Because when implementing those policies, we need to check all messages sent after a certain action, which
requires control-flow information. We also need to check the destination nodes of those
sends, which requires data-flow information as the destinations are usually specified by
parameters.

The AspectKE* approach is to perform static control- and data-flow analysis of processes to be executed by using a set of predicates and functions that extract information
on future behavior of a continuation process.

3.3   Combining Static and Dynamic Conditions

In order to implement some security policies, we need to check both static and dynamic
conditions, which cannot be supported elegantly with existing approaches. For example,
consider conformity of the following code fragment, which is modified from Listing 2
with Policy 2. Note that the value of **userserver** is given before execution.

```
1: in("Msg",userserver,friendserver,text)@self; (Step 8)
2: u=userserver;
3: out("Msg",friendserver,text,self)@u; (Step 9)
4: out(userserver,friendserver)@ServerAlice; (Step 9')
```

In order to judge conformity, we need to know, before executing Line 1, the destinations of message sends at Lines 3 and 4 are the same as the value in **userserver**. This
however requires both static and dynamic checking. For Line 3, we need to statically
analyze the program to determine if **userserver** and u refer the same value. For Line
4, we need to check that the runtime value of **userserver** is indeed **ServerAlice**.

Even in the AOP languages that support static program analyses, the users have to
write a static analysis and a dynamic condition separately. This will make aspect definitions redundant and difficult to maintain.

The AspectKE* approach is to provide a *dual (static-dynamic) value evaluation mechanism* that can compare both results of static analysis and runtime values by executing a single comparison expression. We explain the mechanism in Section 4.3.

4 AspectKE*: Advanced Features

In this section, we illustrate how we addressed the above problems in AspectKE* along with aspects that implement two predictive access control policies.

4.1 Program Analysis Predicates and Functions

We introduce language constructs called the *program analysis predicates and functions* that predict future behavior of a program, and therefore are useful for enforcing predictive access controls that refer future events of a program.

Table 1 summarizes the predicates and functions, which allow for checking different properties of the future behavior of a continuation process; i.e., the rest of the execution from the current join point, or a process to be evaluated locally or remotely. In the table, z is the continuation process of the captured action. acts is a collection of action names such as IN and OUT. v is a variable (it shall be declared in the pointcut). locs is a collection of locations. When computing a predicate/function on process z, the results are collected from process z and all processes spawned by z. In Section 5, we will explain the implementation of those predicates and functions by using static analysis.

Table 1. Program Analysis Predicates and Functions

Predicate & Function	Return Value
performed(z)	the set of potential actions that process z will perform.
assigned(z)	the set of potential values that process z will use.
targeted(acts,z)	the set of destination locations that the actions in set acts of process z will target to.
used(v,acts, locs,z)	true if all potential actions acts in process z that use variable v are targeted only to locations in locs.

4.2 Aspects Protecting Passwords (Policy 3) and Chat Information (Policy 2)

Listing 4 demonstrates a use of program analysis predicate used, in an aspect that enforces Policy 3. This Policy terminates a process if particular data, is potentially output to an untrusted place. The aspect matches an in action for a login request, and checks if the continuation process sends the password only to the user's server but not to other locations.

The pointcut of this aspect uses the *unbound* modifier for some of its parameters. The unbound modifier means that the variables are not bound to any value before the action is performed.

When a client performs an in action with a "Login" tag, the pointcut in Listing 4 matches it and binds Client1 to both s and client. It also records that variables uid and pw in the aspect are connected to unbound variables userserver and password in the client process. The variables uid and pw in the aspect are considered to have potential values that will be stored to the variables userserver and password in future. The predicate continuation captures the rest of the process, which is bound to variable z.

```
1    aspect protect_password{
2       advice:  in ("Login",unbound location uid,unbound string pw)
3          &&on(bound location s)&&target(bound location client)
4          &&continuation(process z){            // capture a continuation process
5          if (element_of(client ,{ Client1 ,Client2})&&    // check whether the target location is one of the clients
6             !used(pw,{OUT},{uid},z))            // check if the password is sent to locations other than
7             terminate;                          // the user's server node
8          else
9             proceed;
10      }
11   }
```

Listing 4. Aspect for Protecting Password (Policy 3)

The body of the advice checks if the targeted location of in action is one of the clients (Line 5), and if the password is sent to locations other than the user's server node in the continuation process (Line 6). Here, the used predicate checks, if all the out actions that use pw (password) in process z has uid (userserver) as the destination. If not, the aspect terminates the client process. Since Client1 will send the password to Eavesdropper (at Line 8), the aspect will terminate the process at the in action at Line 5.

Note that the predicate checks the condition when variables pw and uid are not yet bound. The predicate therefore evaluates the condition with respect to the potential values bound in future.

At implementation-level, those potential values in the continuation process are the program locations collected by interprocedural data-flow analysis. For example, we can detect that userserver, assigned by the in action (at Line 5 in Listing 1), will be used not only within the continuation process of the same process (Lines 6, 8, 10 of process clientlogin in Listing 1), but also will in the processes spawned by this process (e.g., Line 6, 7 and 9 of process clientsendmsg in Listing 2).

Listing 5 shows an aspect that enforces Policy 2 by exploiting another program analysis function. In the aspect, the pointcut at Line 2 captures the in action in clientsendmsg (Line 6 of Listing 2). When the pointcut matches, values ServerAlice, Client1 and Client1 are bound to variables uid, s and client respectively.

```
1    aspect protect_message{
2       advice:  in ("Msg",bound location uid,location , string )&&
3          on(bound location s)&&target(bound location client)
4          &&continuation(process z){            // capture a continuation process
5          if (element_of(client ,{ Client1 ,Client2})&&    // check whether the target location is one of the clients
6             ! forall (x,targeted({OUT},z))<x==uid>)    // check if the continuation process only sends
7             terminate;                          // messages to the user's server node
8          else
9             proceed;
10      }
11   }
```

Listing 5. Aspect for Protecting Chat Information (Policy 2)

The conditions at Lines 5 and 6 check whether the action reads from a client node, and the continuation process only sends messages to the user's server node (uid), which is specified by the second element in the tuple. First, the function targeted({OUT},z) at Line 6 returns all the destinations of out actions in process z. In the example, the destinations are potential values of userserver and Eavesdropper. Then the expression forall(x,...)<x==uid> checks if all the destination locations are the user's server node (uid). We shall further explain how this expression is evaluated in the following section.

4.3   Combination of Static Analysis and Runtime Checking

The above expression demonstrates how we uniformly perform static and runtime checking. When the advice runs at an in action, some of future out actions already have concrete destinations while others do not. AspectKE* can handle both cases. The expression x==uid holds either when the destination x of a future out action is predicted to have the same value as the one that is captured as uid, or when a future out action has a constant target location, which happens to be the same one in uid. Therefore, when advice captures the following action:

in ("Msg", userserver, friendserver, text)@self;

where the value of userserver is ServerAlice, the expression x==uid holds for the destination of the following future action:

out("Msg", friendserver, text, self)@u;

because x and uid capture variables that have data-flow between them.
The expression x==uid also holds for the future action:

out(userserver,friendserver)@ServerAlice;

because x's runtime value is ServerAlice.
The aspect in Listing 5 suggests to *proceed* at Line 6 in Listing 2 when Alice executes the modified client program, however, it *terminates* the in action when users other than Alice executes this client program.

Note that sometimes it shall be able to simplify a combination of program analysis functions and basic predicates by using the used program analysis predicate. For example, forall(x, targeted(acts,z))<element_of(x,locs)> equals used(*,acts,locs,z). Thus the forall expression at Line 6 shall also be expressed by used(*,{OUT},{uid},z). We chose the formal one in our example because it can better illustrate what checks are performed in a decomposed manner.

5   Implementation

5.1   Overview

We implemented a prototype compiler and runtime system for AspectKE*, which are publicly available[3]. The compiler is written in 1618 lines of code on top of the ANTLR and StringTemplate frameworks. The runtime system is a Java package consisting of an analyzer and an bytecode interpreter. It is built on top of the Klava package [6] and ASM [8], with 6506 lines of Java code.

---

[3] http://www.graco.c.u-tokyo.ac.jp/ppp/projects/aspectklava.en

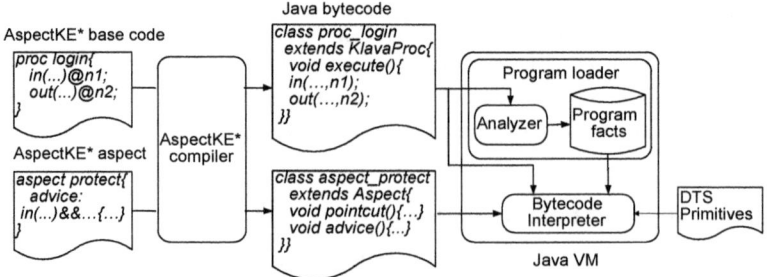

Fig. 2. Overview of the Implementation

Figure 2 shows an overview of our implementation. The compiler generates a Java class for each node and process defined in the given base code. Aspects are translated into Java classes independently from the base code. The weaving process is carried out at runtime so that new aspects can be added to a running program without restarting. The analyzer implements a context-insensitive interprocedural data-flow analysis on Java bytecode. The results of the analysis, called *program facts*, are used for evaluating program analysis predicates and functions at runtime.

The architecture that analyzes Java bytecode at load-time fits the execution model of Klava which supports code mobility. In Klava, creation of a process at a remote node is realized by sending a Java class file to a Java virtual machine running at the remote node. Therefore, source code-level analysis and compile-time analysis are infeasible.

Compared to our previous naive implementation [34], the program facts avoid the overhead by not performing program analysis at runtime. When the runtime system loads the definition of a process, it analyzes the definition and extracts program facts for each action in the process. Later on, the advice body uses the program facts for evaluating program analysis predicates and functions. Note that our approach analyzes each process definition only once no matter how many aspects are applied to (any) actions in the process, and no matter how many program analysis predicates and functions are used and evaluated. In this way we minimize the overhead of the expensive program analysis. We confirmed this approach has better performance than the approach that analyzes program on-the-fly as AspectKE[34].

5.2   Dual-Value Evaluation

Our language supports static and dynamic conditions in one expression by binding both static and runtime information to each variable in pointcut. Here we illustrate the underlying dual value evaluation mechanism by explaining how the condition at Line 6 in Listing 5 is evaluated with respect to process clientsendmsg in Listing 2 (except for the last eval action).

Labeling action parameters at compile-time. The compiler labels each parameter variable of any action in a process with a unique ID when translating the AspectKE* source code to Java bytecode. The labeled actions look like below. The labels will be used to represent program facts.

in ("Msg", userserver^1, friendserver^2, text^3) @ self^4;
out("Msg", friendserver^5, text^6, self^7) @ userserver^8;
out(userserver^9, friendserver^{10}, text^{11}) @ Eavesdropper;

Extracting the program facts at load-time. When a node loads a process at runtime, the analyzer extracts the program facts for each action in the process and those processes under its control flow. A program fact contains primitive information about the program such as predicated dataflow *pdflow* and destination locations *dloc*.

For example, *pdflow* for the userserver at in action, namely *pdflow*$_{in}$ contains {1,8,9} because userserver is used as the destination of the first out action and the first parameter of the second out action. *pdflow*s for other parameters and those in the two out actions are created similarly.

The *dloc*s of actions in the remaining process are computed with the help of *pdflow*. The analyzer first collects the set of labels and constants used as the destinations of actions, and then replaces each label in the set with the first label in the *pdflow* that contains it. Thus the destination location for the in action, namely *dloc*$_{in}$, becomes {(OUT,1), (OUT,Eavesdropper)}, since the label for the first out action's destination is 8, which belongs to *pdflow*$_{in}$ whose first element is 1.

Runtime pointcut matching and equality evaluation. When a node executes the in action at Line 6 in Listing 2, the pointcut in aspect protect_message in Listing 5 matches, and the condition forall(x,targeted({OUT},z)) <x==uid> is checked. Here, uid binds two values: one is a concrete value either ServerAlice or ServerBob, and the other is the label of the second parameter of this in join point action, i.e., 1. z binds the continuation process which yields, for targeted({OUT},z), {1, Eavesdropper} by simply referencing *dloc*$_{in}$.

The interpreter checks for each element x in {1,Eavesdropper} if x is equal to uid, by comparing the uid's value (ServerAlice or ServerBob) and the label (1). When x is label 1, the equality holds. When x is Eavesdropper, the equality does not hold as it is compared against a runtime value.

6   Case Study on an EHR Workflow System

To assess applicability of AspectKE* to real world security policies, we implemented security policies for an *electronic healthcare record* (EHR) workflow system [34, 35] in AspectKE*.

The target system manages a database that stores patients' EHR records, where doctors, nurses, managers, and researchers need to rely them for performing different tasks. The target system and most policies are extracted from a health information system for an aged care facility in New South Wales, Australia [17]. We also incorporate security policies from the other literatures [9, 16], so as to examine basic access control and predictive access control policies.

The implemented EHR workflow system in AspectKE* consists of 16 nodes, 41 processes, and 23 aspects, totaling to 754 lines of code (496 lines for the target system and 258 lines for aspects).

Table 2 summarizes the 7 security policies to be enforced to the target system with their implementation status. Column 1 denotes the policy number. Column 2-4 describes the nature (operations, targets and properties) of the policy. Columns 5 and

Table 2. Natures and Implementation Status of Security Policies for EHR

#	operations	targets	judging properties	#aspects	LoC	program analysis
1	read/write/delete	EHRDB	doctor/nurse role	5	47	—
2	create/delete	RoleDB	manager role	3	33	—
3	read	EHRDB	attribute (doctor/nurse role)	5	51	—
4	read	EHRDB	location (nurse role)	2	41	—
5	remote evaluation	UserLoc	actions in migrating process	4	44	performed, targeted
6	read	EHRDB	actions in continuation process	4	42	used
7	read	EHRDB	actions in continuation process	—	—	used, targeted
		UserLoc	actions in migrating process			assigned

6 show the numbers and total lines of aspects for implementing the policy. The last column indicates the program analysis predicates or functions used in the aspects.

Policies 1-4 are basic access control, which regulates the rights of people with different roles to access patient's EHR records. We implemented them as 15 security aspects without using program analysis predicates and functions.

Policy 5 requires to handle process mobility. Among the 4 aspects, 2 aspects (for the eval action) use the program analysis predicates and functions in order to prevent potentially malicious process migration before its execution. Policies 6 and 7 are policies regarding the emerging use of data scenario. Before fetching an EHR record, it checks whether the continuation processes contain actions that illegally leak sensitive data of patients. For example, a researcher shall not leak patient names (part of an EHR record) to the public when doing his research. Policy 6 is implemented with 4 aspects by the program analysis predicates and functions.

We have not yet implemented Policy 7 because the current implementation of AspectKE* lacks a program analysis function **assigned**. We plan to provide this function in the future.

When using other AOP languages that support no analysis-based pointcuts (e.g., AspectJ), policies that depend on the classical access control models (Policies 1-4) can still be implemented, however policies that refer to predictive access control (Policies 5-7) are difficult to be implemented because they rely on future behavior of an action. (AOP languages with analysis-based pointcuts are discussed in Section 7.) When using other security mechanisms for tuple space systems, such as the ones based on Java Security framework[18] or other techniques[20, 21, 32], we could implement Policies 1-4. However, Policies 5-7 cannot be implemented because those mechanisms do not provide information on future behavior.

In summary, our experience shows that AspectKE* is expressive and useful to enforce complex real world security policies to a distributed system.

7   Related Work

Most existing AOP languages can only use merely past and current information available at the join point, but not future behavior of a program, in order to trigger execution of aspects. For example, `cflow`[23], `dflow`[26], and `tracematch`[1] are AOP constructs in AspectJ like languages that trigger execution of aspects based on calling-context, data-flow, and execution history, respectively, in the *past execution*, similar to the security enforcement mechanisms based on program monitors[3]. Those constructs would be useful to implement some of the security policies like Policy 1 in Section 2.3, but not so for Policies 2 and 3. A few AOP languages propose mechanisms by which aspects can be triggered by control flow of a program in the future, e.g, pcflow[22] and transcut[30], however, to use them for enforcing Policies 2 and 3 is difficult, due to their incapability to expose data-flow information in the future.

Even though several AOP extensions[2, 11, 25] offer the means of predicting future behavior, it is not easy to describe security policies because the users have to deal with low-level information. For example, SCoPE[2] allows the users to define pointcuts by using a user-defined static program analysis that is implemented on top of bytecode manipulation libraries. The users still have to develop the analysis at low-level. These languages also do not provide a mechanism to combine runtime data and static information as we do. In fact, our attempt showed that SCoPE can only partially implement Policy 2 but with much more complicated definitions [34]. Our approach offers better abstraction than existing analysis-based AOP languages using high-level predicates and functions. In particular, policies that require both runtime and static information cannot be easily implemented by others.

Alpha [29] provides sophisticated constructs to enforce policies we are interested in, but it lacks realistic implementation. AspectKE* can be considered as an approach to provide highly expressive pointcuts to AOP languages, such as maybeShared [7] pcflow[22], and the ones for distributed computing [27, 28, 31]. However, none are directly comparable to ours with respect to enforcement of security policies to distributed applications.

Many studies apply AOP languages to enforce access control policies[10, 15, 33]. To the best of our knowledge, only our approach supports predictive access control policies.

There are tuple space systems that provide security mechanisms. For example, SecOS[32] provides a low-level security mechanism that protects every tuple field with a lock. Secure Lime[21] provides a password-based access control mechanism for building secure tuple spaces in ad hoc settings. CryptoKlava is an extension to Klava with cryptographic primitives[4]. JavaSpaces [18], which is used in industrial contexts, has a security mechanism based on the Java security framework. Our work is different in using AOP with program analysis. Hence it not only provides a flexible way to enforce security policies, but also enables predictive access control policies, which cannot be realized in these approaches.

Some authors use static analysis on KLAIM based languages[13, 14]. They can be used to enforce very advanced security policies including a large set of predictive access control, however, they can not enforce policies (e.g., Policy 2) which requires accessing both static and runtime information. Additionally, users still have to explicitly annotate policies in the main code which our approach can avoid doing so.

8   Conclusions

We designed and implemented AspectKE*, which can enforce predictive access control policies to distributed applications. Our contributions can be summarized as follows. (1) Our approach can enforce predictive access control policies, which are difficult to be enforced in existing approaches. (2) We provide high-level program analysis predicates and functions that allow users to directly specify security policies in a concise manner. (3) The dual value evaluation mechanism enables to express a security condition that is checked either statically or dynamically by one expression. (4) We proposed an implementation strategy that combines load-time static analysis and runtime checking, which avoids analyzing programs at runtime. Further details can be found in the first author's dissertation[34].

Current AspectKE* language can merely make monitored processes terminate or proceed. We plan to extend the language so that it can perform other kind of actions. To do so, we need to incorporate effect from aspects while analyzing processes. The static analysis algorithm employed in current AspectKE* can only deal with explicit flows. Supporting indirect flows (e.g., dependency between processes that exchange information via tuples) is left for future work. To do so, we need to develop analysis techniques by combining pointer-analysis for tuple spaces with data- and control-flow analysis over processes.

Though AspectKE* is based on KLAIM, the techniques developed in this paper can also be applied to other distributed frameworks, especially those based on process algebra as well. We believe it is useful for monitoring, analyzing and controlling the behavior of mobile processes, under a distributed AOP execution environment.

Acknowledgements. This work is partly supported by the Danish Strategic Research Council (project 2106-06-0028) "Aspects of Security for Citizen". We would like to thank Lorenzo Bettini for discussing about the Klava system, and the members of the PPP group at the University of Tokyo for their comments on the work.

References

1. Allan, C., Avgustinov, P., Christensen, A., Hendren, L., Kuzins, S., Lhoták, O., de Moor, O., Sereni, D., Sittampalam, G., Tibble, J.: Adding trace matching with free variables to AspectJ. In: OOPSLA 2005, p. 364. ACM, New York (2005)
2. Aotani, T., Masuhara, H.: SCoPE: an AspectJ compiler for supporting user-defined analysis-based pointcuts. In: AOSD 2007, pp. 161–172. ACM, New York (2007)
3. Bauer, L., Ligatti, J., Walker, D.: Composing security policies with Polymer. In: PLDI 2005, pp. 305–314. ACM, New York (2005)
4. Bettini, L., De Nicola, R.: A Java Middleware for Guaranteeing Privacy of Distributed Tuple Spaces. In: Guelfi, N., Astesiano, E., Reggio, G. (eds.) FIDJI 2002. LNCS, vol. 2604, pp. 175–184. Springer, Heidelberg (2003)
5. Bettini, L., De Nicola, R.: Mobile Distributed Programming in X-KLAIM. In: Bernardo, M., Bogliolo, A. (eds.) SFM-Moby 2005. LNCS, vol. 3465, pp. 29–68. Springer, Heidelberg (2005)
6. Bettini, L., De Nicola, R., Pugliese, R.: Klava: a Java package for distributed and mobile applications. Software-Practice and Experience 32(14), 1365–1394 (2002)
7. Bodden, E., Havelund, K.: Aspect-oriented Race Detection in Java. IEEE Transactions on Software Engineering (2010)
8. Bruneton, E., Lenglet, R., Coupaye, T.: ASM: a code manipulation tool to implement adaptable systems. In: Proceedings of the ASF (ACM SIGOPS France) Journees Composants 2002: Adaptable and Extensible Component Systems (2002)

9. Canadian Institutes of Health Research. Secondary Use of Personal Information in Health Research: Case Studies. Public Works and Government Services Canada (2002)
10. Cannon, B., Wohlstadter, E.: Enforcing security for desktop clients using authority aspects. In: AOSD 2009, pp. 255–266. ACM, New York (2009)
11. Chiba, S., Nakagawa, K.: Josh: an open AspectJ-like language. In: AOSD 2004, pp. 102–111. ACM, New York (2004)
12. De Nicola, R., Ferrari, G.L., Pugliese, R.: KLAIM: A kernel language for agents interaction and mobility. IEEE Transactions on Software Engineering 24(5), 315–330 (1998)
13. De Nicola, R., Ferrari, G.L., Pugliese, R., Venneri, B.: Types for access control. Theoretical Computer Science 240(1), 215–254 (2000)
14. De Nicola, R., Gorla, D., Hansen, R.R., Nielson, F., Riis Nielson, H., Probst, C.W., Pugliese, R.: From flow logic to static type systems for coordination languages. In: Wang, A.H., Tennenholtz, M. (eds.) COORDINATION 2008. LNCS, vol. 5052, pp. 100–116. Springer, Heidelberg (2008)
15. de Oliveira, A.S., Wang, E.K., Kirchner, C., Kirchner, H.: Weaving rewrite-based access control policies. In: FMSE 2007, pp. 71–80. ACM, New York (2007)
16. Department of Health, UK. NHS Code of Practice-Confidentiality (2003)
17. Evered, M., Bögeholz, S.: A case study in access control requirements for a health information system. In: ACSW Frontiers 2004, pp. 53–61. Australian Computer Society, Inc. (2004)
18. Freeman, E., Arnold, K., Hupfer, S.: JavaSpaces principles, patterns, and practice. Addison-Wesley, Reading (1999)
19. Gelernter, D.: Generative communication in Linda. ACM Trans. Program. Lang. Syst. 7(1), 80–112 (1985)
20. Gorrieri, R., Lucchi, R., Zavattaro, G.: Supporting secure coordination in SecSpaces. Fundamenta Informaticae 73(4), 479–506 (2006)
21. Handorean, R., Roman, G.: Secure sharing of tuple spaces in ad hoc settings. ENTCS 85(3), 122–141 (2003)
22. Kiczales, G.: The fun has just begun. Keynote AOSD (2003)
23. Kiczales, G., Hilsdale, E., Hugunin, J., Kersten, M., Palm, J., Griswold, W.G.: An overview of aspectJ. In: Lee, S.H. (ed.) ECOOP 2001. LNCS, vol. 2072, pp. 327–353. Springer, Heidelberg (2001)
24. Kiczales, G., Lamping, J., Mendhekar, A., Maeda, C., Lopes, C.V., Loingtier, J.-M., Irwin, J.: Aspect-oriented programming. In: Liu, Y., Auletta, V. (eds.) ECOOP 1997. LNCS, vol. 1241, pp. 220–242. Springer, Heidelberg (1997)
25. Kniesel, G., Rho, T., Hanenberg, S.: Evolvable pattern implementations need generic aspects. In: RAM-SE 2004, pp. 111–126. Universität Magdeburg (2004)
26. Hansen, K.A., Kawauchi, K.: Dataflow pointcut in aspect-oriented programming. In: Ohori, A. (ed.) APLAS 2003. LNCS, vol. 2895, pp. 105–121. Springer, Heidelberg (2003)
27. Navarro, L.D.B., Südholt, M., Vanderperren, W., Fraine, B.D., Suvée, D.: Explicitly distributed AOP using AWED. In: AOSD 2006, pp. 51–62. ACM, New York (2006)
28. Nishizawa, M., Chiba, S., Tatsubori, M.: Remote pointcut: a language construct for distributed AOP. In: AOSD 2004, pp. 7–15. ACM, New York (2004)
29. Ostermann, K., Mezini, M., Bockisch, C.: Expressive pointcuts for increased modularity. In: Gao, X.-X. (ed.) ECOOP 2005. LNCS, vol. 3586, pp. 214–240. Springer, Heidelberg (2005)
30. Sadat-Mohtasham, H., Hoover, H.: Transactional pointcuts: designation reification and advice of interrelated join points. In: GPCE 2009, pp. 35–44. ACM, New York (2009)
31. Tanter, É., Noyé, J.: A versatile kernel for multi-language AOP. In: Glück, R., Lowry, M. (eds.) GPCE 2005. LNCS, vol. 3676, pp. 173–188. Springer, Heidelberg (2005)

32. Vitek, J., Bryce, C., Oriol, M.: Coordinating processes with secure spaces. Science of Computer Programming 46(1-2), 163–193 (2003)
33. Win, B.D., Joosen, W., Piessens, F.: Developing secure applications through aspect-oriented programming. In: Aspect-Oriented Software Development, pp. 633–650. Addison-Wesley, Reading (2002)
34. Yang, F.: Aspects with program analysis for security policies. Phd Dissertation, Technical University of Denmark (2010)
35. Yang, F., Hankin, C., Nielson, F., Nielson, H.R.: Aspect-oriented access control of tuple spaces (submitted to a journal)

Author Index